The Unorthodox Presidency
of Donald J. Trump

The Unorthodox Presidency

of Donald J. Trump

Edited by

Paul E. Rutledge

and

Chapman Rackaway

University Press of Kansas

Published by the University Press of Kansas (Lawrence, Kansas 66045),
which was organized by the Kansas Board of Regents and is operated and
funded by Emporia State University, Fort Hays State University, Kansas State
University, Pittsburg State University, the University of Kansas, and Wichita
State University.

Library of Congress Cataloging-in-Publication Data

Names: Rutledge, Paul E., editor. | Rackaway, Chapman, editor.
Title: The unorthodox presidency of Donald J. Trump / edited by
Paul E. Rutledge, and Chapman Rackaway.
Description: Lawrence: University Press of Kansas, 2021 |
Includes bibliographical references and index.
Identifiers: LCCN 2020048507
ISBN 9780700632312 (cloth)
ISBN 9780700632329 (paperback)
ISBN 9780700632336 (epub)
Subjects: LCSH: Trump, Donald, 1946– | United States—Politics and
government—2017– | United States—Foreign relations—2017– |
Presidents—United States.
Classification: LCC E912 .U56 2021 | DDC 973.933092—dc23
LC record available at https://lccn.loc.gov/2020048507.

British Library Cataloguing-in-Publication Data is available.

Printed in the United States of America

10 9 8 7 6 5 4 3 2 1

The paper used in this publication is acid free and meets the minimum
requirements of the American National Standard for Permanence of Paper
for Printed Library Materials Z39.48-1992.

Rutledge: To Amy, Luke, Ben, Ryan, Max, and Jack,
who inspire me every single day.

Rackaway: For Andrea, Madison, Micheala, Will, and
Cate—my love to you all, for always.

Contents

Acknowledgments

RUTLEDGE

I began my academic career in 1999 as a first-generation college student who did not know the first thing about achieving success in college. I owe more than I could ever repay to Reinhard Heinisch and Raymond Wrabley, who during my time at the University of Pittsburgh at Johnstown saw potential in me that I did not know I had. I also wish to thank Robert DiClerico, who provided invaluable mentorship at West Virginia University and without whom none of what I have accomplished would be possible. I thank the great colleagues at the University of West Georgia, for their constant support and collegiality. While the entire department is more collegial than I could ever imagine, especially noteworthy is my coauthor, Chapman Rackaway. Finally, I thank my father, Ron Rutledge, who probably never imagined that his love of politics and the American presidency in particular had such an effect on me.

RACKAWAY

In 2017, I made the decision to leave an institution where I'd worked for a decade to move to the University of West Georgia. One of the unexpected side benefits of making the move was getting to be in a larger department with great scholars who helped me reinvigorate my research agenda. One of those scholars, Paul Rutledge, has become my coeditor here and I'm thrilled to be able to have my name on a volume alongside his.

Edited volumes like this one are a true team effort. And the team we've been able to assemble in this book includes individuals for whom I have a deep and abiding respect. To every one of the authors, whether you've been a friend and mentor or someone who I have only recently come to know, I'm grateful for your willingness to contribute to this important work.

This work also could not have been done without the stalwart help of the board and staff at the University Press of Kansas. Having lived for some time in Kansas and worked in its university system, it's a point of pride for me to publish with UPK. David Congdon in particular deserves our thanks as our acquisitions editor.

Introduction

Paul E. Rutledge and Chapman Rackaway

The presidency of Donald Trump has been unorthodox from the initial stages of his campaign. To launch his campaign, he descended via a golden escalator in grand representation of his transition from businessman to candidate for the presidency and proceeded with an unprecedented onslaught on the norms of American democracy and political correctness that was equal parts brazen and in character for an individual well-known for his made-for-television personality. Prior to becoming a formal candidate for the presidency, Trump had put himself in the political limelight by flirting with the possibility of running for office several times, only to back out before officially entering the race. Trump had been an outspoken voice on political issues for quite some time, most notably championing the birther movement that insinuated that President Barack Obama was not born in the United States and thus was ineligible to serve in the Oval Office. Such conspiracy theory–driven and seemingly racist rhetoric as a private citizen would not be muffled with the inception of his campaign. Trump's declaration that he intended to seek the Republican nomination for president declared his intention to continue these patterns, railing against illegal immigrants crossing the border from Mexico as criminals and rapists. Later in the primary campaign, he openly mocked the physical disability of a reporter who had criticized him. Trump's banter with his political rivals resorted to elementary if not entertaining name-calling resembling that of a playground bully whose victims, such as Low Energy Jeb (Bush), Lyin' Ted (Cruz), and Little Marco (Rubio), ran more conventional, overshadowed, and eventually ineffective campaigns.

Trump's penchant for playground bullying made for great television, which resulted in a tremendous amount of free advertising that his rivals were never able to overcome. Candidate Trump's success in spite of his obvious flaws questioned the established conventional wisdom of primary elections. Trump's fundraising efforts were quite low compared to those of other candidates. Further, Trump eschewed the use of his personal fortune mostly because there was no need. The campaign, assisted by an onslaught of news coverage, was remarkably efficient at obtaining primary victories with a small campaign war chest. Trump's preference for petty insults and his success in spite of a deficiency in campaign funds or organization would also continue into the general election, where he defeated Democratic presidential nominee Hillary Clinton in the Electoral College despite losing the popular vote by nearly three million votes. The victory was unquestionably one of the greatest upsets in the history of presidential elections. The unorthodox nature of the campaign led to an equally unconventional turnout among lesser-educated white Americans in the Rust Belt, questioning much of the orthodoxy surrounding both polling and election forecasting.

It is clear that Donald Trump, the candidate, exemplified a nontraditional version of American politics. He was a candidate who eschewed the norms of campaign procedure, political correctness, and, in the worst cases, human decency in favor of a rough-and-tumble, take-no-prisoners approach that appealed to those who felt marginalized in a changing society. At the same time, the constitutional design of the presidency has seen political outsiders, even if not as outlandish, rise to the office of the presidency before and has maintained stability. The norms of the office have survived challenge, and the institution persists. A disruptive, outsider candidate with eccentric views has the potential to win the office of the presidency. We have seen that before in American politics. However, never has such a candidate been so alien to political norms. The presidency of Donald Trump represents, in the history of the United States, the most significant test of the constitutional design and boundaries on the office of the presidency by an occupant who is antithetical to everything in its past. As the United States nears the end of Trump's first term, the questions scholars must ask include: To what extent has the Trump presidency been unorthodox? Has the institution of the presidency changed as a result of the Trump presidency? Has the actual operation of the presidency, regardless of the personal penchant for unorthodox behavior of the incumbent, been unorthodox? Finally, has the shock to the system presented by the Trump presidency altered the office of the presidency moving forward? We seek, with the contributions of our esteemed colleagues, to provide insight into these questions throughout this edited volume.

In the pages that follow, scholars of the presidency and American politics generally explore the presidency in the context of Donald Trump, searching for how the office of the presidency has imposed constraints on the Trump administration as well as how Trump has challenged the boundaries of acceptable or expected presidential activity. In the end, the results are a mixed bag. In many ways, the presidency is strong enough to rein in even President Trump, through careful checks and balances that have persevered through those challenges. In yet other ways, however, Trump's actions in the Oval Office have presented direct challenges to the American presidency that have exacerbated long-held problems with checks and balances that Trump's unorthodox style has exposed fully and led to questions regarding the potential for permanent effects of the Trump presidency on the Oval Office.

PREVIEW OF THE BOOK

This volume is divided into three sections. The first section, chapters 1 through 4, explores the Trump presidency in the context of American elections, including Trump as a candidate, the 2016 presidential election, the 2018 midterm elections, and the effect that the election results and the associated political context have had on President Trump's opportunity to govern.

In chapter 1, Chapman Rackaway explores disruption as a tactic that led to Donald Trump's electoral success. Following the primary election success of Congressman Ron Paul in his bid for the presidency in 2012, Republicans felt threatened by insurgent antiestablishment candidates such as Paul and changed the rules of their nominating process. The goal of these modifications was for the nomination process to coalesce around a favorite, presumably from the establishment, earlier in the nomination contest. However, in practice, as Rackaway demonstrates, the proportional awarding of delegates in earlier states actually kept candidates in longer, and the crowded field of seventeen initial candidates originally entered in the Republican primary gave a distinct advantage to a candidate like Donald Trump, who had tremendous name recognition. Benefiting from this recognition and his independent wealth, Trump had a unique opportunity to operate from outside the political mainstream without having to court the high-dollar Republican donors that many candidates depend on for survival and to disrupt the Republican primary in several strategic ways. After exploring the disruptive nature of the Trump candidacy in the primary election, Rackaway details the disruptive nature of the Trump candidacy in the general election, noting that Trump's name recognition and accompanying free media exposure allowed him to ignore polling data, fundraising, and endorsements that are typically critical to a more orthodox candidate's success.

In chapter 2, Wayne Steger explores right-wing populism in the context of the Trump candidacy. While the use of right-wing populism to promote anti-government themes is not new, Candidate Trump brought his own brand of right-wing populism to the fore. Trump is a classic populist in terms of his divisiveness of the public into "us vs. them," whereby the white working and middle classes are pitted against a laundry list of enemies of different racial, ethnic, education, and cultural backgrounds. Supporters of Trump tend to be more likely to lack trust in government and have a penchant for authoritarian values, consistent with previous iterations of populism. Steger explores the extent to which President Trump borrows from the previous iterations of right-wing populism, represented as the "silent majority" under Richard Nixon, as "real Americans" by former vice presidential candidate Sarah Palin, and under the banner of protectionism and immigration policies by Pat Buchanan in his bid for the Republican nomination in 1992 and 1996. Trump borrowed directly from Ronald Reagan in the construction of his campaign theme promising to "Make America Great Again." Trump's version of populism presented more of an emboldened affront to those outside of his core group of supporters, which sets him apart from his right-wing populist predecessors, who, acting within a similar frame, were much subtler.

Russell Brooker details the relationship between President Trump and racial appeals in chapter 3. Donald Trump had taken actions as a private citizen for years that alienated him from African Americans, most notably in his public condemnations of the "Central Park Five" and his leadership in the birther movement, and this alienation continued in his campaign for the presidency. Brooker details how Trump's concept of "the other" to be opposed adopted a style reminiscent of George Wallace's populism, which was centered in racist undertones specifically targeting the opposition and resentment of Black Americans. Donald Trump's electoral success was dependent upon the white vote, which surged in 2016, compared to 2012, especially among lesser-educated white voters in Rust Belt states, while fueling divisiveness and opposition to the Black community and demoralizing the Black vote.

Chapter 4 turns to the 2018 midterm elections in which the Republican Party lost forty seats and control of the House of Representatives. Tyler J. Hughes and Lawrence A. Becker discuss the results of the 2018 midterms, including the aforementioned House elections and the Senate elections, in which the Republicans lost two seats despite the calendar being overwhelmingly in their favor. Despite a Misery Index that was near its lowest point for any midterm election, which should have benefited the Republicans, Democrats were able to turn the tables and win a House majority as well as an unexpected pickup in the Senate. As Hughes and Becker demonstrate, the overarching explanation for the Democratic ability to far outperform expectations based on economic data and the seats that happened to be up for grabs was opposition to President Trump, which increased turnout substantially among important demographic groups nationwide that are predisposed to opposing Trump based upon his policy positions and rhetoric.

Part II focuses on the effect Trump has had on American political institutions. Constitutionally, the president of the United States is compelled to work in some way with the legislative branch, the federal courts, and extensively with the bureaucracy as the head of the executive branch of government. Additionally important is the relationship of the presidency with the media as a venue for the president to reach the public with his policy agenda, to pressure Congress to enact policy, and to communicate with organized interest groups who represent public interests and provide important information and expertise within the legislative branch. It is to the relationships between President Trump and each of these institutional or quasi-institutional actors that the second part turns.

In chapter 5, Paul E. Rutledge explores presidential power in the context of the Trump presidency. The definition of presidential power has over time evolved away from the ability to direct change through persuasion and toward a calculation of the strategic environment in which the president has an opportunity to govern. Despite Trump's unorthodox nature, Rutledge argues that the boundaries placed on the office by the strategic presidency and political time[1] make the president's opportunity structure quite orthodox. Facing a polarized Congress, a fractured Republican Party in Congress, a popular vote loss, and a public mood trending toward liberalism, Trump's opportunity for obtaining legislative success was limited. This opportunity became even more limited following the midterm loss of the House of Representatives and the 2019 impeachment in the House for obstruction of justice and abuse of power. The Trump presidency, then, perfectly fits the model of a disjunctive presidency within the Reagan regime, which could have major implications for 2020 and beyond for the Republican Party.

In chapter 6, Rebecca M. Eissler takes an in-depth look at President Trump's legislative policy agenda. Constitutionally, presidents are given the opportunity to advance a policy agenda in Article II, Section 3, via the State of the Union address. Presidents have a significant incentive to engage actively in the legislative process, seeking to accomplish their goals through passing legislation rather than solely through executive action. Legislative enactment is more permanent because Congress would have to enact another law to counter an established law, whereas executive unilateral approaches to accomplish major policy goals are easily undone by the next president if he or she chooses to do so. Despite both this permanence and serving for the first two years under unified Republican government, President Trump, Eissler demonstrates, devoted more of his energies to his policy agenda on public appeals via Twitter to obtain support for his priorities while engaging in executive action. Eissler argues that, compared to other presidents, President Trump took very little interest in congressional procedure and legislative negotiations. Rather, his approach to the legislative agenda took on more of a "governing by campaigning" motif, where he was most successful at gaining support from those who agreed with him rather than those who were at the margins and crucial to building successful legislative coalitions.

Jonathan Lewallen examines President Trump's bargaining relationship with Congress in chapter 7. The Constitution establishes a significant bargaining relationship between the president and Congress, in terms both of the use of the veto and of appointments to the executive and judicial branches. Lewallen explores President Trump's use of "negative power" through veto bargaining. President Trump's use of veto threats falls in line with those of previous presidents for the most part. However, his use of the veto has been unorthodox in that much of his veto activity has been aimed at the Republican-controlled Senate passing resolutions in opposition to his foreign policies. Further, President Trump has encountered much more difficulty than anticipated getting his nominees passed for both executive branch and judicial vacancies. The Trump presidency is unorthodox, as Lewallen demonstrates, in the number of positions within the executive branch that were left vacant and the amount of time that has passed with those positions remaining vacant. Further, in spite of favorable institutional changes for judicial nominees and Republican control of the Senate, President Trump has faced much more difficulty than his predecessors in getting his nominees out of committee.

In chapter 8, JoBeth Surface Shafran and Heather T. Rimes explore Trump's relationship with the executive branch further. Similar to many of the other ways in which President Trump's leadership style has been unorthodox, Twitter is a major factor in his leadership of the executive branch. Shafran and Rimes chronicle a continuous onslaught of tweets from the president's Twitter account aimed at executive branch agencies and officials. Among these posts on social media, President Trump has announced policy changes that have surprised executive branch officials, has announced personnel changes via Twitter, and has publicly chastised current and former members of the executive branch. Such an approach to executive branch management is unprecedented in the history of the presidency. Despite the pleading among his advisors for the president to stop using Twitter in this way, he has continued unabated.

Thomas Rogers Hunter examines President Trump's relationship with the federal judiciary in chapter 9. In what is becoming a significant theme, Hunter chronicles the president's extensive use of Twitter to criticize both federal courts and their decisions, most notably the Ninth Circuit Appellate Court. Further, the president's use of Twitter to criticize individual decisions and individual justices on a personal level has led to numerous unusually strong public rebukes from justices, most notably from Chief Justice John Roberts. Perhaps the most successful aspect of the Trump presidency from a conservative perspective, though, has been his collaboration with Mitch McConnell in the so-called judges project, which has seen a virtual conveyer belt of judicial nominees rolling through the confirmation process in the Senate. Trump's appointees, despite many receiving a record number of negative votes and an unusual number not emerging from committee, as Lewallen notes, have been among the most numerous, the most ideologically conservative, and the youngest to ever gain positions on the federal bench. In this regard, it is likely that a major lasting effect of the Trump administration will be a significant rightward turn in the composition of federal courts for several decades.

Finally, Part III examines Trump and public policy. Chapters 10 and 11 turn to President Trump's relations with quasi-institutional participants in American democracy, namely, interest groups and the media. In chapter 10, Burdett Loomis explores the former and details the relationship of organized interest groups with Donald Trump's executive branch. Trump campaigned on "draining the swamp" in Washington, which was a pejorative way of describing his arms-length approach to lobbyists as well as his steadfast opposition to the so-called deep state. Rather than draining the swamp, however, Loomis details how the revolving door has shifted from the legislative to the executive branch, with many former Washington lobbyists now being employed in Trump's executive branch. Further, Washington lobbyists have found unprecedented access to the top levels of American government by meeting with the president informally at one of his private clubs. These findings could produce lasting changes for interest group access as well as executive branch staffing that Loomis indicates could greatly enhance the power of interest groups moving forward.

In chapter 11, Matthew Eshbaugh-Soha and Joshua P. Montgomery examine Trump's relationship with the media. To argue that President Trump's relationship with the media has been truculent would be a substantial understatement. Eshbaugh-Soha and Montgomery demonstrate that Trump has experienced more coverage from the media than any other president. It is also clear that Trump has been more combative with the media than any other president, which likely fuels the negative tone of the coverage. Trump's press secretaries have been less engaged with the media than his predecessors, which hampers his ability to control the message. To make up for this, President Trump uses Twitter quite liberally to engage with the news media and promote his policy agenda. In spite of these efforts, as Eshbaugh-Soha and Montgomery demonstrate, the media tends to cover Trump in traditional ways, with more attention given to traditional speeches than to tweets. While Trump's media strategy is quite unorthodox, the authors indicate that his coverage by the media really is not so unorthodox.

In chapter 12, Roy T. Meyers assesses President Trump's negotiations over the nation's budget. President Trump has continued in the establishment of a new Republican orthodoxy that eschews concerns for racking up budget deficits. While this has been a fairly consistent stance on the part of Republican presidents in the post-Reagan era, with George H. W. Bush being a notable exception, it is a substantial departure from the fiscal conservatism espoused by previous Republican presidents like Dwight D. Eisenhower. Trump also, as Meyers describes, has expanded the use of the budget as a political football to achieve policy goals such as funding for the border wall. This includes the sequestration and redirection of budgetary funds provided for defense to procurement of the border wall, which is constitutionally questionable. President Trump also attacked the Federal Reserve repeatedly on Twitter, consistent with the pattern of his Twitter use. Finally, as Meyers indicates, the penchant for deficit spending was a continuation of the fiscal approach of the Reagan Republicans, which was kicked into overdrive with the stimulus package presented as a result of COVID-19, making Trump the greatest deficit spender in the history of the republic.

In chapter 13, Christopher Olds explores the relationship between President Trump's rhetoric, on the one hand, and economic uncertainty, on the other. Specifically, given the president's penchant for tweeting, Olds examines the relationship between President Trump's Twitter activity and several indicators of economic uncertainty. Using vector autoregressive techniques, which establish relationships among closely related time series, Olds demonstrates an important reciprocal relationship between the volume of tweets issued by Trump and the level of economic uncertainty in equity markets. As Trump tweets more, regardless of whether his attention is on the economy or not, the information overload and associated fatigue tends to lead to more economic uncertainty. Interestingly and perhaps not surprisingly, Olds finds that as perceived economic uncertainty increases, President Trump also tweets more, leading to a vicious self-perpetuating cycle of 280-character word salads and economic despair.

Chapter 14 details Trump's approach to foreign policy. There is perhaps no other area of the Trump presidency that is more unorthodox than his approach to foreign policy. As Jeffrey S. Peake indicates in this chapter, Trump has a strange tendency to eschew multilateral trade agreements and relationships with longtime allies, in favor of bilateral and unilateral foreign policy action that has taken unprecedentedly warm steps toward dictators and hostile regimes. Such activities are a major concern moving forward, as Trump's unorthodox approach could indicate to the world that the foreign policy of the United States is dependent on election results and the partisanship of the president. If this is the perception of US foreign and trade policies in the global community, Peake argues, tremendous uncertainty and increased instability could result. This is perhaps the most threatening aspect of the unorthodox presidency of Donald Trump documented in this book.

Finally, the conclusion revisits some of the most important findings from the volume, focusing on the extent to which President Trump's tenure in office has been unorthodox versus the extent to which the office of the presidency and the constitutional constraints imposed by checks and balances have reined in some of Trump's most unorthodox tendencies. With these lessons in mind, the editors focus on the place of the Trump presidency in historical context and offer a preview of what this volume indicates as the nation closes in on the 2020 presidential election.

NOTE

1. For a complete discussion of the concept of political time, see Stephen Skowronek's *Presidential Leadership in Political Time: Reprise and Reappraisal,* 3rd ed. (Lawrence: University Press of Kansas, 2020).

REFERENCE

Skowronek, Stephen. *Presidential Leadership in Political Time: Reprise and Reappraisal.* 3rd ed. Lawrence: University Press of Kansas, 2020.

PART I

Trump and the Electorate

CHAPTER 1

The Disruptive Campaign of Donald J. Trump

Chapman Rackaway

In the world of business, the term "disruption" has become a common buzzword. Disruptive innovators in business take well-established and stable companies or processes and succeed by beating those powerful forces at their own game (Bower and Christensen 1995). Thirty years ago, the idea of retail giant Sears having its dominant market share eaten away by Wal-Mart and online retailers to the point that the company declared bankruptcy and became functionally extinct would have been a shocking assertion. But Wal-Mart (and later Amazon) did disrupt Sears's business model, the old giant did not or would not adapt, and the new upstart took its place as a dominant player. Disruption as a tactic is well-established in the realm of private business, and the paradigm of disruptive innovation has spread to other areas. Southern New Hampshire University, the University of Phoenix, and other online educators, for example, have disrupted higher education.[1]

The realm of American presidential politics is no more insulated from the potential for disruptive innovation than any other industry. Perhaps it is appropriate that the most disruptive force in politics in decades entered with no political experience at all and a background in the private business sector—real estate, specifically—where disruption is a regular occurrence. Donald J. Trump was the most disruptive candidate to successfully pursue the presidency since Franklin Roosevelt argued for significant federal spending and regulatory intervention as a solution to the economic crisis of the late 1920s. Roosevelt changed the political game significantly, not just in policy but in his use of new media as well. In 2016, Donald Trump comprehensively challenged established political strategies and tactics.

When disruptors enter a new environment, they either succeed or fail. In retrospect, Trump appeared to be a candidate who would fail in his efforts to disrupt decades of best practices in presidential campaigning. However, as unlikely a rise to success as he had, Trump did indeed successfully bring disruption to politics through his 2016 campaign. And if the history of disruptive innovation suggests anything for the future, it is that Trump's disruption will significantly shift the strategies and practices of campaigns for some time.

THE ENVIRONMENT OF DISRUPTION

Donald Trump had long been considered a potential candidate for president. As early as 1988, Trump's name was referenced in news accounts and opinion polls to determine his viability compared with other prospective entrants to the race. In 1999, Trump publicly declared himself a candidate for the Reform Party's 2000 presidential nomination but never filed the paperwork or developed a campaign organization to pursue the office (Edsall 1999). Trump made his pronouncement on the *Larry King Live* interview program at a time when presidential candidates would announce their intention at dedicated press conferences. Donald Trump's public persona, as a real estate investor and later as a candidate, would be built using media to promote his brand and interests. Commentators at the time openly questioned whether Trump was a serious candidate or simply engaging in a publicity stunt in the interest of self-promotion (Neal 1999).

The Barack Obama presidency would see Trump pivot to more seriously considering a run for the Republican nomination. Early on in the Obama presidency, Trump openly declared himself a "birther," that is, someone who was skeptical that the president's birth certificate was legitimate (Blow 2016). Trump then changed his voter registration to Republican, and in 2011, he was invited to speak at the Conservative Political Action Conference (CPAC), at the time one of the springboards for Republican presidential hopefuls' campaigns (Milbank 2011). Trump quickly became the front-running Republican in the 2012 nomination pre-polls, but he eventually opted out of pursuing the GOP's nomination that year (Schoen 2011). Trump became progressively more serious about running, including letting his contract for television's *The Apprentice* lapse in 2015 and making a return engagement to CPAC that year (Moody 2013). Despite continued insinuations that Trump was brand-building, he was increasingly serious in his desire to pursue the presidency.

The environment in which Trump ran in 2016 was much more favorable to his candidacy than 2012 was. Obama was a divisive president and not overwhelmingly popular, but he was popular enough to carry roughly 50 percent approval ratings in an improving economy. The eventual nominee, Mitt Romney, could not contest effectively and never came close to the incumbent. The economy was still solid, though not impressive, in 2016, which played more into a Republican nominee's hands. Further, the time-for-change model suggested that after two terms of a Democratic administration, voters were ready to elect the out-party into the White House (Abramowitz 2008b).

Trump also faced a better opportunity within the GOP structure. The Romney/Ryan loss in 2012 led conservatives to a significant period of soul-searching. Worried that the Republican Party's message was not resonating with voters, GOP insiders began discussing concerns that the George W. Bush–era rhetoric of low taxes and cultural conservatism was a losing strategy for elections to come and that a new message with new messengers was necessary to return the White House to Republican hands (Martin 2012). Even more importantly, after a chaotic 2012 primary and convention for the Republicans, national leaders made a number of changes to the nomination system that would unknowingly make Trump's path to the nomination easier. Eager to quell outsider uprisings that led to a strong showing for Ron Paul's campaign for the nomination, the GOP limited the number of unpledged delegates, tightened rules on caucuses, reduced the number of caucus-state delegates, and made earlier states allocate their delegates on a proportional rather than a winner-take-all basis (Guilford 2016). Designed to encourage party mainliners to rally around a consensus candidate more quickly than the prolonged 2012 nomination contest, the rules changes actually made it easier for Trump to emerge as the presumptive nominee despite not being a consensus candidate.

DISRUPTING THE PREPRIMARY

The first phase of a presidential nomination process today is known as the preprimary. In the pre-primary phase, candidates typically seek endorsements from party insiders, demonstrate the ability to fundraise, and establish strong professional campaign organizations (Adkins and Dowdle 2002). The length, cost, and haphazard calendar that make up the primary election season (that time when caucuses and primaries are actually conducted) makes the pre-primary an important vetting process for hopeful candidates. Over the last twenty years, ever more candidates have entered the pre-primary presidential sweepstakes, but until 2012, most of them dropped out well before the primaries began. The Republicans faced a different pre-primary phase in 2012, where ten candidates remained during the primaries. The crowded field presented a problem, spreading support out and throttling the GOP's attempt to find a consensus candidate. The 2012 GOP primary was expensive, long, and arduous and resulted in only a partial consensus nominee, Mitt Romney.

The GOP's rules changes prior to 2016 were supposed to winnow the potential candidates down, but instead they had the opposite effect. A total of seventeen Republican candidates pursued the nomination, with twelve remaining at least into the beginning of primary season. Despite the GOP's early proportionality rule designed to create a consensus candidate, it actually encouraged candidates to stay longer in the race than they would have in a winner-take-all primary system. The proportional allocation of early votes gave marginal candidates small victories they could use to fundraise and continue on with the campaign. The crowded field was thus a ripe opportunity for a candidate with name recognition to enter. Such a well-known candidate would only have to win approximately 30 percent of a given state's votes to have a strong showing and eventually capture the nomination.

Before Trump's entrance into the 2016 race, the field was reflecting a "new generation" of candidates, at least on the Republican side. A mixture of youth and experience, upstarts and mainstream insiders, and candidates with extensive name recognition constituted the field. The only holdovers from 2012 were former senator Rick Santorum and Texas governor Rick Perry. Other governors like Perry who had made national names for themselves by embracing the Tea Party style of conservatism, like Scott Walker and Bobby Jindal, entered the race, and more established mainline Republicans like Mike Huckabee and Chris Christie joined in as well. Longshot moderates George Pataki and John Kasich were outside the Republican primary base. Outsiders Carly Fiorina and Ben Carson added their names to the list. A new wave of US senators including Ted Cruz, Lindsey Graham, Rand Paul, and Marco Rubio also contested the primary. Of all the candidates, former Florida governor and political scion Jeb Bush was considered by most pundits to be the pre-election favorite. But the open seat and new rules meant that a multitude of candidates saw an opportunity to contend for the nomination despite the design of the new delegate allocation rules.

Trump chose to delay entry into the primary until June 2015 and was one of the latest candidates to include their name. Unlike other candidates, Trump had a built-in advantage of existing name recognition that would significantly disrupt the usual practices of politics. Since the 1980s, Donald Trump had curated a media profile that made his name ubiquitous and synonymous with success. Books on business negotiations, constant attention in the media, and since 2004 a prime-time television audience with his show *The Apprentice* (and its spinoff *The Celebrity Apprentice*) gave Trump name recognition that dwarfed that of the other candidates in the field. Trump did not need to run the fusillade of ads or have a hundreds-strong ground team in Iowa to push his name into peoples' minds.

Name recognition was a significant advantage, but it was also symbolic of the disruptive nature of the Trump candidacy. In the McGovern-Fraser era of functionally binding presidential primaries, candidates establish campaign operations nationwide to build up enough name recognition to register on polls and earn media attention. That name recognition is vital, because voters do strongly base their decisions about which candidates they support on name recognition (Kam and Zechmeister 2013). Since the general public does not pay sustained attention to politics, even candidates who are well-known in political circles rarely have high name recognition. Traditionally, candidates have designed their media campaigns around building that familiarity with voters, but it is a difficult, costly, and time-consuming task. Decades in the public eye outside of politics gave Donald Trump a level of name recognition unheard of by political candidate standards. In a 2015 tracking poll, Trump's name recognition was 92 percent, twenty points higher than his next-closest rival, Jeb Bush, who himself benefited from his family's extensive political history (Dugan 2015).

Trump did not need to spend the millions of dollars that candidates typically do in pursuit of presidential nominations. The months of advertising runs with soft-focus biographies and lists of credible accomplishments would have been redundant for Trump. The asset of name recognition allowed Trump to run a different kind of campaign, one for which his opponents were not ready.

Trump's wealth also served as a disruptive factor, allowing him the freedom to deviate from typical Republican presidential primary strategy. Wichita, Kansas, oil tycoons Charles and David Koch have long served as GOP kingmakers, so much so that the pre-primary fundraising phase of the Republican process has become colloquially known as the "Koch primary" because securing Koch financial support would guarantee that candidate the ability to stay in the primary long after others had dropped out. Candidates would expend a significant amount of time and energy to secure the Koch brothers' blessing, but Donald Trump was able to sidestep the "Koch primary" with his own financial backing (Parker 2015).

Candidates for president normally have been members of that party their entire adult lives. Those candidates build careers around eventually seeking the presidency, and party switching is exceptionally rare. When candidates do switch parties, the event is once-in-a-lifetime. Ronald Reagan's conversion from FDR Democrat to Goldwater Republican is the sole example of such a successful transition. But Donald Trump flaunted convention by having oscillated between the Democratic and Republican Parties five times over thirty years. Trump registered as a Republican in the 1980s, switched to New York's Independence Party the following decade, changed his registration to Democrat in 2001, only to change back to the GOP in 2009 (Gillin 2015). By 2011, Trump chose to remove all partisan affiliation from his registration and went back to the Republicans in 2012 (Gillin 2015).

DISRUPTING THE PRIMARY

Prior to Trump's campaign, the conventional wisdom about party primaries came foremost from Cohen et al.'s *The Party Decides*, which showed that between 1980 and 2000, party elites coordinated to provide cues early in the pre-primary process that guided party elites' preferred candidates to victory (Cohen et al. 2009). Donald Trump would upend the theory, since party elites rallied around different candidates and largely avoided him. Trump secured roughly one-third the number of endorsements that party stalwarts Marco Rubio and Ted Cruz earned. John Kasich's long-shot bid even tallied nearly as many significant endorsements as Trump's did (Bycoffe 2016). The Trump campaign intentionally bypassed party elites, which was supposed to be the more direct path to primary victory. The authors of *The Party Decides* said as much in 2020, affirming the theory that Trump had taken party elite control away from the GOP (Anonymous 2020).

Once Trump formally entered the primary in June 2015, he used his strategic name-recognition advantage to disrupt the entire campaign. Four specific areas of disruption are the focus here: 1) policy agenda, 2) business orientation, 3) limited media strategy, and 4) rhetoric. Not all of Trump's disruptions were strategic in nature, however. One particularly noteworthy element of Trump's campaigning was his disruptive, but not necessarily strategic, rhetoric.

Strategic Disruption

Donald Trump's presidential campaign differed from others before it in that he and his campaign team ignored or flaunted established political strategies and tactics long accepted as necessary for competitive presidential nomination campaigns. The unconventional strategy looked like a loser to pundits and analysts accustomed to a specific type of campaigning, but Trump's name recognition advantage would outweigh all of the established conventional wisdom about candidates running for president with no prior electoral experience.

The Trump policy agenda further differentiated him from the rest of the field and established GOP practice. Instead of focusing on establishing bona fides with evangelicals and talking tax cuts, Trump took stands that were unsettled within Republican circles or even antithetical to the rhetoric that GOP candidates had used for the last two decades. Prior to Trump's candidacy, Republican candidates tended to speak in reverential tones about international issues such as NAFTA and trade with China. Outsourcing was generally approved by GOP hopefuls as good for the prices of domestic goods for consumers. Trump would change that completely.

Immigration, with specific attention to immigrants coming to the United States outside of the formal citizenship process, was a position on which the GOP was still divided. In 2012, the Republican nomination hopefuls showed a variety of different approaches to immigration policy, and few took the hardline stance Trump would eventually favor. Eventual nominee Mitt Romney mostly avoided the issue throughout his campaign. Some candidates, like Ben Carson, took stronger stands, pushing for stricter rules on legal immigration and border

control, but they found no added support for taking such stands. After the Romney campaign failed to win the presidency, some Republicans, such as then House Speaker John Boehner, indicated the GOP
might acquiesce to the Obama administration's stated goal of more
lenient immigration policy reforms (Preston 2012).

Trump's approach in 2016 was to focus a significant amount of energy on a clear and divisive strategy on immigration. Blasting what
he saw as an overly lax and permissive immigration practice under
the Obama administration, Trump noted in a fiery speech numerous
Americans who had been killed by illegally residing immigrants. Noteworthy in his speech was reference to Kate Steinle, a young woman
killed by an undocumented immigrant in San Francisco. Trump specifically mentioned San Francisco's status as a "sanctuary city" that
would not turn illegal immigrants over to federal Immigration and
Customs Enforcement (ICE) for deportation if they were arrested. For
Trump, the flow of illegal immigrants into the United States equated
to a Trojan Horse, and he insinuated that this flow was designed to
fundamentally alter the racial and cultural landscape of the country.
The fiery and pointed rhetoric was easily the clearest policy position
Republicans had articulated during a presidential campaign, marking
Trump as a candidate more than willing to flaunt established practices
and conventional wisdom among Republican Party and campaign op-
eratives (Anonymous 2016).

Primary elections encourage candidates to take more extreme,
polarized stances on issues, but before Trump, no Republican candidates with serious designs on the presidency used immigration as
their issue. Trump recognized an opportunity, because a March poll
found that nearly half of Republican voters favored a hard line on
immigration, including deportation of all undocumented immigrants
from the United States. When Trump proposed a wall as a preventative against further immigration, nearly four in five of his supporters
favored building it. Furthermore, Trump supporters were the most
likely group to have negative views about immigrants in general (Doherty 2016).

Trump saw an opportunity to disrupt the campaign by making immigration a central part of his rhetoric. Public opinion had been shifting, from a place in 2012 when immigration opinions were divided
among partisans on both sides to 2016 when views had moved into
significant alignment with partisanship (Gimpel 2016). The freedom
that Trump's campaign felt may have been related to his wealth and

independence from the Koch primary. The Koch brothers had long taken a more immigrant-friendly stance on the policy area than many Republicans, quietly staying out of the fight during the Obama administration while members of the Tea Party embraced a harder line on immigration. Republican candidates likely softened their stances when confronted with the Kochs' preference, but Trump did not need to worry about alignment with the Wichita billionaires (Mider 2015). With Tea Party candidates having established a precedent for hardline immigration rhetoric, Trump seized on an opportunity that prior candidates had lacked.

The primary-phase hardline on immigration was not restricted to the southern US border, either. Trump's campaign rhetoric also mentioned Muslim immigration as a threat to US security. On the campaign trail, Trump likened Mexican gang MS-13 to terrorists such as the Islamic radicals who carried out the 9/11 attacks and promised to secure all borders from any threat (Lind 2016). Trump also voiced opposition to foreign trade agreements and the gradual offshoring of American jobs. Expanded global trade agreements was one of the unifying issues among Republican candidates before 2016, so Trump once again was deviating from the standard set of conservative talking points. Rather than this new approach turning Republican primary voters off, the GOP electorate rallied around Trump.

One notable element of Trump's rhetoric was a common refrain heard among Republican candidates for twenty years beforehand, namely, that Trump would run government more like a business. As only Ross Perot had tried before, Trump ran for president without any electoral experience. Therefore when Trump made overtures to bring more private-sector practices into government, he could speak from authentic experience.

As an extension of Trump's approach to bring more of the business world into politics, he violated standing practice by running against the Republican Party's elite leadership. Party elites are a vital part of winning coalitions for primary candidates (Cohen et al. 2009). For money, endorsements, expanding media coverage, favorable treatment by state and local officials, and many other reasons, the party apparatus is a powerful tool that most candidates revere at best and fear at least. But Trump's primary campaign identified itself as an insurgent attack on the established party elite. Ron Paul tried a similar strategy, if ideologically from a very different origin, and was unsuccessful. Trump took a page out of the Tea Party playbook, however, that had worked effectively in 2010 and 2012 for state-level and congressional candidates (Rosenthal and Trost 2012).

The Trump campaign's most significant deviation from established strategy during the primary phase, though, was his media strategy. Primary campaigns for presidential nominations are expensive endeavors, costing successful candidates around $100 million over the last few campaign cycles. However, Trump's bombastic style and made-for-TV persona allowed him to run a very limited and low-cost advertising campaign. By February 26, 2016, when Trump's momentum was strong enough to virtually guarantee him the nomination, his campaign had spent only about $10 million on advertising (Silver 2016a). Other candidates spent much more for much less. Jeb Bush put eight times as much money into his campaign as Trump, and four other Republicans spent more than the New York real estate mogul. Those five Republicans (Bush, Marco Rubio, Ted Cruz, Chris Christie, and John Kasich) spent a total of $169 million but could never compete with Trump.

In most campaigns, Trump's low spending would have been the mark of an also-ran candidate, someone who would struggle to finish in the top three of any state contest. Instead, Trump got more unpaid media coverage than all of the other candidates combined. The equivalent exposure of Trump's media coverage was estimated to be valued at nearly $2 billion. Trump did not leverage his personal wealth to blanket the primary states with television ads, despite being one of the people most capable of such a level of spending. Cable news programs particularly focused on Trump, with Fox News' coverage providing him access to a core element of the GOP's primary electorate. The other candidates in the GOP field were dwarfed by Trump's unpaid exposure. While Trump received $1.89 billion in non-advertising television exposure, the next highest value total was Cruz at a mere $313 million (Confessore and Yourish 2016).

Name recognition, decades of experience on television, and a larger-than-life reputation combined to make Trump an intriguing character to be the headliner for news programming, and Trump effectively availed himself of that unique advantage. Trump's news media exposure was not all made up of fawning testimonials to his business acumen and leadership. Another disruptive strategy, one that appeared much riskier, would involve the rhetorical style Trump chose to employ.

Rhetoric

Donald Trump used language differently than any of his primary competitors and indeed differently than nearly any candidate who came before him. Trump certainly used a more populist approach in his campaign messaging, but the style of Trump's communication was itself unique and disruptive.

One may speculate as to whether a candidate such as Trump would have succeeded in an age before social networking sites, specifically the 280-character domain of Twitter. Trump's decades as a media figure had helped produce an acerbic personality who was willing to do something political candidates usually tried to avoid: denigrating others in the public spotlight. Prior to his candidacy, Trump was a regular tweeter. Trump's political profile expanded over his willingness to question the veracity of Barack Obama's birth certificate and included critiquing the supposed plastic surgery that celebrities at awards shows had done (Barbaro 2015).

Twitter was the venue but also a mindset. As a platform, Twitter's unique quality has always been the imposed brevity of the content on it, even after they doubled the character limit of a given tweet in 2017. Pithy and snarky content are mainstays of the Twitter ecosystem, and Trump enthusiastically embraced the medium as a campaign tool to supplement his abundant media coverage.

The Trump campaign embraced what Winberg (2017) calls "insult politics." Prior to Trump's candidacy, most candidates strove to be critical of their competing candidates but refrained from becoming personal or insulting. The tone was negative but not denigrating. Political professionals termed the style "comparative" to avoid the common connotation that the candidates were nasty for being "negative." Campaign strategists and candidates alike worried about their public perception and wanted to come across as likable, which usually meant sounding optimistic and being congenial. Trump would not worry about either of those considerations.

Instead of pivoting from his caustic and often insulting persona on Twitter once he entered the 2016 GOP primary, Trump brought his brand of insult politics with him. As Virginia Heffernan, writing for Politico, aptly put it:

> Donald Trump, the crowned social-media virtuoso of the 2016 campaign cycle, is floridly available, grabbing the Internet's lapels

every few hours. With its sheen of raw improv and generous tolerance for subliteracy, Twitter has become Trump's natural home. No surprise: The platform works especially well for anyone who's convinced they've been silenced elsewhere, including those in the midst of losing their minds (think Amanda Bynes, Rupert Murdoch, Curt Schilling) or finding their voices (Marc Andreessen, Mia Farrow, John Podhoretz). Trump, who once claimed he had been called "the best 140 character writer in the world," makes himself heard in fragments, monosyllables and exclamation points, a proud male hysteric with the deafening staccato and hair-trigger immune system that Twitter exists to host. He embraces odd abbreviations, erratic capitalization and typos in his invariably reactive rants: "illegal imm," "Presidential Primaries," "He is do totally biased." The Twitter account @realDonaldTrump is the opposite of aloof, the opposite of polished (Heffernan 2016).

If Twitter was, as Politico intimated, a political Land of Misfit Toys, then Donald Trump crowned himself its king in 2016. Trump began his onslaught of abuse in the primary phase, calling fellow Republican candidates names such as "little Marco Rubio," "low-energy Jeb Bush," and "lyin' Ted Cruz." Such unfiltered and intentional insults were as wide-ranging as they were caustic. Normally, campaign strategy dictates that a campaign attack is launched only against candidates who present as a threat to the attacking candidate. But Trump personally insulted every one of the Republican hopefuls in the nomination phase of the 2016 election. Trump refused to ignore the candidates, like John Kasich, that were nowhere near close to Trump's polling numbers. Among political professionals, there was a sense of trepidation about going negative against other candidates, because there was always the chance the tactic could backfire. But as with so many other established norms of campaigning, Trump flaunted the cautious approach to attack by being almost indiscriminate in his personally negative commentary. The practice was so out-of-the-ordinary that the *New York Times* dedicated a page to cataloging the people, concepts, and entities that Trump insulted on Twitter during his 2016 campaign (Lee and Quealy 2017).

Some of Trump's rhetoric was clearly strategic. One of the rhetorical principles against which Trump railed on the campaign stump was "political correctness." During a *Meet the Press* appearance in 2015,

held a stalwart group of Republican allies at arm's length: religious conservatives. In one more important way, Trump flaunted GOP campaign convention by not immediately seeking support from them. Since Reagan's election in 1980, one of the most powerful elements of the Republican electoral coalition has been composed of religious conservatives. George W. Bush's campaigns were built on a foundation of Christian conservatives, and pundits believed that the reason both John McCain and Mitt Romney lost their bids for the presidency was a lack of enthusiasm from evangelical Protestants (Hagerty 2012). With the evangelical presence looming large for 2016, one would think the Texan son of a well-known evangelical pastor currently serving in the US Senate would be favored among them over a twice-divorced New York real estate mogul with a brash, confrontational, and family-unfriendly caustic style of speaking. Such a juxtaposition made Ted Cruz, bringing pastor father Rafael's imprimatur among evangelicals, a safer bet than Donald Trump going into the campaign (Draper 2016).

The Iowa caucuses reinforced the idea of Cruz's relationship with the evangelical wing of the GOP being a winner. Cruz took first place in Iowa with just over 26 percent of the vote. Trump, however, was only three percentage points behind and running strong despite lacking the important evangelical base. Cruz's win may have seemed as though evangelicals would carry him to eventual victory, but his Iowa victory would not follow with more until the primary calendar shifted westward where more caucuses were held. Trump did worse in caucus states across the board than he did in those with ballot primaries, so Iowa's presence as first on the calendar may have overexaggerated the influence evangelicals would have. Caucuses tend to have lower voter turnout, amplifying those who mobilize, and among Republicans, evangelicals tend to mobilize very well (Gold and Russell 2007).

Trump disrupted the typical Republican voting blocs by making the evangelical wing of the party come to him. From the 1980s until Trump's campaign, the most reliable GOP voting bloc was composed of evangelical Protestants (Smidt and Kellstedt 1992; Rozell and Gupta 2006; Gill and DeFronzo 2013). As Trump accumulated more state wins and convention delegates, evangelicals had to make a choice: stay with the Republicans and embrace Trump, switch to Hillary Clinton, or encourage an independent candidate to run. With no viable independent alternatives, evangelicals began slowly gravitating toward Trump over the course of the primary season.

The alliance between Trump and the evangelical wing of the GOP looked to be an uneasy one, as no Republican candidate (perhaps ever) so appeared to ignore or reject evangelical religious and behavioral norms in their personal life as did Trump. At the time, pundits took to predicting the end of the evangelicals' power within the Republican Party because of the incommensurable differences between Trump and his new faithful compatriots (Turner 2016).

Trump clearly spoke in a way that was different from others before him, but it resonated with the base voters he was trying to reach and activate. Trump's campaign passed on the typical conservative campaign messaging of the last twenty years, basing his appeals on working-class white voters who had felt the government did not see or care about them. By couching his language in a vernacular that connected to the white working class, Trump displayed a discourse of "authenticity" rather than "truth" that provided a crucial cornerstone of Trump's appeal to his electoral base (Montgomery 2017).

The tone and tenor of language was not the only disruption that Trump's strategy foisted upon American politics. A long-standing norm had been violated: presidential media aloofness. While presidents have had difficult relationships with reporters and media outlets since the republic's founding, what makes Twitter unique is that it allows a president to bypass the traditional media entirely. For decades presidents used subtle techniques to try to manipulate the messages the media would communicate about them and their policies, but with Trump's use of social media, he was able to ignore the traditional media outlets and communicate directly with people in a way so innovative it had not been seen since FDR's Fireside Chats (Keith 2016).

The lack of success that Trump had in caucuses like Iowa's was a relative one, and the inverse of that circumstance would be one of Trump's great disruptions. As primaries tend toward low voter turnout, they are mobilization games. Caucus states, where only the most fervent of the political faithful turn out to vote, produce results that are usually more in favor of ideologically polarized candidates (Abramowitz 2008a). Caucus states provide a test of where the most committed voters will follow a candidate, and they often factor prominently in campaign strategy. However, Donald Trump's campaign did not see appealing to the faithful as a winning strategy and thus disrupted conventional Republican campaigning thought. Instead of going for the caucuses, as Cruz did, Trump's chances to win the nomination rested with the least likely primary voters: nonaffiliated voters in open ballot primary states. Turnout in open primary states surged in 2016 over 2012, and in those states Trump had his greatest success (Rackaway 2018).

Finally, a signature rhetorical strategy bears note here in Trump's campaign slogan "Make America Great Again" or MAGA. Typically, presidential campaign sloganeering either reflects the character of the individual running ("Reformer with Results" was George W. Bush's slogan in 2000 and "For People, for a Change" was Bill Clinton's 1992 catchphrase) or an aspirational, optimistic view of the future (Barack Obama's "Yes We Can" in 2008 and George H. W. Bush's "Kinder, Gentler Nation" in 1988). Donald Trump would upend the forward-looking and optimistic sloganeering with Make America Great Again. The most salient word in the slogan is "again," which was engineered to evoke nostalgia for a time past rather than to press on into the future. Pairing the backward look with the two middle words combined to make a critique of the United States' culture that had not been seen before. By wanting to "make America great again," there was an implication in the slogan that America was not great or had somehow failed in its tradition of greatness. Acknowledging or asserting failure in the American ethos was unheard of among campaigns before Trump's, but his slogan effectively said that America was not as great as it could or should be.

The use of MAGA can be seen in other perspectives, in not-so-subtle ways as a repudiation of the rhetorical and strategic approach to his predecessor's presidency. Trump followed a very traditional campaign strategy in separating himself from President Obama, but inherent in Trump's rhetoric was the assertion that America not only was moving in the wrong direction under Obama but also was lesser, weakened, under his leadership.

Campaigns consistently espouse American exceptionalism, a mark of the greatness of the nation evoking national pride. Political campaigns have, over time, played a significant role in the socialization of American exceptionalism (Arceneaux 2006). In that vein, Trump's campaign diametrically opposed itself to the conventional aggrandizement of American culture by suggesting a flaw, or weakness, in it. Much like the other disruptions, implicitly rejecting American exceptionalism was an incredibly risky strategy that paid off for Trump.

Combining the rhetorical and strategic deviations, Trump's campaign should never have had success at all. Despite every rejection of established campaign practice, Trump seemingly bulldozed his way through the primary season. By late May, Donald Trump had won enough delegates to clinch the Republican nomination at July's convention (Kelly 2016). After winning a nomination through disruption, Trump would continue working against expected strategies in the final phase of the campaign.

DISRUPTING THE GENERAL ELECTION

Having established a norm-violating standard in the primary, the Trump campaign continued doing so in the general election against Democratic nominee Hillary Clinton. Some of the same practices carried over. Elite endorsements, or the lack thereof, did not hinder Trump in the primary, and so a lack of newspaper endorsements similarly did not affect his general election campaign.

Newspaper endorsements have long been a staple of presidential campaigns. Most major dailies have tended toward endorsing Democrats, but a number of papers have broken with that standard over the last four decades and endorsed Republicans (Chiang and Knight 2011). Trump's disruptive behavior and campaign may have been the reason that even right-leaning newspapers shied away from supporting him. The *Chicago Tribune,* which had endorsed Republican presidential candidates for decades, decided to support Libertarian Gary Johnson. The *Wall Street Journal* and the *New York Post,* both Republican stalwarts, did not endorse any candidate, which in itself was a repudiation of Trump's candidacy. And without specifically mentioning Clinton, *USA Today* and the *Fort Worth Star-Telegram* specifically endorsed voting for any candidate who was not Donald Trump (Staff 2016). Only two newspapers of national stature endorsed Trump: The *Las Vegas Review-Journal* (owned by Trump friend and ally Sheldon Adelson) and the *Jacksonville (FL) Times-Union* (Gold 2016; Editorial Board 2016).

Among all of Trump's disruptions, perhaps the one that had the most significant and lasting impact was his disavowal or ignorance of polls that strongly suggested Hillary Clinton would defeat him in the general election. In retrospect, Trump was right to ignore the polls, but it appeared at the time as though the Republican nominee was going to lose the general election in one of the most lopsided contests in decades.

Polls have become commonplace in presidential campaigns, and over time they have become increasingly reliable, especially when each state's polls were aggregated algorithmically into predictive models. For the two elections before 2016, the gold standard of poll predictions belonged to Nate Silver and his fivethirtyeight.com website. In 2008 and 2012, Silver predicted only one state going to the wrong victor. Based on aggregated polls, Silver gave Hillary Clinton a 71.4 percent chance of winning the presidency and a slightly better 71.8 percent chance when economic and historical data were added to the model. The final Silver model predicted Clinton would win 302 electoral votes, well beyond the 270 needed for victory (Silver 2016a).

Silver's model was only as good as its data, however, and clearly the polls' source data had gotten things wrong. Not only did Clinton not win, but Trump won more electoral votes than the Silver model predicted she would. Trump took 306 electoral votes, including from some swing states that had turned reliably Democratic for Obama: Michigan, Ohio, and Pennsylvania.

Throughout the fall general election campaign, most polls suggested a Clinton victory. Real Clear Politics aggregated ten tracking polls over the course of the contest, and of them only one pointed to a Trump victory. Even the somewhat-correct *Los Angeles Times* poll was suspect, because it predicted the national popular vote and not the electoral vote. While Trump won the electoral vote, Clinton won the popular vote.

Trump ignored the polls, refused to change his aggressive and unfamiliar campaign style, and remained confident that his campaign would emerge triumphant on election day, as it indeed did. The disconnect between the poll predictions and the election outcome led to great uncertainty about the use of preelection polls as predictors of election results. Pollsters held a special convention just a few months after the election to conduct a postmortem, mostly determining that poll weighting and sampling models were incorrect (Cohn 2017). Academics determined that Trump's support did not materialize until late in the campaign, thus making most polls correct but unable to absorb last-minute variance (McKee et al. 2019).

Silver rose to prominence during the Obama presidency. Another norm that campaign established was the value of field offices. The Obama campaign's use of digital media overshadowed the data-driven operation they employed, using large bases of individual data to develop local profiles of where opening field offices would yield the highest rate of voter turnout (Harfoush 2009; Issenberg 2013; Schrager 2016). The strategic distribution of field offices became similar to advertising strategy: a necessary but not sufficient prerequisite for a successful campaign (Darr and Levendusky 2014).

Trump also ignored the conventional wisdom regarding field offices. The Trump campaign never opened a field office in any location. Even in states where candidates do not expect to win, they usually appoint a state director. In swing states like Ohio, Trump never even named a state director. Instead, Trump relied on the Republican National Committee (RNC) to deploy the entire field operation for his general election campaign. Trump lagged far behind Clinton's campaign on field deployment, putting a significant amount of faith in the RNC's ability to conduct his ground game (Murray and Killough 2016).

At the time, it appeared that Trump simply wanted to focus on the advertising component of presidential campaigning and functionally outsourced the labor-intensive ground game efforts in which he was less interested. However, another perspective suggests that Trump simply adapted more quickly to the changing campaign environment by pivoting from field office deployment to a new strategy with greater emphasis on social media campaigning. Through the general election campaign, the bare-bones Trump campaign apparatus spent their efforts on two primary foci: 1) engaging the state parties to serve as the de facto field offices for the campaign and 2) shifting attention to social media and digital efforts (Martin 2016). News media attention at the time suggested that the lack of a campaign-specific ground operation was a sign of disarray within the operation or of a lack of understanding of what was necessary to win (Graham 2016; Sarlin et al. 2016). Once again, Trump drastically disrupted the standard campaign practices and won despite what seemed to be a losing strategy.

The digital strategy was a significant shock to established practices of campaigning but one that is more likely to be adapted by future organizations. The Trump campaign put multiple times the money and focus into digital than the Clinton campaign did, roughly outspending the Democrat $210 million on digital to just over $30 million. Spending alone did not equate to victory, as Trump digital director Brad Parscale hired the firm Cambridge Analytica to target audiences using the measurement of psychological traits such as openness to new experiences, extroversion, and neuroticism (Winston 2016).

Trump carried forward another break with tradition from the primary into the general: ignoring established Republican ideological orientations and talking points. For decades, the GOP had been a staunch advocate of liberalizing trade policy, but Trump favored the United States leaving established trade partnerships such as the

Arceneaux, K. "Do Campaigns Help Voters Learn? A Cross-National Analysis." *British Journal of Political Science* 36, no. 1 (2006): 159–173.

Arkin, D. "Donald Trump Criticized after He Appears to Mock Reporter Serge Kovaleski." NBC News, 2015. https://www.nbcnews.com/politics/2016 -election/donald-trump-criticized-after-he-appears-mock-reporter-serge -kovaleski-n470016.

Barbaro, Michael. "Pithy, Mean and Powerful: How Donald Trump Mastered Twitter for 2016." *New York Times*, October 5, 2015, 1.

Blow, Charles. "Trump, Grand Wizard of Birtherism." *New York Times*, September 17, 2016, A6.

Bower, Joseph L., and Clayton M. Christensen. "Disruptive Technologies: Catching the Wave." *Harvard Business Review* (January–February 1995): 43–53.

Bycoffe, Aaron. "The 2016 Endorsement Primary." FiveThirtyEight. 2016. https://projects.fivethirtyeight.com/2016-endorsement-primary/.

Cassidy, John. "How Donald Trump Won the GOP Nomination." *New Yorker Online.* 2016. https://www.newyorker.com/news/john-cassidy/how-donald -trump-won-the-g-o-p-nomination.

Chiang, Chun-Fang, and Brian Knight. "Media Bias and Influence: Evidence from Newspaper Endorsements." *Review of Economic Studies* 78, no. 3 (2011): 795–820.

Cohen, Marty, David Karol, Hans Noel, and John Zaller. *The Party Decides: Presidential Nominations before and after Reform.* Chicago, IL: University of Chicago Press, 2009.

Cohn, Nate. "A 2016 Review: Why Key State Polls Were Wrong about Trump." *New York Times*, May 31, 2017, 1.

Confessore, Nicholas, and Karen Yourish. "$2 Billion Worth of Free Media for Donald Trump." *New York Times*, March 16, 2016. https://www.nytimes.com /2016/03/16/upshot/measuring-donald-trumps-mammoth-advantage -in-free-media.html.

Darr, Joshua P., and Matthew S. Levendusky. "Relying on the Ground Game: The Placement and Effect of Campaign Field Offices." *American Politics Research* 42, no. 3 (2014): 529–548.

Diamond, Jeremy. "Trump on Protester: 'Maybe He Should Have Been Roughed Up.'" CNN. 2015. https://www.cnn.com/2015/11/22/politics /donald-trump-black-lives-matter-protester-confrontation/index.html.

Doherty, Carroll. "5 Facts about Trump Supporters' Views of Immigration." Pew Center for People and the Press. 2016. https://www.pewresearch.org/fact -tank/2016/08/25/5-facts-about-trump-supporters-views-of-immigration /ft_16-08-25_immigrationdeport/.

Draper, Robert. "Ted Cruz's Evangelical Gamble." *New York Times Magazine*, January 26, 2016, 1.

Dugan, Andrew. "Among Republicans, GOP Candidates Better Known

Than Liked." Gallup.com. 2015. https://news.gallup.com/poll/184337/among-republicans-gop-candidates-better-known-liked.aspx?utm_source=Politics&utm_medi um=newsfeed&utm_campaign=tiles.

Editorial Board. "Editorial: Trump Is the Change Agent America Needs." *Florida-Union Times*, November 4, 2016, A5.

Edsall, Thomas B. "Trump Set to Join Reform Party." *Washington Post*, October 25, 1999, A1.

Epstein, Reid, and Colleen McCain-Nelson. "Donald Trump Lays Out Protectionist Views in Trade Speech." *Wall Street Journal*, June 28, 2016, 2.

Gill, Jungyun, and James DeFronzo. "Religion, Rational Political Theory, and the 2008 Presidential Election." *Politics and Religion* 6, no. 2 (2013): 303–316.

Gillin, Joshua. "Bush Says Trump Was a Democrat Longer Than a Republican 'in the Last Decade.'" PolitiFact. 2015. https://www.politifact.com/fact checks/2015/aug/24/jeb-bush/bush-says-trump-was-democrat-longer-republican-las/.

Gimpel, James. "Immigration Policy Opinion and the 2016 Presidential Vote." *Center for Immigration Studies.* 2016. https://cis.org/Report/Immigration-Policy-Opinion-and-2016-Presidential-Vote.

Gold, Hadas. "Las Vegas Review-Journal Endorses Donald Trump." *Politico.* 2016. https://www.politico.com/blogs/on-media/2016/10/las-vegas-review-journal-endorses-donald-trump-230225.

Gold, Howard, and Gina Russell. "The Rising Influence of Evangelicalism in American Political Behavior, 1980–2004." *Social Science Journal* 44, no. 3 (2007): 554–562.

Graham, David. "There Is No Trump Campaign." *Atlantic.* 2016. https://www.theatlantic.com/politics/archive/2016/06/there-is-no-trump-campaign/486380/.

Guilford, Gwynn. "How the Republican Elite Tried to Fix the Presidency and Instead Got Donald Trump." Quartz. 2016. https://qz.com/685831/the-republican-crackdown-on-2012s-ron-paul-insurgency-boosted-donald-trumps-delegate-math-and-changed-how-the-party-connects-with-its-supporters/.

Hagerty, Barbara. "For Evangelicals, Romney Is the Lesser of Two Evils." National Public Radio. 2012. https://www.npr.org/2012/05/11/152507126/for-evangeli cals-romney-is-the-lesser-of-two-evils.

Harfoush, Rafah. *Yes We Did! An Inside Look at How Social Media Built the Obama Brand.* New York: New Riders, 2009.

Heffernan, Virginia. "How the Twitter Candidate Trumped the Teleprompter President." *Politico Magazine*, May/June 2016. https://www.politico.com/magazine/story/2016/04/2016-heffernan-twitter-media-donald-trump-barack-obama-telemprompter-president-213825.

Heikkilä, Niko. "Online Antagonism of the Alt-Right in the 2016 Election." *European Journal of American Studies* 12, no. 1 (2017): 12–22.

Issenberg, Sasha. *The Victory Lab: The Secret Science of Winning Campaigns.* New York: Broadway, 2013.

Kam, Cindy D., and Elizabeth J. Zechmeister. "Name Recognition and Candidate Support." *American Journal of Political Science* 57, no. 4 (2013): 971–986.

Keith, Tamara. "Commander-In-Tweet: Trump's Social Media Use and Presidential Media Avoidance." National Public Radio. 2016. https://www.npr.org/2016/11/18/502306687/commander-in-tweet-trumps-social-media-use-and-presidential-media-avoidance.

Kelly, A. "Donald Trump Clinches GOP Nomination." National Public Radio. 2016. https://www.npr.org/2016/05/26/479588197/donald-trump-clinches-gop-nomination.

Kiff, Sarah. "Donald Trump Endorses an Idea Liberals Love: Letting Medicare Negotiate Drug Prices." Vox. 2016. https://www.vox.com/2016/1/26/10835000/trump-medicare-drug-prices.

Lee, Jasmine, and Kevin Quealy. "The 598 People, Places and Things Donald Trump Has Insulted on Twitter: A Complete List." *New York Times*, 2017. https://www.nytimes.com/interactive/2016/01/28/upshot/donald-trump-twitter-insults.html.

Lind, Dara. "Donald Trump's Proposed 'Muslim Registry,' Explained." Vox. 2016. https://www.vox.com/policy-and-politics/2016/11/16/13649764/trump-muslim-register-database.

Martin, Johnathan. "GOP Soul-Searching: 'Too Old, Too White, Too Male?'" Politco. 2012. https://www.politico.com/story/2012/11/gop-soul-searching-must-now-begin-083472.

Martin, Rachel. "How Trump Waged an Under-the-Radar Ground Game." National Public Radio. 2016. https://www.npr.org/2016/12/06/504520364/how-trump-waged-an-under-the-radar-ground-game.

McKee, Seth C., Daniel A. Smith, and MV Trey Hood. "The Comeback Kid: Donald Trump on Election Day in 2016." *PS: Political Science & Politics* 52, no. 2 (2019): 239–242.

Mider, Zachary. "The Koch Brothers Have an Immigration Problem." Bloomberg News. 2015. https://www.bloomberg.com/news/articles/2015-08-27/the-koch-brothers-have-an-immigration-problem.

Milbank, Dana. "The Donald Trumps the Pols at CPAC." *Washington Post*, February 13, 2011, A1.

Montgomery, Martin. "Post-Truth Politics?: Authenticity, Populism and the Electoral Discourses of Donald Trump." *Journal of Language and Politics* 16, no. 4 (2017): 619–639.

Moody, Chris. "Donald Trump to Address CPAC." Yahoo! News. 2013. https://www.yahoo.com/news/blogs/ticket/donald-trump-address-cpac-205409450-politics.html.

Murray, Sara, and Ashley Killough. 2016. "Donald Trump's Unconventional

Approach to Building a Ground Game." CNN. 2013. https://www.cnn.com /2016/06/09/politics/donald-trump-ground-game/index.html.

Neal, Pat. "Trump Flirts with Campaign in Namesake Fashion." CNN. 1999. https://www.cnn.com/ALLPOLITICS/stories/1999/11/15/trump.flor ida/index.html.

Oppel, Richard. "Romney's Adversarial View of Russia Stirs Debate." *New York Times*, May 11, 2012, A2.

Parker, Ashley. "'Koch Primary' Tests Hopefuls in the G.O.P." *New York Times*, January 20, 2015, A1.

Poniewozik, James. "The Real Donald Trump Is a Character on TV." *New York Times*, September 6, 2019, A10.

Preston, Julia. "Republicans Reconsider Positions on Immigration." *New York Times*, November 9, 2012, A3.

Rackaway, Chapman. "Weak Parties and Strong Partisans." In *American Political Parties under Pressure*, ed. Chapman Rackaway and Laurie Rice, 169–187. New York: Palgrave Macmillan, 2018.

Rosenthal, Lawrence, and Christine Trost, eds. *Steep: The Precipitous Rise of the Tea Party*. Berkeley: University of California Press, 2012.

Rozell, Mark J., and Debasree Das Gupta. "'The Values Vote?'" In *The Values Campaign? The Christian Right and the 2004 Elections*, ed. John C. Green, Mark J. Rozell, and Clyde Wilcox. Washington, DC: Georgetown University Press, 2006.

Sarlin, Benjy, Katy Tur, and Ali Vitali. "Donald Trump Does Not Have a Campaign." MSNBC. 2016. http://www.msnbc.com/msnbc/donald-trump -does-not -have-campaign.

Schoen, Douglas. "Obama Hits 50 Percent Approval Rating, According to New Newsweek/Daily Beast Poll." *Newsweek*, February 21, 2011, 18.

Schrager, Adam. *Blueprint: How the Democrats Won Colorado (and Why Republicans Everywhere Should Care)*. Golden, CO: Fulcrum, 2016.

Silver, Nate. "Who Will Win the Presidency?" FiveThirtyEight. 2016a. https:// projects.fivethirtyeight.com/2016-election-forecast/.

———. "How Trump Hacked the Media." FiveThirtyEight. 2016b. https:// fivethirtyeight.com/features/how-donald-trump-hacked-the-media/.

Smidt, Corwin, and Paul Kellstedt. "Evangelicals in the Post-Reagan Era: An Analysis of Evangelical Voters in the 1988 Presidential Election." *Journal for the Scientific Study of Religion* 52 (1992): 330–338.

Staff. "List of Top 50 Newspaper Endorsements for President of the United States." *Chicago Tribune*, November 5, 2016, A12.

Timm, Jane. "After Donald Trump's 'Second Amendment' Comment, Is There Anything He Can't Say?" NBC News. 2016. https://www.nbcnews .com/politics/2016-election/after-donald-trump-s-second-amendment -comment-there-anything-he-n627501.

Turner, Laura. "Will Trump's Nomination Be the End of the Religious Right?"

Politico Magazine. 2016. https://www.politico.com/magazine/story/2016/07/2016-donald-trump-religion-christian-conservatives-republican-party-gop-faith-voters-evangelicals-214037.

Winberg, Oscar. "Insult Politics: Donald Trump, Right-Wing Populism, and Incendiary Language." *European Journal of American Studies* 12 (2017): 12–24.

Winston, Joel. "How the Trump Campaign Built an Identity Database and Used Facebook Ads to Win the Election." Medium. 2016. https://medium.com/startup-grind/how-the-trump-campaign-built-an-identity-database-and-used-facebook-ads-to-win-the-election-4ff7d24269ac#.xp we08w8b.

CHAPTER 2

The Trump Brand of Right-Wing Populism

Wayne Steger

I've watched the politicians. . . . They will never make America great again. They don't even have a chance. They're controlled fully—they're controlled fully by the lobbyists, by the donors, and by the special interests, fully.
—Donald Trump, "Full Text: Donald Trump Announces a Presidential Bid," *Washington Post*

INTRODUCTION

As a candidate, Donald Trump campaigned as a right-wing popu-list. He repeatedly attacked the political establishment during the nomination and general election campaigns (e.g., Trump 2016a). If there was any doubt about the authenticity of Trump's populism, his actions as president put those doubts to rest. He has governed with a profound mistrust of career government officials, replaced policy experts with political loyalists, and disrupted and debilitated multiple agencies. In some ways, however, Trump's right-wing populism looks like a version of anti-government conservatism. After all, Republicans often campaign for office by criticizing government, promising to cut regulations and the size of government. What distinguishes Trump's populism from other anti-government Republicans? This chap-ter offers a brief explanation of what populism is and outlines the contours of the right-wing populist brand that Trump has fostered and promoted.

It should be noted at the outset that right-wing populism has been a growing phenomenon in Republican and conservative circles since the 1950s (Kazin 1995; Postel 2007). Trump's brand of populism builds on this history of Republican politicians who have used right-wing populist themes to promote anti-government attitudes (and advance their own election prospects). Richard Nixon, for example, argued that he represented the "silent majority," framing his supporters as people different from the visible and very liberal anti-war and civil rights activists of the 1960s. He used patriotism and working-class love of country to appeal to those dismayed by the rising "New Left" of the Democratic Party. Ronald Reagan originated the "Make America Great Again" slogan that Trump adopted in 2016. Patrick Buchanan advocated protectionism and anti-immigration policies in his 1992 and 1996 Republican presidential nomination campaigns. Sarah Palin appealed to "real Americans" with populist themes in her role as the vice-presidential running mate of John McCain in 2008. Trump is not an aberration in Republican politics. Populist themes just have been more central to Trump's campaign and governance compared to predecessors who used populist themes to supplement their conservative appeals. Trump thus extends and accelerates trends that began in the 1950s and 1960s and that have helped attract the support of lower-education, working-, and middle-class whites to the Republican Party. In the process, the Republican Party is transforming into something different than the small government party that it used to be.

IS TRUMP A POPULIST?

To understand Trump's populism, we first need to understand what populism is. That is not a simple thing, because populism is a multifaceted concept. In public discourse, populism is often used to describe emotional and simplistic appeals that are directed at the "gut feelings" of the people (Mudde 2004, 54). Trump's simplistic and emotional language in his speeches and on Twitter illustrate populism as "politics of the pub." Populist candidates are authentic to their supporters in part because they talk about things in ways that resonate with them on an emotional level. Critics view populist leaders as demagogues who play on the emotions of poorly informed or misinformed citizens with policy promises that may please voters in the short term but that create long-term problems (Riker 1982). Trump's protectionist trade policies illustrate this usage. Trump appealed to people in communities that had lost manufacturing jobs with promises to bring back jobs through tariffs. Most economists, however, recognize that protecting industries like steel production increases the costs of manufactured goods, decreases competitiveness, and ultimately costs jobs in industries that use steel in their manufacturing—thus risking more jobs than are saved or re-created through these policies (e.g., McGee 1993).

Populism also has multiple meanings in academic discourse. Paul Taggart (2000) views populism as a matter of social movements. Michael Kazin (1995) and Cas Mudde (2004) view populism as a worldview or as a political frame of the average person pitted in a struggle against some elite. Jan Werner-Müller (2016, 19) defines populism as a particular, moralistic imagination of politics pitting a morally pure people against corrupt elites. Richard Hofstadter (1960, 2008) views populism as a social-psychological pathology that motivates a type of political behavior that is characterized by paranoia and conspiracy theorizing. Margaret Canovan (1999) views populism as a style of communication appealing to the average person in a way that has a rivalist mood. Still others portray populism as illiberal, popular democracy unconstrained by rules and institutions that protect political minorities and maintain political stability (Riker 1982; Grattan 2016).

These uses of the term capture aspects of populism, which may be a movement, a conceptual political frame, or a narrative or rhetorical style that frames political conflict as a struggle between a righteous, common group of people (us) and corrupt or illegitimate elites (them). This struggle seeks to enable the "will" of the people to prevail over elite-defined norms and prescriptions or technical rules and procedures that seem to favor elites (or minorities). There is a debate over whether populism threatens liberal democracy or acts as a wake-up call for political elites (Mudde and Kaltwasser 2012; Grattan 2016). Populism involves a rejection of "trustee representation" by political party "establishments" or elected officials. Lack of trust in government was an important component of Trump's appeal among Republicans and Republican leaners who tend to hold authoritarian values (Hetherington 2015).

While populism has a variety of uses, the common threads of populism are a frame of political conflict pitting some group of people against a corrupt and illegitimate establishment in which the people mobilize in support of a political party or leader to change politics-as-usual (Steger n.d.). At the core, populism is a reaction and resistance to perceived power. To these common threads, I add that the discourse, symbolism, and sentiment of victimization characterize populist movements. Populists use the combination of anti-elitism and the politics of victimization to mobilize an aggrieved population against what they see as powerful forces in society in order to win elections and change policy. Left- and right-wing populists are distinguished by the elites that they oppose and the grievances and threats that they perceive (Steger n.d., chapter 2). Left-wing populists like Bernie Sanders oppose primarily economic elites and secondarily the party establishments that serve those elites. Right-wing populists primarily oppose government and cultural elites, as discussed below.

First, all discussions of populism involve anti-elite or antiestablishment sentiment on the part of voters, politicians, or political activists that is embedded in the content of rhetorical appeals or discourse (Mudde 2004; Canovan 1999). Populism is a form of opposition or resistance to perceived power that is in some way unjust or illegitimate (Norris and Inglehart 2019). Richard Hofstadter (2008) argues that populists are prone to conspiracy theorizing. Although Hofstadter's interpretation has been criticized, conspiracy theories serve a couple of important functions. One, conspiracy theories impute evil motives to a powerful other and do so in a manner that delegitimizes the other. Two, conspiracies are a mechanism of populist resistance. For example, right-wing conspiracies accused Obama of being a Muslim who was not a citizen. Hillary Clinton was the subject of numerous conspiracies—from Uranium One to Pizzagate to Benghazi—none of which were substantiated in multiple Republican-directed congressional investigations. Conspiracy theories illustrate the resistance to a powerful, nefarious, and illegitimate other (Nelson 2015, chapter 2; Fenster 2008).

Second, discussions of populism invariably refer to "the people" or the average person in some form of appeal for public mobilization against opposed elites. "The people" consist of a subset of the population whose motives are viewed as righteous and legitimate, while those of the opposing side are corrupt and illegitimate. The "us versus them" framing of conflict forms the contours of an identity politics for the people. For right-wing populists, "the people" refers to a nativist, core population consisting of a dominant ethnic group, such as white people in George Wallace and Sarah Palin's "Real Americans." Paul

Taggart (2000) refers to this focus on a dominant ethnic group as "the politics of the heartland." The framing of political conflict helps create a common identity or solidarity that pits "us" versus "them" to mobilize supporters (Polletta and Jasper 2001, 291). This form of identity politics divides and polarizes society and treats political opponents as "enemies of the people" (Werner-Müller 2016; Mudde 2004). What seems to matter as much as anything is beating "them," which in this case refers to "liberals." Trump's "America First" pits working- and middle-class white Americans against a laundry list of enemies: corrupt government officials, special interests, media executives and reporters, the politically correct left, #BlackLivesMatter activists, Mexicans, Muslims, and people in inner cities (a phrase that refers to people of color).

The sense of righteousness that attends the goals of the in-group against a morally bankrupt or hypocritical opposition creates an emotionally intense, zero-sum conflict in which compromise is a sign of corruption and complicity that cannot be tolerated. The extent to which compromise is disliked is one of the things that differentiates right-wing populists from other Republicans, though in 2016 Republicans of all stripes generally held a dim view of compromise. Right-wing populists can be viewed as uncompromising conservatives whose traditionalist, Christian, and capitalist values are moral and just, while those of the secularist, multicultural, and socialist left are immoral and corrupt. In a divided and polarized world, politics takes on a zero-sum quality, as neither side is willing to accept the legitimacy of the other's values. The stakes in a zero-sum game ratchet up the intensity of partisan emotions, which populist leaders use to mobilize the people against a morally corrupted opposition. Trump's core supporters reviled Clinton and Democrats so much that they could overlook Trump's flaws in an "ends justify the means" mentality befitting a moralistic struggle of good versus evil. For his supporters, Trump may be a flawed messenger, but his cause is right while his enemies are illegitimate and wrong.

A third common element is that populism evokes a desire for change from status quo politics as usual. Calls for political reform invariably imply a change in the power relationships that influence the formation and implementation of public policy. The idea is to mobilize the people in elections to disrupt and take down the "establishment"—the existing networks of powerful elites whose values and grip on government produce policies that are perceived as not helping "the people" or as threatening to the value systems of "the people." Mobilizing the people will empower new leaders who presumably will make government more responsive to the needs and wants of the people as defined above. Populists are willing to accept representative government provided it is their leaders who do the representing and they are the ones being represented (Werner-Müller 2016, chapter 1). The particulars of policy goals may not matter as much as the disruption, if not the destruction, of the establishment in favor of "something" else.

Finally, populist movements and discourse involve resistance to oppression and injustice. This takes two forms. First, the resistance often involves conspiracies about the actions of an evil, immoral or illegitimate adversary as noted above. The second aspect involves using the politics of victimization to mobilize potential supporters against the establishment. American populists view their values and lifestyles as threatened by the prevailing socioeconomic, political, and/or cultural order. Populists see themselves as victims of a system that is unjust, giving rise to a desire to change the social and economic order and value system being institutionalized by political, economic, and cultural elites. While liberals portray economic and cultural power structures as victimizing women, people of color, and LBGTQ populations, right-wing populists see government and liberal cultural elites as threatening their way of life. This is not "woe is me" victimization but a rallying cry to stand up to injustice and to "take our country back."

This idea is implicit in Diana Mutz's (2018) argument that populists are motivated by threats to their social status. Trump supporters were sensitive to threats to their economic and gender- and racially defined status (Norris and Inglehart 2019). Robert Griffin and Ruy Teixeira (2017) similarly find that racial and anti-immigrant attitudes were distinctive characteristics of Trump supporters. The sense of threat is particularly strong in rural areas and smaller cities where the population is largely white (Rothwell and Diego-Rosell 2016). Many Trump supporters saw themselves as under attack by the government and groups aligned with the Democratic Party. Inglehart and Norris (2017) argue that this is part of a long-evolving conflict between people with a cosmopolitan value system that promotes individualism and cultural diversity, on the one hand, and people with a traditional value system that is resistant to changes associated with modernity, on the other. For his part, Trump (2016a, 2016f) repeatedly made claims to victimization—the system is rigged against him and, by extension, his supporters.[1] Populists use the politics of victimization as a mechanism of identity formation, legitimization, and mobilization. Victimization is a powerful motivational mechanism that is common in social movements (Benford and Snow 2000; Polletta and Jasper 2001).

Trump's right-wing populist appeals referenced a multitude of perceived injustices on the grounds of immigration, race, religion, gun ownership, political correctness, and cultural values. Political efforts to open borders and a path to citizenship for unauthorized immigrants were an affront to Americans who were deserving of the jobs taken by immigrants. Trump (2015a) attacked immigrants for "stealing your jobs" and bringing disease, drugs, and crime. These attacks took advantage of attitudes in which opinions about jobs, trade, immigration, and welfare are often biased by prejudicial attitudes toward Black and Latino Americans and all immigrants (Tessler 2016a; Tessler 2016b; Griffin and Teixeira 2017). Trump (2016b, 2016e) similarly used the politics of victimization to appeal to evangelical Christians and Catholics when he claimed that their religious freedoms are under attack by Democrats and government policies that limited for Christians the right to religious speech and practices. Similarly, gun owners were being targeted by Clinton and Democrats who "are trying to take away your guns" (Trump 2016b). Trump's willingness to challenge political correctness and the secular and multicultural value system of urban intellectuals and liberals endeared him to his base (Trump 2016b, 2016c, 2016e). In these cases, Trump took advantage of attitudes that white boys and men in particular were losing out by political, cultural, and economic systems that gave preferences to immigrants and minorities (Mutz 2018). Trump's approach unified various overlapping groups within the Republican Party coalition with his nationalistic Make America Great Again appeals.

Trump's use of the victim card, his signature "trump card" if you will, continued in office. Trump characterized some federal judges as unjustly biased against him to discredit the legitimacy of rulings against his ban on Muslim immigration, the wall, and other administrative actions (Trump 2017b, 2019). The Mueller investigation into Russian interference in the 2016 election and possible collusion by the Trump campaign became "a hoax" and "a witch hunt" (Trump 2018b). The House investigation into his pressure on Ukraine to investigate Hunter and Joe Biden became a witch hunt, a characterization he used on average more than once per day in his tweets (Markham-Cantor 2019). The House impeachment was a "lynching" (Ebbs et al. 2019). Trump frequently accuses most of the national media as being out to get him, occasionally labeling the reporters as "enemies of the people" who have pushed "fake news" to undermine him (Samuels 2019). Critics of Trump often are portrayed as disloyal, unpatriotic, unjust, or unfair. By dismissing unfavorable, factual information as "fake news," Trump gives his supporters a cue to ignore or discount criticism. Trump appeals to his supporters to step up to defend him because he is surrounded and attacked daily by his enemies, who by extension are their enemies. Trump has, in some ways, made himself the embodiment of the perceived victimization of his supporters at the hands of liberal, corporate, media, and government elites.

Trump's play of the victimization card is a very potent strategy given that most party identifiers engage in motivated reasoning, a psychological effect that leads people to ignore, discount, or twist information in ways that allow them to maintain their beliefs and identity (Bolsen et al. 2014; Gastil et al. 2011). Despite an avalanche of news critical of Trump, his supporters maintain and have even increased their support for him. He is more favorably viewed by Republicans since his election than he was during the campaign itself. His strategy of self-aggrievance at the hands of liberal and government elites also fits with the effects of negative partisanship. Feelings of oppression and injustice add intensity to the in-group versus out-group mentality of populism and increasing partisan affect. As the country has polarized along partisan lines, there has been an increase in the intensity of partisan affect—an emotional response associated with partisanship—and in particular, there has been an increase in negative partisan affect in which partisan loyalties are motivated by anger toward, and distrust of, the opposing party (Abramowitz and Webster 2016; Westwood and Iyengar 2015). An important implication of negative partisanship is that weak partisans and independents who identify with a political party are likely to remain loyal to their party regardless of who the nominee is, because these voters are motivated to oppose the other party's candidate as much as they are to support their own party's candidate (Abramowitz and Webster 2016). Trump's supporters may recognize his flaws, but they empathize and defend him because they have common enemies.

Most of the attention given to Trump's right-wing populism focused on the hostile attacks on immigrants, particularly Muslims and Mexicans, and people of color more generally. Anti-immigration and racist appeals, however, were only one aspect of his populist appeals. Trump frequently attacked government for being in the pocket of special interests, including hedge fund managers, Wall Street investors, media executives, and the professional political class (Trump 2016a). He criticized global elites and free trade deals (Trump 2017a, 2017b, 2018a). He attacked government for catering to immigrants and minorities at the expense of (white) working people, adopting a long-standing Republican approach of subtly equating welfare with people of color (Trump 2016d, 2016e). Trump or his surrogates attacked cultural elites and college professors who promote cultural sensitivity toward minorities, women, and LBGTQ populations and whose secularism threatens the Christian identity and rights of Americans (Bowden 2017; Schmid 2019). Trump had a lot of targets, which helped him build a coalition of people who were dissatisfied with the way things are going in the country.

In all of this, Trump's appeals worked because they resonated with the existing value orientations and grievances of a range of people whose predilections incline them toward what might be called social and cultural conservatism (Hetherington 2015; Norris and Inglehart 2019). Trump gave these latent attitudes political relevance and direction, making them a potent force in the 2016 election and beyond. Large numbers of people were dissatisfied with the way things were going in this country because of evolving conditions that made the country ripe for a revival of populism. Elsewhere, I argue that populism is a backlash against economic and socio-cultural change combined with disaffection with the political establishment (Steger n.d., chapter 2). Most theoretical arguments hold that populism is a response or backlash to economic decline, or a backlash against cultural changes that threaten social identity and status (Guiso et al. 2017). The economic backlash argument focuses on white working- and middle-class voters who felt "left behind" as jobs and economic opportunity diminished in communities, resulting in a shift of allegiances of these voters from the Democratic Party to Republican Party (Judis 2016; Porter 2016; Formisano 2016; Rothwell and Diego-Rosell 2016). The cultural backlash argument views populism as a response to the threat to cultural values and status posed by the changing ethnic composition of the country, growing secularism, the continued gains of feminists, and advocacy of diversity that can be subsumed under the label of cosmopolitanism (or one of the uses of the term "liberalism") (Mutz 2018; Norris and Inglehart 2019).

THE DISTINCTIVENESS OF TRUMP'S POPULIST BRAND IN CONSERVATIVE AND REPUBLICAN CONTEXT

To this point, the discussion has focused on populism at a general level while giving examples to illustrate how Trump can be described as a populist. This section offers a categorization of Trump's brand of populism as it relates to governance and policy. Cas Mudde (2004) argues that populism is a "thin" ideology in the sense that populism lacks the interconnected and coherent logic and policy prescriptions of "thick" ideologies like neoliberalism or socialism. That is, populism attaches to and mutates an ideology like conservatism to give it a unique political and policy orientation.

First, American right-wing populists exhibit antipathy toward multiple elites (Judis 2016; Kazin 1995). Trump's supporters are primarily anti-elite or antiestablishment with respect to government officials. They oppose, on a secondary level, those groups that use government to gain special privileges and advantages that they view as disadvantaging them. Right-wing populists like Donald Trump blame government for "rigging the system" in ways that disadvantage working Americans in favor of "special interests" *and* in favor of the "undeserving" poor, minorities, and immigrants at the expense of the "forgotten middle." Trump's supporters tend to be white people in the lower-middle and middle-income brackets, often being self-employed individuals who are better off than others in their communities (Rothwell and Diego-Rosell 2016). Trump's promise to "drain the swamp" was a reference to perceived corrupt relations between government officials and special interests. This includes (undefined) "special interests" who work to distort the market economy. A common framing of the problem is crony capitalism, a concept that can be found in both left- and right-wing populist rhetoric but that is more prevalent in right-wing populist discourse, reflecting the more central place of government in right-wing anti-elitism. Concern with crony-capitalism distinguishes right-wing populism from the neoliberal and supply-side conservatism of the Republican Party that favors and is favored by the business and financial interests that have long been at the core of the party's constituency. Trump's attacks on special interests are inherently disruptive and threatening to the traditional big business constituency of the Republican Party.

Trump's right-wing populism also opposes government policies that benefit the "undeserving" poor (people on welfare) and immigrants. Opposition to welfare is blended with racial antipathy toward Black Americans and minorities, who have long been portrayed in right-wing rhetoric as taking advantage of "welfare" programs while white people have to work for a living and pay taxes to support those programs (Tessler 2016). There are a range of objectionable policies including: immigration laws that enable more Latinos to enter America to "steal jobs" from "real Americans"; affirmative action programs, which they view as giving African Americans, Latinos, and other minorities an advantage at their expense; and redistributive policies that would raise their taxes or reduce their benefits to provide for programs benefiting immigrants and people on welfare. It is brought home by anecdotes of being in a grocery line where a minority purchases items with a Supplemental Nutritional Assistance Program (SNAP) card. Compared to other Republicans, Trump's supporters during the nomination campaign were more extreme in their negative views of immigrants and racial and ethnic minorities (Steger n.d., chapter 9; Griffin and Teixeira 2017).

Many have noted that Trump deviated from traditional Republican positions by supporting Social Security and Medicare and promising a massive infrastructure reconstruction program to create jobs. Trump's economic promises are targeted toward the working middle class. He promised to protect social welfare programs for "deserving" people, defined as those who have paid Social Security and Medicare taxes and which may not include immigrants and welfare recipients. For example, Trump said, "I'm going to save Social Security. . . . There's tremendous waste, fraud and abuse, and we're going to get it. But we're not going to hurt the people who have been paying into Social Security their whole life and then, all of a sudden, they're supposed to get less" (CBS Republican Primary Debate in South Carolina, February 13, 2016). Immigrants—especially refugees and unauthorized immigrants—are portrayed as not contributing to these programs and thus as not deserving. Similarly, people who "live on welfare" do not pay taxes and thus are not deserving. There is a clear demarcation between taxpayers and those who live off the fat of government. Many working- and middle-class people think that they have earned their Social Security and Medicare benefits, so Trump's narrower promise serves them but not undeserving others. Trump's rhetorical appeals are directed toward working- and middle-class Americans who have lived and worked in America their entire lives and thus who have contributed to the programs and can keep them. He could cut these programs for others who "don't pay taxes." Right-wing populists especially dislike Democrats and liberals who are portrayed as privileging these undeserving others at the expense of working, tax-paying people. In many respects, right-wing populist themes about welfare have been integrated into the anti-redistributionist rhetoric of conservatives.

The idea of economic nationalism even more clearly distinguishes Trump's right-wing populism from that of other Republicans and from conservative ideology. The Republican Party has long maintained strong ideological support for the free market and free trade principles. Economic nationalism challenges that philosophy by fusing an economic strategy of protectionism with the emotional appeal of patriotism. Trump attacked free trade agreements and promised to bring mining and manufacturing jobs back to America. He promised to end the Trans-Pacific Partnership (TPP) agreement, renegotiate free trade agreements (i.e., NAFTA), and penalize American manufacturers that move jobs out of the country. He attacked China for unfair monetary and trade policies that gave China access to American markets without sufficient reciprocity (Stracqualursi 2017). Notably, while Trump supporters had a more pessimistic outlook on the economy and on their own economic opportunities, trade protectionism was not a high priority for them (Steger n.d., chapter 9; Griffin and Teixeira 2017). They were more concerned with the economy and jobs, not necessarily Trump's ideas for how to promote jobs and economic opportunity.

Another dimension of the anti-elitism in right-wing populism is the antipathy toward what might be called "cultural elites"—coastal elites, urban elites, and, increasingly, institutions of higher education that promote racial, ethnic, gender, and sexual orientation tolerance. This is most explicitly manifested in right-wing populist opposition to the "political correctness" of urban and intellectual elites whose cultural values and promotion of secularism, diversity, and multiculturalism conflict with their own traditional values and way of life. On a cultural level, right-wing populists resent being told that they should be "politically correct" or that they benefit from "white privilege." The reaction is intense and hostile toward "elites," who they see as demeaning them for the benefit of "others," especially minorities, immigrants, and LBGTQ identifiers. Right-wing populists are more likely than other Republicans to see white Americans as disadvantaged by government while Black Americans are advantaged by government (Steger n.d., ch. 9). On thermometer ratings in the American National Election

Studies pilot survey, Trump supporters rated Muslims, Black Americans, feminists, and scientists less favorably than other Republicans did (Steger n.d., ch. 9). Republicans on average do not see white people as having advantages, nor do they see Black people as being particularly disadvantaged (Steger n.d., ch. 9). Trump supporters during the nomination campaign held even less favorable attitudes toward minorities and immigrants compared to other Republicans. They also generally resent having to give parity to Muslims in a Christian nation; notably, even though Trump supporters tend not to attend church frequently, they do self-identify as Christians (Scala 2018; Rapoport et al. 2018). Lower church attendance and education increasingly distinguish right-wing populists from other Republicans.

On a cultural dimension, Trump's populist appeals reflected cultural exclusivity and nativism. Trump campaigned more as an identity conservative than as a philosophical conservative (Noel 2016). Trump often used the term "they" or "them" when talking about immigration, crime, welfare, and the double standards inherent in norms of politically correct speech (Ball 2016). Trump began his campaign with a speech in which he characterized (most but not all) Mexican illegal immigrants as drug dealers, criminals, and rapists (Trump 2015a). Trump proposed building a wall along the Mexican border, deporting illegal immigrants, and banning Muslim immigrants. The wall and deportation promises were the same populist appeals that Patrick Buchanan used in his 1996 Republican presidential nomination campaign. These promises attracted considerable support from leaders of white supremacist groups (Bump 2017).

White identity sentiment was visible in the reaction to the #BlackLivesMatter movement spurred by police killings of unarmed Black men. #BlackLivesMatter provoked a strong, negative reaction among lower-education whites and others who rallied under the banner of #BlueLivesMatter and #AllLivesMatter.[2] Trump sided with the backlash movement with his calls for tougher law enforcement to deal with what he (falsely) claimed were increasing crime rates, which he characterized as problems caused by immigrants and people in inner cities (references that implied Latinos and African Americans). In an interview during the Republican nominating convention, Trump criticized the #BlackLivesMatter movement for instigating violence against police and called the group a threat that must be watched carefully (Diamond 2016). During the presidential debate at Hofstra University, Trump answered a question about how to improve race relations in America by calling for tougher law-and-order policies like stop and frisk, a racially charged policy shown to result in racial and ethnic profiling.[3] Law and order has long been a strong Republican theme, which also corresponds to the more authoritarian personality characteristics of the majority of Republican Party identifiers (Hetherington and Weiler 2009). Calls for law and order also can be viewed as an element of white identity politics that uses law enforcement and the penal code to keep minorities in check (Alexander 2012).

Critics of Trump interpreted the racial, ethnic, and religious undertones of some of his rhetoric as indicative of white nationalism, if not racism (Hajnal and Abrajano 2016). On several occasions, Trump retweeted posts by white supremacy groups, and he failed to condemn violence against racial, ethnic, and religious (Muslim) minorities (McCaskill 2016; Kharakh and Primack 2016). Trump attracted substantial support from white nationalist, white supremacy, and neo-Nazi groups, one of whom called Trump a "real opportunity" for white nationalists (Smith 2016; Holley 2016). These aspects of Trump's rhetoric and support drew intense and sustained criticism from Democrats and from a few Republicans. Trump responded to criticisms of his rhetoric by attacking "political correctness."[4] Political correctness, with its emphasis on acceptance of racial, ethnic, religious, gender, and sexual orientation differences, has long been anathema to some Republicans, going back to George H. W. Bush in the 1988 presidential campaign (Itkowitz 2015). Trump's attacks on political correctness resonated with white middle-class voters and demonstrated his willingness to challenge cultural elites (those with a cosmopolitan value system) (Dreher 2016).

Trump's "Make America Great Again" directly borrowed Ronald Reagan's 1980 campaign slogan (Margolin 2015). Trump's use of the theme was generally consistent with Republican campaigns since Reagan. Trump differed in that he talked about Making America Great Again (MAGA) for "real Americans," a concept that connotes a greater degree of "cultural exclusivity." This term has percolated in right-wing political discourse since George Wallace's populist campaigns in the 1960s. The concept of real Americans has been common in Republican discourse for more than a decade and was popularized by Sarah Palin in the 2008 presidential election campaign. Trump, with Palin by his side in January 2016, talked about "Real America." Numerous Tea Party candidates adopted the slogan in 2010, 2012, and 2014 congressional elections (Skocpol and Williamson 2013). "Real America" expresses a nostalgic vision of America in a simpler, more prosperous era when people with a high school education could get middle-class wages through manual labor or owning a small business; when male role models headed traditional families; when local communities were centered around churches; and when diversity and sexual orientation were not even afterthoughts. Real America is blue-collar traditionalism found in rural, small town, and neighborhood communities. MAGA thus has a meaning for audiences that connotes making America great again for real Americans, who are Americans of European descent who hold traditional and authoritarian values that Hetherington and Weiler (2009) argue is a prevalent characteristic of the Republican Party coalition.

Real America is America outside the beltway. The federal government is an enemy. The concept of Real America is the functional equivalent of the left-wing populists' slogan, "ninety-nine percent against the one percent." For the right, the establishment is federal government—a government that caters to special interests and is responsive to minorities and immigrants at the expense of the middle class. In Trump's right-wing perspective, government is the evil, the swamp that must be drained or even destroyed. There is little good that government would do in Trump's approach, which seemed to require the undoing of government. The disruptiveness of Trump's administration and policy is the subject of other chapters in this volume.

CONCLUSION

Political commentators often dismiss populists as demagogues offering simplistic policy ideas that may be appealing in the short term but may be bad for people and the country in the long run. Critiques of populist leaders, however, dismiss the power of populism at their own peril. Republican elites and candidates for the 2016 Republican presidential nomination repeatedly dismissed the potency of Donald Trump, only to find Trump winning pluralities of the vote in primary after primary until it was too late for anyone to stop him (Steger 2017). Hillary Clinton and the Democrats repeated the pattern in the general election.

Public discontent, anger with political leaders, and widespread desire for change do not in themselves enable populists to change the political system. Public desire for something different to shake things up—a throw-the-bums-out mentality—often fails to upend patterns of government. Trump helped invigorate right-wing populism in America by being sensitive to public attitudes and opinions of his potential supporters and then shaping these attitudes in ways that helped him get elected. Trump bypassed traditional media by speaking directly to his supporters through social media and endorsing opinions expressed in right-wing digital and cable/radio media. Trump used Twitter effectively, steadily growing his number of followers to more than 12 million by Election Day.[5] Trump benefited from an extensive communications infrastructure on the political right, where leading conservative political commentators such as Sean Hannity, Mark Levin, Laura Ingraham, Glenn Beck, Ben Shapiro, and Ann Coulter promoted Donald Trump and his populist messages. In doing so, they helped shape and reinforce Trump's populist messaging aimed at millions of angry Republicans and Republican leaners.

As president, Donald Trump finds the checks and balances of government to be too constraining. Right-wing populists like Trump believe that governing should be a simple process in which the government acts to fulfill the wants of their electoral coalition, rather than serving "others" who populists see as being unfairly or unjustly privileged by government policies. Trump's election and his behavior in office poses a serious threat to the rule of law and to liberal democracy (defined as a majority rule system that is limited in ways intended to protect political minorities). Trump and his supporters act as if they are the majority, but his base is not a majority of the public. During the 2016 Republican nomination, Trump was the preferred choice of less than 45 percent of caucus and primary voters. He won the presidency with less than 47 percent of the popular vote in the general election. Since being elected, he has maintained presidential approval ratings that have hovered between 39 and 43 percent of respondents in national polls. Despite support from only a minority of the public, Trump has fought against the normal constraints on presidential power to enact policies that he wants enacted regardless of the wisdom of those policies. The notions of limited government, the rule of law, and liberal democracy require a balancing of majority and minority interests and groups. This balance is fragile and susceptible to subversion in favor of antidemocratic policies enacted by democratically elected officials (Levitsky and Ziblatt 2018).

NOTES

1. Unless noted otherwise, references to Trump rhetoric and speeches were obtained from an electronic search of addresses, miscellaneous comments, Twitter posts, campaign speeches, addresses, or interviews. The American Presidency Project, https://www.presidency.ucsb.edu/documents/app-categories/elections -and-transitions/campaign-documents.

2. The PEW Research Center documented a substantial partisan divide on these movements. http://www.pewresearch.org/fact-tank/2016/07/08/how -americans-view-the-black-lives-matter-movement/.

3. For Trump's comments at the debate, see: http://www.cnn.com/videos /politics/2016/09/27/clinton-trump-debate-hofstra-stop-and-frisk-sot-five .cnn/video/playlists/2016-presidential-debate-donald-trump-hillary-clinton/.

4. Political correctness emerged in the late 1980s as a movement that promoted avoidance of expression or actions perceived to exclude, marginalize, or insult groups of people who are socially disadvantaged or discriminated against. It promotes cultural inclusivity and diversity. From the right-wing perspective, political correctness is an effort to censor freedom and suppress traditional social values and social relationships, which includes implicit social hierarchies along gender and racial lines.

5. See https://www.socialbakers.com/statistics/twitter/profiles/detail /25073877-realdonaldtrump, accessed February 15, 2021.

REFERENCES

Abramowitz, Alan I., and Steven Webster. "The Rise of Negative Partisanship and the Nationalization of U.S. Elections in the 21st Century." *Electoral Studies* 41, no. 2 (2016): 12–22.

Alexander, Michelle. *The New American Jim Crow: Mass Incarceration in an Era of Color Blindness.* New York: New, 2012.

Ball, Molly. "The Resentment Powering Trump." *Atlantic,* March 15, 2016. https://www.theatlantic.com/politics/archive/2016/03/the-resent ment-powering-trump/473775/.

Benford, Robert D., and David A. Snow. "Framing Processes and Social Movements: An Overview and Assessment." *Annual Review of Sociology* 26 (2000): 611–639.

Bolsen, Toby, James N. Druckman, and Fay Lomax Cook. "The Influence of Partisan Motivated Reasoning on Public Opinion." *Political Behavior* 36, no. 2 (2014): 236–262.

Bowden, John. "Trump Jr. Slams Liberal Universities in Speech." Hill. October 7, 2017. https://thehill.com/blogs/blog-briefing-room/news/354236 -trump-jr-rails-against-liberal-universities-in-speech.

Bump, Philip. "A Brief History of Donald Trump Addressing Questions of Racism and Anti-Semetism." *Washington Post*, February 21, 2017. https://www.washingtonpost.com/news/politics/wp/2017/02/17/a-brief-history-of-donald-trump-addressing-questions-about-racism-and-anti-semitism/.

Canovan, Margaret. *Populism*. New York: Harcourt Brace, 1981.

———. "Trust the People! Populism and the Two Faces of Democracy." *Political Studies* 47, no. 1 (1999): 2–16.

Diamond, Jeremy. "Trump: Black Lives Matter Has Helped Instigate Police Killings." July 19, 2016. http://www.cnn.com/2016/07/18/politics/donald-trump-black-lives-matter/.

Dreher, Rod. "Trump: Tribune of Poor White People." *American Conservative*. July 22, 2016. http://www.theamericanconservative.com/dreher/trump-us-politics-poor-whites/.

Ebbs, Stephanies, Karen Travers, and Elizabeth Thomas. "Trump Defends Calling Impeachment Inquiry a 'Lynching.'" October 25, 2019. ABC News. https://abc news.go.com/Politics/trump-defends-calling-impeachment-inquiry-lynching/story?id=66531405.

Fenster, Mark. *Conspiracy Theories: Secrecy and Power in American Culture*. Minneapolis: University of Minnesota Press, 2008.

Formisano, Ronald. "The Populist Tsunami of the Second Gilded Age." *Forum* 14, no. 3 (2016): 281–294.

Gastil, John, Don Braham, Dan Kahan, and Paul Slovic. "The Cultural Orientation of Mass Political Opinion." *PS: Political Science and Politics* 44, no. 3 (2011): 711–714.

Grattan, Laura. *Populism's Power: Radical Grassroots Democracy in America*. New York: Oxford University Press, 2016.

Griffin, Robert, and Ruy Teixeira. "The Story of Trump's Appeal." Washington, DC: Democracy Fund Voter Study Group, 2017.

Guiso, Luigi, Helios Herrera, Massimo Morelli, and Tommaso Sonne. "Populism: Demand and Supply." 2017. https://www.heliosherrera.com/populism.pdf.

Hajnal, Zoltan, and Marisa Abrajano. "Trump's All Too Familiar Strategy and Its Future in the GOP." *Forum* 14, no. 3 (2016): 295–309.

Hetherington, Marc J. "Trust in Trump Comes from a Lack of Trust in Government." Brookings. 2015. https://www.brookings.edu/blog/fixgov/2015/09/16/trust-in-trump-comes-from-lack-of-trust-in-government/.

Hetherington, Marc J., and Jonathan D. Weiler. *Authoritarianism and Political Polarization in America*. Cambridge University Press, 2009.

Hofstadter, Richard. *The Age of Reform*. New York: Vintage, 1960.

———. *The Paranoid Style in American Politics*. New York: Vintage, 2008.

Holley, Peter. "Top Nazi Leader: Trump Will Be a 'Real Opportunity' for White Nationalists." *Washington Post*, August 7, 2016. https://www.washing

tonpost.com/news/post-nation/wp/2016/08/07/top-nazi-leader-trump
-will-be-a-real-opportunity-for-white-nationalists/.

Inglehart, Ronald F., and Pippa Norris. "Trump and the Populist Authoritarian Parties: *The Silent Revolution* in Reverse." *Perspectives on Politics* 15, no. 2 (2017): 443–554.

Itkowitz, Kolby. "Donald Trump Says We're All Too Politically Correct: But Is That also a Way to Limit Speech?" *Washington Post*, December 9, 2015. https://www.washingtonpost.com/news/inspired-life/wp/2015/12/09/donald-trump-says-were-all-too-politically-correct-but-is-that-also-a-way-to-limit-speech/.

Judis, J. B. "Us v. Them: The Birth of Populism." *Guardian*, October 13, 2016. https://www.theguardian.com/politics/2016/oct/13/birth-of-populism-donald-trump.

Kazin, Michael. *The Populist Persuasion: An American History.* New York: Basic, 1995.

Kharakh, Ben, and Dan Primack. "Donald Trump's Social Media Ties to White Supremacists." *Fortune*, March 22, 2016. https://fortune.com/longform/donald-trump-white-supremacist-genocide/.

Levitsky, Steven, and Daniel Ziblatt. *How Democracies Die.* New York: Broadway Books, 2018.

Margolin, Emma. "'Make America Great Again'—Who Said it First?" September 9, 2015. https://www.nbcnews.com/politics/2016-election/make-america-great-again-who-said-it-first-n645716.

Markham-Cantor, Alice. "What Trump Really Means When He Cries Witch Hunt." October 29, 2019. https://www.thenation.com/article/archive/trump-witch-hunt/.

McCaskill, Noland D. "Trump Retweets Another White Supremacist." Politico, February 27, 2016. https://www.politico.com/blogs/2016-gop-primary-live-updates-and-results/2016/02/donald-trump-white-supremacist-retweet-219915.

McGee, Robert W. "The Cost of Protectionism: Should the Law Favor Producers or Consumers?" *Georgia Journal of International and Comparative Law* 23, no. 3 (1993): 529.

Mudde, Cas. "The Populist Zeitgeist." *Government and Opposition* 39, no. 4 (2004): 542–563.

Mudde, Cas, and Cristóbal Rovira Kaltwasser. "Populism and (Liberal) Democracy: A Framework for Analysis." In *Populism in Europe and the Americas: Threat or Corrective for Democracy?* ed. Cas Mudde and Cristóbal Rovira Kaltwasser, 1–26. New York: Cambridge University Press, 2012.

Mutz, D. C. "Status Threat, not Economic Hardship, Explains the 2016 Presidential Vote." *Proceedings of the National Academy of Sciences* 115, no. 19 (2018): E4330–E4339.

Nelson, J. S. "The Corporate Conspiracy Vacuum." *Cardozo Law Review* 37, no. 249 (2015): 101–156.

Noel, Hans. "Maybe Faux Conservatives Are Still Conservatives." Vox, January 25, 2016. http://www.vox.com/mischiefs-of-faction/2016/1/25/10828656 /faux-conservatives-trump-national-review.

Norris, Pippa, and Ronald Inglehart. *Cultural Backlash: Trump, Brexit, and Authoritarian Populism*. New York: Cambridge University Press, 2019.

Polletta, Francesca, and James M. Jasper. "Collective Identity and Social Movements." *Annual Review of Sociology* 27 (2001): 283–305.

Porter, E. "Where Were Trump's Votes? Where the Jobs Weren't." *New York Times*, December 13, 2016. https://www.nytimes.com/2016/12/13/busi ness/economy/jobs-economy-voters.html.

Postel, Charles. *The Populist Vision*. New York: Oxford University Press, 2007.

Rapoport, Ronald B., W. Henry Crossman, and Rachel Lienesh. "From Tea Party to Trump Party." Paper presented at the annual meeting of the Midwest Political Science Association. Chicago 2018.

Riker, William H. *Liberalism against Populism: A Confrontation between the Theory of Democracy and the Theory of Social Choice*. San Francisco: Freeman, 1982.

Rothwell, Jonathan T., and Pablo Diego-Rosell. "Explaining Nationalist Political Views: The Case of Donald Trump." Working paper. 2016. http://pelg .ucsd.edu/2.rothwell_2016.pdf.

Samuels, Brett. "Trump Ramps Up Rhetoric on the Media, Calls Press 'the Enemy of the People." Hill. April 5, 2019. https://thehill.com/homenews/ad ministration/437610-trump-calls-press-the-enemy-of-the-people.

Scala, Dante. "Holier Than Thou: Ted Cruz and the Puzzle of Evangelical Voters." Paper presented at the annual meeting of the Midwest Political Science Association. Chicago 2018.

Schmid, Julie. "Response to President Trump's Executive Order on Denial of Research Funds." 2019. https://www.aaup.org/news/response-president -trumps-executive-order-denial-research-funds#.XpSisFxKhTs.

Skocpol, Theda, and Vanessa Williamson. *The Tea Party and the Remaking of Republican Conservatism*. New York: Oxford University Press, 2013.

Smith, Candice. "The White Nationalists Who Support Donald Trump." March 10, 2016. https://abcnews.go.com/Politics/white-nationalists-sup port-donald-trump/story?id=37524610.

Steger, Wayne P. "Populist Challenges in the 2016 Presidential Nominations." In *The 2016 Presidential Elections: The Causes and Consequences of a Political Earthquake*, ed. Amnon Cavari, Richard Powell, and Kenneth R. Mayer, 23–42. Lanham, MD: Lexington Books, 2017.

———. *Resurgence of American Populism: Socio-Economic Change and Political Discontent*. Abingdon, UK: Routledge, forthcoming.

Stracqualursi, Veronica. "Ten Times Trump Attacked China and Its Trade Relations with the US." November 9, 2017. https://abcnews.go.com/Politics/10-times-trump-attacked-china-trade-relations-us/story?id=46572567.

Taggart, Paul. *Populism: Concepts in the Social Sciences.* Philadelphia: Open University Press, 2000.

Tessler, Michael. "The Education Gap among Whites This Year Wasn't about Education: It Was about Race." *Washington Post,* November 16, 2016a. https://www.washingtonpost.com/news/monkey-cage/wp/2016/11/16/the-education-gap-among-whites-this-year-wasnt-about-education-it-was-about-race/.

———. "Views about Race Mattered More in Electing Trump Than in Electing Obama." *Washington Post,* November 22, 2016b. https://www.washingtonpost.com/news/monkey-cage/wp/2016/11/22/peoples-views-about-race-mattered-more-in-electing-trump-than-in-electing-obama/.

The American Presidency Project. University of California Santa Barbara. https://www.presidency.ucsb.edu/documents/app-categories/elections-and-transitions/campaign-documents.

Trump, Donald. "Full Text: Donald Trump Announces a Presidential Bid." June 16, 2015a. https://www.washingtonpost.com/news/post-politics/wp/2015/06/16/full-text-donald-trump-announces-a-presidential-bid/.

———. "Full Text: Donald Trump Campaign Speech in Wisconsin." August 17, 2016a. https://www.politico.com/story/2016/08/full-text-donald-trumps-speech-on-227095.

———. "Remarks at Saint Anselm College in Manchester, New Hampshire." June 13, 2016b. American Presidency Project. https://www.presidency.ucsb.edu/documents/.

———. "Address Accepting the Presidential Nomination at the Republican National Convention in Cleveland, Ohio." July 21, 2016c. American Presidency Project. https://www.presidency.ucsb.edu/documents/.

———. "Remarks on Immigration at the Phoenix Convention Center in Phoenix, Arizona." August 31, 2016d. American Presidency Project. https://www.presidency.ucsb.edu/documents/.

———. "Remarks at High Point University in High Point, North Carolina." September 20, 2016e. American Presidency Project. https://www.presidency.ucsb.edu/documents/.

———. "Remarks at the Southeastern Livestock Pavilion in Ocala, FL." October 12, 2016f. American Presidency Project. https://www.presidency.ucsb.edu/documents/.

———. "Remarks at a 'Make America Great Again' Rally in Melbourne, Florida." February 18, 2017a. American Presidency Project. https://www.presidency.ucsb.edu/documents/.

———. "Remarks at a National Republican Congressional Committee Dinner." March 21, 2017b. American Presidency Project. https://www.presidency.ucsb.edu/documents/.

———. "Remarks at the Conservative Political Action Conference in Oxon Hill, Maryland." February 23, 2018a. American Presidency Project. https://www.presidency.ucsb.edu/documents/.

———. "Remarks at a "Make America Great Again" Rally in Fargo, North Dakota." June 27, 2018b. American Presidency Project. https://www.presidency.ucsb.edu/documents/.

———. "Remarks at the National Rifle Association Institute for Legislative Action Leadership Forum in Indianapolis, Indiana." April 26, 2019. American Presidency Project. https://www.presidency.ucsb.edu/documents/.

Werner-Müller, Jan. *What Is Populism?* Philadelphia: University of Pennsylvania Press, 2016.

Westwood, Sean J., and Shanto Iyengar. "Fear and Loathing across Party Lines: New Evidence on Group Polarization." *American Journal of Political Science* 69, no. 3 (2015): 690–707.

CHAPTER 3

Real Americans: White Identity and the Election of Donald Trump

Russell Brooker

INTRODUCTION

How did he do it? How did Donald Trump win the presidential election in 2016? In 2015, many observers, including some prominent Republicans, perceived him to be unqualified by experience and unsuitable by temperament to be president (Quirk 2018). He had no government or military experience, only the second such major party presidential candidate in more than one hundred years (Wendell Willkie was the other). He was the most unpopular major party candidate since polling began (Hillary Clinton was second) (Ceaser, Busch, and Pitney 2017, 101, 128). Yet he won.[1] Analysts have offered many explanations, including people's economic anxiety, Trump's massive free publicity, his campaigning style, and Hillary Clinton's unpopularity. In this chapter, we will focus on Trump's appeal to white voters and their identity as being white, on how Donald Trump used white identity and a narrow conception of who were real Americans as a tool for appealing to white voters. During the campaign, he emphasized issues that distinguished white Americans from "other" Americans, focusing on African Americans, Latin American immigrants, and Muslims. He successfully contrasted the interests of white Americans with the interests of nonwhites. He won 57 percent of the white vote and 21 percent of the nonwhite vote.

Ironically two of the three groups are "white" by Census standards, if not by the standards of many American voters. There is no necessary "nonwhiteness" component to immigration status or religion, but Trump managed to conflate race, immigration, ethnicity, and religion into a vaguely coordinated threat to American life. Trump did not do anything that had not been done many times before. Throughout American history, race, immigration, ethnicity, and religion have often been conflated. At various times, Catholics, Jews, Orthodox Christians, Hindus, and Muslims have been considered "nonwhite" by American custom and sometimes by American law. During the 2016 election, a group of white supremacists unintentionally illustrated this practice when they placed robocalls saying, "We don't need Muslims. We need smart, educated, white people" (Bronstein and Griffin 2016).

REAL AMERICANS

Who is a real American? In 1944, Gunnar Myrdal and his associates wrote about an American dilemma: we know that the American creed says we are *all* real Americans with equal rights, yet we also know that we are not equal. Some of us are more equal—or considered more "real"—than others (Myrdal, Sterner, and Rose 1944). To understand "real" Americans and white identity today, it is necessary to trace white identity through American history. Race, ethnicity, citizenship, immigration, and religion have played out in countless permutations in this area since the Republic began. In 1790, the US immigration law provided for the naturalization of "free white person[s] . . . of good character," but no others. At the time of the American Revolution, the franchise was generally limited to white men with property, but over the following decades, the vote was extended to all white men.

Except in rare circumstances, the vote was not extended to African Americans, who had been enslaved in American colonies since the seventeenth century. After the end of the Civil War and slavery, Black Americans gained citizenship and the vote, but segregation and discrimination have continued in many areas, including voting, to the present day.

In the following centuries, the issue of "real" Americans versus "other" Americans played out in various ways through immigration. Political scientist Ashley Jardina wrote, "Each subsequent wave of immigration has provoked national conversations around the preservation of America's identity as a white nation, and one in which whites maintain political, social, and economic power" (2019, 10). In the 1840s and 1850s, Irish Catholics immigrated to the United States in large numbers, prompting the growth of the American, or Know-Nothing, Party. According to their opponents, the Irish were not "white." At about the same time, the United States annexed about half of Mexico, and the Mexicans, who suddenly became Mexican Americans, faced discrimination as if they were nonwhite immigrants. Decades later, in 1882, Congress passed the Chinese Exclusion Act to prevent "pagan" Asian immigrants from entering the United States.

In the late 1800s and early 1900s, a massive immigration of Southern and Eastern Europeans took place, mostly Catholics and Jews. Again, anti-immigration forces conflated religion and race, referring to the new immigrants as nonwhite. President Theodore Roosevelt lamented about the possibility of white Americans committing "race suicide" (Minnesota Public Radio 1997). From 1915 through the 1920s, the second Ku Klux Klan arose, and while the Klan was anti-Black, as its origins would predict, it was also opposed to Catholics, Jews, and immigrants.

During the last few decades, people from all over the world have immigrated to the United States, but the focus in the 2016 election was on those from Latin America. By the time of the 2016 election, the United States, and the voting public, had become more diverse than ever before. In the eight years between the election of Barack Obama in 2008 and the election of Donald Trump in 2016, the proportion of Americans who were white declined from 66 percent to 62 percent (by 2018, it had further declined to 60.4 percent) (US Census). America's increasing diversity, while nothing new, has upset some "real" white Americans and set the stage for Donald Trump's run for the presidency.

POPULISM AND REAL AMERICANS

Donald Trump did not explicitly say that he was appealing to white voters' resentment. He said he was fighting for the welfare of the common people who had lost out to sinister forces. His claim placed him in the long tradition of politicians and political activists who are now called "populists" (Ceaser, Busch, and Pitney 2017, 4–10).

Some of the most important populists in American history have included Andrew Jackson, who mobilized poor white voters, especially those in the West and the South, against Eastern interests, symbolized by the Bank of the United States. Jackson brought people into power who had not previously had authority; he benefited from, and helped expand, the vote among common white men. Two decades later, the Know-Nothings fought as outsiders, people who were being pushed aside by establishment politicians who were abetted by an influx of Irish Catholics. In the 1880s and 1890s, the Populist movement (from which the word "populist" gets its name) organized Black and white cotton, wheat, and tobacco farmers to resist Wall Street, the railroads, and financial manipulators who "farmed the farmers." The official name of the political party was the People's Party, and the Populists wanted "the people" to take back control of the government.

During the Great Depression, Louisiana senator Huey Long portrayed himself as the hero of the poor whom President Franklin Roosevelt had not helped. Long developed a Share Our Wealth program to redistribute money from the wealthy to the needy.

In the 1960s and early 1970s, Alabama Governor George Wallace claimed to "stand up for America," against civil rights "agitators" and "pointy-headed intellectuals." He benefited tremendously from white resentment of Black voting as a result of the Voting Rights Act.

There has not necessarily been a connection between populism and racial or ethnic prejudice. Racial appeal was not important for Andrew Jackson, the People's Party, or Huey Long. However, racism was an important part of the appeal of the Know-Nothings and George Wallace. During the 2016 election, Trump's brand of populism followed a combination of his predecessors' approaches. Like Jackson, he threatened the Wall Street elites and promised to "drain the swamp." Like the original Populists, he promised to protect the "common people" by maintaining Social Security, Medicare, and Medicaid, in defiance of traditional Republican orthodoxy. He also followed the racist model of George Wallace in attributing the cause of the woes of the "real" Americans to other, marginalized, Americans.

THREE TRENDS

The 2016 election took place in the midst of three reinforcing trends that affected voting dramatically. The first trend was a gradual shift of whites to the Republican Party and minorities to the Democratic Party. Political scientists Edward G. Carmines and James A. Stimson noted in the 1980s that whites' opinions on racial segregation were leading to a growing partisan division between Democrats and Republicans, with anti-segregationist whites moving to the Democratic Party (1981, 1989). In the 1990s, Clem Brooks and Jeff Manza pointed to liberal attitudes toward social issues—such as abortion, women's roles, and civil rights—as explanations of educated white professionals moving toward the Democratic Party (1997). More recently, Marisa Abrajano and Zoltan L. Hajnal showed that more positive attitudes toward immigration by college-educated whites led them to vote more Democratic, while those without college degrees tended to vote more for Republicans (2015). Brian Arbour (2018) has pointed to a "new" ethnic group, unhyphenated Americans, who are white people who identify their ethnicity as simply "American," instead of English, German, Irish, or some other nationality. They tend to be native-born, less-educated Protestants who vote heavily Republican. By the 2010s, there were about 21 million of them, concentrated in an area roughly in the Appalachian part of the country, from West Virginia to northern Mississippi.

These changes have led to growing polarization (Abramowitz 2019, 57–71). There are fewer conservative Democrats and liberal Republicans than there were in decades past. People are becoming more consistent in their party preferences, issue positions, and general outlook on politics. This trend began in the 1950s, when liberal Republican members of Congress were replaced by Democrats and conservative Democrats were replaced by Republicans—or politicians in the "wrong" parties switched sides. With the coming of the civil rights movement in the 1950s and 1960s, a Democratic Party that had been split between white Northern liberals and white Southern conservatives lost most of the white Southerners to the Republicans and gained millions of Black liberals who had previously been kept from voting.

The movement to increased consistency between political opinions and party identification has been reinforced by modern technology that has allowed the creation of a multitude of media outlets so that each person can listen only to his or her own opinions; liberals can watch MSNBC and conservatives can watch Fox News, with neither group ever needing to hear a conflicting point of view. Personal preferences may be enhanced on the Internet with algorithms that act as "filter bubbles" to direct people to content they already agree with (Flaxman, Goel, and Rao 2016, 299). Looking at online news consumption, Seth Flaxman, Sharad Goel, and Justin M. Rao found "strong evidence" that people tended to read only sources that

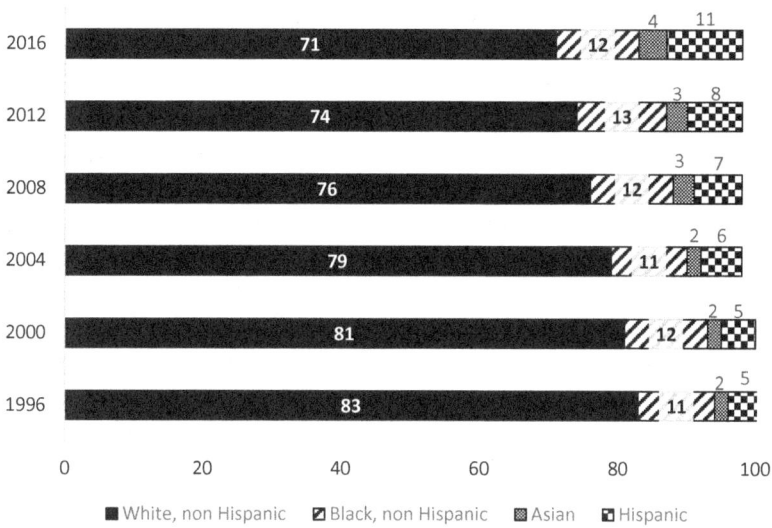

Figure 3.1: Composition of the American Electorate. *Sources:* "Current Population Survey (1996–2012)," cited in Brown and Clemons (2015); and "Election 2016: Exit Polls" (2016).

are ideologically compatible with their opinions. They write, "Users who predominately visit left-leaning news outlets only very rarely read substantive news articles from conservative sites, and vice versa for right-leaning readers, an effect that is even more pronounced for opinion articles" (2016, 300).

The second trend in the 2016 election was increasing ethnic diversity of the country, including in the electorate (Abramowitz 2019, 49–50). In the 1990s, well over 80 percent of the voters in presidential elections had been non-Hispanic whites. The proportion of non-Hispanic whites decreased in every subsequent election so that by 2016, they made up only 71 percent of presidential voters. The proportion of African Americans remained about the same, but the percentages of Latinos and Asians increased. Because of their large numbers, the increase in the Latino vote was particularly important and promises to be more important in the future.

The election of Barack Obama was an unmistakable indicator that the country was changing demographically. To some white Americans, Obama's election was a threat to their dominant status in society. For Americans most opposed to Obama, he did not meet the criteria as a person who "counts" as American—white, English-speaking, native-born, and Christian (Theiss-Morse 2009). To them, he was Black, born in Kenya (or another country), and Muslim. He did, however, speak English.

Obama's election led to the dramatic rise of the Tea Party, a mass movement that emphasized both libertarian economics and white identity. Political scientists Christopher S. Parker and Matt A. Barreto describe people who supported the Tea Party based on a belief that the "real" America was being threatened: "People are driven to support the Tea Party from the anxiety they feel as they perceive the America they know, the country they love, slipping away, threatened by the rapidly changing face of what they believe is the 'real' America: a heterosexual, Christian, middle-class, (mostly) male, white country" (Parker and Barreto 2013, 3).

Diversification is not stopping. The American population is inexorably becoming less white, and demographers predict that sometime in the 2040s, non-Hispanic whites will make up a minority of the US population. Again, some whites view this inevitable development as a threat to the America they know (more on this later).

The third trend has been an increase in identity politics. Economic differences are still important—Democrats on the left, Republicans on the right—but now people's noneconomic identities are increasing in importance. Sometimes identity politics are easy to recognize, such as with lesbian, gay, bisexual, and transgender (LGBT) rights, as well as the BlackLivesMatter and #MeToo movements.[2] The left has found value in identity politics, and now much of the right is embracing it, including many whites who identify as "white."

"Whiteness" has recently increased as an identity important to politics. Earlier research on "whiteness" had shown a lack of feeling of being "white." Being white was considered "normal," not "ethnic" (Hayward 2013).[3] Ashley Jardina wrote about the "invisibility of whiteness" (2019, 47). She wrote that whites' dominant status meant "that whites have come to accept this arrangement as 'normal'; they view themselves as the 'default category'" (2019, 22). "However," she wrote, "since the election of Barack Obama, white identity and ethnocentrism has grown" (2019, 2). White identity is connected to education. Among whites, college-educated voters have been moving toward the Democrats, while those without college degrees have been moving toward the Republicans (Sides, Tesler, and Vavreck 2017, 38).

Trump was dominant among white voters who did not graduate from college.

These three trends culminated in the 2016 election. The drift of less-educated white voters to the Republican Party, increased diversification, polarization, and white identity all contributed to the election of Donald Trump. Political scientist John Sides looked at panel data from 2011, 2012, and 2016. He concluded that trends such as lesser-educated whites moving to the Republican Party and increased polarization continued into 2016. He wrote that "compared to the 2012 election, the 2016 election was distinctively about attitudes related to racial, ethnic, and religious minorities." He also looked at the connection between identity and "being truly American." Only a few Democrats (16 percent) and Republicans (23 percent) said European heritage was important. But 30 percent of Trump supporters said European heritage was important. More strikingly, 63 percent of Trump supporters said it was important to be a Christian, compared to 30 percent of Democrats and 56 percent of Republicans (Sides 2017). Sides and two colleagues note in another place that "the overall pattern is clear: whites' attitudes about race, ethnicity, and religion came to play a larger role in 2016 than other recent elections" (Sides, Tesler, and Vavreck 2019, 172).

The findings of Sides and his colleagues study raise the question of why the 2016 election was so distinctive. After all, if the trends were already underway, why did they manifest themselves so vividly in 2016 instead of 2012, when Obama, the (supposedly foreign-born Muslim) African American candidate, was running? The clear answer is that Donald Trump was the one politician who knew how to harness those trends. He entered the political arena as a partisan entrepreneur and knew how to mobilize white people's anxieties and resentments. As Sides and his colleagues wrote, "What gave us the 2016 election . . . was not changes among voters. It was changes in the candidates" (Sides 2017, 220).

For the last few years, political scientists have discussed the term "dog whistle politics," referring to politicians using coded racial appeals to whites to "manipulate hostility toward nonwhites" (Lopez 2013, ix). The idea is to mobilize white prejudice without explicitly mentioning race. Although the term is new to the twenty-first century, the practice is not. Politicians have long referred to "law and order" and "welfare queens." Donald Trump also used dog whistle appeals, but what distinguishes him from other presidential candidates is that often he did not. He frequently spoke in plain English about Mexican rapists or Muslim terrorists. In fact, he prided himself in being "politically incorrect" by frankly using non-coded words.

Trump's performance raises two questions. First, is he just another Republican who got lucky, benefiting from trends underway? None of his racial, ethnic, immigrant, or religious attacks are new in American history; did he just happen to use the methods that work now? Is he just the "same old" right-wing populist, or is he something unique? Second, now that Trump has uncovered the key to Republican victory, will future candidates follow his lead? The same demographic and political trends are continuing and appear likely to continue for the foreseeable future. What will the Republicans do with them? The answers to both of these questions require the perspective of history, something we do not have now. Any of us could speculate, but we really need to wait and see.

ETHNICITY AND THE VOTE

Here, we examine the effect of race, ethnicity, immigration, and religion on Trump's election. But first it is important to note that partisanship, not race, was the most important factor in the election. Approximately 90 percent of Republicans voted for Trump and 90 percent of Democrats voted for Clinton. The changes from 2012 to 2016 were not monumental. Approximately 89 percent of those who had voted for Romney and voted in 2016 voted for Trump. Likewise, 86 percent of Obama voters who voted in 2016 voted for Clinton (Sides 2017).

Ethnically, the vote was consistent with votes of the past. Trump won the white vote, with 57 percent going to him, as Republicans have since 1968, and Clinton won the Black vote, with a massive 89 percent going to her, as Democrats have since 1936. About two-thirds of Latinos and Asians voted for the Democratic candidate.[4]

Turnout of different ethnic groups was roughly the same as in 2012. However, one major difference was that in 2012, the Black turnout had been slightly higher than the white turnout, but in the 2016 election the white turnout surpassed the Black turnout. The Black turnout was not especially low; it was about the level it had been in 2004 and higher than in 1996 and 2000. But considering that the election was so close—fewer than 80,000 votes in Michigan, Pennsylvania, and

Table 3.1: Presidential Vote Percentage in 2016 by Ethnicity

Candidate	Total Vote (%)	Ethnicity (%)				
		White	Black	Latino	Asian	Other
Trump	46	57	8	28	27	36
Clinton	48	37	89	66	65	56
Other/No Answer	6	6	3	6	8	8

Source: "Election 2016 Exit Polls," CNN, https://www.cnn.com/election/2016/results/exit-polls, accessed August 21, 2019, n = 24,558.

Wisconsin gave the electoral vote to Trump—the decline in Black voting was possibly fatal to Hillary Clinton. She received the support of 89 percent of the African Americans who did vote. It is possible that higher turnout levels by African American voters in those three swing states could have won the election for Clinton.

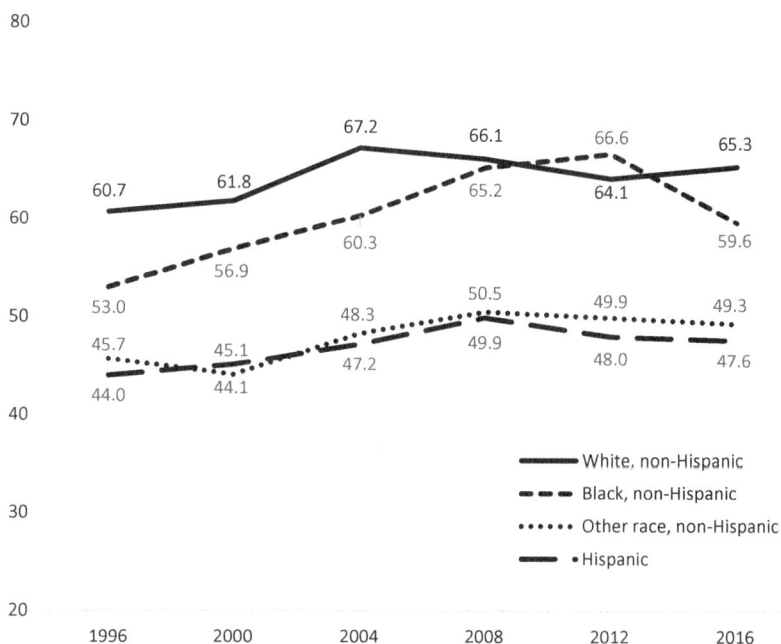

Figure 3.2: Reported Voting Rates by Ethnicity, 1996–2016. *Source:* File (2017).

The White Vote

Overall, Trump won 57 percent of the white vote but only 21 percent of the nonwhite vote. Analysts have divided those white voters into subgroups. One division is gender. Since 1980, women have voted more Democratic than men have. In 2016, although women voted for Hillary Clinton more than men did, most white women (52 percent) voted for Trump, compared to 62 percent of men (CNN 2016).

Separating whites into those who graduated from college and those who did not, Trump did much better with the nongraduates. He won the white graduates 48 percent to 45 percent but the white nongraduates 66 percent to 29 percent (American National Election Studies 2016).

Religious orientation was important. Since the 1970s, Christian evangelicals have been important in electing mostly Republicans to the presidency. (Democrat Jimmy Carter was an exception.) Data from the American National Election Studies (ANES) show that Trump won 76 percent of the vote of whites who considered themselves "born again," compared to only 52 percent of those who did not (American National Election Studies 2016).

Donald Trump's voter constituency was much whiter than Hillary Clinton's. Table 3.2 shows that while most—60 percent—of Clinton's voters were white, almost all—88 percent—of Trump's voters were white. Four years before, 88 percent of Romney's vote had been white (Scocca 2012). Clearly, Trump, like Romney, was dependent on the white vote. As the white vote declines in proportion to the other vote, it is not plain to see how the Republicans will adjust. A constituency that is 88 percent white may be enough when white voters make up more than 70 percent of the electorate, but it is not likely to be enough when the white share declines.

Table 3.2: Ethnic Profiles of Trump's and Clinton's Voters

Ethnic Group	Trump	Clinton
White, non-Hispanic	88%	60%
Hispanic	6%	14%
Black, non-Hispanic	2%	19%
Other	4%	7%

Source: Pew Research Center, survey conducted November 29–December 12, 2016.

The Black Vote and White Resentment

During the 2016 campaign, Donald Trump did make appeals for Black votes. He told Black voters they had nothing to lose with him as president. He addressed the African American voter by saying, "What do you have to lose? You're living in poverty. Your schools are no good. You have no jobs. Fifty-eight percent of your youth is unemployed. What the hell do you have to lose?" (LoBianco and Killough 2016). Although Trump did make attempts to win Black votes, before the 2016 campaign, he had spent years alienating African Americans. In the case of the "Central Park Five," in which five Black and Latino teens were falsely accused of raping a white woman and have since been exonerated, Trump took out a full-page ad in four newspapers in 1989 calling for the return of the death penalty. The ad implied the four teens should be executed (Davidson 2014). During the Obama administration, he was one of the most prominent "birthers," people who—incorrectly—said Obama was born outside the United States and was a Muslim (Whitworth 2016). During the 2016 campaign, he went out of his way to criticize rap music and made fun of Jay-Z and Beyoncé (Le Vine 2016). During the primaries, former Ku Klux Klan leader David Duke endorsed Trump. Trump claimed, implausibly, that he did not know anything about Duke and took two days to disavow Duke's support (Qiu 2016).

Writing three years after the election, journalists Reid J. Epstein and Jonathan Martin summarized their take on Trump and African Americans. Although they were writing about his presidency and the upcoming 2020 campaign, the description applies to his 2016 campaign: "President Trump's entire approach to people of color—his attacks on political leaders, his campaign's social media strategy targeting the black electorate, his ability to fuel black opposition but also demoralize some black voters—is one of the most extraordinary political dynamics of the Trump era. No modern president has ever vilified black America or sought to divide people along racial lines like Mr. Trump" (Epstein and Martin 2019).

In the 1980s, political scientists began using a "racial resentment scale" that purports to capture feelings of racism without explicitly mentioning racism and without the survey respondents necessarily even consciously thinking racist thoughts. The idea behind the scale is that since the civil rights movement, politicians and voters have refrained from using explicitly racist terms to describe opinions that have racial components. Some analysts have claimed that the "old" racism has been replaced by a "new" racism—still racism but worded politely in a kind of code such as "law and order."

Different items can be used to construct a scale, but the most common ones were included in the 2016 ANES. They involve degrees of agreement with four statements, from "Agree Strongly" to "Disagree Strongly." The four statements are:

1. Irish, Italian, Jewish, and many other minorities overcame prejudice and worked their way up. Blacks should do the same without any special favors.
2. Generations of slavery and discrimination have created conditions that make it difficult for blacks to work their way out of the lower class.
3. Over the past few years, blacks have gotten less than they deserve.
4. It's really a matter of some people not trying hard enough; if blacks would only try harder they could be just as well off as whites.

The four statements are combined into one scale by using a multivariate statistical technique called principal components analysis (PCA) that creates the scale based on survey respondents' answers to the four questions and how those answers correlate with each other. PCA forces the scale to have a mean of zero and a standard deviation of one. Any values above zero indicate more resentful answers, and negative values indicate less resentful answers. Table 3.3 divides the total sample and four ethnic groups into quartiles. By definition, for the entire sample, 25 percent of the respondents are in each quartile. Table 3.3 shows that 30 percent of whites were in the most conservative quartile, and 57 percent are in the two most conservative quartiles. The proportions of Latinos and Asians are much lower, with less than 20 percent in the most conservative quartile. As one might expect in a scale about African Americans, only 3 percent of Black respondents are in the most conservative quartile.

Table 3.3 also shows the mean values for each of the four ethnic groups examined in this chapter. Not surprisingly, whites show the highest levels of racial resentment, while Blacks show the lowest. Since the questions are focused on African Americans, not minorities in general, Latinos and Asians are in the middle. People in both these groups could reasonably think of themselves as being in the "many other minorities [that] worked their way up."

Table 3.3: Racial Resentment Composition by Ethnicity

Quartile	Total Sample (%)	Ethnic Group (%) White	Latino	Asian	Black
Highest Quartile	25	30	18	16	3
Second Quartile	25	27	24	33	11
Third Quartile	25	22	37	27	31
Lowest Quartile	25	21	20	25	54
Sample Size	3,647	2,510	430	101	385
Mean Value	0	0.1309	–0.0427	–0.0634	–0.7586

Source: 2016 American National Election Study.

Tables 3.4a and 3.4b show whites and Latinos separately. It is clear that for white voters, the level of racial resentment was clearly linked with the vote for Trump. Table 3.4a shows that 87 percent of white voters with the highest levels of resentment voted for Trump, compared to only 9 percent of those with the lowest levels. Table 3.4b shows the same relationship for Latinos, although the numbers are lower at every level of resentment, from a high of 63 percent to a low of 2 percent. There were not enough African Americans with "resentful" views and not enough Asian Americans in the sample to analyze these two groups.

Political scientists Sean McElwee and Jason McDaniel conducted a similar analysis of ethnic attitudes and voting. They used three scales: the racial resentment scale; a "black influence animosity" scale, using questions about the US government favoring African Americans and how much political influence Black people have; and an immigration scale about immigrants potentially taking jobs from Americans. They found that "both racial resentment and black influence animosity are significant predictors of Trump support among white respondents." They concluded that all three factors taken together—racial resentment, black influence animosity, and anti-immigration attitudes—have a cumulative effect comparable in importance to partisan identification. Finally, they predicted that two of the trends we have already examined—polarization and identity—would increase as the Democrats stood for diversity and the Republicans stood for resentment (McElwee and McDaniel 2017b).

A study asked 510 white millennials (Americans born 1981–1996) about whites losing ground in American society, discrimination

Table 3.4a: Percentage Vote for Trump and Clinton by Racial
Resentment Quartile, Whites Only

| | | Racial Resentment Scale (%) | | | |
Candidate	Total Sample* (%)	Highest Quartile	Second Quartile	Third Quartile	Lowest Quartile
Trump	54	87	65	42	9
Clinton	39	9	26	49	83
Sample Size	1,855	552	480	367	453

Source: 2016 American National Election Study.
*The "Total Sample" percentages in this table are not the same as total vote
because only those respondents who answered the four "racial resentment"
questions are included.

against whites, and minorities overtaking whites. The findings of the
study showed that the more threatened by minorities the subjects
were, the more likely they were to vote to Trump. The researchers
used an 11-point scale, ranging from those who felt least vulnerable
to those who felt most vulnerable. Of those who felt most vulnerable,
77 percent reported voting for Trump, while only 3 percent of those
who felt least vulnerable did. The researchers also found a link with
education; 95 percent of the most vulnerable who had not gone to
college voted for Trump, but only 28 percent of those who had gone
to college did (Fowler, Medenica, and Cohen 2017).

Table 3.4b: Percentage Vote for Trump and Clinton by Racial
Resentment Quartile, Latinos Only

| | | Racial Resentment Scale (%) | | | |
Candidate	Total Sample* (%)	Highest Quartile	Second Quartile	Third Quartile	Lowest Quartile
Trump	24	63	28	17	2
Clinton	69	33	67	77	87
Sample Size	255	46	61	85	60

Source: 2016 American National Election Study.
*The "Total Sample" percentages in this table are not the same as total vote
because only those respondents who answered the four "racial resentment"
questions are included.

Immigrants and Diversity

One factor that helped Trump was that many voters were concerned about the growing number of immigrants and the possibility that they could threaten American values, a feeling sometimes linked with "cultural anxiety." Political scientists Marc Hooghe and Ruth Dassonneville examined racist resentment and anti-immigration sentiments and concluded that they were equally important in explaining votes for Trump (2018, 532). The study by McElwee and McDaniel, just mentioned, found that immigration attitudes were more important for the vote than were anti-Black attitudes for white people (2017b).

Some of Trump's anti-immigrant views were plain to see. In his announcement for the presidency in 2015, Trump talked about Mexico sending "criminals" and "rapists" to the United States (Washington Post Staff 2015). During the campaign, he suggested that a judge of Mexican ancestry who had been born in Indiana could not be fair to him because of his ethnicity (Kendall 2016). One of his main campaign promises was to build a wall between the United States and Mexico and force Mexico to pay for it.

John Sides and his colleagues (2017) looked at panel data from 2011 in which survey respondents had been asked about their opinions on immigration. They found that five years later, Hillary Clinton had kept almost all of Obama's voters who had positive opinions on immigration but lost about one-third who had negative views.

Sociologist Arlie Russell Hochschild connects the anxiety of the white working class about good, steady jobs to resentment toward minorities (2016a, 135–139). She uses the metaphor of Tea Party members standing in line for the American Dream. As they waited, other people cut in the line, aided by liberals and the federal government. These line-cutters included many types of people, including Black people, immigrants, and refugees who might be ISIS terrorists. She writes (2016b) that the "structural stress upon the white working class has led whites to fear that what they have seen affect the black lower class could hit them next. This fear also exacerbates preexisting fear and disdain for nonwhites and non-Christians—especially Mexicans and Muslims."

Using "feeling thermometers," in which survey respondents rated Trump on a 0–100 scale, a Pew research study found that Republican voters who thought that the presence of new immigrants "threatens traditional American customs and values" gave Trump higher (or "warmer") ratings than other Republicans did. A total of 59 percent who thought immigrants threatened America had "warm" feelings of over 50 toward Trump, with 42 percent giving ratings between 76 and 100. Among the Republican voters—21 percent of them—who said that new immigration "strengthens American society," only 30 percent gave him ratings above 50 and only 14 percent above 75 (Jones and Kiley 2016).

Sean McElwee and Jason McDaniel developed a scale on people's opinions about an increasingly diverse nation. The scale was much like the "racial resentment" scale used by many analysts and included in this chapter. After informing survey respondents that census projections predicted that by the year 2043 nonwhites would be a majority of the US population, they gave them four statements to agree or disagree with:

- Americans will learn more from one another and be enriched by exposure to many different cultures.
- A bigger, more diverse workforce will lead to more economic growth.
- There will be too many demands on government services.
- There will not be enough jobs for everybody.

They concluded "that probability of support for Trump increases sharply with negative views on rising diversity, and positive views towards diversity decrease the probability of voting for Trump." They used the same scale with a panel of voters who had voted in 2012 and 2016 and found that viewing racial diversity as a threat predicted voters switching from Obama to Trump and that a more positive view toward diversity predicted a switch from Romney to Clinton or another candidate (McElwee and McDaniel 2017a).

Religion

Religion has long been used as a basis to label people as less than really American. Since the 1980s, and especially since the terrorist attacks on September 11, 2001, Muslims have become the most frequent targets. Trump used Muslims to motivate his white base. During the campaign, he read from a card and spoke of himself in the third person: "Donald J. Trump is calling for a complete and total shutdown of Muslims entering the United States until our country's representatives can figure out what the hell is going on!" Prominent Republicans, such as House Speaker Paul Ryan, spoke out against Trump's proposed Muslim ban, but a majority of Republican voters supported it (Wadsworth 2016). In 2015, Trump suggested that he would consider a special registry for some or all Muslims in the United States (Carroll 2015). He recounted watching thousands of American Muslims cheer as the World Trade Center towers fell on September 11, 2001— although the cheering had not taken place (Mackey 2015). Later, after his election, his administration suggested reinstating a database of immigrants from Muslim-majority countries; such a database had existed after September 11, 2001, but was ended two years into the Obama administration (Lind 2016). Trump also ridiculed Khizr Khan, a Muslim whose son had been a US Army captain killed in Iraq, after he criticized Trump at the Democratic National Convention. Trump also criticized Islam for oppressing women because, he implied, Khan's wife, Ghazala, had not been allowed to speak (Haberman and Oppel 2016).

During Trump's leadership of "birtherism," to prove that Barack Obama was really a Muslim, a 2014 poll showed that 29 percent of Americans, and 45 percent of Republicans, said that Obama was a Muslim (Wadsworth 2016). Before the 2016 election, Michael Tesler analyzed surveys that linked Obama's alleged Muslim religion to Trump's support. He found that "Trump's strongest support in the polls has come from Americans who question Obama's Christian faith." His research showed that the greater the respondents perceived the Muslim "threat" to be, the more likely they were to support Trump (Tesler 2016).

CONCLUSION

Many factors contributed to Donald Trump's successful run for the presidency. The contest was mainly a partisan one, with Republicans and Democrats voting in overwhelming proportions for their candidates. Economics and other issues were important. The miniscule margins in Michigan, Pennsylvania, and Wisconsin were vital. But among the other factors, race, immigration, ethnicity, and religion were important. The trends of increasing demographic diversity, intensifying polarization, and growing white identity gave him the opportunity to be successful with his appeals. Yet, everything Trump did with white and minority voters had been done before, usually for more than one hundred years.

What was unorthodox about Trump's election? Not his vote totals (Rudalevige 2018). His electorate was very white (88 percent), but no whiter than Romney's. He received 46 percent of the popular vote, while Romney received 47 percent. Compared to Romney, he received about the same percent of white voters (59 percent for Romney versus 57 percent for Trump), Black voters (6 percent versus 8 percent), Latino voters (27 percent versus 28 percent), and Asians (26 percent versus 27 percent) (al-Gharbi 2018). He was not unorthodox in his appeal to white hostility toward nonwhites. That appeal has been used many times for many years.

What was unorthodox about Trump is that he used the issues involving white identity so explicitly and so often—and so well. He tied them together into an almost seamless whole that appealed to millions of voters. George W. Bush, John McCain, and Mitt Romney had had the same issues and the opportunities to use them in the same way, but they did not. Within the entire scope of American history, Trump does not seem so unorthodox, but in the context of the twenty-first century he does.

What about the future? Tomorrow never knows, but at this point it seems logical that Trump will use the same techniques in the 2020 election and future candidates will follow his lead. After all, American demographics are not likely to change in the foreseeable future (Denison 2016), the economic system is probably not going to restore industrial jobs, and less-educated whites are unlikely to "regain" their old place in society. White resentment does not seem likely to go away. Will anybody in 2024 have the skill to mobilize white identity as well as Trump did? Will anybody want to mobilize white identity as well as Trump did?

Of course, things will change. Things always change. As the proportions of Latino and Asian voters increase, appeals to white racial resentment may accelerate, but there may not be enough resentful whites to swing elections. James W. Ceaser and his colleagues note that an approach based on white identity "will likely have a short shelf-life in a country that is becoming less white by the year" (2017, 180). The Electoral College will continue to be important. If the Latino and Asian populations increase dramatically in California, the presidential calculations may not be affected, but if they appear in Michigan, Pennsylvania, and Wisconsin, presidential politics may change a great deal.

NOTES

1. In determining why Trump won the election, it is good to keep in mind that Clinton received almost three million more popular votes than Trump did. In an election of 137 million votes, approximately 78,000 votes in Wisconsin, Michigan, and Pennsylvania determined that Trump would be president.

2. BlackLivesMatter is a Black-founded, decentralized activist movement that began in 2012, in reaction to the acquittal of George Zimmerman after he killed Trayvon Martin. It gained in prominence after the police killings of Michael Brown in Ferguson, Missouri, and Eric Garner in New York City in 2014. Its main focus in the United States is on police killings of unarmed African Americans. #MeToo is a feminist decentralized movement opposed to sexual harassment and sexual assault. The movement gained prominence after movie producer Harvey Weinstein was accused of numerous sexual assaults.

3. Hayward's book was published in 2013, but she conducted her interviews in 2003, five years before Obama was elected president. Ali Rattansi (2007) pointed out that in the United Kingdom in the 1960s, whiteness was seen as a "*colourless* and invisible norm."

4. Interestingly, Trump received a lower percentage of white votes than Mitt Romney had in 2012 (59 percent for Romney versus 57 percent for Trump) as well as higher percentages from African Americans (6 percent versus 8 percent), Latinos (27 percent versus 28 percent), and Asians (26 percent versus 27 percent) (al-Gharbi 2018).

REFERENCES

Abrajano, Marisa, and Zoltan Hajnal. *White Backlash: Immigration, Race, and American Politics.* Princeton, NJ: Princeton University Press, 2015.

Abramowitz, Alan I. *The Great Alignment: Race, Party Transformation, and the Rise of Donald Trump.* New Haven, CT: Yale University Press, 2019.

al-Gharbi, Musa. "Race and the Race for the White House: On Social Research in the Age of Trump." *American Sociologist* 49, no. 4 (2018): 496–519. https://doi.org/10.1007/s12108-018-9373-5.

American National Election Studies. 2016 Time Series Study, accessed April 27, 2021. https://electionstudies.org/data-center/2016-time-series-study/.

Arbour, Brian. "This Is Trump Country: Donald Trump's Base and Partisan Change in Unhyphenated Americans." In *American Political Parties under Pressure: Strategic Adaptations for a Changing Electorate,* ed. Chapman Rackaway and Laurie L. Rice, 15–42. New York: Palgrave Macmillan, 2018.

Arbour, Brian K., and Jeremy M. Teigen. "Barack Obama's 'American' Problem: Unhyphenated Americans in the 2008 Elections*." *Social Science Quarterly* 92, no. 3 (2011): 563–587.

Bronstein, Scott, and Drew Griffin. "Trump's Unwelcome Support: White

Supremacists" CNN.com. February 6, 2016. https://www.cnn.com/2016/02/05/politics/donald-trump-white-supremacists-new-hampshire/index.html.

Brooks, Clem, and Jeff Manza. "The Social and Ideological Bases of Middle-Class Political Realignment in the United States, 1972 to 1992." *American Sociological Review* 62, no. 2 (1997): 191.

Brown, Donathan L. and Michael L. Clemons. *Voting Rights under Fire: The Continuing Struggle for People of Color.* Santa Barbara, CA: Praeger, 2015.

Carmines, Edward G., and James A. Stimson. "Issue Evolution, Population Replacement, and Normal Partisan Change." *American Political Science Review* 75, no. 1 (1981): 107–118.

———. *Issue Evolution: Race and the Transformation of American Politics.* Princeton, NJ: Princeton University Press, 1989.

Carroll, Lauren. "In Context: Donald Trump's Comments on a Database of American Muslims." *Politifact,* November 24, 2015. https://www.politifact.com/article/2015/nov/24/donald-trumps-comments-database-american-muslims/.

Ceaser, James W., Andrew E. Busch, and John J. Pitney, Jr. *Defying the Odds: The 2016 Elections and American Politics.* Lanham, MD: Rowman & Littlefield, 2017.

Davidson, Amy. "Donald Trump and the Central Park Five." *New Yorker,* June 23, 2014. https://www.newyorker.com/news/amy-davidson/donald-trump-and-the-central-park-five.

Denison, Benjamin. "The Appeal to Ethnic Resentment." In *The Science of Trump: Explaining the Rise of an Unlikely Candidate,* ed. John Sides and Henry Ferrell, chapter 23. Washington, DC: Monkey Cage, 2016.

"Election 2016: Exit Polls." CNN. 2016. https://www.cnn.com/election/2016/results/exit-polls.

Epstein, Reid J., and Jonathan Martin. "Why a Race-Baiting Trump Is Courting Black Voters." *New York Times,* August 3, 2019. https://www.nytimes.com/2019/08/03/us/politics/black-vote-trump.html.

File, Thom. "Voting in America: A Look at the 2016 Presidential Election." US Census Bureau, May 10, 2017. https://www.census.gov/newsroom/blogs/random-samplings/2017/05/voting_in_america.html.

Flaxman, Seth, Sharad Goel, and Justin M. Rao. "Filter Bubbles, Echo Chambers, and Online News Consumption." *Public Opinion Quarterly* 80, S1 (2016): 298–320.

Fowler, Matthew, Vladimir E. Medenica, and Cathy J. Cohen. "Analysis: Why 41 Percent of White Millennials Voted for Trump." *Washington Post,* December 15, 2017. https://www.washingtonpost.com/news/monkey-cage/wp/2017/12/15/racial-resentment-is-why-41-percent-of-white-millennials-voted-for-trump-in-2016/.

Haberman, Maggie, and Richard Oppel, Jr. "Donald Trump Criticizes Muslim

Family of Slain U.S. Soldier, Drawing Ire." *New York Times*, July 31, 2016. https://www.nytimes.com/2016/07/31/us/politics/donald-trump-khizr -khan-wife-ghazala.html.

Hayward, Clarissa Rile. *How Americans Make Race: Stories, Institutions, Spaces.* New York: Cambridge University Press, 2013.

Hochschild, Arlie Russell. *Strangers in Their Own Land: Anger and Mourning on the American Right.* New York: New, 2016a.

———. "The Ecstatic Edge of Politics: Sociology and Donald Trump." *Contemporary Sociology: A Journal of Reviews* 45, no. 6 (2016b): 683–689.

Hooghe, Marc, and Ruth Dassonneville. "Explaining the Trump Vote: The Effect of Racist Resentment and Anti-Immigrant Sentiments." *PS: Political Science & Politics* 51, no. 3 (2018): 528–534.

Jardina, Ashley. *White Identity Politics.* New York: Cambridge University Press, 2019.

Jones, Bradley, and Jocelyn Kiley. "More 'Warmth' for Trump among GOP Voters Concerned by Immigrants, Diversity." Pew Research Center. June 2, 2016. https://www.pewresearch.org/fact-tank/2016/06/02/more-warmth-for -trump-among-gop-voters-concerned-by-immigrants-diversity/.

Kendall, Brent. "Trump Says Judge's Mexican Heritage Presents 'Absolute Conflict.'" *Wall Street Journal*, June 3, 2016. https://www.wsj.com/articles /donald-trump-keeps-up-attacks-on-judge-gonzalo-curiel-1464911442.

Le Vine, Lauren. "Donald Trump Against Beyonce, Jay-Z." *Vanity Fair*, November 8, 2016. https://www.vanityfair.com/style/2016/11/donald-trump -against-beyonce-jay-z.

Lind, Dara. "Donald Trump's Proposed 'Muslim Registry' Explained." Vox. November 16, 2016. https://www.vox.com/policy-and-politics/2016/11 /16/1364 9764/trump-muslim-register-database.

LoBianco, Tom, and Ashley Killough. "Trump Pitches Black Voters: 'What the Hell Do You Have to Lose?'" CNN. August 20, 2016. https://www.cnn .com/2016/08/19/politics/donald-trump-african-american-voters/index .html.

Lopez, Ian Haney. *Dog Whistle Politics: How Coded Racist Appeals Have Reinvented Racism and Wrecked the Middle Class.* Oxford, UK: Oxford University Press, 2013.

Mackey, Robert. "Claim That Video Backs Donald Trump's Assertion of Mass 9/11 Celebration Is Debunked." *New York Times*, December 2, 2015. https://www.nytimes.com/politics/first draft/2015/12/02/video-report -cited-as-evidence-of-trumps-claim-of-mass-911-celebrations-is-debunked/.

McElwee, Sean, and Jason McDaniel. "Fear of Diversity Made People More Likely to Vote Trump." *Nation*, March 14, 2017a. https://www.thenation .com/article/fear-of-diversity-made-people-more-likely-to-vote-trump/.

———. "Economic Anxiety Didn't Make People Vote Trump, Racism Did." *Nation*, May 8, 2017b. https://www.thenation.com/article/economic-anxi ety-didnt-make-people-vote-trump-racism-did/.

Minnesota Public Radio. "Race Suicide." Minnesota Public Radio. November 20, 1997. news.minnesota.publicradio.org/features/199711/20_smiths _fertility/part1/f4.shtml.

Myrdal, Gunnar, Richard Sterner, and Arnold Marshall Rose. *An American Dilemma*. New York: Harper and Brothers, 1944.

Parker, Christopher S., and Matt A. Barreto. *Change They Can't Believe In: The Tea Party and Reactionary Politics in America*. Princeton, NJ: Princeton University Press, 2013.

Qiu, Linda. "Donald Trump's Absurd Claim That He Knows Nothing about Former KKK Leader David Duke." *Politifact*, March 2, 2016. https://www .politifact.com/factchecks/2016/mar/02/donald-trump/trumps-absurd -claim-he-knows-nothing-about-former-/.

Quirk, Paul J. "The Presidency: Donald Trump and the Question of Fitness." In *The Elections of 2016*, ed. Michael Nelson, 189–216. Thousand Oaks, CA: Sage/CQ, 2018.

Rattansi, Ali. *Racism: A Very Short Introduction*. Oxford, UK: Oxford University Press, 2007.

Rudalevige, Andrew. "The Meaning of the 2016 Election: The President as Minority Leader." In *The Elections of 2016*, ed. Michael Nelson, 217–238. Thousand Oaks, CA: Sage/CQ, 2018.

Scocca, Tom. "Eighty-Eight Percent of Romney Voters Were White." *Slate*, November 7, 2012. https://slate.com/news-and-politics/2012/11/mitt -romney-white-voters-the-gop-candidates-race-based-monochromatic-cam paign-made-him-a-loser.html.

Sides, John. "Race, Religion, and Immigration in 2016." *Democracy Fund Voter Study Group*. April 19, 2017. https://www.voterstudygroup.org/publica tion/race-religion-immigration-2016.

Sides, John, Michael Tesler, and Lynn Vavreck. "How Trump Lost and Won." *Journal of Democracy* 28, no. 2 (2017): 34–44.

———. *Identity Crisis: The 2016 Presidential Campaign and the Battle for the Meaning of America*. Princeton, NJ: Princeton University Press, 2019.

Tesler, Michael. "Candidate of the Islamophobes." In *The Science of Trump: Explaining the Rise of an Unlikely Candidate*, ed. John Sides and Henry Ferrell, chapter 21. Washington, DC: Monkey Cage, 2016.

Theiss-Morse, Elizabeth. *Who Counts as an American? The Boundaries of National Identity*. New York: Cambridge University Press, 2009.

US Census. "QuickFacts." Census.gov/quickfacts/fact/table/US#.

Wadsworth, Nancy D. 2016. "Since When Is Religious Persecution Anti-American?" In *The Science of Trump: Explaining the Rise of an Unlikely Candidate*, ed. John Sides and Henry Ferrell, chapter 19. Washington, DC: Monkey Cage, 2016.

Washington Post Staff. "Donald Trump Announces a Presidential Bid." *Washington Post*, June 16, 2015. https://www.washingtonpost.com/news/post

-politics/wp/2015/06/16/full-text-donald-trump-announces-a-presiden
tial-bid/.

Whitworth, Chris. "A Short History of Donald Trump's 'Birther' Conspiracy."
Guardian, September 16, 2016. https://www.theguardian.com/us-news
/video/2016/sep/16/donald-trump-barack-obama-birther-theory-video.

CHAPTER 4

Trump and the 2018 Midterms

Tyler J. Hughes and Lawrence A. Becker

INTRODUCTION

On January 3, 2019, Sharice Davids became the first American Indian woman to serve in Congress (a distinction shared with Deb Haaland [NM-01], also elected in 2018). She also became the first openly LGBTQ person elected by the state of Kansas, the second Democrat to represent Kansas's Third Congressional District since 1963, and the first Democrat elected to the House from Kansas since 2010. In many ways, Davids's victory—and many similar victories across the country—represents the apparent anti-Trump sentiment displayed during the 2018 midterms: a woman of color defeating a white, male incumbent in a traditionally Republican state. Kansas's Third Congressional District was one of forty gained by Democrats in the 2018 elections.

This "blue wave" of 2018 was sizable, but it was far from being the largest House seat change in modern congressional elections. Such dramatic changes in partisan control of Congress are often accompanied by negative events or policy indicators attributed to the president's party, such as war, economic distress, or major scandals. The 2018 midterms lack these exogenous shocks to the system. Instead, the electoral gains made by Democrats in 2018 are connected by a single, unique factor: President Trump. This chapter examines the effect of President Trump—that is, his policy decisions, involvement in specific campaigns, and divisive rhetoric—on the 2018 midterm elections.

We begin with an overview of the size of the 2018 blue wave in historical context. The Democratic gains in the House—and the party's net loss of two seats in the Senate—is compared against other examples of significant seat gain/loss in modern congressional elections. We then examine record-breaking numbers in 2018 for voter turnout, campaign fundraising, and the number of general election candidates from historically underrepresented groups. These trends highlight Trump's influence on the midterm elections, beyond party control of Congress. Finally, we provide brief case studies on specific races from two different parts of the country to better understand how Democrats recaptured the House with such a large seat margin. The results suggest Democrats were likely to perform well in the 2018 midterms—due to favorable sociopolitical and demographic change—but the environmental factors cannot fully explain the size of the party's victory. Instead, President Trump, who was not even on the ballot, had the single greatest impact on the elections.

DEMOCRATIC SUCCESS IN THE 2018 MIDTERMS

The 2018 "Blue Wave" in Context

At first glance, the "blue wave" of 2018 appears large but nothing like the massive change in partisan representation seen in some previous elections. The president's party tends to lose seats in midterm elections due to a variety of factors, including a regression-to-the-mean after gains in presidential elections, a referendum on presidential performance, or a simple penalty voters place on parties for holding political power (Kernell 1977; Campbell 1985; Erikson 1988). Additionally, research on recent wave elections (1994 and 2010) suggests that opposition voters become more energized as the president and Congress attempt to enact unpopular legislative initiatives or fail to solve pressing policy issues, such as a stagnant economy (Brady et al. 1996; Campbell 2011). Given these dynamics, the Democratic takeover of the House in 2018 is not a historic outlier or terribly surprising.

Figure 4.1 displays the partisan makeup of the House and Senate from 1946 to 2018.[1] Of the nineteen post–World War II midterms, the House seat change of 2018 ranks sixth. Across these midterms, the president's party gained House seats only twice (1998 and 2002), so losses for the president's party are the norm. In fact, the president's party lost an average of twenty-five House seats over this timespan. The

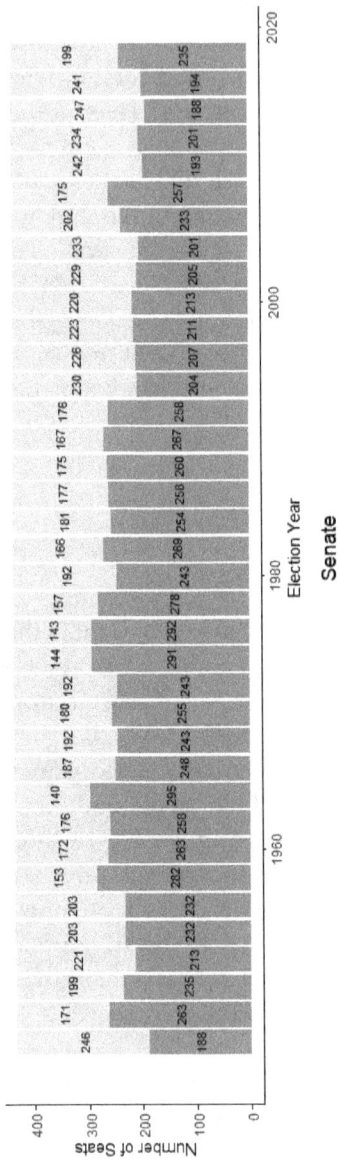

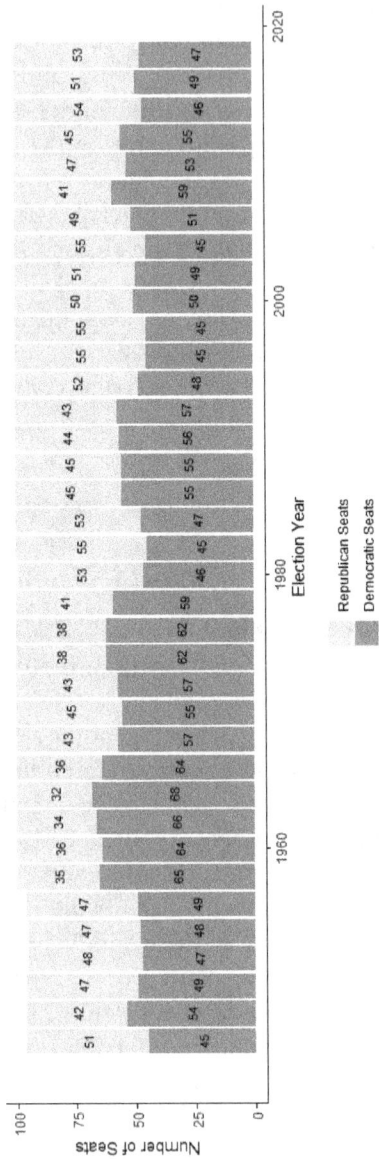

Figure 4.1: Number of Congressional Seats by Party and Chamber, 1946–2018.

net gain of forty seats by Democrats in 2018 is above average but far from being the largest turnaround in modern congressional elections. Surprisingly, Republicans gained two seats in the Senate in 2018—an unlikely scenario, given the concurrent changes in the House.

On the other hand, the net gain of forty seats was the largest for Democrats in the House since the "Watergate" class of 1974, when House Democrats gained forty-eight seats. This comparison is striking, considering the comparable gains of 1974 came amid a near perfect storm of a presidential scandal and resignation, a weak economy, and lingering war fatigue. There were only two other post-1946 elections in which Democrats had larger House seat gains: 1948 (+75 seats) and in 1958 (+50 seats). Conversely, Republicans claimed significant House victories in three post–World War II elections: 1966 (+47 seats), 1994 (+54 seats), and 2010 (+64 seats).

As mentioned above, the Democrats' forty-seat gain in the House was accompanied by a two-seat loss in the Senate. This result was more a function of the peculiar Senate playing field in 2018 than anything else. Democrats held twenty-six of the thirty-five Senate seats up for election in 2018, so Democrats were largely playing defense through-out the 2018 Senate election cycle. Republicans defeated four Dem-ocratic Senate incumbents in Florida (Nelson), Indiana (Donnelly), Missouri (McCaskill), and North Dakota (Heitkamp), but Democrats picked up seats in Arizona (open seat) and defeated an incumbent Re-publican in Nevada (Heller). All four of the Republican pickups were in states Trump had won in 2016 (by margins of 1.19 percent, 19.01 percent, 18.51 percent, and 35.73 percent, respectively), and Trump performed better in 2016 (margin of victory) in all of these states than Republican candidates did in 2018 (Republican Senate candi-dates won in these states by 0.12 percent, 5.92 percent, 5.81 percent, and 10.84 percent, respectively). In fact, the margin for Democrats was better in almost every one of the thirty-five Senate races around the country, with a few exceptions.[2] The political geography of the 2018 Senate map created a stacked deck for Republicans, so, despite a net loss of two Senate seats, Democrats dramatically outperformed their 2016 margins.

In comparison to other "wave" elections, the House gains made by Democrats in 2018 are particularly impressive, because most pre-vious elections with larger seat changes were accompanied by some combination of economic distress (1958, 1974, 2010) and war (1948, 1966, 1974). In 2018, the US economy was healthy by most standards, including a historically low unemployment rate (3.9 percent). The "Misery Index,"[3] which is calculated by adding unemployment and inflation rates, provides another point of economic comparison. In the eighteen midterm elections between 1950 and 2018, the only year in which the Misery Index was lower than 2018 was 1954. A robust and healthy economy in 2018 should have insulated the president's party from electoral losses; the Republican losses of 2018 clearly went against expectations.

Presidents typically receive credit for a healthy economy and blame for economic loss (Waterman, Silva, Jenkins-Smith 2014, 75). Trump is an exception to this pattern of presidential approval. In early 2018, Harry Enten (2018) pointed out that Donald Trump was the most unpopular president at the one-year mark of a presidential term since 1945, when pollsters started measuring presidential approval. Trump entered his second year with a net approval rating of negative 15 points, and his approval and disapproval ratings have also been more stable than any president before him. It was this lack of public confidence in Trump, more than anything else, that led to the Democratic Party's upset victory. A simple OLS regression between House seat gains/losses and presidential approval between 1946 and 2018 suggest Trump's Election Day approval of 44 percent would translate to a gain of thirty-three seats for Democrats in 2018.[4] Democrats obviously out-performed historic trends.

The Democratic gains in the House were impressive when we account for disadvantages House Democrats faced due to gerrymandering and the concentration of Democratic voters in urban areas. The culmination of these factors left Democrats with very few "easy" pickups in 2018. For example, heading into the 2018 elections, House Republicans held only nine seats that voted for the Democratic candidate in both of the previous two presidential elections (Cohn 2018). By comparison, in advance of the "red wave" of 2010, Democrats held sixty-seven seats that voted for the Republican candidate in both of the two previous presidential elections. Given this context—and economic downturn created by the Great Recession—the 2010 results were largely predictable. The electoral landscape became slightly better for Democrats after 2016, when Hillary Clinton won twenty-seven districts that also elected a Republican representative.[5] Democrats would go on to win all but two of these districts (NY-24 and TX-23) in 2018. In contrast, there were only fourteen districts won by Trump in 2016 that also elected a Democrat—Republicans won four of these seats in 2018. While many Republican-controlled districts shifted their presidential vote in 2016, Democrats overperformed with their forty-seat gain. Significant gains by Democrats were further hindered by district maps that "packed" Democratic voters into solid blue Democratic districts and scattered Republican supporters more evenly across a state's remaining districts. The concentration of partisan voters is partly a function of Democrats clustering in urban centers and Republicans being spread out over rural areas. But this geographic division was exacerbated by Republican-led gerrymandering, which "wastes" Democratic votes in many states, such as North Carolina and Wisconsin (Stephanopoulos and McGhee 2015).[6] For example, in 2018, Republicans received 50.4 percent of the total vote in North Carolina, but Republicans won ten of the state's thirteen House districts (Astor and Lai 2018).

Surprising Trends from 2018

The context of the "blue wave" described in the previous section tells only part of the story of Trump and the 2018 midterms. The elections were record-breaking across many fronts, beyond the significant seat gains made by Democrats. In 2018, we saw record turnout and fundraising and the most diverse field of candidates in history. Some of these dynamics can be explained as backlash to an unpopular president. The culmination of these trends was a hyper-motivated electorate that exceeded expectations. All of the records broken in 2018 are connected by a single thread: The specific rhetorical and policy controversies caused by President Trump.

The most prominent feature of 2018 was voter turnout. Across the country, 50 percent of the voting-eligible population voted in 2018—more than an 11-point increase from the 2014 midterms.[7] This was the highest turnout rate in a midterm election since 1974 (another notable "wave" election). The increase in turnout was a full 10 points higher than any midterm election after the 1994 Republican takeover of the House. In the aggregate, there was something clearly different about the 2018 midterms compared to past midterms (and even past "wave" elections). While we expect the president's party to take a loss during the midterm, an 11-point swing in turnout from midterm-to-midterm is shocking.

The record turnout of 2018 was driven by groups that traditionally vote for Democratic candidates. For example, turnout among

Hispanic voters increased by 13 points from 2014 to 2018—a 50 percent increase.[8] Asian Americans showed a comparable increase. These changes are especially noteworthy, because Hispanic and Asian American voters typically display lower levels of voter turnout, compared to white and Black voters. There were also large differences in motivation across age groups. The youngest age group (18–29) voted at a rate of 35.6 percent—a 79 percent increase from 2014. Older age groups also displayed increases, but the gains were not nearly as large as those displayed by the younger voters.

Both women and men voted at higher rates than either group did in 2014—an increase of 12 and 11 percentage points, respectively. However, turnout among women was 55 percent compared to 51.8 percent among men in 2018. The gender gap was more apparent across age and racial categories. Younger women (18–29 years old) out-voted men of the same age group, 38 percent to 33 percent. White, non-Hispanic women voted at a slightly higher rate than white, non-Hispanic men: 57.5 percent to 55.5 percent. Other racial categories display a much larger gender gap. Hispanic women out-voted Hispanic men by more than six percentage points in 2018 (43.7 percent to 37.3 percent). Black women displayed the largest difference compared to men of the same racial category—54.9 percent of eligible Black women voted compared to 46.4 percent of eligible Black men. These differences in voter turnout by gender and race are at least partly due to these groups being the targets of President Trump's most damning rhetorical statements and policy decisions.

A cornerstone of his 2016 campaign was undocumented immigration and a proposed border wall with Mexico. The language used to describe these plans was vitriolic and targeted directly at immigrants from Latin America. Among other examples, President Trump infamously launched his campaign by declaring, "When Mexico sends its people, they're not sending their best. . . . They're bringing drugs. They're bringing crime. They're bringing rapists" and "Some people call it an 'invasion.' It's like an invasion. They have violently overrun the Mexican border" (Scott 2019). Likewise, African Americans were often the brunt of Trump's racially coded language. Throughout the 2016–2018 National Football League seasons, many players—mostly Black players—protested police brutality and racism by kneeling during the national anthem. Trump used these protests as fuel in his many rallies during his first two years in office. At one rally, the president said in response to the protesters "get that son of a bitch off the field." He then praised the NFL for passing a policy that forbid players from kneeling on the field during the anthem (Coaston 2018). Trump also made many disparaging comments toward women during his campaign; the most salient example was then-candidate Trump's comments on the *Access Hollywood* tape, where he described grabbing women's genitalia without consent. At the time of this writing, Trump has been publicly accused of sexual misconduct by seventeen women (Brice-Saddler 2020).

In addition to this rhetoric, the policy decisions made by the president's administration disproportionately affected the groups mentioned above. The administration terminated the Deferred Action for Childhood Arrivals (DACA) program in 2017 and aggressively pursued a policy of family separation for people crossing the southern border and seeking asylum in the United States. Given these policy actions, it is not surprising that Hispanic voters participated at historic rates in 2018.

The first two years of the Trump presidency also saw many attempts to repeal or undermine the Affordable Care Act (ACA), a policy that particularly benefited women and racial minorities. For instance, after the implementation of the ACA, the proportion of the uninsured among racial minorities dropped more than it did among whites (Buchmueller et al. 2016). Likewise, women benefited more than men from the ACA's protections for preexisting conditions and preventative care requirements. These aspects of the policy decreased the out-of-pocket medical spending for women on a variety of services, such as contraception (Becker and Polsky 2025). In 2017, the Trump administration cut the advertising budget for the ACA by 90 percent and the policy's in-person outreach program by $23 million—a move meant to undermine the success of the ACA (Kliff 2017). The biggest blow to the ACA came in December 2017 when Trump signed the Tax Cuts and Jobs Act (TCJA) into a law, which removed the ACA's "individual mandate."

A final policy-related move that helped motivate minority groups in 2018 was the nomination—and subsequent appointment—of two conservative judges to the Supreme Court, creating a conservative majority in the court. The ideological change led many to believe the court could overturn the landmark *Roe v. Wade* decision related to abortion access. The Brett Kavanaugh confirmation hearings were particularly galvanizing for women. A key part of Kavanaugh's Senate hearings revolved around alleged sexual misconduct, and the hearings included witness testimony from a survivor of a sexual assault allegedly perpetrated by Kavanaugh. Despite these claims, the Senate approved Kavanaugh 50–48, in a mostly party-line vote.[9] This confirmation served as a lightning rod for many women voters, who led multiday protests throughout the process (Witt 2018).

Turnout was not the only indicator of increased voter mobilization in 2018. The elections also saw record-breaking campaign fundraising numbers in multiple races. Table 4.1 lists the twenty House races with the highest combined fundraising levels since 2009[10]—eleven of the top twenty elections took place in 2018. The Center for Responsive Politics (Mayersohn 2019) estimated that a total of $5.7 billion[11] was spent by "candidates, parties, committees, PACs, and outside groups" in 2017 and 2018, a 50 percent increase over 2014. These record-breaking numbers further highlight public enthusiasm surrounding the 2018 midterms.

Democrats were the driving force behind many of these fundraising records. The Democratic candidate outraised their Republican opponent in nine of the twelve post-2016 elections listed in table 4.1 (including Georgia's Sixth Congressional District's 2017 special election). Additionally, each of the twelve elections featured either a Republican incumbent or an open seat. In the aggregate, Democratic House candidates outspent their Republican House counterparts by $300 million (Mayersohn 2018). The ability of Democrats to outraise Republicans in these races is noteworthy, because incumbents typically enjoy a large fundraising advantage, due to an established donor network and name recognition (Erikson 1971; Jacobson 2009; Ansolabehere and Snyder 2002; Fouirnais and Hall 2014). Despite this advantage, Republican incumbents in these races did not fare well. Seven elections in table 4.1 featured a Republican incumbent,[12] and only two Republican incumbents—Devin Nunes (CA-22) and Barbara Comstock (VA-10)—outraised their Democratic challenger. Nunes would go on to win reelection, but Comstock lost to Democrat Jennifer Wexton. In fact, five of these seven Republican incumbents lost their bid for reelection in 2018.[13] Campaign spending is also correlated with vote share and turnout (Jacobson 1978, 1990, 2009), so the fundraising success of Democratic challengers may have translated into electoral victory. It is impossible to determine a causal relationship between turnout and campaign fundraising. Regardless, the overall fundraising records and the specific record-breaking elections listed in table 4.1 highlight yet another dimension of Democratic mobilization and excitement in 2018.

A final surprising trend from 2018 connected to the anti-Trump

Table 4.1: Top Twenty Fundraising Totals in House of
Representatives Elections, 2009–2018

Year	District	Total (millions $)
2017	GA-06	44.8
2012	OH-08	32.1
2018	PA-01	27
2012	FL-18	24.2
2018	CA-22	22.2
2018	MD-06	21.9
2016	WI-01	21.4
2018	CA-39	20.7
2014	OH-08	20.3
2016	MD-08	19.9
2010	MN-06	19
2018	CA-49	18.6
2016	FL-18	18.1
2018	NY-19	18
2018	VA-10	17.8
2012	MN-06	17
2018	KY-06	15.4
2018	CA-45	15.2
2018	CA-48	15.1
2018	CA-10	15

sentiment present in the election was the record number of candidates
from historically underrepresented groups. As previously stated, many
of Trump's statements and policies had a direct, negative impact on
gender and racial minorities. The diversity of the 2018 candidate field
was largely driven by Democratic candidates. White men comprised
only 42 percent of the Democratic Party's candidate pool in congressional seats,[14] while 77 percent of Republican nominees were white
men. The percent of white, female Democratic nominees increased
from 21 percent of congressional candidates in 2016 to 30 percent in
2018. There was also an increase in the number of Democratic female
candidates of color from 8 percent of the field in 2016 to 11 percent
in 2016. The diversity of the Republican pool of congressional candidates saw little change between 2016 and 2018.

The diverse field of candidates made the 116th Congress (2019–
2021) the most diverse Congress in US history.[15] Once again, the
changing diversity of Congress was led by the Democratic Party. The

number of women in Congress grew to 102 after the 2018 midterms—a 23 percent increase in female representation from the 115th Congress (2017–2019). Democrats held eighty-nine of these seats. Black representation also saw gains, increasing from fifty to fifty-six Black members over the same period. Democrats held fifty-four of these seats. Hispanics made fewer gains between the 115th and 116th Congresses, increasing from forty-two seats to forty-three. However, the number of Hispanic Democrats increased from thirty to thirty-four during this time, meaning the number of Hispanic Republicans in Congress decreased. The 2018 midterms were a high-water mark for women and racial minorities. Descriptive representation tends to increase turnout among minority groups, and the changing electoral landscape may have influenced the historic turnout of 2018 (Griffin and Keane 2006; Uhlaner 2012). It is not a coincidence that these historic demographic changes took place in the first midterm after Trump's election.

Taken together, the impressive seat gain by Democrats and the various election records broken in 2018 displayed a clear referendum on President Trump and the Republican Party. The Democratic victory in the House is noteworthy, considering that many economic and political factors seemed to favor the president's party. Regardless, a healthy economy was not enough to insulate Republican candidates from nationwide voter mobilization caused by Trump's divisive rhetoric and policy decisions.

Surprise Victories in the "Blue Wave"

Any wave election is decided by the handful of truly competitive seats and another group of surprising upset victories. To better understand the role of President Trump in the 2018 midterms, we compare Democratic victories across two very different electoral landscapes: Orange County, California, and South Carolina's First Congressional District. These more granular examinations help to explain the large-scale dynamics described in the previous section, and the individual cases show the 2018 blue wave was due to more than just ongoing incremental political and demographic change.

ORANGE COUNTY

In 2016, 51.5 percent of voters in Orange County, California, cast their vote for Hillary Clinton, compared to just 42.9 percent for Donald

Trump. The last time a majority of votes in this traditional Republican stronghold went for a Democratic presidential candidate was 1936, during the landslide reelection campaign of Franklin D. Roosevelt (Krishnakumar et al. 2016). In many ways, Orange County is an ideal locale for Republican candidates: the district contains many upper-income voters, and the population is centered around suburban areas. While the Clinton victory came as a shock to many, the Republican stranglehold on Orange County had been loosening since the 1990s. Barack Obama lost the county by only 2.5 percent in 2008 and by 6.3 percent in 2012 (compared to a 30-point loss by John Kerry in 2004). Despite the success of Clinton in 2016, four of the six congressional districts at least partly contained in Orange County remained under Republican control at the start of the 115th Congress (2017–2019). All six congressional districts would be held by a Democrat after the 2018 midterm elections.

The story of Orange County's political change has less to do with Democratic gains and more to do with Republican losses. In 2010, 43.8 percent of the county's voters were registered as Republican, compared to just 31.9 percent registered as Democratic. By 2018, Republican registration had dwindled to 34.7 percent, while Democratic registration increased to only 33.5 percent. The county was also undergoing a change in demography during this period. The percent of non-Hispanic, white residents decreased from 51.3 percent to 44.1 percent between the 2000 and 2010 census. The trend is expected to continue with the 2020 census.[16] This change is mostly due to an influx of Hispanic residents to the county—an unsurprising change in a majority-minority state. The US Census Bureau estimates that Orange County will have a population composed of 40 percent non-Hispanic, white and 34 percent Hispanic, non-white in 2020.

The change in demographics is especially noteworthy, given the issue environment and rhetoric of the 2016 presidential election. As described earlier in the chapter, immigration—undocumented immigration across the US southern border, in particular—was a staple of Trump's campaign rhetoric, and the issue remained a focus of the president throughout his first term in office. California was also the focus of much of President Trump's anti-immigration ire. In 2017, California governor Jerry Brown signed Senate Bill 54, the California Values Act—the so-called sanctuary state law. This law prevented both state and local law enforcement officers from coordinating with federal agencies when encountering most undocumented immigrants in the state of California. After passing the law, California Senate president Kevin de León, who represented the state's Twenty-Fourth Senate District (East Los Angeles), said, "SB 54 will prevent state and local law enforcement officers from being commandeered by President Trump to enforce federal laws" (Phillips 2017). Immigration and actions by the Trump administration were clearly on the minds of many in Southern California heading into the 2018 midterms.

Aside from immigration, policy discourse in Trump's first term was dominated by health-care and tax reform. As previously discussed, much of the health-care debate centered around reforming and dismantling the Affordable Care Act. The first attempt to do so was the Republican-sponsored American Health Care Act of 2017 (AHCA), which included provisions to eliminate the expansion of Medicaid, replace subsidies for insurance premiums for low-income families, allow states to opt out of many ACA requirements, and eliminate the "individual mandate." While the AHCA did not become law, the legislation did spark controversy for Republican legislators who supported the effort, prompting voter protests outside Darrell Issa's (CA-49) district office in San Diego (Figueroa et al. 2017).

The biggest legislative success of the Trump administration, the Tax Cuts and Jobs Act of 2017 (TCJA), also directly affected many in Southern California, and the law remained a salient issue heading into the 2018 midterms. Specifically, the capping of the state and local property, income, and sales tax deduction (SALT) to $10,000 disproportionately affected California, particularly upper-income and high property value areas of the state, like Orange County. Unlike the AHCA, the TCJA would become law, but two of the four Orange County Republicans (Rohrabacher [CA-48] and Issa [CA-49]) opposed the bill. Taken together, the potential for the 2018 Democratic takeover of Orange County was precipitated by the interaction between political and demographic change, divisive rhetoric from the president on immigration, and salient policy decisions by the Trump administration.

To gain a deeper understanding of the dynamics in Orange County —and the likelihood of sustained Democratic control—we also consider specific district-level electoral trends. Table 4.2 contains the percent of general election votes cast for the Democratic and Republican candidates for president and the House of Representatives in the 2016 and 2018 elections. The remaining four districts reveal shifting political divisions in Orange County, and the results suggest the possibility

Table 4.2: Comparing the Percentage of Presidential and District-Level Votes in Orange County, by Majority Party, 2016–2018

2016 Presidential Election		*2016 House Election*		*2018 House Election*	
Democratic	*Republican*	*Democratic*	*Republican*	*Democratic*	*Republican*
51.5	42.9	57.2	42.8	51.6	48.4
49.8	44.4	58.6	41.4	47.9	52.1
66.3	27.9	70	—	69.1	30.9
62.6	31	63.7	36.3	64.9	35.1
47.9	46.2	58.3	41.7	53.6	46.4
50.7	43.2	49.7	50.3	56.4	43.6

Source: Information available through www.ballotpedia.org.
Note: The Forty-Sixth and Forty-Seventh Districts were held by Democrats prior to 2016. The 2016 general election in the Forty-Sixth District featured two Democratic candidates.

of continued Democratic control in some districts and political parity in others.

Based on recent election results, the most surprising Democratic gains were the Thirty-Ninth and Forty-Fifth Congressional Districts. Clinton won each of these districts by a wide margin in 2016. These two districts also elected a Republican House candidate in the same election (and these candidates won by a larger margin than Clinton). In the Thirty-Ninth Congressional District, Republican Ed Royce won the 2016 general election with 57 percent of the vote (he was first elected in 1993). After the retirement of Royce in 2018, Democrat Gil Cisnernos defeated Republican Young Kim 51.6 percent to 48.4 percent in the 2018 general election—a significant shift in district alignment, even in the absence of an incumbent. It is notable that Trump did not endorse the Republican candidates in either the Thirty-Ninth or the Forty-Fifth Congressional District.[17] The election in the Forty-Fifth District contained an incumbent, Mimi Walters, who won reelection in 2016 by 17 points. Despite the advantages of incumbency, Walters lost her bid for reelection to Democrat Katie Porter 47.9 percent to 52.1 percent. These two districts represent large deviations from previous elections in terms of partisanship and the House vote—a relatively safe incumbent (Walters) was even defeated.

A less surprising outcome was the defeat of Republican incumbent Dana Rohrabacher in the Forty-Eighth Congressional District. Clinton narrowly won this district in 2016 by 1.7 points, and Rohrabacher won reelection by less than a percentage point in the same election. The marginality of the seat was also affected by Rohrabacher's controversial votes on the ACHA, several attempted repeals of the ACA, and a resolution supporting the Immigration and Customs Enforcement office. Rohrabacher also received an endorsement from President Trump. These factors culminated in a stunning defeat of the incumbent: a 12-point loss to the Democratic challenger Harley Rouda. The defeat of Rohrabacher was not shocking. However, the margin of the defeat was greater than expected, and the election followed the same trend as other Orange County seats.

Taken together, the four Democratic House pickups in Orange County represent an interaction between Trump's influence and the potential for sustained Democratic control of the seats. On the one hand, the political and demographic landscape of Orange County has been undergoing dramatic change over several decades. The weakening grasp of the Republican Party is partly the result of decades-long incremental change. While these dynamics help explain increasing partisan competitiveness in Orange County, changes in voter registration and demographics cannot explain the complete Democratic takeover in a single election. The effect of Trump's rhetoric and his administration's policy choices also played a factor in these unexpected results.

SOUTH CAROLINA'S FIRST CONGRESSIONAL DISTRICT

In 2018, Joe Cunningham became the first Democrat since 1978 to win an election in South Carolina's First Congressional District, which includes parts of five different counties across the state's southern shoreline. From a strictly demographic and geographic standpoint, this district is solid ground for Republican candidates. The First Congressional District is mostly rural but also contains parts of the city of Charleston. Most of the area covered in Charleston County includes affluent suburbs, such as Sommerville and Mount Pleasant. The district's population is overwhelmingly white and upper-income; the US Census Bureau estimates the district's 2018 population to be 73.6 percent white, with a median family income of $70,000[18] (78.7 percent of registered voters in the district are white, non-Hispanic[19]). The district also contains many wealthy tourist destinations along the coast, including Hilton Head Island and Folly Beach. Given these dynamics, it is not surprising the district had been represented by a Republican since 1981.

Cunningham's surprising victory—and the effect of Trump on the election—began in the Republican primary. Former South Carolina governor Mark Sanford started his political career as the representative of the First District in 1995. After two tumultuous, scandalous terms as governor (2003–2011), Sanford again represented the area by winning a special election in 2013. He then ran unopposed in 2014, and he won reelection in 2016 with 58.5 percent of the vote. Sanford carried political baggage into office with him, but he was well-liked in his district. Despite his electoral success, Sanford was challenged by state representative Katie Arrington in the 2018 primary. Sanford also received severe, public criticism from President Trump, who endorsed Arrington on the day of the primary election. On June 12, 2018, President Trump tweeted: "Mark Sanford has been very unhelpful to me in my campaign to MAGA. He is MIA and nothing but trouble. He is better off in Argentina. I fully endorse Katie Arrington for Congress in SC, a state I love. She is tough on crime and will continue our fight to lower taxes. VOTE Katie!" Arrington would go on to beat Sanford by 4 points. The actual impact of this late endorsement on the day of the primary was negligible. However, it is clear Trump maintained a visible presence in the district before the general election, potentially energizing Democrats in an overwhelmingly Republican area.

Democrat Joe Cunningham was not a strong candidate by most standards: he never held public office and carried little name recognition in his home district. While he did not face an incumbent in the general election, he was running against a state representative who won her 2016 election with 70 percent of the vote. For all intents and purposes, this should have been an easy win for Arrington, but the primary election upset—and Trump's public endorsement—brought a new level of attention to a typically overlooked Republican seat. Trump's presence also remained a factor, as he recorded a robocall for Arrington's campaign in November. Cunningham would go on to win the seat by 1.4 percent—a margin of nearly four thousand votes. This was a competitive race, but it was also a shocking win and margin for a Democrat in what was originally thought to be a safe Republican district.

Rather than shoring up support for Arrington, Trump's intervention in the election appears to have motivated Democratic voters in the district. Comparing turnout in 2018 to the previous midterm election is difficult, because Sanford ran unopposed in 2014. However, Cunningham won the election by running up a large tally in

Charleston and the surrounding suburbs (including some precincts won by Trump in 2016), the most Democratic portion of the district (Parker 2018). Arrington beat Cunningham in four of the five counties within the district, but Cunningham held an overwhelming majority in Charleston County—more than enough to overcome his deficits in other counties. Fundraising totals also point to a highly motivated Democratic electorate. Cunningham raised $2.4 million over the course of the election—nearly $1 million more than Arrington's campaign.[20] Clearly, Democratic supporters found a new sense of enthusiasm in 2018, and the only change to the electoral landscape precipitating the Democratic victory was President Trump.

The outcome in South Carolina's First District was shocking, even during a wave election. Compared to Orange County, California, the prospects of Democrats holding onto this seat in the long run are in doubt. After all, Republicans held this seat for nearly forty years. There are no large-scale trends—either political or demographic—pointing to continued electoral parity in the district. Instead, an unpopular president intervened in what would normally be a safe Republican seat, motivating Democrats accustomed to seeing a Republican elected year after year. It is clear Trump's direct involvement—and larger-scale dynamics surrounding the presidency—played a major role in this surprise Democratic victory in 2018.

CONCLUSION

The 2018 midterms do not represent the largest House seat gain for a party in modern congressional elections, but it is clear Democrats over-performed, relative to historic patterns. These elections also displayed historically high levels of voter mobilization, indicated by record turnout, campaign fundraising, and the most diverse field of candidates in US history. The intensity surrounding the 2018 midterms can only be explained by the divisiveness and antipathy engendered by Trump's 2016 campaign for president and his first two years in office. Trump's impact on election outcomes was felt at the national level and within individual races. In some places, like Orange County, the changing demographic and political landscape exacerbated problems for Republican candidates caused by Trump. In other places, like South Carolina's First District, a Democrat pulled off a huge upset due to the direct intervention of Trump. Of course, a multitude of factors affect election outcomes, and the 2018 midterms are no exception.

However, a clear theme emerged after Democrats reclaimed the House majority: Trump, with his controversial rhetoric and policy agenda, was a major liability for Republican candidates across the country.

NOTES

1. Seat totals gathered from the House's History, Art, and Archives and the Senate's respective websites (https://history.house.gov/Home/ and https://www.senate.gov/history/partydiv.htm). Independent and third-party legislators are included with major-party totals only if the websites indicate that the legislator caucused with one of the two parties. For this reason, the totals in each year may not equal the total number of seats in each chamber.

2. We consider Maine senator Angus King and Vermont senator Bernie Sanders as Democratic candidates because they caucus with the Democrats in the Senate even though they are not Democrats. Clinton's margin in 2016 was better than Democratic Senate candidates in Massachusetts, New Jersey, and Utah. In New Jersey, this was likely the result of Sen. Robert Menendez having been on trial for corruption earlier in 2018 and in Utah, Trump's 2016 margin was reduced because of the presence of Utah native, Evan McMullin, on the ballot. McMullin received 21.3 percent of the vote. In addition, in California, there was no Republican Senate candidate on the ballot in 2018.

3. See *A Dictionary of Economics* (4th ed.), ed. John Black, Nigar Hashimzade, and Gareth Myles (Oxford: Oxford University Press, 2012).

4. The regression coefficient and data were obtained from the University of California, Santa Barbara's "The American Presidency Project": https://www.presidency.ucsb.edu/node/332343/.

5. District-level results for presidential elections were obtained from the Daily Kos: https://www.dailykos.com/stories/2018/2/21/1742660/-The-ultimate-Daily-Kos-Elections-guide-to-all-of-our-data-sets#1.

6. The district maps in these states were the subjects of federal lawsuits in 2019.

7. Election data was obtained from the United States Election Project (www.electproject.org).

8. Turnout data by gender and race was obtained from the US Census Bureau's Current Population Survey (Voting and Registration Supplement).

9. All Republicans voted to confirm (two Republican senators voted "present"). Joe Manchin (D-WV) was the only Democrat to vote for Kavanaugh's confirmation.

10. Campaign fundraising data was obtained from www.followthemoney.org. The website tracks individual races starting in 2009. The data in table 4.1 only includes fundraising by candidate campaign committees. The campaign with the highest fundraising totals listed in table 4.1 was a special election in Georgia's Sixth Congressional District in 2017. This race gar-

nered significant national attention when the incumbent, Republican Tom Price, resigned to become the Secretary of Health and Human Services. Democratic candidate Jon Ossoff raised a record $29.5 million (over four times more than his opponent) in a losing effort.

11. This total was publicized by www.opensecrets.org, and the figure includes spending by outside groups, such as SuperPACs.

12. The 2018 races featuring a Republican incumbent were: CA-22, NY-19, VA-10, KY-06, CA-45, CA-48, and CA-10.

13. Nunes went on to win reelection, along with Andy Barr (KY-06).

14. Data on race and gender of candidates was obtained from the Reflective Democracy Campaign's 2018 "A Rising Tide?" report. The final report contains information on general election candidates as of September 21, 2018.

15. Demographic information on Congress was obtained from the Brooking Institution's "Vital Statistics of Congress" report.

16. Voter registration and Census information was obtained from the Center for Demographic Research, California State University, Fullerton and the US Census Bureau 2019 projections.

17. Information on endorsements is gathered from Ballotpedia.org, which includes appearances in television ads, radio ads, at fundraising events, and at campaign rallies. Endorsements were also recorded for President Trump's tweets.

18. Estimates obtained from the 2018 American Community Survey.

19. Information obtained from www.scvotes.org.

20. According to www.opensecrets.org, the average Democratic House candidate raised $1.95 million in 2018.

REFERENCES

Ansolabehere, Stephen, and James M. Snyder, Jr. "The Incumbency Advantage in US Elections: An Analysis of State and Federal Offices, 1942–2000." *Election Law Journal* 1, no. 3 (2002): 315–338.

Astor, Maggie, and K. K. Rebecca Lai. "What's Stronger Than a Blue Wave? Gerrymandered Districts." *New York Times*, 2018.

Becker, Nora V., and Daniel Polsky. "Women Saw Large Decrease in Out-of-Pocket Spending for Contraceptives after ACA Mandate Removed Cost Sharing." *Health Affairs* 24, no. 7 (2015): 1204–1211.

Brady, David W., John E. Cogan, Brian Gaines, and R. Douglas Rivers. "The Perils of Presidential Support: How the Republicans Captured the House." *Political Behavior* 18 (December 1996): 345–368.

Brice-Saddler, Michael. "New York Writer Who Accused Trump of Raping Her Wants a Sample of His DNA." *Washington Post*, January 30, 2020.

Buchmueller, Thomas C., Zachary M. Levinson, Helen G. Levy, and Barbara L.

Wolfe. "Effect of the Affordable Care Act on Racial and Ethnic Disparities in Health Insurance Coverage." *American Journal of Public Health* 106, no. 8 (2016): 1416–1421.

Campbell, James E. "The Midterm Landslide of 2010: A Triple Wave Election." *Forum: A Journal of Applied Research in Contemporary Politics* 8, no. 4 (2011): (online).

———. "Explaining Presidential Losses in Midterm Congressional Elections." *Journal of Politics* 47, no. 4 (1985): 1140–1157.

Coaston, Jane. "2 Years of NFL Protests, Explained." Vox. September 4, 2018.

Cohn, Nate. "Why Democrats' Gain Was More Impressive Than It Appears." *New York Times*, November 7, 2018.

Enten, Harry. "How Trump Ranks in Popularity vs. Past Presidents." FiveThirty Eight. January 19, 2018.

Erikson, Robert S. "The Advantage of Incumbency in Congressional Elections." *Polity* 3, no. 3 (1971): 395–405.

———. "The Puzzle of Midterm Loss." *Journal of Politics* 50, 4 (1988): 1011–1029.

Figueroa, Teri, Joshua Stewat, and Sarah Wire. "Issa Appears on Rooftop as Hundreds Protest outside His Vista Office." *San Diego Union-Tribune*, May 30, 2017.

Fouirnais, Alexander, and Andrew B. Hall. "The Financial Incumbency Advantage: Causes and Consequences." *Journal of Politics* 76, no. 3 (2014): 711–724.

Gelman, Andrew, and Gary King. "Estimating Incumbency Advantage without Bias." *American Journal of Political Science* 34, no. 4 (1990): 1142–1164.

Griffin, John D., and Michael Keane. "Descriptive Representation and the Composition of African American Turnout." *American Journal of Political Science* 50, no. 4 (2006): 998–1012.

Hirano, Shigeo, and James M. Snyder, Jr. "Using Multimember District Elections to Estimate the Sources of the Incumbency Advantage." *American Journal of Political Science* 53, no. 2 (2009): 292–306.

Jacobson, Gary C. "The Effects of Campaign Spending in Congressional Elections." *American Political Science Review* 72, no. 2 (1978): 469–491.

———. "The Effects of Campaign Spending in House Elections: New Evidence for Old Arguments." *American Journal of Political Science* 34, no. 2 (1990): 334–362.

———. *The Politics of Congressional Elections*. New York: Longman, 2009.

Kernell, Samuel. "Presidential Popularity and Negative Voter: An Alternative Explanation of the Midterm Congressional Decline of the President's Party." *American Political Science Review* 71, no. 1 (1977): 44–66.

Kliff, Sarah. "Trump Is Slashing Obamacare's Advertising Budget by 90%." Vox. August 31, 2017.

Krishnakumar, Priya, Jon Schleuss, and Joe Fox. "For the First Time since

Franklin D. Roosevelt, a Majority in Orange County Voted for a Democrat." *Los Angeles Times*, November 11, 2016.

Mayersohn, Andrew. "Most Expensive Midterms in History Set Several Spending Records." www.opensecrets.org. November 8, 2018.

Parker, J. Emory. "Detailed Map Reveals How Joe Cunningham Won SC-1 by Flipping Charleston Suburbs." *Post and Courier*, November 28, 2018.

Phillips, Kristine. "In Message of Defiance to Trump, Lawmakers Vote to Make California a Sanctuary State Law." *Washington Post*, September 16, 2017.

Schneider, Elena. "'Something Has Actually Changed': Women, Minorities, First-Time Candidates Drive Democratic House Hopes." *Politico*, September 11, 2018.

Scott, Eugene. "Trump's Most Insulting—and Violent—Language Is Often Reserved for Immigrants." *Washington Post*, October 2, 2019.

Stephanopoulos, Nicholas O., and Eric M. McGhee. "Partisan Gerrymandering and the Efficiency Gap." *University of Chicago Law Review* 82, no. 2 (2015): 831–900.

Uhlaner, Carole J. "Potentiality and Representation: The Link between Descriptive Representation and Participation in the United State." *Politics & Gender* 8, no. 4 (2012): 535–541.

Waterman, Richard, Carol L. Silva, and Hank Jenkins-Smith. *The Presidential Expectations Gap: Public Attitudes Concern the Presidency*. Ann Arbor: University of Michigan Press, 2014.

Witt, Emily. "The Final Days of the Brett Kavanaugh Protests." *New Yorker*, October 7, 2018.

PART II

Trump and American Institutions

CHAPTER 5

Understanding Trump's Strategy and Opportunity

Paul E. Rutledge

INTRODUCTION

Much like his predecessors, President Donald Trump came to office
with an expectation of a transformative presidency. Trump's campaign
was structured with transformative, albeit divisive, rhetoric decrying
the accomplishments of his immediate predecessor, Barack Obama.
In doing so, Trump promised to "Make America Great Again" with
proposals that were somewhat opaque and at times alienated supporters of his own party. However, as Stephen Skowronek (2020) notes,
president-centered reconstructions in American politics have been
less the result of the president's ambition and more based on the
structure of opportunity within which the president operates. This
chapter will investigate the Trump presidency in terms of the opportunity structure he faces.

To understand presidential power in the context of the Trump
presidency, we must first understand the evolving understanding of
presidential power. Such a discussion will also lead to the ability to
gauge the extent to which President Trump had the opportunity to
lead. The first section of this chapter will detail the contemporary
understanding of presidential power and leadership opportunities,

before detailing the leadership potential that existed for the Trump presidency as indicated by mandate perceptions, public mood, and the composition of Congress. The evidence indicates that Trump's ability to bring about the transformation he desired was significantly constrained by his opportunity structure, and his misunderstanding of that opportunity coupled with his unfamiliarity with the policy process or substantive policy details has led to little legislative accomplishment. In conclusion, the Trump opportunity will be placed in historical context, with an eye toward where the Trump presidency falls in American political development and what it possibly indicates regarding the future of the American presidency.

UNDERSTANDING PRESIDENTIAL POWER

In his groundbreaking work, Richard Neustadt described presidential power as the power to persuade (Neustadt 1990). Neustadt's assertion has become by far the most cited and recognized formulation of presidential power and presidential research generally. Prior to Neustadt's novel conception of presidential power in 1960, presidential power was generally considered only within the bounds of the institution, having little to do with the person occupying the institution. Rather, presidential power was a function of the institution itself and both the constraints and opportunities presented in Article II of the Constitution. Scholars such as Edward S. Corwin (Corwin 1957) and Clinton Rossiter (1960) dominated presidential scholarship prior to Neustadt with primarily institutional conceptions of presidential power. Of course, Neustadt's conception of presidential power gave birth to the recognition within scholarship on the presidency of inherent powers, a series of extraconstitutional advantages that fundamentally dominate most presidential activity within the governance structure. Neustadt's power approach can also be contrasted with several other styles of presidential power. Neustadt's approach is a focus on the strategy of presidents in obtaining influence. Progressing with scholarship on the individual president, rather than the institution of the presidency, such an approach is different from the legal and institutional conceptions discussed above but also and perhaps more importantly is different from the focus on the characteristics of the individual in the office, such as a psychological approach (Barber 2019).

The biggest difference among the conceptions of presidential power and approaches to studying the presidency is change. The constitutional opportunities and constraints placed upon and within the presidency are rather constant. The psychological makeup of a president, given the advanced age of most presidents when they reach the office, is also rather constant. However, Neustadt's approach permits change. As one observer notes, Neustadt's interest is less on what causes success in one instance and more on what affects the probabilities of success in every instance. Strategically, how the president masters Congress in a certain instance is of less interest than what presidents can do to consistently master Congress (Edwards 2000).

Bargaining is a key component of the Neustadt approach to presidential power. Neustadt conjures images of the president as "chief bargainer," a negotiator who is getting his hands dirty in a pluralist decision-making setting. The chief bargainer is not perfect. While there is some advantage in being the president for persuasive ability, there is no assurance that the president will be successful in bargaining with others, such as members of Congress, who have their own diverse set of political interests and preferences. The ability of the president to make use of the prestige of his office, for Neustadt, is quite personal and is dependent not only on his persuasive abilities but also on his professional reputation. Such a focus on the personal president gives birth to the notion that some individuals will fare differently than others in the office. Presidents such as Franklin Roosevelt with his New Deal program, Lyndon Johnson with his Great Society, and Ronald Reagan with his desires for devolution and downsizing the federal government have been credited by presidential historians with tremendous abilities to persuade, directing and inspiring great change in American politics. On the other hand, presidents who presided over less productive times have not been afforded such high praise on their personal abilities to persuade or direct change.

Neustadt's approach to presidential power remains one of the most influential contributions to the study of the presidency for good reason. The "power as persuasion" approach has sparked tremendous scholarship that transcends the formal office, gives life to the inherent powers found in the office, and moves beyond the personal characteristics found in the psychological approach that are inert. However, the power as persuasion approach to studying the presidency is not without its flaws. Several scholars have noted the shortcomings with the Neustadt approach and built upon the foundation to move toward a more nuanced understanding of presidential power without taking away from the Neustadt contribution.

One problem with the power to persuade is that it is, in fact, *too* personal. Neustadt's book details many anecdotes on specific instances of presidential persuasion that are not conducive to future hypothesis testing. Such an approach is a successful shift from the previous paradigms that governed presidential scholarship, but in essence the shift may have been too far. As Lyn Ragsdale notes, one of the central problems with Neustadt's conception of presidential power is that it ignores the broader institutional context within which the president operates. Presidents are quite constrained by the policies and issues that carry over from one president to the next, requiring much of the president's attention to be on issues where there is not much wiggle room for personal ingenuity. An example is a president's foreign policy "doctrine." While every president has a unique name for their approach to foreign policy, the foreign policy priorities of the president are normally governed by national interest within the setting of world politics. Presidents from Truman through Reagan had different names for their approach to foreign policy, but as Ragsdale notes, the overarching goal regardless of the framing efforts was the containment of communism (Ragsdale 2000). Trump has largely continued in this tradition in many ways, though his unorthodox style has had consequences. Trump has broken with many of our longstanding alliances by labeling friends as foes, establishing troubling relationships with enemies, and removing the United States from participation in multilateral agreements. While this is detailed further in chapter 14 of this volume by Jeff Peake, it is worth mentioning here that Trump has presented a significant challenge to the boundaries that institutional history has placed on a president to be an agent of change. Trump's presidency has been disruptive to foreign policy and has the potential to have vast consequences on the stability of international affairs for decades.

Paul Light expresses further skepticism regarding the ability of the modern presidents to lead, even at the agenda-setting stage in which a volume of literature indicates the president has the best prospects for success (Rutledge and Larsen-Price 2014). Light notes that the post-Watergate presidency starting in the 1970s has faced increased competition from Congress, which reasserts itself to restore the checks and balances between the institutions following changes from the New Deal and Great Society eras. Further, at the same time, Congress developed a robust subcommittee system that led to increased complexity faced by presidents in their attempt to persuade members of Congress to enact their agendas. Finally, Watergate in and of itself did irreparable damage to the prestige of the office and the level of trust that would be afforded to leaders following Watergate, which, coupled with congressional reforms in both approach and structure, led to a presidential agenda that would be met with skepticism upon arrival. Taken together, Light asserts that the contemporary institution is a no-win presidency, which is far afield from the presidency as a director of change through persuasive ability as posited by Neustadt (Light 1999).

Finally, recent scholarship has posited a more nuanced understanding of presidential power that moves away from persuasion and more toward opportunity. George C. Edwards (2012) questions the ability of presidents to persuade in as much as Neustadt's work suggests that presidents can be directors of transformative change through their persuasive abilities. While Edwards concedes that presidents may have persuasive abilities, such persuasion to direct change is usually found at the margins, is the exception rather than the rule, and operates within the constraints of the opportunity calculation within which all presidents must operate. Edwards focuses more on opportunity than persuasion, and his notion of presidential power is focused on the president as a facilitator rather than as a director of transformative change. This conception of presidential power can be understood through three primary examples detailed by Edwards.

First, President Franklin D. Roosevelt has been credited with transformative change in American government and politics as a result of his New Deal program. In fact, it is Roosevelt who is credited with the creation of the ever important "first one hundred days" that leads to pressure on every president to get as much accomplished as quickly as possible. Much of Roosevelt's New Deal program for economic recovery was accomplished in his first one hundred days. Further, there is specific lore about Roosevelt reaching into the living rooms of the American people through his Fireside Chats. However, as Edwards details, there is little tangible evidence that Roosevelt exerted any form of transformative leadership in enacting the New Deal. Roosevelt discussed major legislative proposals on only four occasions in Fireside Chats, which were happening weekly. This means that an infinitesimal percentage of his Fireside Chats were focused on moving the needle toward his policy. Further, as Edwards details, two examples of Roosevelt proposals that he most actively tried to lead through persuasion were his Lend-Lease program and the court packing plan.

The Lend-Lease program experienced a bump, but it was only after foreign events dictated a movement toward more involvement on the allied side of World War II. On the court packing plan, there is little evidence that Roosevelt was able to move the needle in his favor. In fact, the most notable movement was against Roosevelt's plan over time, and the plan was eventually defeated.

Next, President Lyndon Johnson has been accorded tremendous ability to lead Congress through his knowledge of congressional procedure as a former Senate majority leader and also through his ability to give recalcitrant legislators "the Johnson treatment," using his intimidating size and personality to persuade.[1] Following his landslide election victory in 1964 over Republican Barry Goldwater, Johnson presided over one of the most productive periods in legislative history. Sweeping policy changes were made in accordance with his Great Society program to combat poverty, bring equal rights both in politics and society to African Americans, and broaden the social safety net provided by the New Deal. However, once again Edwards finds very little evidence of Johnson using his persuasive ability to gain traction anywhere that the public and Congress were not already prepared to go. In fact, Edwards goes on to provide comments from those inside both the Kennedy and Johnson administration who felt that President Kennedy would have accomplished just as much as Johnson did. Those inside the administration agreed that were it not for his assassination, Kennedy, despite his differing approach to dealing with Congress, would have been just as adept at maximizing the opportunity as Johnson was, given Kennedy's sizable electoral landslide and accompanying congressional majority.

Finally, President Ronald Reagan is widely known for his persuasive abilities as the "Great Communicator." Without question, President Reagan did have an unusual ability to speak directly to the American people in terms they could understand and connect with. He also had considerable skill in charming members of Congress personally. However, these qualities, while admirable, do not necessarily translate into transformative persuasion. Rather, transformative persuasion in the Neustadt conception would involve President Reagan using his ability to communicate and gain support for his preferred programs. However, once again, Edwards finds very little evidence of Reagan being able to lead either the public or Congress to favor his preferred programs. Rather, the evidence suggests that Reagan's best skill was leading people where they already wanted to go. Conservative Democrats supported his tax cuts, according to Edwards, because they agreed with them. Following initial successes in spending cuts domestically and spending increases on the military, Reagan was met with frustration throughout the majority of his tenure because the preferences of the public and Congress moved in the opposite direction, favoring spending increases domestically while refusing to increase defense spending during his entire second term.

In summary, Edwards (2012; 2016) advances a different understanding of presidential power. Given the lack of evidence Edwards finds to support the notion that presidents can use their persuasive abilities to transform American government, even in the best test cases, we are left with a presidency that is governed more by opportunity than persuasion. It is not transformative leadership that leads to presidential success. Rather, according to Edwards, it is facilitation governed by the opportunities available to lead that dictate presidential power. What Roosevelt, Johnson, and Reagan have in common is great opportunities to facilitate change that both the public and Congress were already primed for. This is not to suggest that leadership skills are not important. Instead, the focus of leadership is on the ability of presidents to facilitate change by exploiting the opportunities when they arise (Edwards 2012). Such conceptions of leadership are more consistent with prominent theories of public policy, such as John Kingdon's three streams approach. When the policy, political, and solutions streams intersect in his Garbage Can Model, policy windows open for transformative change to occur (Kingdon 2010). Following periods of stability and incremental change, policy windows open for policy punctuations and settle in at new equilibrium points that transform the trajectory of public policy (Baumgartner and Jones 2009).

It follows that a president's strategic opportunity for leadership is governed by three things. First, the size of the president's electoral victory is an important factor in the perception of a mandate to govern. A mandate perception is present under the conditions in which there is broad consensus in the media, the public, and perhaps most importantly, in Congress that the election is a mandate to enact policy platforms on behalf of the voting public (Grossback et al. 2006). Second, presidential opportunity for leadership is governed by the composition of Congress. Presidents have a much stronger opportunity to lead when their co-partisans are in control of both chambers of the legislature and have much more difficulty leading under periods of divided government. Additionally, co-partisans do not offer guaranteed success, as ideological congruence is also a prerequisite to presidential leadership. Finally, the public mood in conservative-liberal terms provides an important constraint on presidential opportunities to lead. Presidents will experience their best opportunity to exert leadership when the public mood is consistent with the ideology of the president. In each of the three cases detailed by Edwards above, Presidents Roosevelt, Johnson, and Reagan had tremendous opportunities to lead according to these indicators. However, the opportunity structure is not equal, or, more importantly, promising, for all presidents.

In the next section of this chapter, the leadership opportunity available to President Donald Trump will be evaluated in historical context. As the reader will see, President Trump's opportunity to govern was limited according to these dimensions. However, opportunities for the type of sweeping, transformative change discussed above are rare and fleeting. Presidents must learn to operate within this environment of leadership, which is constrained to facilitating and making the best of the opportunity available to them. President Trump has shown very little understanding of the political context within which he operates, has refused opportunities to work across the aisle, and has failed to rally the fractured Republican Party behind the vast majority of his legislative agenda. He campaigned on broad, if vague, themes to bring transformative change and "make America great again." All presidents claim a mandate publicly. However, most presidents have either made adjustments to their agenda or learned from the difficulties they have faced within the legislative process. Trump has demonstrated very little ability to learn from defeat, instead lashing out at the media, members of Congress, or any number of others that he can pass blame to rather than accepting responsibility and showing any form of personal or presidential growth.

TRUMP AND PRESIDENTIAL POWER

Given the evolving understanding of presidential power described above, it is important to transition into what the concept of presidential power means for the Trump presidency. What factors are important in determining the opportunity available to President Trump to govern? Edwards (2016) provides scholars of the presidency with several important questions to ask when attempting to understand, and perhaps even predict, the opportunities available for presidential success. Each of these questions will be analyzed in the context of the Trump presidency in this section.

Electoral Mandate Perception

First, Edwards asks if there is a perception of an electoral mandate for presidents to enact their policies. All presidents claim, following their elections, that the people have spoken. Presidents are emboldened by winning the ultimate political prize in the nation and the chance to be seated in perhaps the most powerful position in the world. Coming off of the high of this victory, all presidents will be confident and bold in exclaiming and perhaps exaggerating the political capital gained by their victories. Scholarly work on the understanding of electoral mandates gives us some understanding of what to look for when investigating potential mandate conditions. Grossback, Peterson, and Stimson (2006) look to media accounts and comments by members of Congress in the days following elections and also find a notable deviation in the voting patterns of members of Congress in moving toward the direction of the electoral mandate.

The 2016 election was certainly a surprise; nearly every political science model and even models outside of academia predicted a Hillary Clinton victory, some even comfortably (Campbell et al. 2017). Only Helmut Norpoth's primary model (2016) and Alan Abramowitz's time-for-change model (2016) predicted a Trump victory. With that said, the models that predicted a Clinton victory were closer to the actual election result, and the Norpoth and Abramowitz models overestimated the percentage of the vote won by Trump in terms of the popular vote. President Trump was able to win the election in spite of losing the popular vote by a margin of more than 2 percent. President Trump won several key states in the upper Midwest that went for Obama in 2008 and 2012. These states included Pennsylvania, Iowa, Michigan, Ohio, and Wisconsin. Coupled with Florida as a Southern swing state and Maine's Second Congressional District, a total of one hundred electoral votes swung in the direction of the Republican candidate. Additionally, several of the states that were won by Trump had very close margins. In Michigan, Trump defeated Hillary Clinton by less than eleven thousand votes out of the nearly five million cast statewide. In Wisconsin, Trump's victory over Clinton was still modest, though greater than the victory in Michigan (and perhaps even more surprising) with a margin of approximately twenty-two thousand votes of a total of just under 3 million cast. President Trump carried Pennsylvania by just over forty-four thousand votes of the more than 6 million votes cast in the Keystone State. Taken together, these three states were crucial to the Trump victory, flipping a crucial forty-six electoral votes from the Clinton to Trump column with the combined margin in the popular vote total of the three states of only approximately seventy-seven thousand votes of over 136 million votes cast nationwide.

President Trump won the Electoral College and the presidency generally based on the votes of roughly 0.0005 percent of the population in three states, all while losing the popular vote by just under 3 million votes nationally. One concession regarding these numbers, of course, is that Democratic candidate Hillary Clinton won the popular vote in part by running up huge margins in several blue states, most notably the nation's most populous state of California. The story of the 2016 election is that of a contest between the two least likable candidates in the history of public opinion polling. Were it not for Donald Trump, as Gary C. Jacobson (2017) points out, Hillary Clinton would have been the candidate with the lowest favorability ratings of all time. This is particularly true among rival partisans and independents, with majorities in both groups viewing both of the candidates unfavorably. What is perhaps more telling is the low favorability ratings that each candidate had among their own parties, with voters in each party having to swallow hard and vote for their candidate because of how unacceptably they viewed the prospect of casting a vote for the candidate of the rival party (Jacobson 2017).

The Trump victory in 2016, although it was a surprise, is hardly a typical landslide election that would be consistent with a mandate perception. Additionally, George C. Edwards (2017) discusses a litany of polling data that casts serious doubt over the possibility of a Trump mandate. Polling just prior to the 2016 election indicated strongly that the majority of voters who cast a vote *for* Donald Trump were actually casting their vote *against* Hillary Clinton.[2] Further polling indicated that just 29 percent of the American public agreed that President Trump was given a mandate to govern, while 59 percent saw the election results as a basis for Trump to work across the aisle with Democrats.[3] Doing so would be difficult, however, given that the margin of approval between Republicans and Democrats toward Trump was astonishing, with 90 percent among Republicans compared to 14 percent among Democrats.[4] Finally, President Trump began his term with a record low approval rating, according to Gallup, of 45 percent.[5] The evidence indicates that in spite of claims made by a victorious Trump, following a tradition of his predecessors, that the American voting public had given life to a mandate perception on behalf of Trump's policies, there is no tangible evidence to indicate that President Trump had a mandate to govern. In fact, the majority of evidence found in the 2016 election, the transition, and the beginning of the president's first term indicate quite the opposite. The Trump presidency would begin following a campaign that contained little in terms of specific policy proposals for the public to support, shrouded in a record level of unfavorability within his own party, the rival party, and among independents.

Composition of Congress

The second dimension of presidential opportunity according to Edwards (2016) is the composition of Congress. There is a long scholarly debate over the impact of unified versus divided government. Presidents typically can have high expectations of support from within their own party. As such, unified government is a desirable condition within which every president hopes to govern.

The composition of Congress was much more favorable to the opportunity to govern presented to President Trump on January 20, 2017. President Trump benefited from a Republican majority of a fairly comfortable forty-seven seats in the House of Representatives to begin his first term. Such a margin in the House of Representatives is key, because the hierarchically structured House allows the party leadership of the chamber to exert considerable influence over its agenda and procedures. Further, the limits placed on amendments and debate that come with majority control over House procedures allow a majority that is cohesive to run roughshod over dissenting minorities, especially in comparison to the Senate.

President Trump also found a favorable situation in the Senate, where the Republicans had majority control at a margin of fifty-two to forty-eight. While presidents would certainly prefer a majority in the Senate compared to a minority, the supermajoritarian procedures in the Senate demand a much wider margin for majority control to truly be effective, as Krehbiel's (2010) work demonstrates in extraordinary detail. A filibuster-proof majority, for example, would require a majority of sixty votes or more, something that the Republicans were far from at the beginning of President Trump's first term.

However, the condition of unified government falls far short of guaranteeing presidential success. The volume of literature on unified government lends some evidence to this. David Mayhew (2004) casts the original doubt on the importance of unified government, finding that divided government does not guarantee less legislative productivity. In fact, Mayhew finds that just as many examples of significant legislation have derived from divided government as we have seen from unified government over the period 1946–2002. This does bring into question two assumptions regarding unified government. First, that presidents facing unified government will find it significantly easier to get legislation passed. Second, that presidents facing divided government will automatically face a greater resistance and gridlock. According to Mayhew's findings, both assumptions are highly questionable.

Additional investigation of the importance of unified government for presidential success further validates these long-held assumptions. Sundquist (1992) challenges Mayhew's findings in suggesting that Mayhew's focus on the number of significant enactments only ignores the broader picture of the legislation that passes under divided government, which can be significantly delayed or diluted as compared to significant enactments that pass under unified government. Edwards et al. (1997) challenge Mayhew further in suggesting that Mayhew's focus on significant legislation that passed ignores the potentially significant legislation that did not pass. Their findings suggest that presidents do hold an advantage when presiding over unified government in several ways. Presidents oppose more legislation, thus taking more negative action, under the condition of divided as opposed to unified government. As a result, they find that presidents are more likely to oppose legislation and that potentially significant legislation that the president opposes is less likely to pass under divided government. However, their findings do suggest that presidents are equally likely to support legislation and see that legislation enacted under conditions of unified and divided government. As such, the assumptions regarding divided government causing gridlock are upheld, somewhat, in that divided government leads to the failure of more significant legislation than does unified government. But the results also clearly indicate that the amount of significant legislation that will pass under unified and divided government are similar. This means that divided government may increase the prospect of failure, but unified government does not offer a greater prospect of success.

There is some evidence, however, that unified government under

Republican presidents is not as productive as divided governments in which Democrats control Congress or unified governments in which Democrats control both chambers and the presidency. Coleman (1999) suggests that parties are responsive to the public mood. The public policy mood is a measure created by James A. Stimson (1999) that measures the desires of the public for more, less, or about the same level of government activity (measured as spending in the public opinion question) on specific policy areas. Stimson then aggregates these measures across the comprehensive list of policy areas provided in the NES General Social Survey to come up with an overall disposition and public desire for more or less government productivity on a 0–100 scale, with higher numbers indicating a more liberal public mood. During periods of heightened liberalism, both unified Democratic government and divided government led by a Republican president lead to increased legislative productivity. This indicates party responsiveness to the public desires for more or less government. Typically, unified Republican government would produce less legislation both in terms of ideology of the party and in terms of the public mood generally being less favorable to significant enactments when the public chooses unified Republican government, with the Reagan Revolution of 1980 being the most obvious example.

Facing a unified Republican government at the beginning of his term, then, President Trump's success was far from guaranteed. His margin in the House was relatively comfortable, but his margin in the Senate was relatively thin, especially when considering the supermajoritarian procedures inherent in the Senate. Matters are further complicated for Trump in that the public mood, as shown in figure 5.1 below, provides a rare disconnect between the election results and the public desire for activism. Leading up to his inauguration in 2017, the public mood for activism was actually increasing even from the time of the election just two months earlier,[6] jumping from 61.7 to 65.6 in just one quarter. When President Trump took office, he had unified Republican government, but the public policy mood was actually the least favorable to the conservative policy agenda than at any other time that Republicans controlled the presidency and Congress. Other periods of unified Republican control of the presidency and Congress include 1953–1955, when Republican President Dwight D. Eisenhower began his presidency with a policy mood of approximately 53, and 2003–2007, when President George W. Bush faced a public mood that generally was comparable to the mood faced by Trump but

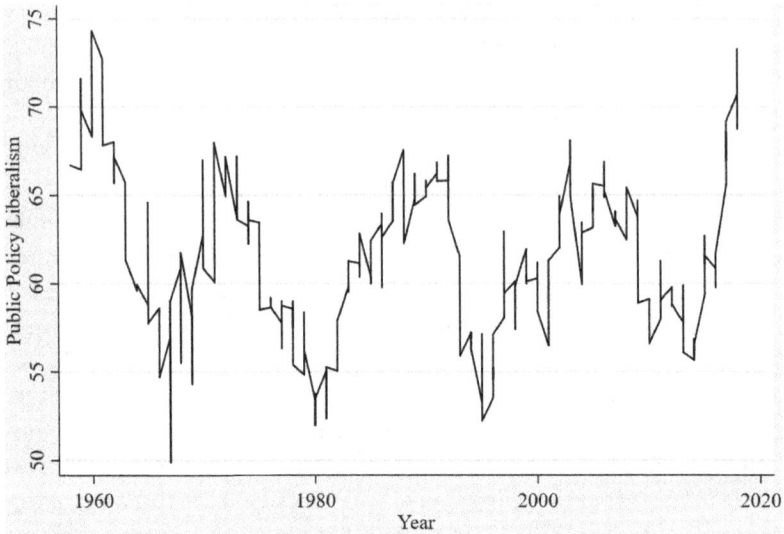

Figure 5.1: Public Policy Mood, 1958–2018. *Source:* James Stimson, "Data," accessed April 28, 2021, http://stimson.web.unc.edu/data/.

relatively steady. What sets the public mood President Trump faces apart is the general and immediate trend away from conservatism. According to Coleman (1999), while the public is demanding more activism on the part of the government during the first two years of Trump's term, the unified Republican government is the least likely to produce what the public wants.

President Trump's unified government is further complicated by the extent of discord within the Republican Party. Part of this is easily demonstrated in the primary contest, in which seventeen Republican candidates ran for the Republican nomination and Trump prevailed over the noted objection of many establishment Republicans. Then-candidate Trump was very hard on establishment Republicans such as Jeb Bush and also similarly sparred with candidates like Ted Cruz, who like Trump was running outside of the Republican mainstream. As a result, many prominent Republicans such as both former presidents Bush refused to endorse Donald Trump. Ted Cruz, who upon finishing second was provided with a prime speaking slot at the Republican National Convention that would eventually nominate candidate Trump, gave a speech in which he clearly was focused on elevating his own profile and rallying the conservative cause, but nowhere in his

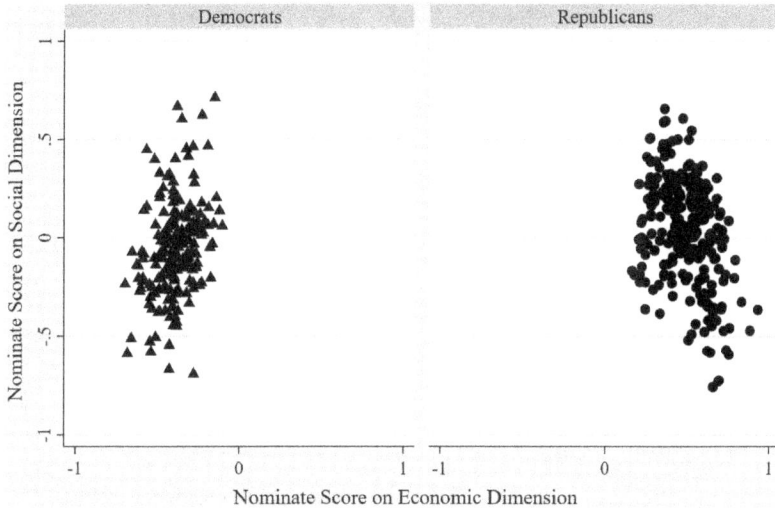

Figure 5.2: NOMINATE Scores for the 115th House. *Source*: Jeffrey B. Lewis, Keith Poole, Howard Rosenthal, Adam Boche, Aaron Rudkin, and Luke Sonnet. Voteview: Congressional Roll-Call Votes Database. https://voteview.com/.

speech did he endorse Donald Trump. The rough and tumble primary campaign left a lot of bitterness toward Trump with Republicans of all ideological dispositions, and as discussed above there was very little enthusiasm in voting for Trump as compared to the strong desire to vote against his opponent. While the rabid opposition to Hillary Clinton proved a semi-successful campaign strategy for winning the election, it would be far more difficult to actually govern.

The extensive Republican field is but one, and not even the best, indicator of the divisions in the Republican Party. To evaluate the extent of the Republican Party's cohesiveness, we turn to Poole and Rosenthal's (1985) NOMINATE scores for each of the Republican and Democratic members of the 115th Congress.[7] Figures 5.2 and 5.3 above show the NOMINATE scores for each party in the 115th Congress for the House and the Senate, respectively. As figures 5.1 and 5.2 demonstrate, there is no overlap among the parties, indicating the polarization between them. Very few Democrats or Republicans can be found close to the 0, centrist value for NOMINATE scores. Such polarization makes it very difficult for President Trump to work across party lines and build bipartisan coalitions. To examine the extent of

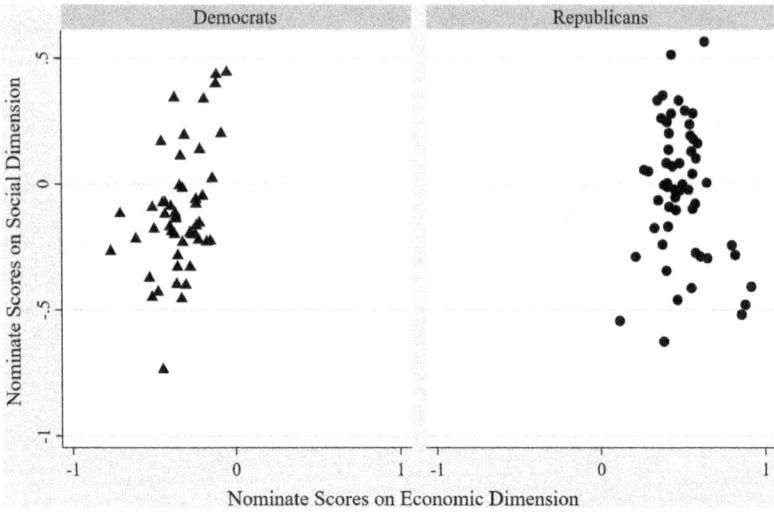

Figure 5.3: NOMINATE Scores for the 115th Senate. *Source:* Jeffrey B. Lewis, Keith Poole, Howard Rosenthal, Adam Boche, Aaron Rudkin, and Luke Sonnet. Voteview: Congressional Roll-Call Votes Database. https://voteview .com/.

partisan cohesion among the parties in Congress, tables 5.1 and 5.2 provide summary statistics for the 115th House and Senate, respectively. The Democrats in both chambers have a mean and minimum closer to zero than do their Republican counterparts, indicating a more moderate caucus than the Republicans. Further, the Republicans' NOMINATE scores have a higher standard deviation than the Democrats' NOMINATE scores, indicating much less partisan cohesion among congressional Republicans. Such conditions would make it difficult for President Trump to keep the unified Republican coalition together to pass legislation. Additionally, the majority of Republicans in Congress ran ahead of Trump in their districts in terms of their vote percentage (Edwards 2017; Jacobson 2017). This weakened the notion of any coattail effects from his election. As Edwards (2017) points out, Donald Trump inherited the most polarized Congress ever faced under unified Republican government. These data demonstrate that Trump also had a much more fractured Republican Party in Congress, making it difficult to obtain consistent support even from his own party.

Of course, it is noteworthy that President Trump did not help his

Table 5.1: Summary of 115th House NOMINATE Scores by Party

Party	Mean	Standard Deviation	Minimum	Maximum
Democrats	−0.39	0.114	−0.7	−0.1
Republicans	0.49	0.149	0.16	0.93

Source: Jeffrey B. Lewis, Keith Poole, Howard Rosenthal, Adam Boche, Aaron Rudkin, and Luke Sonnet. Voteview: Congressional Roll-Call Votes Database. https://voteview.com/.

own cause. His divisive rhetoric during the campaign did little to endear Democrats to the idea of working with him to pass his agenda. However, Democratic members of Congress did find some hope in Trump's uncharacteristically non-partisan proposals for opportunities to reach across the aisle. Specifically, President Trump expressed a desire to pass a substantial infrastructure improvement package, which has long been a proposal favored more by Democrats than Republicans. However, rather than working across the aisle at the beginning of his term to secure a potential legislative victory on infrastructure, President Trump chose the more divisive proposals such as securing funding for the border wall across the Southern border, repealing and replacing the Affordable Care Act, and passing a tax cut that would disproportionately benefit top income earners. Taken together, these proposals had little hope of securing any Democratic support in Congress, and with the exception of the tax cut, they were quite divisive among Republicans as well (Edwards 2017).

The 2018 elections would prove even more damaging to the Trump opportunity, as the public policy mood (shown in figure 5.1 above) continued to increase to a more liberal disposition, reaching a near all-time high of 73 during quarter four of 2018. Only in the third and

Table 5.2: Summary of 115th Senate NOMINATE Scores by Party

Party	Mean	Standard Deviation	Minimum	Maximum
Democrats	−0.34	0.15	−0.77	−0.06
Republicans	0.49	0.16	0.11	0.91

Source: Jeffrey B. Lewis, Keith Poole, Howard Rosenthal, Adam Boche, Aaron Rudkin, and Luke Sonnet. Voteview: Congressional Roll-Call Votes Database. https://voteview.com/.

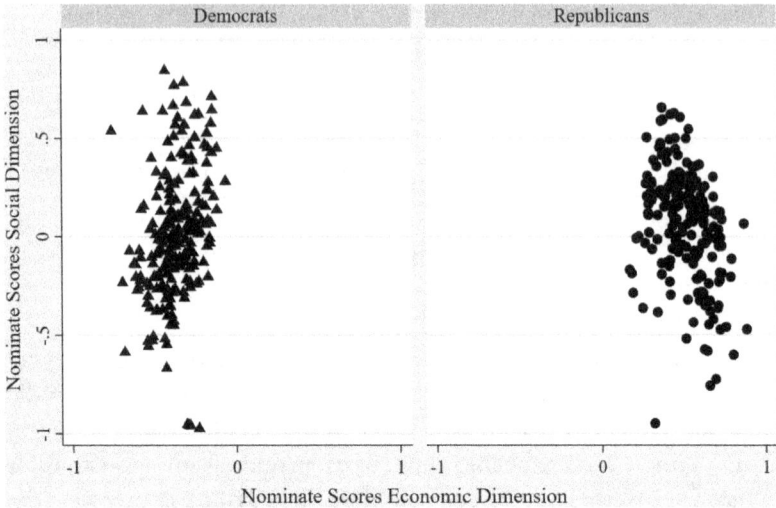

Figure 5.4: NOMINATE Scores for the 116th House. *Source:* Jeffrey B. Lewis, Keith Poole, Howard Rosenthal, Adam Boche, Aaron Rudkin, and Luke Sonnet. Voteview: Congressional Roll-Call Votes Database. https://voteview .com/.

fourth quarters of 1960 was the public policy mood recorded to be more liberal. President Trump and the Republicans experienced substantial losses in the House of Representatives, with Democrats gaining a total of forty seats including the defeat of twenty-nine incumbent Republicans and fourteen open seats. Many incumbent Republicans, feeling the losses coming, did not seek reelection, including most prominently House Speaker Paul Ryan. The forty-seat gain in the 2018 midterms was the largest Democratic gain in the House since the elections of 1974, an election that took place less than three months after Republican President Richard Nixon resigned as a result of Watergate.

To call the relationship between the Trump White House and the Democratic-controlled House of the 116th Congress contentious would be an understatement equivalent to saying that the Titanic took on a little water. Polarization in Congress continued to be significant, as demonstrated by the NOMINATE scores in figures 5.4 and 5.5 above. Similar to what was observed in the 115th Congress, Republicans also remained much further from the center and much less cohesive compared to the Democrats, as the summary statistics provided in table 5.3 and 5.4 demonstrate. Given the midterm election results, there

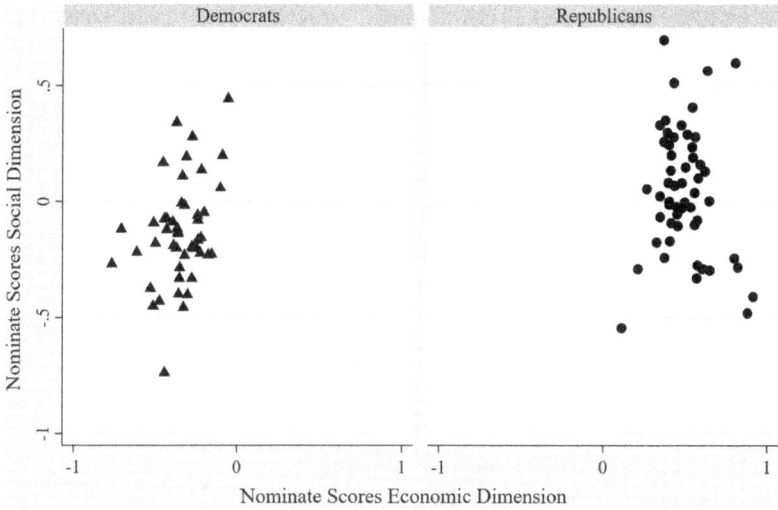

Figure 5.5: NOMINATE Scores for the 116th Senate. *Source:* Jeffrey B. Lewis, Keith Poole, Howard Rosenthal, Adam Boche, Aaron Rudkin, and Luke Sonnet. Voteview: Congressional Roll-Call Votes Database. https://voteview .com/.

was little reason for Republicans to perceive coattail effects from Donald Trump similarly to the 115th Congress. Democrats in the House also ramped up their investigation of President Trump's dealings with Ukraine, in which he threatened to withhold aid to Ukraine if they refused to investigate the business dealings of his 2020 Democratic challenger, former vice president Joe Biden. On December 18, 2019, the 116th Congress voted to impeach Trump on charges of abuse of power and obstruction of justice, making him the third president in US history to be impeached. The impeachment vote went straight on

Table 5.3: Summary of 116th House NOMINATE Scores by Party

Party	Mean	Standard Deviation	Minimum	Maximum
Democrats	−0.37	0.12	−0.76	−0.07
Republicans	0.5	0.14	0.16	0.88

Source: Jeffrey B. Lewis, Keith Poole, Howard Rosenthal, Adam Boche, Aaron Rudkin, and Luke Sonnet. Voteview: Congressional Roll-Call Votes Database. https://voteview.com/.

Table 5.4: Summary of 116th Senate NOMINATE Scores by Party

Party	Mean	Standard Deviation	Minimum	Maximum
Democrats	–0.35	0.15	–0.77	–0.06
Republicans	0.49	0.16	0.11	0.91

Source: Jeffrey B. Lewis, Keith Poole, Howard Rosenthal, Adam Boche, Aaron Rudkin, and Luke Sonnet. Voteview: Congressional Roll-Call Votes Database. https://voteview.com/.

party lines, and the Republican majority in the Senate followed suit with acquittal on February 5, 2020, the lone Republican vote to convict coming from Utah senator Mitt Romney.

The impeachment permanently damaged President Trump's ability to work with the House Democrats, particularly House Speaker Nancy Pelosi. The relationship between Trump and Pelosi has always been chilly, in part due to the public comments he has made about her from his Twitter account. The conflict between the two has played out quite publicly, with reports surfacing in late March that the president and the Speaker had not spoken in five months (Raji 2020). Following President Trump's 2020 State of the Union address on February 4, 2020, House Speaker Pelosi shredded her copy of the speech on national television.

In spite of Trump's cold relationship with the 116th Congress, particularly Democrats, his largest piece of legislation was delivered by the 116th Congress when he signed the CARES Act into law on March 27, 2020. The economic stimulus package that carries up to a $6 trillion price tag to combat the COVID-19 pandemic and associated shutdown passed the Senate in a 96–0 vote, and the House followed suit by passing the bill overwhelmingly by voice vote. This was the third stimulus package, and by far the largest, passed by Congress and signed by President Trump in response to the COVID-19 pandemic. If there is reassurance to be had regarding the fractured politics of Trump's relationship with Congress, it is that both parties can put aside differences to pass necessary legislation during times of crisis.

In summary, President Trump's opportunity for success in Congress was limited in spite of unified government to begin his term. Facing a highly divided Republican Party and a small majority in the Senate, unified government did not do much to help Trump's legislative productivity in Congress. The president also did not help himself in his legislative choices, as detailed in the two chapters to follow by Rebecca M. Eissler and Jonathan Lewallen, respectively. President Trump campaigned on prioritizing several (admittedly vague) policies, including most notably the repeal and replacement of the Affordable Care Act, the building of a Southern border wall, tax cuts, and infrastructure. With the exception of infrastructure, each of these policy proposals is quite divisive and unlikely to garner bipartisan support. Rather than moving on infrastructure first, which could potentially have secured an early bipartisan accomplishment, Trump chose to focus on the other three priorities, which alienated congressional Democrats (Edwards 2017). Further, with the exception of the proposed tax cuts, even the congressional Republicans were hesitant to act on Trump's other legislative priorities. Prospects for success only became worse following the 2018 midterms, when the Democrats took over the House majority after gaining forty seats in what was considered a national referendum on the Trump presidency (Jacobson 2017). It would take an emergency brought on by a global pandemic to have any claim to noteworthy legislation for the Trump administration, with the exception of the Tax Cuts and Jobs Act of 2017, which passed the House and Senate strictly on party lines and was signed by the president on December 22, 2017. The lack of legislative productivity during the Trump first term is in large part due to a misunderstanding, similar to many of his predecessors, of the opportunities and constraints of presidential power.

DISCUSSION

A useful way to examine presidential power in terms of President Trump's opportunity to lead is to compare his opportunity structure, defined above, to those of his predecessors. It is clear that President Trump lacked the electoral landslide component of a mandate perception, similar to Presidents Franklin Roosevelt, Lyndon Johnson, and Ronald Reagan detailed above.

Perhaps the closest comparison we have to the Trump opportunity structure among modern presidents is the presidency of George W. Bush. Similar to Trump, Bush was elected with less than a majority of the popular vote but was still able to win the Electoral College vote. In fact, President Trump won a larger share of the Electoral College vote than did President Bush, but President Bush lost the popular vote by far less. In terms of the Electoral College, President Bush's victory came as a result of 537 votes in Florida, a much more tenuous victory than that of President Trump across three states. Bush also was benefited by unified Republican government, similar to President Trump, but the similarities end there. As George Edwards (2009) details, President Bush intended to be a domestic president focused on education reform, which resulted in a bipartisan coalition passing No Child Left Behind, and tax cuts, which enjoyed Republican support. In reaching across the aisle for larger legislation and working on modest alterations to existing policy that were consistent with his Republican base, the Bush administration demonstrated some understanding of how to exploit opportunities for success during his first term. President Bush benefited from political experience in this regard, surrounded himself with folks holding tremendous political experience like Deputy Chief of Staff Karl Rove, and perhaps most importantly, faced a better opportunity structure than President Trump. The 107th and 108th Congresses were much less divided along party lines than the 115th and 116th, and further, the Republican Party was much less fractured within Congress. President Bush also began his term, in spite of the controversial election victory, with much less disdain from registered Democrats and an approval rating of 57 percent to begin his presidency. His approval rating would rise to 63 percent in Gallup polls by mid-March. President Trump's public approval has, as of this writing in April 2020, never risen to or above 50 percent.[8] It is likely, then, that the biggest difference between the Bush and Trump opportunities, and a deeper understanding of the Trump opportunity in historical context, is found in an exploration of the opportunity structure faced by President Jimmy Carter.

Perhaps owing in part to Trump's lack of experience in government, Trump's understanding of his lack of a mandate is not surprising. He came to the Oval Office seeking to enact a broad, even if vague, agenda for change. The promise to "Make America Great Again" placed him squarely in the America First doctrine that befits his association with the Reagan regime. Trump's business background propelled him confidently in his ability to make deals, both domestic and abroad, that would advance his agenda in domestic and foreign policy respectively. However, Trump did not understand the legislative process, expresses little interest in direct involvement in the bargaining inherent in advancing an agenda, and failed to understand the polarization both within his own party and between the parties. It is not unprecedented for a president to claim a mandate to govern publicly. Trump's approach in public has matched that in private, however, proceeding as if he had a mandate when he did not. This stands in stark contrast to his two immediate predecessors. Barack Obama's agenda perhaps undersold his mandate to govern in size and scope. George W. Bush, on the other hand, had an opportunity quite similar to Trump and acted according to a thorough understanding of his opportunity, working across the aisle and advancing smaller scale changes to existing programs that had some level of bipartisan support. Perhaps most importantly, both Obama and George W. Bush showed a significant willingness to learn from their failures in the legislative process, whereas Trump's most unorthodox trait has been an unwillingness to learn from mistakes. The reaction of Trump to setbacks has been, time and again, to lash out at others, deflect and place blame, and not accept any responsibility. The extent to which his experience with presidential power is unorthodox relates mostly to his penchant for petulance.

Both Presidents Bush and Trump find themselves situated in the Reagan regime according to Stephen Skowronek's (2020) construct of presidential leadership within the constraints of political time. According to Skowronek's work, presidential leadership is also governed by opportunity structures more so than personal capabilities. Presidents will have opportunities for success or entrapments of failure based in large part according to where they fall in a given political time cycle. The advantage that President George W. Bush holds in comparison to Donald Trump is found in political time. Bush's presidency occurred far earlier as an articulator of the Reagan Regime, whereas Donald Trump's time as president is coming as the Reagan regime is seemingly fracturing. His presidency is much more similar, accordingly, to the presidency of Jimmy Carter. Like Trump, President Carter faced a seemingly fracturing New Deal coalition marked by a deeply divided Democratic Party. In spite of unified government, Carter had a very difficult time working with Congress. Carter's presidency would be significantly constrained, in spite of his best efforts, because he was unable to navigate Congress successfully. Similarly to Trump, Carter was largely a political outsider, who was less than adept at navigating the very swamp President Trump promised to drain. Like Carter, Trump also faces a public mood that is reaching a high point for the opposition party and continuing to climb in a direction opposite of his partisan leanings. In running for a second term, beleaguered and light on legislative accomplishment, Carter's loss began the Reagan regime to which President Trump is haphazardly clinging. If history is any indication and political time has not been replaced by secular time (Skowronek 2020), the prospects of President Trump bringing an end to the Reagan Regime and ushering in a new Democratically led reset of the political clock seems likely in 2020.

NOTES

1. An example can be found at the University of Virginia's Miller Center, https://millercenter.org/the-presidency/educational-resources/albert -thomas-gets-the-johnson-treatment.

2. ABC News Polls conducted October 20–22, 2016. Also cited by Edwards (2017).

3. *Washington Post* Schar School Poll, November 11–14, 2016. Also cited by Edwards (2017).

4. Gallup Poll, January 20–22, 2017. Also cited by Edwards (2017).

5. Gallup Poll, January 20–29, 2017. Also cited by Edwards (2017).

6. Data pulled from James A. Stimson's professional website. The data can be obtained at Stimson.web.unc.edu.

7. Lewis, Jeffrey B., Keith Poole, Howard Rosenthal, Adam Boche, Aaron Rudkin, and Luke Sonnet (2019). Voteview: Congressional Roll-Call Votes Database. https://voteview.com/.

8. Polling results obtained from the Gallup website: https://news.gallup .com/interactives/185273/r.aspx.

REFERENCES

Abramowitz, Alan. "Will Time for Change Mean Time for Trump?" *PS: Political Science & Politics* 49, no. 4 (2016): 659–660.

Barber, James David. *The Presidential Character.* London: Routledge, 2019.

Baumgartner, Frank R., and Bryan D. Jones. *Agendas and Instability in American Politics.* 2nd ed. Chicago: University of Chicago Press, 2009.

Campbell, James E., Helmut Norpoth, Alan I. Abramowitz, Michael S. Lewis-Beck, Charles Tien, Robert S. Erikson, Christopher Wlezien, Brad Lockerbie, Thomas M. Holbrook, Bruno Jerôme, Véronique Jerôme-Speziari, Andreas Graefe, J. Scott Armstrong, Randall J. Jones, and Alfred G. Cuzán. "A Recap of the 2016 Election Forecasts." *PS: Political Science & Politics* 50, no. 2 (2017): 331–338.

Coleman, John T. "Unified Government, Divided Government, and Party Responsiveness." *American Political Science Review* 93, no. 4 (1999): 821–835.

Corwin, Edward S. *The President, Office, and Powers, 1787–1957,* 4th rev. ed. New York: New York University Press, 1957.

Edwards, George C. III, Andrew Barrett, and Jeffrey Peake. "The Legislative Impact of Divided Government." *American Journal of Political Science* 41, no. 2 (1997): 545–563.

———. "Neustadt's Power Approach." In *Presidential Power: Forging the Presidency for the Twenty-First Century*, ed. Robert Y. Shapiro, Martha Joynt Kumar, and Lawrence R. Jacobs, 9–15. New York, Columbia University Press, 2000.

———. *The Strategic President: Persuasion and Opportunity in Presidential Leadership*. Princeton, NJ: Princeton University Press, 2012.

———. *Predicting the Presidency: The Potential of Persuasive Leadership*. Princeton, NJ: Princeton University Press, 2016.

———. "No Deal: Donald Trump's Leadership of Congress." Paper presented at the Annual Meeting of the American Political Science Association. September 2, 2017.

Grossback, Lawrence J., David A. M. Peterson, and James A. Stimson. *Mandate Politics*. New York: Cambridge University Press, 2006.

Jacobson, Gary C. "The Triumph of Polarized Partisanship in 2016: Donald Trump's Improbable Victory." *Political Science Quarterly* 132, no. 1 (2017): 9–41.

Kingdon, John W. *Agendas, Alternatives, and Public Policy*. 2nd ed. London: Pearson, 2010.

Krehbiel, Keith. *Pivotal Politics: A Theory of U.S. Lawmaking*. Chicago: University of Chicago Press, 2010.

Lewis, Jeffrey B., Keith Poole, Howard Rosenthal, Adam Boche, Aaron Rudkin, and Luke Sonnet. *Voteview: Congressional Roll-Call Votes Database*. https://voteview.com/. 2019.

Light, Paul C. *The President's Agenda: Domestic Policy Choice from Kennedy to Clinton*. Baltimore, MD: Johns Hopkins University Press, 1999.

Mayhew, David R. *Divided We Govern: Party Control, Lawmaking, and Investigations, 1946–2002*. 2nd edition. New Haven, CT: Yale University Press, 2004.

Neustadt, Richard. *Presidential Power and the Modern Presidents*. New York: Free Press, 1990.

Norpoth, Helmut. "Primary Model Predicts Trump Victory." *PS: Political Science & Politics* 49, no. 4 (2016): 655–658.

Poole, Keith T., and Howard Rosenthal. "A Spatial Model for Legislative Roll Call Analysis." *American Journal of Political Science* 29, no. 2 (1985): 357–384.

Ragsdale, Lyn. "Personal Power and Presidents." In *Presidential Power: Forging the Presidency for the Twenty-First Century*, ed. Robert Y. Shapiro, Martha Joynt Kumar, and Lawrence R. Jacobs, 31–46. New York: Columbia University Press, 2000.

Raji, Manu. "Pelosi and Trump Haven't Spoken in Five Months." CNN.com. 2020. https://www.cnn.com/2020/03/24/politics/nancy-pelosi-trump-talks/index.html.

Rossiter, Clinton L. *The American Presidency*. 2nd ed. New York: Harcourt Brace, 1960.

Rutledge, Paul E., and Heather A. Larsen-Price. "The President as Agenda-Setter-in-Chief: The Dynamics of Congressional and Presidential Agenda Setting." *Policy Studies Journal* 42, no. 3 (2014): 443–464.

Skowronek, Stephen. *Presidential Leadership in Political Time: Reprise and Reappraisal*. 3rd ed. Lawrence: University Press of Kansas, 2020.

Stimson, James A. *Public Opinion in America: Moods, Cycles, and Swings*. 2nd ed. Boulder, CO: Westview, 1999.

Sundquist, James L. *Constitutional Reform and Effective Government*. Rev. ed. Washington, DC: Brookings Institution, 1992.

CHAPTER 6

The Trump Legislative Agenda in Historical Perspective

Rebecca M. Eissler

INTRODUCTION

The presidency of Donald J. Trump is a puzzle. This presidency has been characterized by controversial decisions but not by a prominent policy agenda. Most presidents run for office with a clear policy platform and then immediately set about trying to enact it, often by trying to get laws passed. Voters want to know what a candidate will do in office to make their lives better. From Franklin Roosevelt's first hundred days in office to President Obama's focus on health-care reform, presidents pursue legislation as a solution to policy problems because it is a clear, decisive, and enduring way to change the country. That change, that promise of a better tomorrow under their leadership, is a key motivator for many who pursue the highest office in the land.

Often, the president is a dominant actor in national policy making. Many scholars have pointed out that there is no one quite as powerful as the president for focusing attention on policy issues, and thus no single person quite as consequential for passing legislation (Baumgartner and Jones 2010; Kingdon 1984). Presidents engage with the policy-making process in a number of different ways: by highlighting problems and proposing solutions, by negotiating with legislators, by communicating with the public, and by taking independent executive action. Many of these activities center around legislation. Legislation has the most enduring effect on policy, as it requires either new legislation or the courts declaring the law unconstitutional for it to be overturned (Ragusa 2010). Consequently, this has been a long favored, and often required, route for policy change.

The first three years of the Trump presidency featured a very different role for the president in the legislative and policy-making process. Instead of focusing his energies on a few big pieces of legislation and actively fighting to get them to his desk for signature, President Trump took an alternative tactic, one focused on public appeals via Twitter and executive action. He was also less engaged in legislative negotiations than other presidents. This chapter examines how President Trump's policy approaches compare with those of other presidents, in order to consider the role that the president has played in policy change in the second half of the twentieth century.

WHAT IS THE LEGISLATIVE AGENDA?

To compare the Trump legislative agenda with the agendas of other presidents, it is first necessary to define the legislative agenda. In studies of the policy process, the agenda is "the list of subjects or problems to which governmental officials and people outside of government closely associated with those officials, are paying some serious attention at any given time" (Kingdon 1984, 3). Consequently, we can understand a legislative agenda as those policy areas that are being attended to *in* Congress. Presidents have a strategic advantage over Congress and the courts. The president can take a wide range of actions in pursuit of their preferred policy outcomes, while members of Congress *must* work through the legislative process, and the courts can change policy only when a related case comes before them. The president has the option to push for policy legislatively or he can take executive action. That choice makes it important that we examine how presidents choose to use the legislative track and, when they do, how they engage with the legislative process.

There are a number of reasons why a president might choose to pursue policy change via the legislative process. One reason is that legislation is more durable. As scholars of the legislative process can attest, legislation survives in part because it has already gone through a rigorous process. Along the legislative road, a bill faces many veto points; moments in which, if there is not enough support, the bill will die. Any time a bill becomes a law it does so because there is enough agreement and momentum to push the bill to the point of enactment (Krehbiel 1998). That consensus gives the law durability (Mayhew 1974; Ragusa 2010).

In this way, the legislative process is very different from the avenues available to the president to make policy unilaterally. Executive actions, whether they take the form of executive orders, memoranda, or proclamations, can be issued by the president acting alone but can be overridden with legislation or the issuance of a new executive action (Chu and Garvey 2014). One consequence is that policy change via executive action is much less durable than change that comes via legislation. For example, due to the less durable nature of presidential action, there has been considerable volatility during the Obama and Trump administrations regarding the status of legal protections for undocumented immigrants who came to the United States as minors. After many unsuccessful attempts at a legislative remedy, President Obama directed the Department of Homeland Security to create the Deferred Action for Childhood Arrivals (DACA) program (Napolitano 2012). The order was overturned early in the Trump administration (Shear and Davis 2017), and although that decision is still working its way through the courts, the lack of a legislative remedy created a great deal of uncertainty for those affected by the program (de Vogue et al. 2017). The chaos around the DACA program is a clear example of how people are affected when a policy change is undermined because of the manner in which the change was enacted. A president who wants to see their policies become a part of their legacy may choose to pursue that change legislatively, as unwinding legislation is more difficult than ending executive action.

A second reason why we might see presidents pursue change via the legislative process is that it is the legally required path. Executive action cannot override legislation, so if presidents want to change policy that is enshrined in law, such as the Trump administration's desire to get rid of the Affordable Care Act (ACA), they have to do it through Congress (Chu and Garvey 2014). The requirement for policy change via legislation presented a challenge for the Trump administration because, although there had been a significant change in the makeup of Congress since the ACA became law, the policy had generated popular support for some provisions, which made it difficult to repeal despite Republican majorities in both the House and Senate.

Regardless of what reason motivates a president to make policy via the legislative process, it is clear that to understand the role of the president in policy, we must understand the choices presidents make about how they engage legislatively.

THE LEGISLATIVE AGENDAS OF MODERN PRESIDENTS

To compare the legislative agenda of President Trump to the agendas of other presidents, it is important to understand some of the characteristics of presidential involvement in the legislative process. Over time, there has been considerable variation in how presidents have engaged in policy, just as there has been considerable variation in the personalities and leadership styles of our presidents. First, every president has pursued a number of important policy changes. Using Mayhew's dataset of important enactments (2005), we know that from 1945 to 2016, on average, presidents see 34.6 important bills become law during their presidencies. Even if we limit this analysis to the first two years of a president's time in office, we see a great deal of legislation; the average number of significant enactments in the first two years is 14.5. Figure 6.1 shows us the number of major enactments that became law during the first two years of each president's term. We see considerable variation, with President Johnson's time in office resulting in the greatest number of pieces of legislation (24 major enactments), and Presidents Eisenhower, Reagan, and George H. W. Bush tied for the least (9 major enactments each). President Trump's first two years in office come close to the average of 14.5, with 12 major enactments. But the quantity of major enactments does not tell the whole story; it is also important that we examine the quality of presidential legislative behavior. After all, not all of these pieces of legislation saw the same level of presidential involvement, as some of the 415 pieces of legislation during this period were more congressionally motivated, and not all of the presidential involvement was in support of the legislation's passage; this is particularly true of the fifteen pieces of legislation that became law after a presidential veto. But even with these caveats, it is clear evidence of a significant role for presidents in the legislative process.

Given that the president's formal powers in the legislative process are limited to signing or vetoing the bills that come to their desks, they have a number of other ways to engage in the process. First, presidents propose policy. The ability to propose policy ideas is established in the Constitution by the charge that presidents should

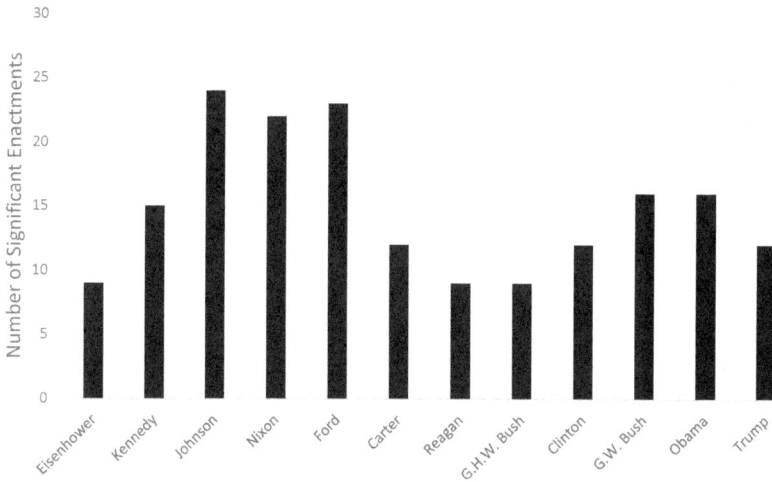

Figure 6.1: Number of Significant Enactments for Each President in Their First Two Years in Office

"recommend to their Consideration such Measures as he shall judge necessary and expedient" (Article II, Section 3), but presidents must work with members of Congress to transform these recommendations into bills. Presidential policy proposals have the potential to be significant, if they are acted on, or to be toothless, if they are ignored (Cohen 2012).

Second, presidents can communicate directly with the public. Public support for legislation can be a significant factor in determining whether a bill will become law (Calvo 2007; Canes-Wrone and De Marchi 2002). Constituents and other interest groups can lobby members of Congress to sway their vote on issues, and presidents can be very good at activating public pressure campaigns among those who already agree with the policy or support the president, more broadly (Canes-Wrone 2010). Ronald Reagan pushed through the largest tax cut in American history with the Economic Recovery Tax Act of 1981. Reagan's strategy to build support relied on a pair of prime-time televised addresses to the nation, one from the Oval Office and one, the very next day, given from the well of the House of Representatives to a joint session of Congress, in which he set out his justification for the legislation and his broader plan of economic reforms. These two high-profile speeches allowed him to communicate directly with the public, creating a narrative of urgency. Communicating directly with the public can be a significant force in the legislative process, particularly when a president is able to gain support for their narrative.

Third, presidents often play an important role in the legislative process through negotiations with Congress. The legislative process culminates in the president's decision to sign or veto legislation. The president's position on policy is important because gaining enough support in Congress to marshal the two-thirds majority required in both the House and the Senate to override the president's veto is quite rare, particularly as the chambers have become much more polarized (Krehbiel 1998). Legislative negotiation can take two main forms. The first is direct negotiations. These can be presidential meetings or calls with legislators, either to discuss the content of the policy before it has been introduced or to exert pressure on legislators about a bill as it is coming to a vote. It can also take the form of statements about policy, which allow the president to publicly stake out a position. The second form of negotiation is through the use of formal veto threats. A Statement of Administration Policy is a formal opportunity for an administration to state their position about a piece of legislation before it comes to a vote (Kernell 2006). This chapter will focus primarily on the first kind of negotiation, where the president is working directly with Congress. These two types of action have the power to influence the legislative agenda, as Congress may choose not to move on a piece of legislation if they think there is a strong chance that the president will veto it. President Lyndon Johnson was famous for his involvement in the legislative process, particularly in the Senate, where he had served for a long time. Johnson's knowledge of senators and legislative procedure, as well as his willingness to negotiate and "twist arms" to get support for his bills, has been credited with his ability to get a great deal of important legislation passed (Beckmann et al. 2017). But his forceful style of negotiation is not the only kind that presidents have engaged in. President Obama was famous for consulting with Republican members of Congress regarding aspects of the ACA, ultimately including 188 Republican-generated amendments to the legislation to try to make it possible for them to vote for it (Carlsen and Park 2017). Over time, presidents have taken many different approaches to negotiation, but it is safe to say historically that presidents have used the veto power to shape policy, not just to approve or disapprove.

Finally, presidents have a non-legislative way to involve themselves in the legislative process: through the use of executive action. As discussed previously, unilateral executive action might seem completely separate from the president's legislative agenda, but it can play an important role in shaping that agenda. Every time the president changes policy via executive action, he is presenting an option to Congress: let this action stand and you don't need to deal with this issue. One characteristic of the imperial presidency is the expansion of executive action as a solution to policy problems. For some, this is a gross overreach of presidential authority (Williamson 2019). For others, this is a response to a trend in Congress that, whether for electoral concerns or reasons of polarization, has members who are unwilling or unable to come together and take on challenges (Cooper 2014). Actions such as President Obama's DACA program or President Clinton's executive order banning sexual orientation–based discrimination in the federal civilian workforce were explicit challenges to positions held by Congress at the time. Despite the backlash those orders produced, in neither instance was Congress able to overturn the presidential action. Executive orders and other forms of presidential action can be a force for shaping both the issues that will appear and the issues that won't appear on the legislative agenda.

As this discussion makes clear, modern presidents have always had a significant role in shaping the legislative agenda. Through a variety of actions, presidents engage in the policy process by proposing policy changes, communicating with the public, negotiating with legislators, and taking independent action. Though there has been considerable variation in the ways that presidents have used these actions, it has been conventional wisdom that modern presidents will engage in the policy process robustly. President Trump presents a challenge to that wisdom.

THE LEGISLATIVE AGENDA OF DONALD J. TRUMP

The legislative agenda of the Trump administration presents presidency and policy scholars with a number of challenges. In some ways, President Trump's behavior is significantly different from past presidents, but in other ways it represents a logical extension of patterns we have seen in past presidents. As the discussion on the size of the legislative agenda showed, it is not enough to talk about the Trump administration in raw numbers. Figure 6.1 showed that, in terms of the passage of significant legislation, the Trump administration is similar to other presidents. Instead, it is illustrative to look at the manner in which President Trump has engaged with the legislative process. We are able to detect a number of important differences and similarities that help us to understand the Trump legislative agenda.

President Trump's Approach to Policy Proposals

All presidents come to office having made promises about what policies they will tackle. Some get to work on those issues right away; President Clinton, for example, created the Health Care Task Force in January 1993. Others are forced to delay their attention to campaign promises in response to other exigent circumstances, a position President Obama found himself in due to the Great Recession. President Trump's position on taking office was much more like President Clinton, where there were no crises requiring him to diverge from his campaign plans. However, just because he was free to focus on those issues he campaigned on does not mean they all resulted in his preferred policy change.

On the campaign trail, President Trump made many promises: he promised to build a wall at the southern border with Mexico, to enact broader immigration reform, and to cut off immigration from places that he claimed could not conduct "sufficient screening"; to renegotiate the North American Free Trade Agreement (NAFTA) and other trade arrangements; to end the Affordable Care act; and to cut taxes (list drawn from McCammon 2016 and the 2016 Republican Party Platform). While this sounds like a robust agenda of policy proposals, when we consider only those that were acted on by Congress, we see that the president's ability to propose policy change was much weaker. The border wall, immigration reform, NAFTA renegotiation, the Affordable Care Act repeal, and tax reform all came before Congress, but only a few of them have been successful.

President Trump's two most successful policy proposals were his plan to cut taxes and the renegotiation of NAFTA. Yet they were successful largely because the ideas had wide bases of support. The Republican Party, particularly after Paul Ryan took over as Speaker of the House, had long supported the idea of tax code reform. Although there were challenges in getting this piece of legislation through the House, the beliefs of some members of the Freedom Caucus, Republican orthodoxy, and the majorities in both the House and the Senate made it likely that it would be a successful policy proposal. The success of the United States-Mexico-Canada Agreement (USMCA), which was the replacement for NAFTA, likewise, was meaningful. During the

2016 election, concern about free trade agreements had become salient talking points for both Democrats and Republicans. Thus, it is unsurprising that the USMCA was able to pass the House and the Senate, even after Democrats took control. The proposal was successful because it enabled both Democrats and Republicans to deliver on issues that were important to their political bases (Cochrane 2020).

The policies the president has proposed, but that have not succeeded in Congress, are also quite interesting. The Republican Party had long been in support of "repealing and replacing" the Affordable Care Act, but had been foiled by President Obama's veto during his time in office (Riotta 2017). Once President Trump took office, repeal supporters went into high gear to develop a replacement plan, as they knew they would now receive the president's signature on anything they could get passed through Congress. However, one major problem remained; while there was support for repealing the ACA in Congress, there was significant public opposition to the replacement plan (Blendon and Benson 2019). While the bill passed by a narrow margin in the House of Representatives, receiving 217 yeas and 213 nays, it failed in the Senate, 49–51, largely on the grounds that the replacement legislation would undo many of the accomplishments of the ACA, such as increased coverage and protections for those with preexisting conditions (Scott 2017).

Immigration reform and border wall plans proposed by Donald J. Trump on the campaign trail received even less action and support in Congress, although in different ways. Immigration has been a thorny policy area for quite some time, particularly how to handle those who came to the country without documentation as children, also known as Dreamers. At various times, President Trump seemed willing to trade protections for Dreamers for funding for the border wall in his negotiations with Congress; however that deal was a nonstarter for Democrats, whose support was necessary due to dissenting factions within the Republican Party (Karni and Stolberg 2019). The back-and-forth between the parties resulted in a number of government shutdowns but ultimately has resulted neither in comprehensive immigration reform nor in legislative appropriations for the border wall. It is worth noting, however, that policy failures such as these are not unique. President Clinton failed to pass his own attempt at health-care reform, and President George W. Bush failed to privatize Social Security, among many, many others. All of this goes to show that it is not enough to have a majority in the House and Senate. Unified government did not, in and of itself, make President Trump's policy proposals more successful. Success depended on the nature of the policies and whether there was a sufficient coalition of support in Congress, not just to take up the issue but also to see it through to passage.

President Trump's Communication Styles

President Trump uses his public communications quite differently from other presidents. Past presidents tended to rely heavily on speeches and press conferences to get their message, whether policy or political, out to the public. Whether we are thinking of Franklin Roosevelt's Fireside Chats, Ronald Reagan's televised addresses about economic policy, or President George W. Bush's sixty stops in sixty days tour to talk about Social Security reform, presidents have used a wide array of tools to communicate with the public. Despite still having access to many of those tools, President Trump seems to prefer the more informal communication style of Twitter.

Twitter is a relatively new medium for politicians and in some ways represents a significant evolution in political communications, as it permits presidents to reach out to the public directly. For much of the twentieth century, presidents had no choice but to communicate via the press. Prominent journalists, such as Walter Cronkite, Tom Brokaw, and Helene Cooper, reported on the presidency, telling the public about his actions and distilling and contextualizing the president's message. Social media have given President Trump the ability to get around these gatekeepers and speak directly to the public. New technology means that it is not necessary for the Trump administration to transmit their messages through anyone else; they have the power and the audience to transmit it directly, leaving the traditional news media to covering the president's tweets as a way to provide context. This is a challenge for the media, as there is a pattern of false or misleading information in the tweets (Politifact 2020).

Another difference between President Trump and past presidents is visible in the types of public speeches that he gives. The most visible speech that a president gives each year is the State of the Union address. The Constitution mandates that presidents report on the state of the country, and though it does not require the president to use the speech to "recommend to their Consideration such Measures as he shall judge necessary and expedient," modern presidents have largely done so. State of the Union addresses are traditionally long lists of policy proposals, allowing the president to set out his legislative agenda for the coming year and to herald the successes of the year before. During a president's first address before Congress, he may echo campaign proposals, but successive speeches expand, refine, and develop the proposed policy agenda. President Trump's State of the Union addresses are much different, much more like campaign events than opportunities to propose policy. Trump's 2020 State of the Union address did focus on accomplishments of the past year and ways that the administration has tackled issues important to the president, but it did so without proposing many legislative solutions. This is critical, because while the White House and the bureaucracy can tackle some issues on their own, without the support of Congress through appropriations and legislation, there are limits to the power of executive branch problem-solving.

Additionally, President Trump used the opportunity for some "made for TV" moments. Three moments, in particular, were incredibly unusual: awarding a scholarship to Janiyah Davis, to highlight school choice; awarding of the Presidential Medal of Freedom to Rush Limbaugh, nominally in recognition of his radio show and his recent advanced cancer diagnosis; and the reunification of Sgt. First Class Townsend Williams and his wife, Amy. These moments were each at a part of the speech about a related policy area but were much more tools for the president to appear benevolent and to evoke emotion than they were about broader policy goals and administration proposals. These moments, among many others, highlight how President Trump uses the trappings of the White House to advance his own image, rather than his policy agenda.

Other than the State of the Union address, most of President Trump's public speeches have been more politically than policy oriented, in support of his legislative agenda. In his first three years in office, he has given no policy speeches before a joint session of Congress, and only one of two televised addresses have been about matters of policy decision-making, focusing on border security. While these numbers are low, they are not extremely below the rate at which other presidents used these tools, as these particular communication tools are designed to be used sparingly to denote their seriousness.

What is unusual are the kinds of public addresses President Trump gives at rallies. Rallies and town halls are traditional venues for talking directly to the public about policy or politics, but President Trump's "Make America Great Again" rally speeches are largely politically focused, used to promote either other candidates or himself as a candidate for president. Policy is largely a secondary concern at these events. The president's use of these events is quite different from past presidents who have used rallies to talk to people about policy; whether we look at President Obama's rally for Dreamers in Arizona, President George W. Bush's town halls around the country about Social Security, or President Johnson's remarks through spring 1964 talking about the War on Poverty, all of these speeches were primarily in support of a policy outcome, with no mention of a political campaign for office. President Trump uses his communications with the public largely for political purposes, rather than to advance his legislative agenda.

Legislative Negotiation between President Trump and Congress

Negotiation is a routine and constant part of the relationship between the president and Congress. It can take many forms: presidents can negotiate the shape policy might take before it is introduced in Congress, they can persuade individual members to support or oppose a bill, or they can use the threat of a veto to influence the evolution of a bill through the legislative process. With so many avenues available to them, it is understandable that negotiation plays an important role in understanding the president's legislative agenda.

President Trump's relationship with Congress surrounding negotiation is somewhat unusual. It is important to note that negotiation is important even during periods of unified government. Factions within parties can make it difficult for policy to pass. In this case, factions within the House of Representatives presented a challenge to important pieces of the president's legislative agenda. A conservative wing within the Republican Party, the House Freedom Caucus, almost toppled the president's tax plan, requiring the president to exert pressure on members of his own party to gain their support (Becker et al. 2017). What is more unusual is the way the president engaged in negotiation with Democrats. President Trump repeatedly tied funding for the border wall to a solution for Dreamers and more comprehensive immigration reform. Yet despite many moments in which the president seemed to come to an agreement with the Democratic leadership, he routinely backed away, causing bipartisan reforms to fail (Lind 2019). The result of this repeated failure was the longest government shutdown in US history. The inability to reach agreements with Democrats prevented President Trump from achieving many of his policy goals.

Although President Trump prides himself on his ability to negotiate, his time in office suggests that he is more successful at negotiating with people who already agree with him, rather than finding compromise with those who disagree. The difficulty to negotiate directly with Congress is not all together surprising. While many presidents in the mid-twentieth century were able to find compromise with legislators, the heightened levels of party polarization in the House, Senate, and electorate over the last thirty years have reduced the ability of any president, not just President Trump, to engage in direct negotiation and compromise with Congress. Instead, the Trump negotiation strategy has relied much more heavily on mobilizing Republican base voters so that they either force members of Congress into cooperation with Trump or risk Trump endorsing a challenger in the next election cycle (Plott 2020).

The Preferred Strategy: Executive Action

The tool that President Trump has used to implement some of his most prized policy outcomes is, in fact, not the legislative process at all. Presidents have the ability to change policy via executive action. As discussed earlier, executive actions have limits including where they can be used and their durability, but they are a powerful, and increasingly popular, way for presidents to get their desired policy change. In many ways, President Trump is very similar to Presidents Obama, George W. Bush, and Clinton.

Presidents have always had the power to issue executive actions. President Washington used a proclamation to declare the United States neutral in the war between Britain and France in 1793. Increasingly, presidents have relied on executive action to change policy where they have been unable to get it changed in Congress (Cooper 2014). President Clinton used executive orders to make the federal government more environmentally friendly (Clinton 1996), President George W. Bush made faith-based organizations eligible for federal funds (Bush 2001), and President Obama made changes to the immigration system with executive actions to set up the DACA program (Napolitano 2012). The choice to move policy off the legislative agenda has largely been a response to heightened partisanship in

Congress, which has prevented presidents of the minority party from achieving their policy goals.

President Trump has similarly used executive action to achieve some of his policy goals. On the campaign trail, he talked extensively about preventing people from entering the country, saying that they posed a national security risk due to improper vetting. President Trump's executive order initially banned the entry of people from seven Muslim-majority countries, but the ban was then expanded to include other non–Muslim majority countries. Despite sharp criticism that the ban promoted xenophobia (National Immigration Law Center 2019), the Supreme Court upheld the president's authority to issue the ban due to the national security justification (Liptak and Shear 2018). President Trump has also used executive action to acquire money for the border wall with Mexico. Through the first two years of the Trump administration, requests to Congress for the appropriation of funds to build a wall at the southern border were frequent but unsuccessful. Instead, President Trump redirected approximately $5 billion in funds from the Department of Defense to pay for the project, jump-starting a legal challenge to the president's ability to use funds for purposes other than those for which they were appropriated (Miroff 2020).

The manner in which President Trump has used executive action is one of the more interesting puzzles surrounding the Trump legislative agenda and its relationship to the legislative agendas of past presidents. On the one hand, his use of executive action is quite similar to that of recent presidents, who increased their use of this tool in response to greater polarization and gridlock in Congress. Additionally, President Trump's background as a business executive makes it reasonable to believe that he would be most comfortable using executive action to implement his preferred policy; he decides what policy change he wants and it is put into action. On the other hand, it is somewhat remarkable that the president has relied so heavily on executive action, as the first two years of his administration were marked by unified party control of Congress. Past presidents largely leaned on executive orders when their party was in the minority (Cooper 2014; Gitterman 2017; Mayer 2002). The fact that the president's policies could not pass Congress, even though his party was in the majority, reinforces the idea that partisan majorities are not enough to get policies passed (Mayhew 2005). Legislative policy making requires negotiation and compromise even with one's own party members, two things that the president did not engage in much during his first two years in office, choosing instead to leave legislative control to the leadership teams in Congress. It is hard to know whether this struggle to get policy passed via legislation is special to President Trump or a reflection of the high levels of polarization within and across parties.

CONCLUSION

This chapter has highlighted the differences between President Trump's legislative agenda and policy-making strategy and the approach that many past presidents have taken. President Trump has had less success getting his policy proposals enacted, he has focused less of his public communication on advancing his legislative agenda, and he is less effective at negotiating across party lines than other presidents, historically speaking. The one area in which President Trump is quite similar to other modern presidents is his increased reliance on executive action, freeing himself from the constraints of working with Congress to pursue his policy goals under his own power. These behaviors reflect the heightened levels of polarization in Congress and a further extension of the imperial presidency, which have shaped the policy landscape of the last seventy years.

The differences between President Trump and other past presidents are strong enough to make it worthwhile to contemplate why it is that President Trump takes this approach to policy making. I offer two potential explanations to help us understand why he might engage in the legislative process differently. First, President Trump came to politics directly from the business world. The career paths of past presidents are quite varied, but it is common for them to have been involved in public service or elected office prior to assuming the job as president. Whether they were a former governor, a senator, a congressperson, a general, a union president, an ambassador, or a judge, all presidents since the start of the modern presidency came to office with prior public service, with some of them having devoted their entire adult lives to the endeavor.

President Trump, however, came to the presidency directly from the business and entertainment world, where he had been the head of a real estate development and television enterprise for more than forty years. As a private executive, Donald Trump was able to have the final word on all matters, but as the chief executive of the United States, his actions are subject to checks from other institutions and other such constraints. President Trump is not the only president to come to power without this practice. Richard Neustadt famously retells the story of President Truman's prediction that General Eisenhower would, if elected, find the presidency frustrating because of the fact that commands don't always result in actions (Neustadt 1990, 10). It is reasonable to believe that this inexperience with limitations may create some frustration. This frustration may cause President Trump to form his legislative agenda differently than many past presidents, causing him to rely instead on those actions he can use to make policy unilaterally, as it is a path that would seem to offer the greatest potential to mimic the decision-making style he used prior to the White House.

Another reason why President Trump may take such a different approach to policy making is related to just how unchanged he is by the presidency. The institution of the modern presidency offers the people who have held the position unparalleled power and importance, not just nationally but on an international scale. The desire to seem presidential and to create a positive legacy so that they are remembered as being great can haunt presidential decisions, causing presidents to pursue ambitious legislative agendas (Gergan 2002). But those ambitions are also what drive individuals to run for the office in the first place, which may have been what prompted President Obama's warning that "who you are, what you are—it doesn't change after you occupy the Oval Office. It magnifies who you are" (2016). President Trump's behavior in office is, arguably, unchanged from his behavior before he took office; he seems to hold the same beliefs and impulses that he campaigned on. Some might argue that this is good, as he is living up to the promises that he campaigned upon.

But from a legislative perspective, this raises some concerns. President Trump's mantras "drain the swamp" and "I alone can fix America" have put him in direct conflict with Congress, making him less effective at enacting major policy changes. Whether that be the refusal of Congress to directly fund the border wall, or the inability of a unified Congress to pass comprehensive health-care reform, or the failure to negotiate comprehensive immigration reform, President Trump's legislative agenda has been hampered. The origin of that limitation could be the source of endless debate, but what is not arguable is the fact that President Trump's choice to buck the norms of the presidency has had consequences for his legislative policy agenda.

REFERENCES

Baumgartner, Frank R., and Bryan D. Jones. *Agendas and Instability in American Politics.* Chicago: University of Chicago Press, 2010.

Becker, Bernie, Sarah Ferris, Colin Wilhelm, Sarah Ferris, and Jennifer Scholtes. "House Conservatives Almost Topple Tax Vote." Politico.com. December 4, 2017. https://www.politico.com/story/2017/12/04/house - conservatives-tax-plan-206549.

Beckmann, Matthew N., Neilan S. Chaturvedi, and Jennifer Rosa Garcia. "Targeting the Treatment: The Strategy behind Lyndon Johnson's Lobbying." *Legislative Studies Quarterly* 42, no. 2 (2017): 211–234.

Blendon, Robert J., and John M. Benson. "Public Opinion about the Future of the Affordable Care Act: NEJM." *New England Journal of Medicine*, December 26, 2019. https://www.nejm.org/doi/full/10.1056/NEJMsr1710032.

Bush, George W. Executive Order 13199: Establishment of White House Office of Faith-Based and Community Initiatives. Washington, DC: Government Printing Office, 2001.

Calvo, Ernesto. "The Responsive Legislature: Public Opinion and Law Making in a Highly Disciplined Legislature." *British Journal of Political Science* 37, no. 2 (2007): 263–280.

Canes-Wrone, Brandice. *Who Leads Whom?: Presidents, Policy, and the Public.* Chicago: University of Chicago Press, 2010.

Canes-Wrone, Brandice, and Scott De Marchi. "Presidential Approval and Legislative Success." *Journal of Politics* 64, no. 2 (2002): 491–509.

Carlsen, Audrey, and Haeyoun Park. "Obamacare Included Republican Ideas, but the G.O.P. Health Plan Has Left Democrats Out." *New York Times*, July 21, 2017. https://www.nytimes.com/interactive/2017/07/21/us/health -care-amendments.html.

Chu, Vivian S., and Todd Garvey. "Executive Orders: Issuance, Modification, and Revocation." Congressional Research Service, April 16, 2014. https:// fas.org/sgp/crs/misc/RS20846.pdf.

Clinton, William J. Executive Order 12844: Procurement Requirements and Policies for Federal Agencies for Ozone-Depleting Substances. Washington, DC: Government Printing Office, 1993.

Cochrane, Emily. "Senate Passes Revised NAFTA, Sending Pact to Trump's Desk." *New York Times*, January 16, 2020. https://www.nytimes.com/2020 /01/16/us/politics/usmca-vote.html.

Cohen, Jeffrey E. *The President's Legislative Policy Agenda, 1789–2002.* Cambridge: Cambridge University Press, 2012.

Committee on Arrangements for the 2016 Republican National Convention. "Republican Platform 2016." Republican Platform 2016. Cleveland, OH: Republican Party, 2016.

Cooper, Phillip J. *By Order of the President: The Use and Abuse of Executive Direct Action*. Lawrence: University Press of Kansas, 2014.

de Vogue, Ariane, Madison Park, Artemis Moshtaghian, and Mary Kay Mallonee. "Immigrant Protected under 'Dreamer' Program Stays in Custody." CNN. February 17, 2017. https://www.cnn.com/2017/02/14/politics/daniel-ramirez-medina-daca-detention/index.html.

Gergan, David. "The West Wing Documentary Special." *The West Wing*. Directed by William Couturié. 2002. Los Angeles: NBC.

Gitterman, Daniel P. *Calling the Shots: The President, Executive Orders, and Public Policy*. Washington, DC: Brookings Institution, 2017.

Karni, Annie, and Sheryl Gay Stolberg. "Trump Offers Temporary Protections for 'Dreamers' in Exchange for Wall Funding." *New York Times*, January 19, 2019. https://www.nytimes.com/2019/01/19/us/politics/trump-proposal-daca-wall.html.

Kernell, Samuel. "Presidential Veto Threat as a Negotiating Instrument with the Bicameral Congress." Available at SSRN 1154103 (2006).

Kingdon, John W. *Agendas, Alternatives, and Public Policies*. Vol. 45. Boston: Little, Brown, 1984.

Krehbiel, Keith. *Pivotal Politics: A Theory of US Lawmaking*. Chicago: University of Chicago Press, 1998.

Lind, Dara. "Trump Is the Obstacle to a Shutdown Deal." Vox.com. January 4, 2019. https://www.vox.com/policy-and-politics/2019/1/4/18168652/shutdown-border-immigration-wall-daca.

Liptak, Adam, and Michael D. Shear. "Trump's Travel Ban Is Upheld by Supreme Court." *New York Times*, June 26, 2018. https://www.nytimes.com/2018/06/26/us/politics/supreme-court-trump-travel-ban.html.

Mayer, Kenneth. *With the Stroke of a Pen: Executive Orders and Presidential Power*. Princeton, NJ: Princeton University Press, 2002.

Mayhew, David R. *Congress: The Electoral Connection*. New Haven: Yale University Press, 1974.

———. *Divided We Govern: Party Control, Lawmaking and Investigations, 1946–2002*. New Haven, CT: Yale University Press, 2005.

———. "Major Enactments." Data from Divided We Govern (2005). Yale University. Accessed April 16, 2020. http://campuspress.yale.edu/davidmayhew/datasets-divided-we-govern/.

McCammon, Sarah. "Inside Donald Trump's Stump Speech, Annotated." NPR. September 15, 2016. https://www.npr.org/2016/09/15/493915412/inside-donald-trumps-stump-speech-annotated.

Miroff, Nick. "Trump Planning to Divert Additional $7.2 Billion in Pentagon Funds for Border Wall." *Washington Post*, January 14, 2020. https://www.washingtonpost.com/immigration/trump-planning-to-divert-additional-72-billion-in-pentagon-funds-for-border-wall/2020/01/13/59080a3a-363d-11ea-bb7b-265f4554af6d_story.html.

Napolitano, Janet. "Exercising Prosecutorial Discretion with Respect to Individuals Who Came to the United States as Children." Washington, DC: Department of Homeland Security, 2012.

National Immigration Law Center. "Understanding the Muslim Ban and How We'll Keep Fighting It." June 2019. https://www.nilc.org/issues/immigration-enforcement/understanding-muslim-ban-one-year-after-ruling/

Neustadt, Richard. *Presidential Power and the Modern Presidents.* New York: Free, 1990.

Plott, Elaina. "A Primary from the Right? Not in Trump's G.O.P." *New York Times,* January 28, 2020. https://www.nytimes.com/2020/01/28/us/politics/pennsylvania-republicans-trump.html.

Politifact. "Donald Trump." Politifact.com. Accessed April 16, 2020. https://www.politifact.com/personalities/donald-trump/.

Ragusa, Jordan Michael. "The Lifecycle of Public Policy: An Event History Analysis of Repeals to Landmark Legislative Enactments, 1951–2006." *American Politics Research* 38, no. 6 (2010): 1015–1051.

Riotta, Chris. "GOP Aims to Kill Obamacare Yet Again after Failing 70 Times." *Newsweek,* July 29, 2017. https://www.newsweek.com/gop-health-care-bill-repeal-and-replace-70-failed-attempts-643832.

Scott, Dylan. "Why Senate Republicans Couldn't Repeal Obamacare." Vox.com. July 28, 2017. https://www.vox.com/policy-and-politics/2017/7/28/16054700/senate-obamacare-repeal-john-mccain-susan-collins-lisa-murkowski.

Shear, Michael D., and Julie Hirschfeld Davis. "Trump Moves to End DACA and Calls on Congress to Act." *New York Times,* September 5, 2017. https://www.nytimes.com/2017/09/05/us/politics/trump-daca-dreamers-immigration.html.

Williamson, Kevin D. "Pruning the Presidency." *National Review,* November 27, 2019. https://www.nationalreview.com/2019/11/executive-overreach-imperial-presidency-congress-must-reclaim-proper-place-constitutional-order/.

CHAPTER 7

Trump and Congress: Bargaining and the Power to Say "No"

Jonathan Lewallen

INTRODUCTION

For someone writing about Trump's unorthodox relations with Congress, the question is where to start. Many features of Trump's relations with Congress might be considered unorthodox, including the Senate majority leader's spouse serving in the cabinet and the president's feud with former Republican Speaker of the House Paul Ryan. In this chapter I focus on the use of negative power and bargaining between the two institutions, specifically in Trump's use of veto threats and in the Senate fates of his nominees. These arenas of conflict are built into the American political system, explicitly mentioned in the US Constitution rather than a consequence of changing interpretations of "executive power," so they provide consistent opportunities to compare Trump and his predecessors.

Bargaining is at the core of a president's relationship with Congress because they share formal powers (Neustadt 1991). While presidents can and do act unilaterally (see Howell 2003), such actions tend to be more limited in reach, and they often are signs of a president's failure to convince other actors that his interests are also their interests (Neustadt 1991). Bargaining between presidents and Congress specifically arises from the presence and potential use of vetoes. While the word "veto" itself does not appear anywhere in the US Constitution, Article

I states that presidents must approve of bills for them to become law, while Article II requires the advice and consent of the Senate on presidents' nominees. The veto is a *negative* power: it is the ability to decline a choice (Tsebelis 2003)—the power to say "no."

Negative power leads to bargaining not through its use but through the potential or threat of its use. Time, attention, and other resources are limited. A president's ability to veto legislation forces Congress to bargain earlier in the process lest they spend months or years overcoming collective action problems and building a coalition to pass legislation that the president then rejects. The Senate's ability to withhold consent or "veto" nominations similarly forces presidents to bargain over who those nominees will be. Veto and nomination bargaining exhibit some key differences, but they both represent institutional conflict over the direction of law and public policy.

The broad contours of Trump's bargaining with Congress appear orthodox in many respects: he issued very few veto threats when fellow Republicans held a majority of seats in both the House and the Senate and significantly more veto threats after Democrats won the House majority, both consistent with previous presidents. The percentage of Trump's veto threats devoted to spending bills represents the median among presidents since Reagan. Trump has struggled at times to get his nominees confirmed in a same party-majority Senate, but so did Reagan and George W. Bush.

Closer inspection shows where bargaining and the use of negative power in the Trump administration have significantly differed from his recent predecessors: Trump has not needed to bargain with a Senate supermajority to end filibusters and confirm his nominees; and Congress, particularly the Senate, have both used their own negative power and forced Trump to use his vetoes on foreign policy legislation and nominees to a greater degree than any president over the past forty years. The chapter proceeds in three sections: I first discuss veto bargaining and the importance of the legislation over which Congress and presidents bargain, and then I present data that compares the legislation on which Trump has threatened vetoes to that of his recent predecessors and to his own priorities. The second section examines bargaining over nominations and how and where the Senate has exercised its "veto" with Trump compared to presidents beginning with Reagan. The final section concludes with a discussion of the dynamics of negative power during the Trump administration.

PRESIDENTS, CONGRESS, AND VETO BARGAINING

Veto bargaining involves "real stakes: redistributing wealth, creating rights, making war" (Cameron 2000). Section 7 of the US Constitution's Article I gives presidents the power to say "no" to legislation: "Every Bill which shall have passed the House of Representatives and the Senate shall, before it become a law, be presented to the President of the United States: If he approve he shall sign it, but if not he shall return it . . ." Veto threats appear in statements of administration policy (SAPs), though SAPs can also praise legislation or express concern and state the president's preferences for amending pending bills without going so far as to threaten a veto. Presidents can issue veto threats on bills at any stage of the legislative process, and they can issue multiple veto threats on the same bill: when a bill is pending in the House and again if it advances to the Senate, for example. Because they are SAPs, and not personal messages from a president, the specific veto threat language that appears is either "if [bill number] were presented to the president, he would veto the bill" or "if [bill number] were presented to the President, his advisors would recommend that he veto the bill."

The two-thirds voting threshold in each chamber required to override a president's veto helps give real weight to the president's negative power and encourages majority coalitions to bargain with him lest they need to organize a supermajority coalition later (Cameron 2000; Deen and Arnold 2002; Hassell and Kernell 2016). The president is not always successful in using veto threats to achieve his preferred policy; the success of veto threats depends on institutional and policy contexts like the number of seats the president's party holds in cither chamber, how far a president is into his tenure, and what issue is at question (Barrett and Eshbaugh-Soha 2007; Copeland 1983; Rohde and Simon 1985).

While research on veto threats typically focuses on how Congress and presidents bargain over specific legislative language and policy outputs, they also bargain over the issue agenda. Issue attention in government and politics is an important feature of both representation and agenda setting; controlling what issues are given attention determines which conflicts become salient and how those conflicts are structured (Light 1991). While Cameron as quoted above refers to conflict over shaping policy solutions—how much money to spend, on which programs to spend it, which agencies will be responsible for implementation—the issues on which presidents threaten to veto legislation help define the salient conflicts and thus shape the contours of the US federal government's agenda. Conversely, Congress can influence the political system's agenda and draw presidents into conflict and bargaining by advancing bills on particular sets of issues that may differ from the president's own priorities. By threatening to veto legislation, presidents risk mobilizing opposition and receiving blame for government inaction (Groseclose and McCarty 2001). Veto threats often upend the legislative process by generating Senate filibusters in response and influencing conference committee negotiations between the chambers (Hassell and Kernell 2016).

Congress undoubtedly can "invite" threats by passing legislation it knows the president opposes, as with the Republican-led House's (and eventually Senate's) repeated efforts during the Obama administration to pass bills that would repeal some or all of the Patient Protection and Affordable Care Act after its enactment in 2010. But the responsibility for defining the salient conflicts—and thus shaping the federal government's issue agenda—does not fall solely on the legislature. Presidents have to certify or make visible that conflict, even if doing so merely is a formality (Jones 2000). Making veto threats public through SAPs either invites or certifies conflict more so than privately issued veto threats (Conley 2003). The issues on which presidents have threatened vetoes thus indicate which conflicts have been prioritized. In a previous study of the issue politics surrounding veto bargaining, I find that threats are more likely in four circumstances: under divided government (when the presidential out-party has a chamber majority); on foreign and defense policy, particularly on spending bills; on issues that correspond to the president's own priorities as expressed in the annual State of the Union address; and on issues higher in public salience and importance (Lewallen 2017).

To examine veto bargaining during the Trump administration's first three years, I coded his Statements of Administration Policy that threaten to veto pending legislation according to the Policy Agendas Project issue scheme. The Policy Agendas Project uses a system of twenty major topic codes and 220 minor topic codes to study public policy, issue attention, and agenda setting across time, across different political institutions, and across countries.[1] Samuel Kernell collected SAPs from 1985 to 2008 to study presidential rhetoric and bargaining strategies; I have updated the veto threat data through 2019 and coded them according to the Policy Agendas scheme. Veto threats both depend on legislative movement in Congress and are somewhat discretionary; while presidents cannot threaten to veto bills that do

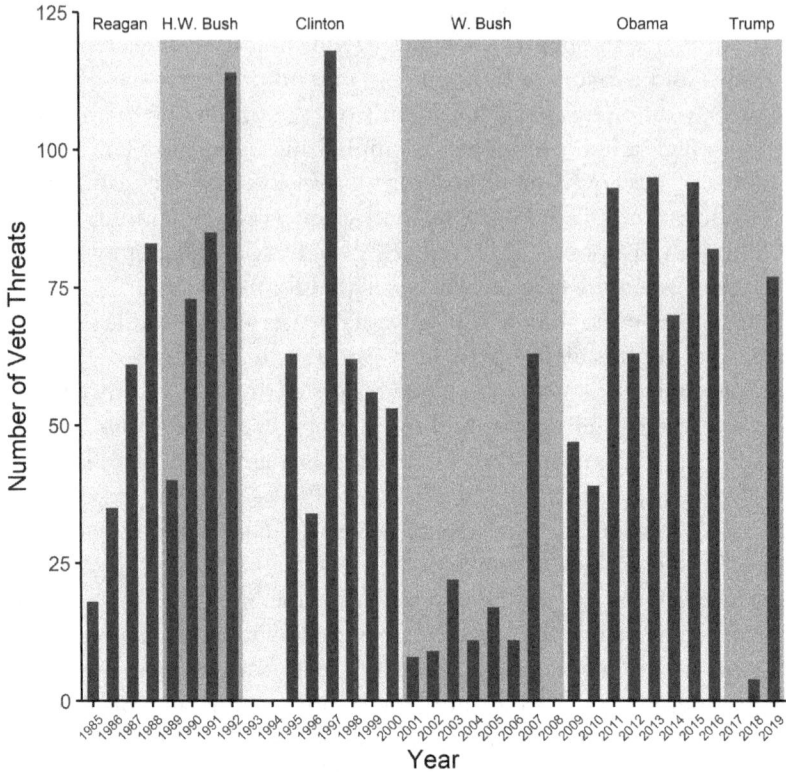

Figure 7.1: Veto Threats since 1985

not exist, they can choose the bills on which to issue SAPs, which in turn elevates attention to the issues those bills would address. Comparing the policy topics underlying President Trump's veto threats to those of his predecessors can help us understand where his veto bargaining remains orthodox and where we have seen real differences.

The first three years of Trump's veto threats are in line with previous empirical findings. Trump issued zero veto threats in 2017 and just four in 2018 when Republicans held a majority of seats in both chambers of Congress (see figure 7.1). The closest he came to issuing a veto threat in 2017 were the fiscal 2017 and fiscal 2018 defense authorization bills (both sponsored by Sen. John McCain, R-AZ, in his capacity as Armed Services Committee chairman), which received SAPs that expressed multiple concerns but did not say whether Trump's advisors would recommend he sign or veto the bill if it was sent to his desk. Two previous presidents in this period also issued zero veto threats

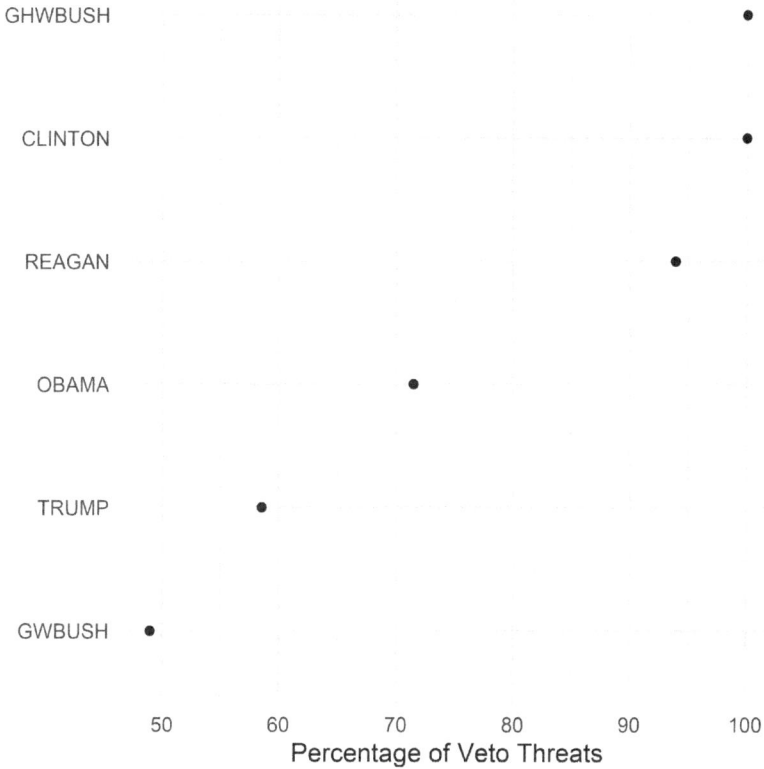

Figure 7.2: Veto Threats under Divided Government

in a year: Clinton in 1993 and 1994, also during unified government, and George W. Bush in 2008, when Democrats had a majority of seats in both chambers. The number of veto threats Trump has issued in a year significantly increased to seventy-seven in 2019, but this number is still well below the 118 Clinton issued in 1997 and the 114 issued by George H. W. Bush in 1992.

In his first three years as president, about 59 percent of Trump's veto threats have been issued to a chamber where the out-party holds a majority of seats (in this specific case, Democrats in the House of Representatives). That figure is low among presidents serving since 1985, though not the lowest; less than half (49 percent) of George W. Bush's veto threats were issued to a Democratic-majority chamber. Conversely, 100 percent of George H. W. Bush's and Bill Clinton's veto threats and 94 percent of Ronald Reagan's veto threats were issued to a chamber with an out-party majority (see figure 7.2).

Jonathan Lewallen

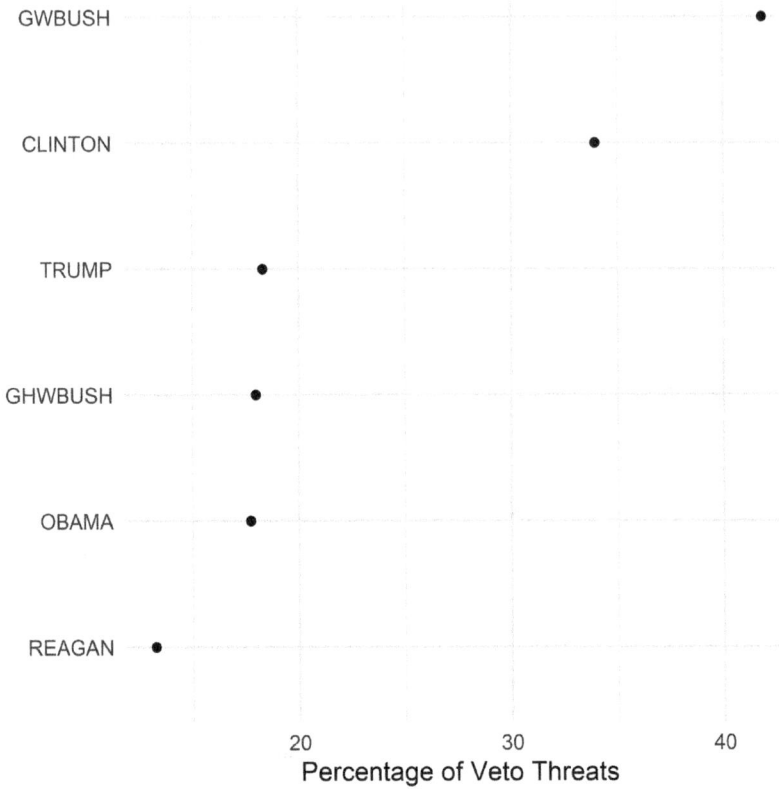

Figure 7.3: Spending Veto Threats

Agency appropriations bills represent a significant arena for veto bargaining. Presidents want to both shift spending toward their preferred levels and protect executive branch priorities and prerogatives. Congress, for its part, wants to protect its own "power of the purse" granted in Article I of the Constitution and also uses spending bills for credit-claiming opportunities for projects in members' states and districts; vetoed appropriations bills potentially deny members those opportunities. With about 18 percent of his veto threats coming against spending bills, Trump represents the median among presidents serving since 1985 (see figure 7.3). The remaining presidents range from a high of about 42 percent of George W. Bush's veto threats and a low of about 13 percent of Ronald Reagan's veto threats coming against appropriations bills.

Because the number of veto threats varies from year to year, per-

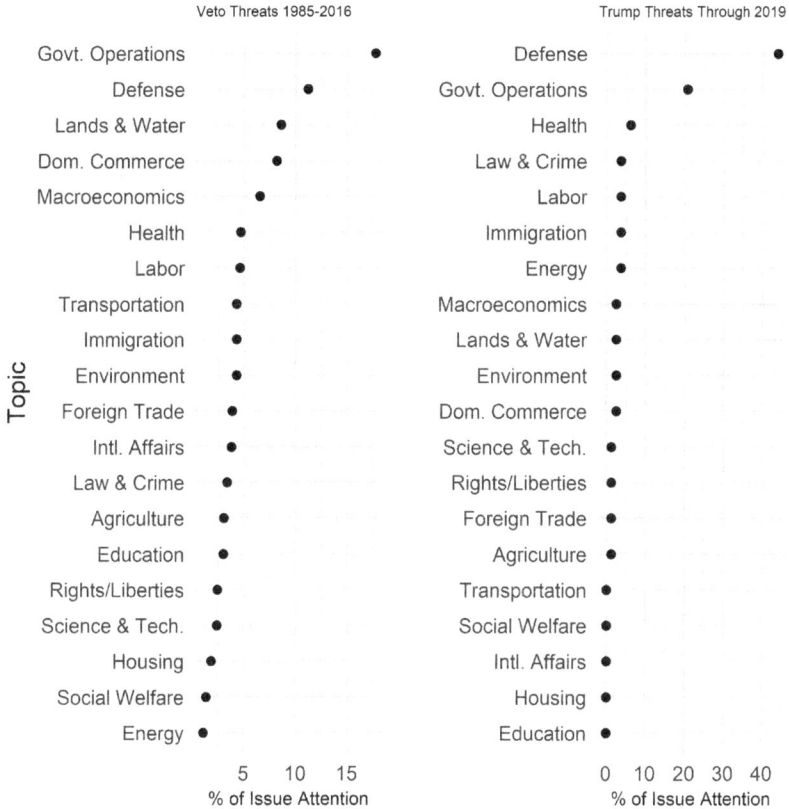

Figure 7.4: Veto Threats by Issue

centages are a better measure of attention than are counts. Issues with higher percentages of veto threats represent higher priorities within veto bargaining, and we can again compare Trump with his predecessors since 1985 to identify whether and where the Trump administration has deviated from previous trends. In the succeeding analysis, the relative ranks of each policy topic are more pertinent than the specific percentages.

The issue politics of veto bargaining during the Trump administration have been fairly orthodox in terms of overall priorities and attention, with a few exceptions. The two major topics on which Trump has threatened to veto the most legislation—defense and government operations—match the top two overall issues from 1985 to 2016 and are consistent with longitudinal trends in veto threat issue attention (Lewallen 2017). Public lands and water policy made up a significant

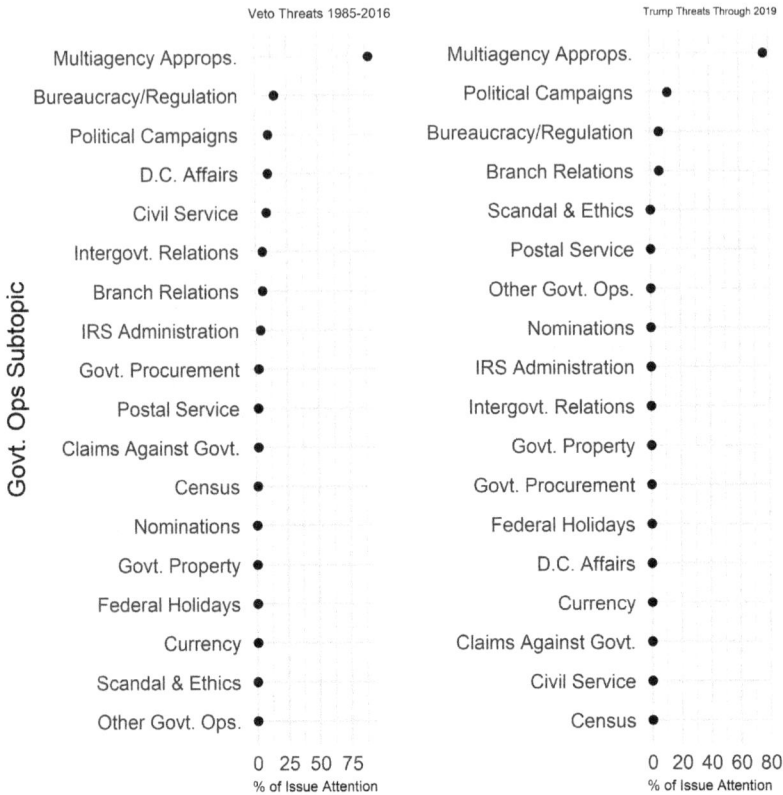

Figure 7.5: Government Operations Veto Threats

percentage of veto threats during the George H. W. Bush and Clinton administrations, though this has declined since; Trump devoting less than 5 percent of his veto threats to Lands and Water legislation is consistent with that trend (see figure 7.4).

Contrary to his predecessors, however, Trump has issued relatively fewer veto threats on domestic commerce and more veto threats on bills related to energy (see figure 7.4). The latter ranks last among all policy topics from 1985 to 2016 and seventh among Trump's first three years of veto threats. The former ranks fourth among all veto threats through 2016, with a slight upward trend prior to the Trump presidency, but eleventh out of twenty topics among Trump's veto threats so far.

The government operations category is fairly broad and includes subtopics such as omnibus appropriations, federal elections and campaign finance, and nominations to currency and commemorative coins. We can disaggregate Trump's veto threats by subtopic to further examine where his attention has focused in his first three years. Trump has issued veto threats on just four government operations subtopics, and those specific subtopics—significant attention to multi-agency appropriations bills, followed by elections and campaigns, the bureaucracy and the regulatory process, and interbranch relations—are consistent with his predecessors (see figure 7.5).

The data presented thus far indicate that the Trump administration's veto bargaining of Congress has been relatively orthodox. Disaggregating Trump's Defense veto threats by subtopic starts to reveal where Trump's veto threats have deviated from his recent predecessors. About 55 percent of the Defense veto threats issued from 1985 to 2016 dealt with Department of Defense appropriations or other general matters, with intelligence, arms control, veteran affairs, and homeland security completing the top five subtopics receiving veto threat attention before the Trump presidency (see figure 7.6, left panel). Trump's veto threats, by contrast, have focused to a much greater degree (80.6 percent) on legislation related to foreign aid and weapons sales, with a few veto threats devoted to war and foreign operations and one each (3 percent of his veto threats) on homeland security and defense appropriations (see figure 7.6, right panel).

The twenty-five bills on weapons sales that Trump has threatened to veto are all joint resolutions providing for congressional disapproval of proposed military sales and exports of technical data and defense services. In this case, then, proposed executive actions led to a congressional response, which in turn produced a counterresponse. All of the joint resolutions regarding weapons and technology sales originated in the Republican-majority Senate, though most were introduced by Foreign Relations Committee ranking member Robert Menendez (D-NJ). Kentucky Republican Rand Paul introduced three of the congressional disapproval resolutions Trump threatened to veto, none of which advanced past the committee stage. All but one of the disapproval resolutions came in 2019; twenty-two of the resolutions passed in the Senate and three also passed in the House, after which Trump did veto them and Congress did not override any of those vetoes. With Democrats in the Senate minority, the twenty-two resolutions that passed the upper chamber received some Republican support, though not enough to create a two-thirds supermajority.

Trump's veto threats through his first three years in office are un-

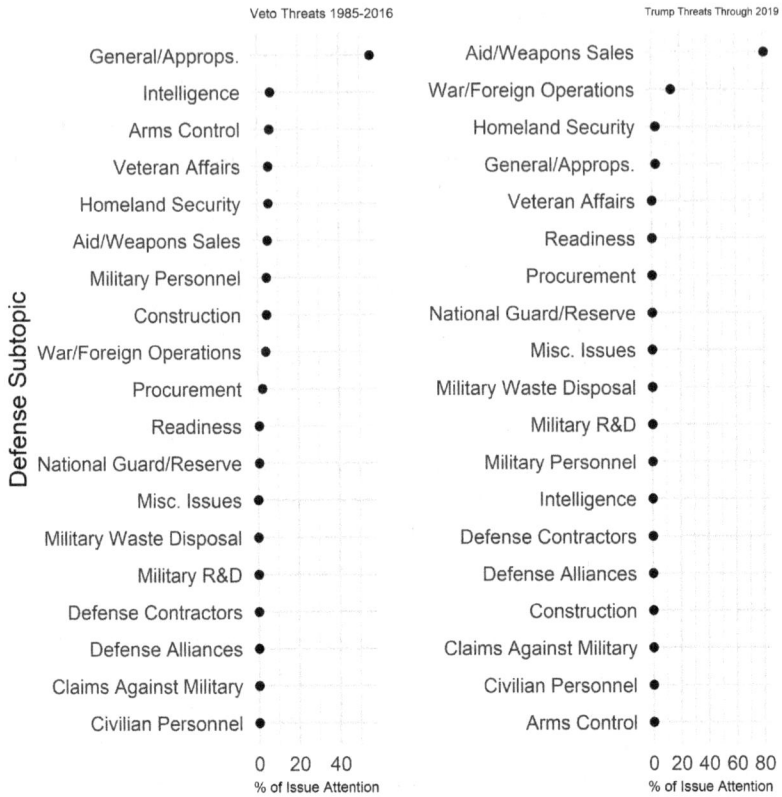

Figure 7.6: Defense Veto Threats

orthodox in another sense: whereas previous research finds that veto threats tend to correspond to issues that receive more attention in the State of the Union address, Trump's veto threats show some deviation from his own priorities. Defense, health, law, and crime have been top-four issues for Trump's State of the Union addresses as well as his veto threats, but international affairs, civil rights and liberties, transportation, and to a lesser extent immigration and macroeconomics have been relatively lower priorities for Trump's veto threat attention than within his annual State of the Union addresses. Conversely, government operations, labor, energy, public lands and water, and science and technology have been much more prominent issues among his veto threats than they have been within his State of the Union speeches (see figure 7.7).

Presidential vetoes represent an exercise of formal power, but Con-

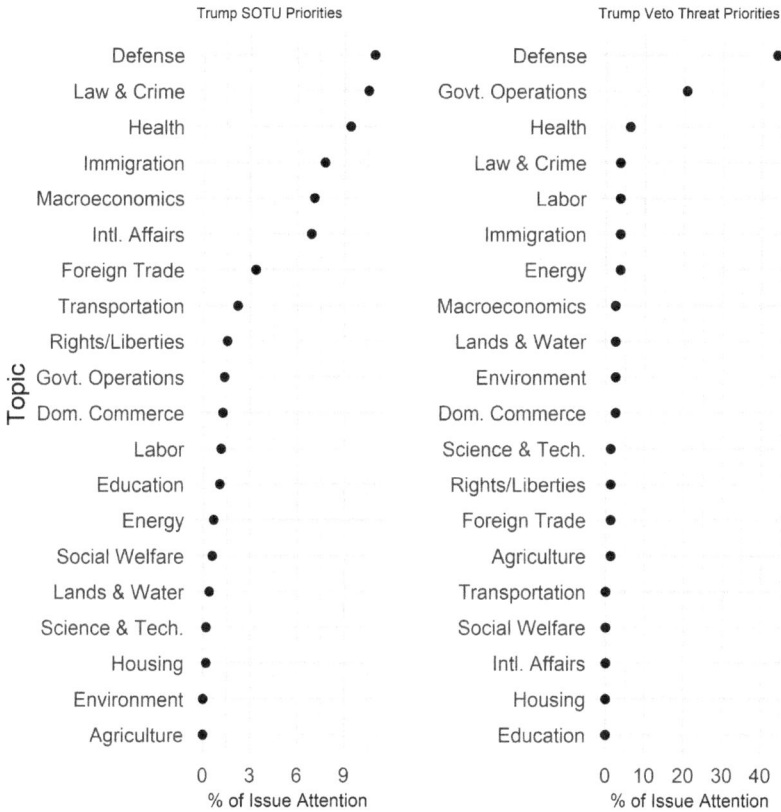

Figure 7.7: State of the Union Veto Threats

gress can still exert agenda-setting influence by drawing presidents into conflict over some issues and not others, which then defines the nature of the bargaining relationship between the two institutions and the scope of the broader policy conflict within those issues. While Trump's veto threat activity appears largely orthodox when compared to his immediate five predecessors, we have seen a shift in veto conflict toward arms sales and military aid and war-related operations. Congress, particularly the Senate, has been willing to challenge Trump on foreign policy issues even to the extent of some Republicans supporting passage of Democratic-sponsored resolutions that would disapprove of arms sales and other administration actions. Congress's influence over Trump's veto threat attention is also suggested by some disconnect between his veto threats and his priorities as expressed in the State of the Union. Even if Congress is unable to override Trump's vetoes, they have drawn Trump away from bargaining over some of his preferred priorities, like immigration and trade. The next section considers how President Trump has bargained with the Senate over nominations to executive and judicial branch positions.

NOMINATIONS AND THE SENATE'S NEGATIVE POWER

While Article I provides presidents with veto power over legislation, Article II, Section 2 gives the Senate the power to say "no" to nominations: "And [the president] shall nominate, and by and with the Advice and Consent of the Senate, shall appoint Ambassadors, other public Ministers and Consuls, Judges of the supreme Court, and all other officers of the United States whose Appointments are not herein otherwise provided for, and which shall be established by Law."

The possibility of withholding Senate "consent" over nominations leads to bargaining earlier in the process, just as presidential veto threats lead to bargaining over legislative content. When a president submits a nomination to the Senate, the nomination typically is referred to a committee with jurisdiction over the agency or court in which the nominee would serve. Nominations may be discharged from committee, but more often the committee will vote on whether to favorably report the nomination, at which point the nomination is placed on the Senate Executive Calendar and scheduled for debate by the whole chamber. Senators thus can "veto" nominations at multiple stages: by preventing the nomination from advancing past the committee stage, by simply not considering a nomination on the Executive Calendar, or by a majority of those present voting not to confirm the nominee. Presidents may withdraw nominations unlikely to be confirmed, but the Senate also can "return" nominations to the president when the chamber recesses or adjourns, after which the president must either resubmit the nomination or nominate someone new (Rybicki 2017).

The Constitution makes Congress responsible for organizing the federal bureaucracy, so the legislature and the president act as joint principals over agencies. The appointment stage is an important tool of congressional oversight (Calvert, McCubbins, and Weingast 1989). In terms of principal-agent theory often used to understand the political direction of the bureaucracy, "selecting the right agent" is often a more efficient way for the principal to obtain her preferred outcome; if the agent and principal agree on desirable outcomes, the latter does not need to spend time monitoring the former. Given the discretion over policy implementation that Congress has delegated to the bureaucracy over time, the initial appointment stage often is most important for determining what policy outcomes will be reached through agency action. A nominee's specific future actions are unknown when Congress considers the nomination; they must use any research conducted into a nominee's background, questions posed to nominees at hearings, and heuristics such as interest group ratings and presidential party identification to predict how the nominee would act in office. Confirmed federal judges outlast the presidents who nominate them and (often) the senators who confirm them, so judicial groups and presidents (and some senators) have increasingly emphasized nominations as a way to cement long-term judicial philosophies and control over policy outcomes. The nominations process thus represents bargaining over the administrative and judicial process both in the present and in the uncertain future.

In writing the *Federalist Papers*, Publius (a combination of James Madison, Alexander Hamilton, and John Jay) sought to address many concerns that some elites had with the newly proposed Constitution. One of those concerns was that the "advice and consent" clause in Article II, Section 2 would give the Senate too much power over the executive. Hamilton defended that provision in *Federalist*, no. 76, noting that the Senate's negative power in this circumstance was essentially reactive: a president could always send another nominee, and the Senate would have no guarantee that individual would be more satisfactory (Madison et al. 1987). In this sense, the Senate's "veto" over nominations differs from the president's veto over legislation. While Congress can either override the veto or advance a new bill, it must overcome the collective action problems inherent in the legislative process to do so; submitting a new nomination requires fewer resources of a presidential administration.

Nominations, like legislation, are subject to Senate debate rules. One of the features that distinguishes the Senate from the House of Representatives is that the upper chamber's standing rules lack a provision that allows senators to "move the previous question"—end debate and immediately vote on the pending issue. So long as one senator does not yield the floor, she can talk for as long as she wants about any subject (or "filibuster"), whether or not it is relevant to the legislation or nomination pending on the calendar. Similarly, an individual senator can place a "hold" on a pending bill or nomination that prevents it from being considered on the floor (Rybicki 2017).

In 1917, senators adopted a rule (Rule 22) meant to provide a means for ending filibusters. A senator must first file a motion to invoke cloture (cosigned by at least fifteen colleagues). If the motion is agreed to, debate continues for a prescribed period of time before the Senate votes on the pending question. Filibusters historically have been a costly form of obstruction since they require sustained opposition, and senators moved to limit filibusters several times during the twentieth century's latter half, including creating a "two-track" system for debating legislation in 1964 that allows a filibuster on a bill or nomination to continue while the Senate considers other pending business; voting to require a three-fifths vote threshold to invoke cloture on measures that would not amend Senate Rules; and voting to limit post-cloture debate time to one hundred hours in 1979 and to thirty hours in 1986 (Binder and Smith 1996; Koger 2010; Sinclair 1989; Wawro and Schickler 2006). While these changes were designed to reduce obstruction's cost to Senate business, in so doing they made obstruction "cheaper" for filibustering senators.

More recent debates over the filibuster have centered on nominations. In 2005, Senate majority leader Bill Frist (R-TN) proposed invoking a "nuclear option" (alternately referred to as the "Constitutional option") to counteract Democratic filibusters of President George W. Bush's judicial nominees, though the idea had existed for a few years prior (VandeHei and Babington 2005). The procedure requires only a simple majority vote to support a point of order against the Senate rules regarding filibusters. Senate Democrats finally invoked the "nuclear option" in 2013 but limited the rules changes to executive and judicial branch nominations, excluding nominations to the Supreme Court. Senate Republicans later invoked the "nuclear option" for Supreme Court nominations in order to confirm Neil Gorsuch in 2017.

The preceding discussion of Senate cloture rules and the reduced threshold for ending filibusters on nominees is important for considering the president's bargaining relationship with Congress, because the rules determine the scope of the Senate's negative power and with whom (or at least, the size of the coalition with whom) presidents must bargain over nominations. Prior to 2013, presidents often had to bargain with a supermajority of senators, and therefore a wider array of represented interests, which helped reinforce the Senate's negative power. But the post-2013 reduced cloture threshold may not necessarily enhance a president's bargaining status in a polarized Congress (Cameron 2002). Committee chairs may exert more of their own negative power and gatekeeping (or threaten to do so to encourage bargaining) once they cannot count on a supermajority threshold for ending filibusters on the chamber floor. If withholding consent is a reactive power, as Hamilton argues, then delaying a nomination—particularly for an extreme length of time as Senate Republicans did with Supreme Court nominee Merrick Garland in 2016 and earlier with Ninth Circuit Appeals Court nominee Richard Paez during President Clinton's second term—could be interpreted as the Senate strengthening its bargaining position. "Strategic delay" prevents presidents from sending a new nominee also not amenable to the Senate and takes the repeated proposal power out of a president's hands (Bell 2002; McCarty and Ragazian 1999; Ostrander 2016).

The remainder of this section compares the fate of Trump's nominees in Congress to those of his recent predecessors. The Library of Congress tracks nominations through its Congress.gov website from 1981 to the present, so the time period largely is comparable with the veto threats data. Congress.gov separates nominations into two categories: civilians and military/foreign service/public health. The majority of military nominations involve routine appointments at rank, so the data presented here focus specifically on civilian nominations. President Trump has not completed his first term as of this writing, so I include only his first three complete years of data (2017–2019). The lack of a complete term means Trump has made fewer nominations than any other president since 1981, but he is not dramatically below one-term president George H. W. Bush (see figure 7.8). Despite numerous high-profile examples of Trump leaving positions vacant, the data suggest that phenomenon is not happening to a significant degree; on this matter the unorthodox behavior is more likely which positions he is leaving vacant and the amount of time they are left vacant.

Comparing the fates of presidents' nominations since 1981 illustrates how Trump differs from his recent predecessors. I specifically provide three measures: whether nominees advanced past the committee stage; whether nominees were confirmed; and whether presidents withdrew a nomination. Of the six presidents serving since 1981, Trump has the lowest percentage of nominees advance past the committees to which they were referred (about 72 percent; see figure 7.9, left panel) and the lowest percentage of confirmed nominees (about 62 percent; center panel). Presidential "success" on these

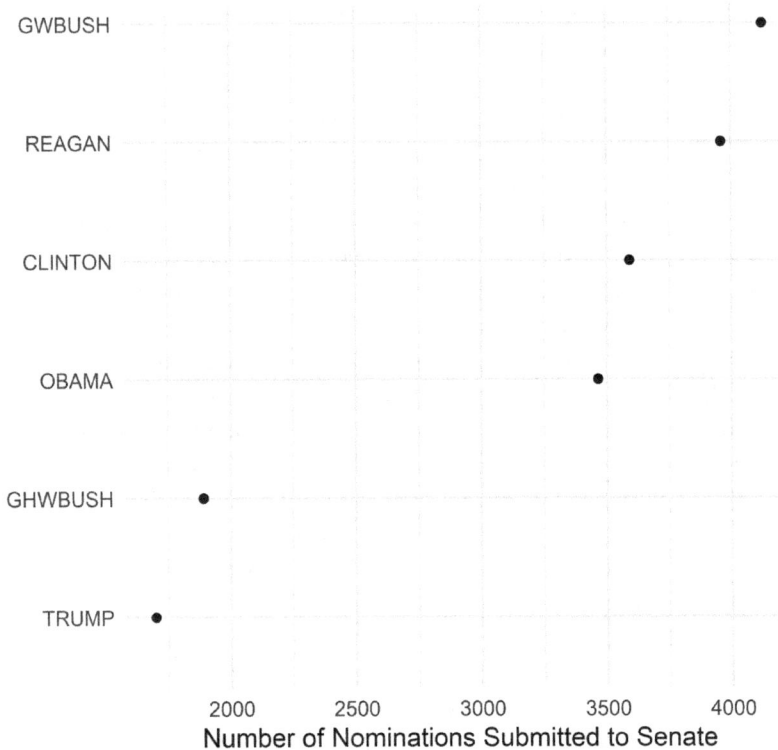

Figure 7.8: Nominations

measures, however, has been trending downward over time, with Reagan experiencing the highest percentages, George H. W. Bush the second-highest, and so on through Trump. While Trump's nominees have experienced more difficulty advancing and gaining Senate consent, the downward trends call into question whether the fate of Trump's nominees can be considered unorthodox or the product of other institutional dynamics set in motion decades before Trump's presidency. Trump has withdrawn just under 5 percent of his nominations, the second-highest percentage after George W. Bush (see figure 7.9, right panel). No other president serving since 1981 withdrew more than 3 percent of his nominations, which indicates that Trump has been less successful in bargaining over nominations than most of his recent predecessors.

The previous two figures group nominations by president, but some presidents have faced a same-party majority Senate, some an out-

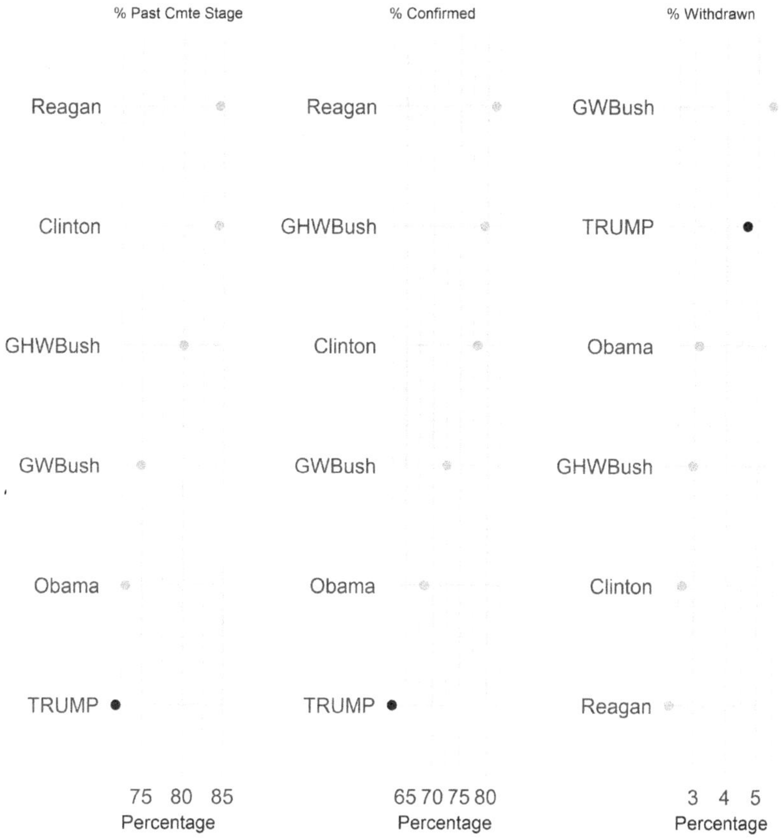

% Past Cmte Stage		% Confirmed		% Withdrawn	
Reagan	●	Reagan	●	GWBush	●
Clinton	●	GHWBush	●	TRUMP	●
GHWBush	●	Clinton	●	Obama	●
GWBush	●	GWBush	●	GHWBush	●
Obama	●	Obama	●	Clinton	●
TRUMP	●	TRUMP	●	Reagan	●
75 80 85		65 70 75 80		3 4 5	
Percentage		Percentage		Percentage	

Figure 7.9: Fate of Nominations

party majority Senate; the Senate circumstances for some presidents changed within their terms. Examining only those congresses for which the president's party held a majority of Senate seats highlights Trump's relative lack of success in bargaining over nominations under favorable conditions (see figure 7.10). Only Obama in 2013–2014 had lower percentages of nominations that advanced past committee (top panel) and nominations that were confirmed (middle panel). Recall that the lack of supermajority support for many of President Obama's nominees helped lead to the cloture threshold's reduction for non–Supreme Court nominations. Trump has needed only a simple majority of the Republican-majority Senate to invoke cloture and proceed to a vote on his nominees but still struggles relative to his predecessors, who faced arguably more difficult bargaining arrangements. In 2017–

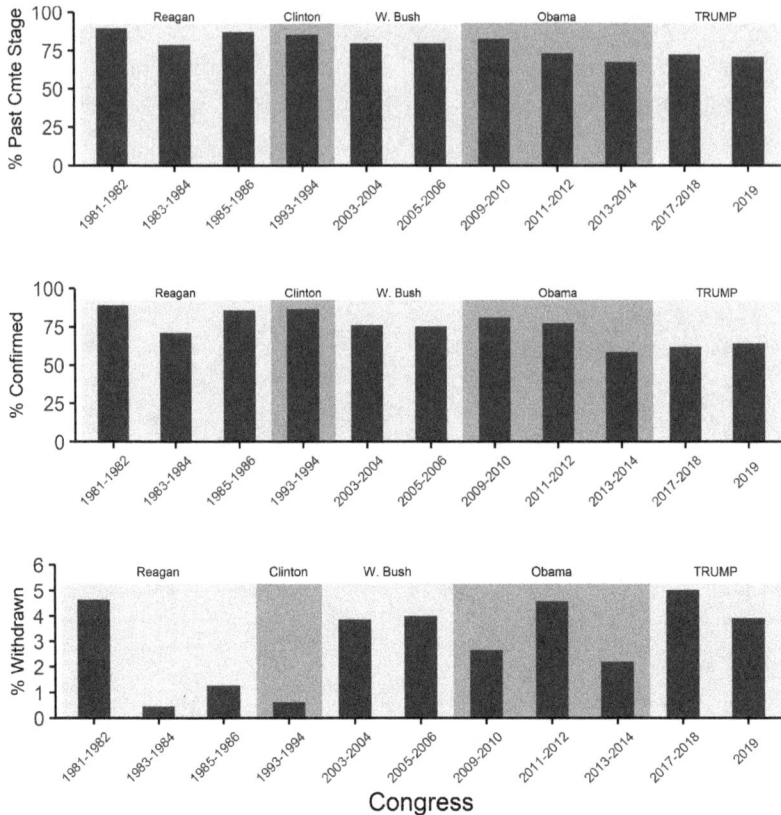

Figure 7.10: Unified Fate of Nominations

2018, President Trump also had the highest percentage of withdrawn nominations among presidents who faced same-party Senate majorities, and his 2019 percentage is the fifth-highest, behind Reagan's first two years in office and George W. Bush's first four years in office, both of whom needed to bargain with supermajorities that included Senate Democrats (see figure 7.10, right panel).

We can further examine the nominations data according to the committees to which the nominations are referred. Differences in committee jurisdictions do not perfectly correspond to differences across policy issues, but they can give us a general sense of where presidents have been more or less successful in bargaining with the Senate over nominations and where Trump may differ from his predecessors. For most committees' jurisdictions, Trump nominees' fate in advancing

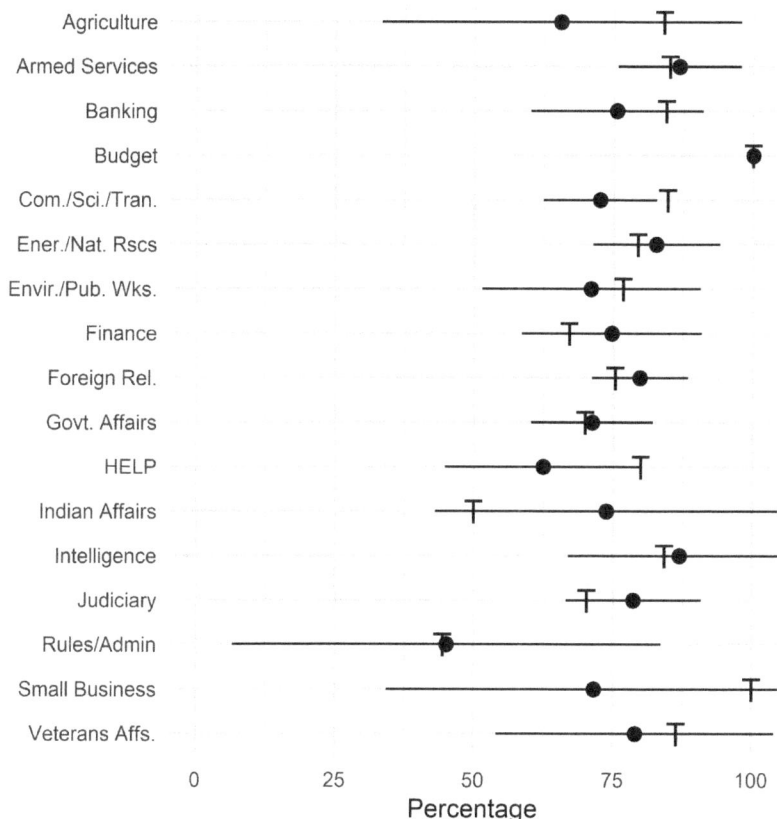

Figure 7.11: Nominations Reported by Committee

past the committee stage largely are in line with his predecessors with a few exceptions. Across Senate committees, the percentage of Trump nominees who were reported favorably (represented on the graph with a "T") fall within one standard deviation of the average percentage from 1981 to 2016 (represented with a dot; see figure 7.11). One notable exception: Trump nominees under the Commerce, Science, and Transportation Committee's jurisdiction were more likely to be reported favorably than those of his predecessors. Trump nominees referred to the Health, Education, Labor, and Pensions Committee also were reported favorably at a rate more than one standard deviation above his predecessors' average, though only just.

Although Trump's nominees have been about as successful at the committee stage as those of the previous five presidents, he has faced

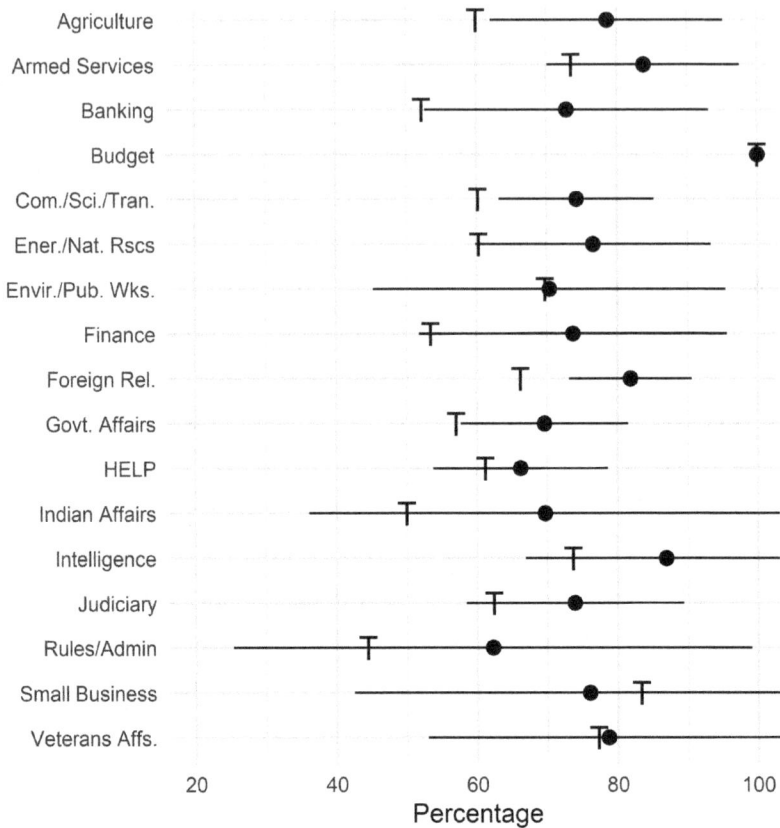

Figure 7.12: Nominations Confirmed by Committee

more difficulty in getting his nominees confirmed, as shown in figure 7.8. When those data are disaggregated by committee, we see that Trump's lower confirmation rates are more pronounced for nominees referred to five committees in particular: agriculture; banking (which also has jurisdiction over housing and urban affairs), commerce, science, and transportation; foreign relations; and government affairs and homeland security (see figure 7.12). Two of these differences are particularly notable; first, the percentage of Trump nominees referred to the commerce, science, and transportation committee and later confirmed is about 14 points lower than his predecessors' average despite Trump having greater success in seeing his nominees favorably reported by that panel. Second, about 82 percent of presidential nominees referred to the Senate Foreign Relations Committee from 1981

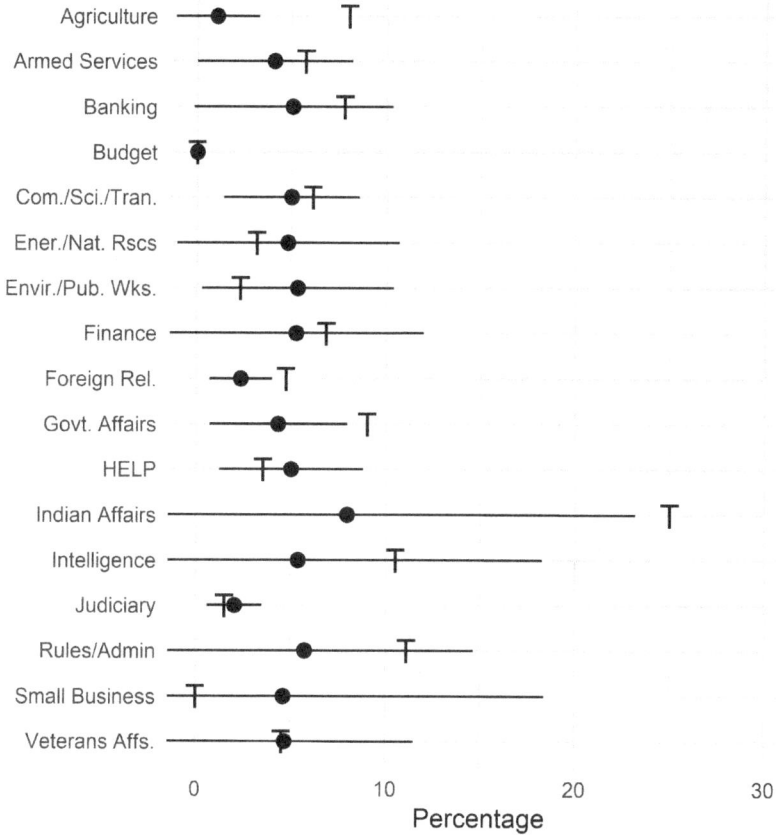

Figure 7.13: Nominations Withdrawn by Committee

to 2016 ultimately were confirmed, second only to Armed Services, but for Trump's nominees that figure is about two-thirds.

Trump has withdrawn nominations at higher rates than his predecessors for nominees referred to four committees: agriculture; foreign relations; government affairs and homeland security; and Indian affairs (see figure 7.13). Fewer than five nominees are referred to the latter panel in any given Congress, and typically just one or two, which helps produce more variability in its numbers from one president to the next. Nevertheless, President Trump has withdrawn one-quarter of his nominations that were referred to the Indian Affairs Committee, compared to an 8 percent average for his predecessors since 1981. Trump also has withdrawn 9 percent of his nominations that were referred to the Government Affairs and Homeland Security Committee and 8 percent of his nominations referred to the Agriculture Committee, higher than his predecessors' averages of about 4 percent and 1 percent, respectively. Trump has withdrawn about 5 percent of his nominations that were referred to the Senate Foreign Relations Committee, twice the average rate of his predecessors. Trump's twelve withdrawn Foreign Relations–referred nominations in 2017–2018 are the second-highest since 1981, behind only George W. Bush's thirteen withdrawals in 2007–2008 when the latter faced a Democratic-majority Senate.

The nominations data presented in this section show that senators are "vetoing" Trump nominees more often than most of his predecessors, particularly nominations related to agriculture, banking and commerce policy, American Indian affairs, homeland security, and foreign policy. Trump has been less successful than many of his recent predecessors in bargaining with the Senate over nominations, even though Republicans have held a majority of seats throughout his presidency and filibuster-related barriers to confirmation were lowered significantly before he took office. The final section concludes with a summation of the chapter's findings and a brief discussion of bargaining and negative power between Congress and the Trump administration.

CONCLUSION

This chapter has examined President Trump's relations with Congress through the lens of negative power and bargaining, specifically in veto threats and nominations. Data from the 1980s to 2019 show that Trump's bargaining relationship with the House of Representatives is fairly orthodox; he issued few-to-no veto threats when Republicans held a majority of seats and has threatened to veto more legislation after Democrats gained the majority in the 2018 elections. The Senate, however, is where we see more deviations from Trump's predecessors, not only in Trump's success (or lack thereof) but in the issues on which Congress has drawn Trump into bargaining and the use of negative power. The Senate has been more assertive with Trump in foreign and defense policy, particularly in scheduling (and mostly passing) resolutions to limit proposed weapons and technology sales to other countries that force Trump to engage and threaten vetoes and in confirming fewer nominees and forcing Trump to withdraw more nominees under the Foreign Relations Committee's jurisdiction.

Congress has asserted itself in a few other policy areas: agriculture (by confirming fewer nominees and forcing more withdrawals), banking and commerce (by confirming fewer nominees), labor policies separate from immigration, and energy (the latter two in forcing Trump to issue relatively more veto threats than his recent predecessors). Congress's willingness to force Trump to bargain over issues that are not his highest priorities and even to veto his nominations is not simply about partisanship. More than 40 percent of Trump's veto threats have been issued to a Republican-majority chamber, and even with the benefit of a lower cloture threshold, his nominee confirmation rates are the lowest or among the lowest for recent presidents who also worked with a same-party Senate.

Bargaining between Congress and presidents over legislation and nominations is a fundamental part of the American political system. Those bargaining relationships are encouraged and reinforced by vetoes and the use of negative power by both institutions. Even if Congress does not always "win" when it withholds its consent over nominations or fails to override a presidential veto, the legislature still can exert influence by shifting the president's time, attention, and other resources toward and away from certain issues and vacancies. In doing so, Congress helps set not only the president's agenda but also that of the broader system by influencing how political conflict organizes.

Trump has not completed his presidential term as of this writing; we will need more information before concluding how unorthodox his relations with Congress really are. The relatively low rates at which Trump nominees advance past the committee stage and are confirmed may be part of longer trends extending at least as far back as the 1980s. Trump also is the first president to begin his tenure with a simple-majority threshold for ending filibusters on all nominations; do his relatively higher rates of withdrawn nominations reflect bargaining failures unique to his administration, or will future presidents face similar challenges as committee gatekeeping becomes more important for exercising the Senate's negative power? Will future Senates build on their current attitude toward weapons sales and foreign operations and contribute to the trend toward more legislative bargaining and confrontation over foreign and defense policy? At least thus far, both Trump's and Congress's use of negative power has been fairly orthodox; the issue arenas in which that negative power has been exercised have not.

NOTE

1. More information can be found at https://www.comparativeagendas .net/pages/About.

REFERENCES

Barrett, Andrew W., and Matthew Eshbaugh-Soha. "Presidential Success on the Substance of Legislation." *Political Research Quarterly* 60, no. 1 (2007): 100–112.

Bell, Lauren Cohen. "Senatorial Discourtesy: The Senate's Use of Delay to Shape the Federal Judiciary." *Political Research Quarterly* 55, no. 3 (2002): 589–608.

Binder, Sarah A., and Steven S. Smith. *Politics or Principle: Filibustering in the United States Senate.* Washington, DC: Brookings Institution, 1996.

Calvert, Randall L., Mathew D. McCubbins, and Barry R. Weingast. "A Theory of Political Control and Agency Discretion." *American Journal of Political Science* 33, no. 3 (1989): 588–611.

Cameron, Charles M. *Veto Bargaining: Presidents and the Politics of Negative Power.* New York: Cambridge University Press, 2000.

———. "Studying the Polarized Presidency." *Presidential Studies Quarterly* 32, no. 4 (2002): 647–663.

Conley, Richard S. "George Bush and the 102d Congress: The Impact of Public and 'Private' Veto Threats on Policy Outcomes." *Presidential Studies Quarterly* 33, no. 4 (2003): 730–750.

Copeland, Gary W. "When Congress and the President Collide: Why Presidents Veto Legislation." *Journal of Politics* 45, no. 3 (1983): 696–710.

Deen, Rebecca E., and Laura W. Arnold. "Veto Threats as a Policy Tool: When to Threaten?" *Presidential Studies Quarterly* 32, no. 1 (2002): 30–45.

Groseclose, Tim, and Nolan McCarty. "The Politics of Blame: Bargaining Before an Audience." *American Journal of Political Science* 45, no. 1 (2001): 100–119.

Hassell, Hans J. G., and Samuel Kernell. "Veto Rhetoric and Legislative Riders." *American Journal of Political Science* 60, no. 4 (2016): 845–859.

Howell, William G. *Power without Persuasion: The Politics of Direct Presidential Action.* Princeton, NJ: Princeton University Press, 2003.

Jones, Charles O. "Reinventing Leeway: The President and Agenda Certification." *Presidential Studies Quarterly* 30, no. 1 (2000): 6–26.

Koger, Gregory. *Filibustering: A Political History of Obstruction in the House and Senate.* Chicago: University of Chicago Press, 2010.

Lewallen, Jonathan. "The Issue Politics of Presidential Veto Threats." *Presidential Studies Quarterly* 47, no. 2 (2017): 277–292.

Light, Paul C. *The President's Agenda: Domestic Policy from Kennedy to Reagan.* Baltimore, MD: Johns Hopkins University Press, 1991.

Madison, James, Alexander Hamilton, John Jay, and Isaac Kramnick. *The Federalist Papers.* New York: Penguin, 1987.

McCarty, Nolan, and Rose Ragazian. "Advice and Consent: Senate Responses to Executive Branch Nominations 1885–1996." *American Journal of Political Science* 43, no. 4 (1999): 1122–1143.

Neustadt, Richard. *Presidential Power and the Modern Presidents: The Politics of Leadership from Roosevelt to Reagan.* Revised. New York: Free, 1991.

Ostrander, Ian. "The Logic of Collective Inaction: Senatorial Delay in Executive Nominations." *American Journal of Political Science* 60, no. 4 (2016): 1063–1076.

Rohde, David W., and Dennis M. Simon. "Presidential Vetoes and Congressional Response." *American Journal of Political Science* 29, no. 3 (1985): 397–427.

Rybicki, Elizabeth. "Senate Consideration of Presidential Nominations: Committee and Floor Procedure." *Congressional Research Service*, April 11, 2017. https://fas.org/sgp/crs/misc/RL31980.pdf.

Sinclair, Barbara. *The Transformation of the U.S. Senate.* Baltimore, MD: Johns Hopkins University Press, 1989.

Tsebelis, George. *Veto Players: How Political Institutions Work.* Princeton, NJ: Princeton University Press, 2003.

VandeHei, Jim, and Charles Babington. "From Senator's 2003 Outburst, GOP Hatched 'Nuclear Option.'" *Washington Post*, May 19, 2005. https://www.washingtonpost.com/wp-dyn/content/article/2005/05/18/AR2005051802144.html.

Wawro, Gregory J., and Eric Schickler. *Filibuster: Obstruction and Lawmaking in the U.S. Senate.* Princeton, NJ: Princeton University Press, 2006.

CHAPTER 8

Trump and the Administrative State

JoBeth Surface Shafran and Heather T. Rimes

INTRODUCTION

In the summer of 2015, shortly before he formally launched his 2016 presidential campaign, Donald Trump tweeted, "Bureaucratic red tape and overregulation are discouraging the American dream. It's time for a bold new direction!" (Trump 2015). Trump's stance evolved into a series of campaign promises that championed deregulation and elimination of what the Trump campaign claimed were administrative barriers to US business interests (Lipton and Applebaum 2017). When President Donald Trump took office in 2017, his former chief strategist Steve Bannon described the president's plan for the federal executive branch as "deconstruction of the administrative state" (Rucker and Costa 2017). The term "administrative state" refers to the federal bureaucracy, the collection of executive branch agencies that act as extensions of the president, which have been tasked with implementing the laws passed by Congress and given a variety of regulatory and enforcement powers. As such, these entities hold an integral, yet complex, status (Rohr 1986; Waldo 1948) within the US federal system, as unelected bureaucrats serve in organizations that maintain often overlapping executive, legislative, and judicial powers (Rosenbloom 1983). Their status generates several constitutional issues related to the relationship between bureaucracy and democracy (Etzioni-Halevy 2013; Meier, O'Toole, and O'Toole 2006), and, as the

180

role of the federal bureaucracy has grown, modern presidents have developed approaches to facilitating political control of the bureaucracy and to using the administrative state as a tool for policy change (Durant and Warber 2001).

The tension between President Trump and the administrative state is no surprise. His intention of "deconstructing the administrative state" is not dissimilar to approaches to the executive branch promulgated by many other presidents. For instance, President Richard Nixon accused federal bureaucrats of not being responsive enough to elected officials, a threat to the democratic nature of the American political system, and attempted, unsuccessfully, to disrupt the power of the federal bureaucracy through reorganization efforts (Rung 1999). Ronald Reagan, although similarly unsuccessful, had plans to eliminate the Departments of Energy and Education (Hechinger 1982; Raines 1981). Efforts to disrupt the effectiveness of the bureaucracy are not confined to Republican presidents; President Bill Clinton also advanced ideas to shrink the size of the administrative state. Influenced by *Reinventing Government* (1992), by David E. Osborne and Ted Gaebler, he had Vice President Al Gore lead a national performance review whose culminating report called for reducing the size of the federal workforce, simplifying administrative regulations, and emphasizing customer service (Gore 1993).

In spite of these executive calls for diminishing the bureaucracy, scholars find that many modern presidents, particularly Republican ones, turn to the bureaucracy as a key element of their policy-making strategy (Hult and Maranto 2010)—an approach known as the "administrative presidency" (Nathan 1983). Durant and Warber (2001, 221–222) describe the approach as follows:

The administrative presidency is premised on three assumptions (Nathan 1983). First, congressional opposition to presidential legislative initiatives is the rule rather than the exception. Second, federal agencies make policy as they exercise bureaucratic discretion when implementing statutes. Consequently, presidents have another opportunity to "legislate" that does not require them to mobilize legislative majorities or supermajorities in Congress. Third, and premised on conventional notions of hierarchical control, presidents indirectly can influence policy by naming political appointees to agencies who either substantively or ideologically share their policy agendas. These appointees, in turn, can change agency rules, budgets, structures, and personnel requirements to suit presidential policy goals. In contrast to this more "indirect" (or "contextual") approach of acting through agents, presidents can take a more direct (or "unilateral") approach. They do so when issuing executive orders, proclamations, presidential signing statements, national security directives, and presidential memoranda.

In sum, decrying bureaucratic pathology and being apprehensive of bureaucratic loyalty (Rourke 1987) while simultaneously employing administrative strategies to promote presidential policy prerogatives (Durant and Warber 2001) is common ground for modern presidents, including President Trump.

Each president craves a responsive administrative system that, while remaining loyal to presidential preferences, will maintain its legitimacy and functionality (Moe 1989). Presidents and their staff, then, tend to be skeptical of the motivations and policy preferences of unknown careerists (Edwards, Mayer, and Wayne 2020). President Nixon, for example, was quoted as telling his cabinet, "We can't depend on people who believe in another philosophy of government to give us their undivided loyalty or best work" (Gvosdev, Blankshain, and Cooper 2019, 206). President Carter expressed similar sentiments when he said, "Before I became president, I realized and I was warned that dealing with the federal bureaucracy would be one of the worst problems I would have to face. It has been even worse than I had anticipated" (Edwards, Mayer, and Wayne 2020, 287).

President Trump's skepticism of the administrative state echoes these sentiments. However, Trump's attacks on the "deep state" are often more extreme in tone and, at times, even fueled by conspiracy theories and content from illegitimate sources (McIntire, Yourish, and Buchanan 2019). We argue that President Trump's approach exhibits a different style and character than that of his predecessors, particularly given his novel use of social media as a tool for interacting with the administrative state. For instance, President Trump has frequently attacked federal bureaucrats, particularly careerists, referring to them as "rogue bureaucrats of the Deep State" (Trump 2019e) and the "Criminal Deep State" (Trump 2018a). According to the *New York Times*, Mr. Trump has retweeted a number of unverified Twitter accounts that promote either "conspiracy or fringe content," including content originating from QAnon, a group labeled by the Federal Bureau of Investigation as a potential domestic terror threat (McIntire,

Yourish, and Buchanan 2019). In particular, Trump reused the hashtag #FakeWhistleblower, originally attributed to QAnon, to discredit the bureaucrat(s) claiming presidential misconduct in regard to the distribution of Ukrainian military aid in 2019.

Other recent scholarship (Lewis 2019, 779) describes President Trump's approach to managing the federal bureaucracy as unorthodox largely because it is more strident and contentious than previous administrations, with the president intentionally working to disassociate himself from the actions of the bureaucracy by "eschewing the role of chief executive and his continual posture as president but not chief executive." This chapter focuses on President Trump's actions in three areas that are fundamental to presidential control of the administrative state: indirect strategies of managing political appointments and influencing careerists, direct strategies of shaping policy change through agency regulatory and rulemaking processes, and bureaucratic responses to these efforts. We utilize examples of statements from Mr. Trump's Twitter account to illustrate that although his rhetoric or delivery is more extreme than that of his predecessors, his skepticism, appointment priorities, and use of the bureaucracy to achieve policy goals is largely consistent with previous approaches. We conclude with a discussion of the political and managerial implications of President Trump's approaches and strategies to bureaucratic control.

INDIRECT STRATEGIES: MANAGING POLITICAL APPOINTEES AND INFLUENCING CAREERISTS

In the US federal government, there are approximately four thousand positions that are filled by political appointment (GAO 2019). Krause and O'Connell (2019, 528) describe the dilemma that presidents face as they attempt to fill these positions: "In their role as chief administrator, presidents both desire that the bureaucracy complies with their policy goals (loyalty) and want agency officials to possess sufficient expertise and capacity for effectively executing tasks relating to policy administration (competence)" (Edwards 2001; Lewis 2008). The need for loyal allies who will steer administrative programming in the direction of the president's policy agenda has come to be known as "responsive competence," and to achieve it, presidential tactics include centralizing control in the White House and maximizing presidential appointments (Moe 1989). Political appointees represent the most effective source of bureaucratic control for presidents (Wood and Waterman 1994) because through the careful and strategic use of appointees, the president can shape agencies within his administration (Lewis 2008), directing them in line with presidential policy (Wood and Waterman 1994) and changing agency performance (Moynihan and Roberts 2010).

The Trump Administration's Approaches to Appointees

The Trump administration appears to follow patterns similar to those of other presidential administrations, with trade-offs in loyalty versus competence being more acute for top-level positions and within executive agencies as opposed to independent regulatory commissions (Krause and O'Connell 2019). However, while appointee background characteristics and dimensions of loyalty (Ouyang, Haglund, and Waterman 2017) are crucial, the Trump administration has highlighted another critical element of political appointment: turnover. Numerous headlines detail exceptionally high turnover levels among Trump appointees (Joung 2019; Lu and Yourish 2018). Kathryn Dunn Tenpas (2020) of the Brookings Institution tracks and analyzes presidential administration turnover data, and according to her findings, turnover in the Trump administration in both the president's cabinet as well as within influential offices in the Executive Office of the President is higher when compared to any one of the past five presidential administrations. A number of offices have also seen serial replacements—at the extreme end, the Deputy National Security Advisor position has been held by six different individuals since President Trump took office (Tenpas 2020).

Additionally, the Trump administration has not attempted to fill many key executive branch positions; slightly more than three years into his term, there are 153 positions requiring Senate confirmation (out of a total 714) that have no nominee (Partnership for Public Service 2020), thus impeding the administration's ability to fully realize the utility of political appointees. While overall his agency nominations lag slightly behind the Obama, George W. Bush, and Clinton administrations, the biggest difference is in President Trump's ability to secure Senate confirmation for his nominees (see O'Connell [2018] for a comparison of the Trump administration with the past four presidential administrations). Lewis, Bernhard, and You (2018) detail six factors that contribute to a complex explanation for President Trump's staffing delays: 1) the president's outsider status that afforded him a smaller network of connections than previous presidents, 2) flaws in the newly minted Trump administration's decision-making process for making hiring recommendations for administrative positions requiring Senate confirmation, 3) a chaotic transition period in which fewer nominations than usual were submitted immediately following the President's inauguration during the period the Senate sets aside specifically for those considerations, 4) a number of unusually controversial nominees, 5) partisan delays in the Senate, and 6) intentional decisions made by the president to leave some positions unfilled.

President Trump has also used a number of temporary or acting appointments to sidestep the need for Senate approval of nominations and to ensure greater loyalty to himself (Graham 2019), and recent research finds that his reliance on acting appointments has surpassed that of his predecessors in both extent of use and level of controversy surrounding these appointments (O'Connell 2020). Acting Attorney General Matt Whitaker was one such example of allowing someone who is unlikely to gain Senate approval to hold an important position that would typically be responsive to both Congress and the president. Those appointed to acting positions are therefore much more reliant on presidential opinion and, as a result, more likely to be inclined toward presidential loyalty than their Senate-confirmed counterparts.

Further differentiating his administration in this respect is the president's use of social media as a human resource tool; Shear and colleagues (2019) report that more than two dozen executive branch official departures have been announced through Twitter, some even being fired by tweet, a novel presidential use for the medium. Many of the most contentious departures are also accompanied by a parting shot from the president's Twitter account. For instance, President Trump tweeted about firing former secretary of state Rex Tillerson: "Mike Pompeo is doing a great job, I am very proud of him. His predecessor, Rex Tillerson, didn't have the mental capacity needed. He was dumb as a rock and I couldn't get rid of him fast enough. He was lazy as hell. Now it is a whole new ballgame, great spirit at State!" (Trump 2018c). Similarly, in a stream of tweets following James Comey's departure, Trump made statements such as "James Comey will be replaced by someone who will do a far better job, bringing back the spirit and prestige of the FBI" (Trump 2017a). These tweets are aimed at politicizing the bureaucracy, signaling the president's stance to new appointees, and keeping others in line.

The use of appointments to politicize a bureaucracy is not without trade-offs (Lewis 2008). Appointees can be ill-suited for their jobs, leave after short stays, and even delegitimize the bureaucracy. President Trump is no stranger to ill-suited appointments, arguing that "[his] life would've been a lot easier" had he originally appointed William Barr rather than Jeff Sessions as the US attorney general (Ward 2020). The appointments of Jeff Sessions and Homeland Security Secretary Kirstjen Nielsen are two examples of ill-suited appointments (Graham 2019). Sessions angered the president by not un-recusing himself from the Russia investigation and not only eventually lost his position as attorney general but also continues to be attacked by Trump on social media months later. Nielsen, on the other hand, refused to carry out a Trump policy of preventing migrants from seeking asylum, arguing that such a policy was illegal. She, too, found herself unemployed. As Cohen (1998) points out, even political appointments can bring their own political agendas that do not always match that of the president. Nothing can guarantee the president complete responsive competence, even from those handpicked bureaucrats.

The Trump Administration's Approaches to Careerists

The ultimate goal of the president is to mobilize the neutral competence of an agency without compromising it. While political appointees are expected to keep agencies on target with presidential prerogatives and can be hired or fired at the will of the president, systems such as the merit system are designed to insulate careerists from the same political pressures. This does not however mean that the president has no ability to influence career bureaucrats. Many careerist positions are also remaining unfilled longer under President Trump's administration than his predecessors (Corrigan 2018). Doherty, Lewis, and Limbocker (2019) examine the likelihood of turnover among career bureaucrats in the Senior Executive Service (SES) during the transition between the Obama administration and Trump administration. They argue that because these administrators are in positions to affect agency policy and decision making, they are likely to be targeted as threats by an incoming presidential administration. The administration may seek to work around civil service protections by employing tactics to influence these bureaucrats to leave their jobs. Doherty and colleagues (2019) find that both efforts on the part of the administration to marginalize key employees as well as strategic exit choices on the part of the employees themselves led to increased turnover among career bureaucrats. The departure rate of SES employees in their study was close to 7 percent six months after the Obama–Trump transition, compared to 9.6 percent an entire year after transition in the previous four presidential administration transitions. Additionally, the Department of State (DOS), in particular, saw a decrease of 5.4 percent of foreign-affairs positions in Trump's first year in the White House. This is much lower than the prior two presidential transitions for hiring for State positions. During the one-year transition from Bush to Obama, the DOS saw a growth of 0.6 percent and an increase of 3.4 percent during the transition from Clinton to Bush for the same positions (Corrigan 2018).

While arguably careerists' departures between administrations result in realignment that is beneficial to developing bureaucratic support for the president's agenda and thus smoothing the friction associated with bureaucratic policy resistance (Doherty, Lewis, and Limbocker 2019), such departures also represent significant organizational costs. For instance, loss of institutional memory, the collective knowledge held within an organization, can inhibit organizational performance (Moynihan and Pandey 2008). Additionally, hiring or promoting and then subsequently training employees demands large resource expenditures of both time and money (Cho and Lewis 2012). Other costs include deleterious effects on employee morale as well as organizational productivity issues (Kim and Fernandez 2017). In sum, there may be a tipping point at which the turnover rate of senior careerists is too high for a presidential administration to fully reap the benefits of responsive competence in the face of the consequences of the loss of technical expertise.

DIRECT STRATEGIES: EXECUTIVE DIRECTIVES AND BUDGET GUIDANCE

In addition to indirectly pushing for change via presidential appointments and influencing careerist behavior, presidents can also be more actively involved in shaping policy change. Lewis and Moe (2013) discuss how presidents can alter policy by influencing the way bureaucracies interpret and implement legislation. While strategic political appointments offer the most sweeping approach to accomplish these goals, presidents also opt to utilize strategies that are more direct and targeted. Direct administrative strategies are characterized as uses of unilateral presidential power (Lowande and Milkis 2014; Waterman

2009) to shape policy by exerting influence on management and implementation processes (Rudalevige 2009). In general, a president has several tools for more directly controlling or, at least, influencing bureaucratic behavior at his disposal, including various forms of presidential directives and budgetary guidance (Durant and Warber 2001). We discuss President Trump's utilization of both of these types of tools.

Executive Directives

First, presidential memoranda and executive orders can be a particularly powerful tool for influencing agency rulemaking and regulatory processes (Thrower 2018). To illustrate, the Environmental Protection Agency (EPA) has been subjected to several presidential directives since 2000. Early in his administration, President Obama utilized the administrative rulemaking processes to address energy independence and climate change in lieu of engaging heavily with Congress on those issues, including increasing Corporate Average Fuel Economy (CAFE) standards (Lowande and Milkis 2014). Further, President George W. Bush shaped environmental policy by altering how the EPA interpreted the new-source review laws (Barcott 2004). Bush spoke to the public as a moderate and strongly encouraged Congress to pass sweeping environmental legislation, such as the Clear Skies Initiative. In private, however, Bush used executive orders, memoranda, and appointees in the EPA to achieve change, causing the new-source review program to be reversed without any legislation being passed in Congress.

President Trump has similarly worked through the rulemaking process to influence the way the EPA implements legislation. In fact, by December 2019, ninety-five environmental rules and regulations had been rolled back under his direction (Popvich, Albeck-Ripka, and Pierre-Louis 2019). Mr. Trump's strategy for change is in direct contrast with Bush's in that he does not have a moderate approach with the public. There is no effort to hide his bypass of Congress for the pursuit of deregulation. For instance, during his campaign he vowed to dismantle "every unconstitutional executive action, memorandum, and order issued by President Obama" (Noah and Schneier 2016) and declared that what the EPA does is a "disgrace" (Schoen 2016). While President Trump's use of executive orders is slightly elevated compared to other recent presidents, the biggest differences appear to be his polarizing rhetoric and insistence on advertising their promulgation (Freking 2019).

Executive Budgetary Guidance

Presidential initiation of the federal budget proposal process is another direct administrative strategy that allows the president to influence policy trajectories. Presidents frequently use the budgetary process to try to influence administrative and regulatory behavior (see Carpenter 1996; Wood and Waterman 1994). By restricting, increasing, or even reapportioning an agency's budget, the president is essentially signaling policy preferences and setting that agency's agenda (Carpenter 1996). For example, in 2018, President Trump's budget requested increases for the Departments of Veterans Affairs (VA), Homeland Security (DHS), and Defense (DOD) and funding decreases for the EPA, Department of State (DOS), and Department of Agriculture (DOA) (Milkis and Jacobs 2017). The 25 percent proposed budgetary cut to the DOS was a clear signal of President Trump's policy preferences. Those cuts in conjunction with increased spending for the VA, DHS, and DOD clearly demonstrated Trump's commitment to the use of military rather than diplomacy for protecting US national security interests (Aleem 2018). As discussed above, the two prior presidential administrations had grown the DOS (see Corrigan 2018). The DOS, though, is not without powerful allies in Congress, which has made presidential control via the budget process difficult. Both Republicans and Democrats in Congress defended against the slashing of the Department of State's budget.

Centrality of Social Media

As with his indirect strategies, President Trump has the tendency to use social media alongside his direct strategies of bureaucratic control. In addition to using Twitter as a human resource tool to fire appointees (e.g., Secretary of State Rex Tillerson), Trump has used the platform to signal budgetary preferences and direct agencies to change policy. For instance, in a stream of tweets on May 13, 2019, the president announced his support in his proposed budget for increases for NASA (Trump 2019c), the Special Olympics (Trump 2019b), and the Great Lakes Restoration Initiative (Trump 2019d). He has also frequently used Twitter to signal policy preferences to agencies, including the DOD and the Department of Justice (DOJ). In July 2017, President Trump tweeted that transgender members of the military would no longer be accepted or allowed to serve (Thompson 2019). The tweet represented a significant policy change to the military and appeared to catch the DOD, including the Joint Chiefs of Staff, by surprise. The DOD seemed unsure of how to handle a clear policy directive sent through such an informal fashion, and former senator John McCain, then chairman of the Senate Armed Services Committee, released a statement condemning the tweet as "yet another example of why major policy announcements should not be made via Twitter" (Mark 2017). President Trump has continued to use Twitter to signal policy preferences to DOD, including advocating for a new Space Force (Trump 2018b) and increased spending for the border wall (Trump 2019a). Most recently, President Trump turned to Twitter to signal policy preferences to DOJ on the Russia investigation, potential political corruption in the Ukraine (Trump 2020), and sentencing in the Roger Stone case (Trump 2019f). To date, only limited empirical work discusses the implications of President Trump's political signaling through Twitter for agency direction (Michaels and Williams 2017; Tillmann 2019), and his relative success in influencing administrative behavior through this medium remains unknown.

BUREAUCRATIC RESPONSES TO PRESIDENT TRUMP

In spite of the numerous direct and indirect administrative strategies available, the president should not expect bureaucratic control to come easily. Individual bureaucratic responses to principal control can vary from complete cooperation to resignation (see Golden 2000; Wilson 1989). Likewise, the responses of agencies themselves can range from compliance to sabotage (see Brehm and Gates 1999; Moe 1985). Each agency has its own agenda, support base, and an information advantage that empower agency resistance (Moe 1985).

Agency Agendas and Protest

Aligned with the exit, voice, and loyalty options posited in Hirschman's (1970) treatise, bureaucrats during the transition to the Trump administration utilized both exit and voice to protest a political agenda that they saw conflicting with their own agency agenda. For instance, one of Trump's campaign promises was to do away with "unnecessary" regulations, especially those within the EPA (Schoen 2016). Since taking office, President Trump followed through on this promise by rolling back regulations on water pollution from coal-fired power plants, coal ash disposal, and methane pollution on federal lands (Popvich, Albeck-Ripka, and Pierre-Louis 2019). EPA workers committed to environmental protection left in droves to protest these policy changes. By September 2018, 1,600 workers had left the agency, with only 400 positions filled, reducing the agency's workforce by 8 percent (Dennis, Eilperin, and Ba Tran 2018). Several veteran EPA employees said that the president's "profound policy shifts" influenced their choice to resign (Dennis, Eilperin, and Ba Tran 2018). The Department of State has also seen several employees resign in protest of the president's policies (see discussion in the Direct Strategies section).

Agencies tend to hire like-minded people who are committed to their mission and goals (Edwards, Mayer, and Wayne 2020). When the president interferes with an agency's agenda or tries to redirect agency attention, resistance through voice (Hirschman 1970) is almost guaranteed. During the Trump administration's transition, some federal agencies were ordered by memo to halt external communications as the administration controversially updated content to align with its viewpoints (Davenport 2017). In response, a number of "rogue" agency Twitter accounts such as AltUSNatParkService, Rogue NASA, and StuffEPAWouldSay, most not claiming connection to the real agencies, proliferated on Twitter, sharing opposition stances such as information about climate change (Davis 2017). Rosemary O'Leary in *The Ethics of Dissent* (2019) applies the term "guerrilla government" to these types of protest activities carried out by career bureaucrats intending to undermine or resist orders from their political superiors.

Agency Support Base and Defiance

Beyond the individual protest actions of career civil servants within agencies, President Trump has also experienced more collective responses to undercut political control. Sources of resistance to presidential interference can include jurisdictional power struggles, direction from congressional principals, and responsiveness to agency publics. First, agencies are very protective of their turf and do not usually respond positively when their jurisdiction is threatened (Peters 2014). The clearest illustration of jurisdictional protectiveness impeding presidential policy prerogatives might be captured within federal reorganization efforts in response to the terrorist acts of September 11, 2001; the Bush administration sought to restructure the federal bureaucracy, redefining jurisdictions, missions, and goals for several agencies. The goal was to facilitate more cohesive policy across a number of issue areas, including transportation, border security, and natural disaster preparedness with the creation of the Department of Homeland Security (DHS). Agencies such as the Federal Bureau of Investigation, the National Security Agency, and the Central Intelligence Agency were able to maintain their dominance within their respective jurisdictions and avoid being merged with the new DHS. Each of the major intelligence bureaus was also able to maintain independence and autonomy by engaging their political capital and arguing that they had represented critical functions that may be negatively impacted by a merge with the new department. While the Trump administration has not attempted a reorganization of this scale, a similar sense of jurisdictional ownership has resulted in obstacles and infighting across numerous agencies. For instance, Isenstadt and Restuccia (2017) depict tension between career bureaucrats and former Trump campaign staffers assigned to agencies to help with the administration's transition; they describe actions taken against the former staffers including shutting them out of agency meetings and deliberations, leaking reputation-damaging information, and reassigning them to other parts of the government to prevent them from encroaching on careerists' turf.

In addition to their internal jurisdictional battles, bureaucracies also frequently enjoy the support of powerful allies, including congressional committees and interest groups, and, as such, the president is not the only political principal from whom bureaucrats take direction. Congress controls both an agency's budget and the legislation that agency is responsible for implementing. Therefore, presidential influence is constrained not just by bureaucratic preferences but also by the legislative branch, which may or may not be sympathetic to the president's agenda (Lewis 2003; Moe 1985). For instance, President Trump's budget proposals have continually called for deep cuts to the Department of State budget (23 percent in the 2020 budget proposal), and Congress has repeatedly rejected these drastic cuts (George 2019).

Finally, agencies must balance direction from Congress and the president with the influence of their own constituents. Scholarship on mass publics suggests that programs can create powerful, politically influential publics (see Campbell 2012). The American Association of Retired Persons (AARP) is a powerful interest group representing the interests of Americans aged fifty-five and older. The AARP is a political ally of a variety of political programs that benefit their members, such as the Social Security Administration (SSA). Former president George W. Bush can attest to the political power of a constituency group, such as the AARP, in protecting programs from presidential interference. In the early 2000s, then President Bush pushed for the privatization of Social Security retirement accounts. The AARP mobilized against the reform and "launched a multimillion-dollar campaign to defeat Bush's plan using newspaper ads, phone banks, pollsters and an army of activists" (Zuckman 2005). Bush's campaign for Social Security reform lasted roughly six months before he gave up, and during this time he saw his disapproval rating rise 16 percentage points (Galston 2007). Bush was less popular and Social Security policy remained untouched. In February 2020, President Trump released a budget proposal in which the SSA would see budget cuts for disability insurance rather than retirement payments (Picchi 2020). It is unclear how this will pan out for an agency that has historically been protected by an influential constituency.

Information Advantage of Agents

Bureaucratic agencies also tend to have an informational advantage over the president. In the principal–agent theory, information asymmetry between the president and the bureaucracy often leaves the president at a disadvantage. Bureaucracies have policy specialization and accumulated knowledge that the president does not possess. The principals (the president or Congress) do not have enough information regarding the policy problem or the actions of the agents, both of which help make controlling bureaucracies impossible and influencing bureaucracies difficult (Brehm and Gates 1999; Moe 1989). The research in this area is often focused on how principals (the president and/or Congress) can ensure bureaucratic compliance (see Lewis and Moe 2013; Miller 2005) and agency response to such attempts at control (see Brehm and Gates 1999; Golden 2000; Wilson 1989).

The expertise of an agency gives it some power against political interference, and Thurber (1996) argues that information is power in subsystem policy making. Information, after all, is a necessary ingredient for the policy-making process, from problem definition and agenda setting to formulation and evaluation. Bureaucrats supply information to policymakers throughout the policy process (for example, see Workman [2015] for the role of federal bureaucrats in agenda setting). In fact, in times of crisis, members of Congress, in particular, are more likely to rely on (and prioritize) bureaucrats as information suppliers (Workman, Shafran, and Bark 2017). Both Democratic and Republican members of Congress requested that the president allow an expert, such the director of the National Institute of Allergy and Infectious Diseases, Dr. Anthony Fauci, to take the lead on the public information campaign and provide a *consistent* message to the public (Lutz 2020).

President Trump at times seems unappreciative of bureaucratic expertise, the Centers for Disease Control and Prevention (CDC) being one such example. During each year of his tenure, Trump has requested cuts to the CDC's budget (Alesse 2020). Again, in early 2020, Mr. Trump proposed more cuts to the agency's budget, proposing a 16 percent overall decrease in agency funding. By the beginning of March 2020, a pandemic caused by a novel coronavirus (COVID-19) was sweeping the globe (Chappell 2020). COVID-19 was moving quickly from country to country, and many countries, like Italy, were struggling to manage the devastation. The CDC quickly proved its expertise was invaluable for confronting the COVID-19 crisis and for US public health, more generally. Within weeks of calling for cuts to the CDC, President Trump walked back requests for funding cuts (Elis 2020).

The information asymmetry between the president and the administrative state is exacerbated by problems of adverse selection (the inability of the principal to have full information about the agent) and moral hazard (the inability of the principal to determine if the agent's actions are in the principal's best interests) (Brehm and Gates 1999; Moe 1989). Further, the principal's moral hazard, the possibility that the principal's goals are self-destructive, is another obstacle for controlling bureaucracies (Miller 2005). Sometimes a decision that seemingly goes against the principal's interests is necessary for reaching long-term policy goals (Miller 2005). President Trump's former chief of staff, John Kelly, claims that before he resigned in January 2019, he warned Mr. Trump against hiring "yes men" (Romero 2019). Kelly argued that if the president did not have a capable chief of staff, impeachment would follow. President Trump was formally impeached by the US House of Representatives on December 18, 2019. While no one will ever know if a different chief of staff could have more successfully steered the president through his dealings with Ukraine or the subsequent investigation by the House, Kelly's argument illustrates that well-informed administrators are sometimes necessary for protecting the president from acting against his own self-interest.

CONCLUSION

In many ways, much of President Trump's appeal to his supporters is his unique persona and "tell-it-like-it-is" style. He says what he thinks and has an unconventional management style. Compared to his predecessors, his tone and approach to communication with his administration is very distinctive. However, neither his skepticism of bureaucrats, particularly careerists, nor his use of the bureaucracy to influence policy is unorthodox. While President Trump has not sought to offer an overarching vision for his administrative strategy (Milkis and Jacobs 2017), as with most modern presidents, he has capitalized on a number of direct and indirect tools—not to deconstruct the administrative state but rather to direct administrative services and influence policy.

One of the most unique aspects of the Trump administration is the president's frequent use of Twitter as a mode of official communication. This approach fits with populist characterizations of President Trump as he uses social media to connect directly to his constituents and avoid the "gatekeeping and interpretation functions of the media" (Boucher and Thies 2019, 712). However, while supporters of President Trump may endorse his use of social media to communicate, it does not appear that this sentiment is shared by bureaucrats—careerist or otherwise. According to the *Wall Street Journal*, Attorney General William Barr has pleaded with Mr. Trump to cease tweeting and talking about the US Department of Justice cases, specifically the case of Roger Stone (Viswanatha and Gurman 2020). Barr argued that the president's tweets and comments were counterproductive for the agency.

Further, while it may be a preferred method for President Trump, his tweets to direct administrative actions have been legally used against him on more than one occasion. Two such examples are the legal disputes over Affordable Care Act (ACA) subsidies and the travel ban (Rucker and Costa 2017). The US Court of Appeals for the District of Columbia Circuit ruled in late July 2017 that a group of state attorneys general had legal standing to fight for ACA subsidies, which both the Trump administration and House Republicans had suggested be abandoned. The court cited "accumulating public statements by high-level officials" as part of their reasoning, alluding to presidential tweets (Goldstein 2017). In the case of the travel ban, the Trump administration was arguing that the ban was necessary for public safety and was *not* aimed at entire countries (Rucker and Costa 2017). The US Court of Appeals for the Ninth Circuit ruled against the ban in June 2017, citing, in part, a tweet from President Trump that said, "That's right, we need a TRAVEL BAN for certain DANGEROUS countries, not some politically correct term that won't help us protect our people!" (Trump 2017b). In both of these examples, the president's tweets hurt his efforts to direct policy change.

In other instances, such as the transgender ban in the military, tweets attempting to change administrative behavior have backfired by catching key managers off guard or being undermined by the agency itself (Thompson 2019). In the case of the transgender ban, in the days following Trump's tweets declaring a ban on transgender military members in July 2017, the Joint Chiefs of Staff declared that no change would be made without formal White House guidance. Coast Guard Commandant Admiral Paul Zukunft publicly stated that he supported those transgender members serving alongside him (Mitchell 2017).

For President Trump, his personality and public appeal is supported by both the use of social media and his tone of communication. It is unlikely that this strategy is effective universally. It is difficult to imagine this style of communication being effective for a more soft-spoken or less charismatic presidential candidate. Most likely, future presidents who were to try to employ such a managerial strategy would have all of the risks: tweets used against them in legal battles and lack of bureaucratic response—without the rewards of public support.

REFERENCES

Aleem, Zeeshan. "Trump Wants to Gut the State Department by 25 Percent: You Read That Right." Vox, February 12, 2018. https://www.vox.com/pol icy-and-politics/2018/2/12/17004372/trump-budget-state-department -defense-cuts.

Alesse, Liz. "Did Trump Try to Cut the CDC's Budget as Democrats Claim?: Analysis." ABC News, February 28, 2020. https://abcnews.go.com/Politics /trump-cut-cdcs-budget-democrats-claim-analysis/story?id=69233170.

Barcott, Bruce. "Changing All the Rules." *New York Times Magazine.* April 4, 2004. https://www.nytimes.com/2004/04/04/magazine/changing-all-the -rules.html.

Boucher, Jean-Christophe, and Cameron G. Thies. "'I Am a Tariff Man': The Power of Populist Foreign Policy Rhetoric under President Trump." *Journal of Politics* 81, no. 2 (2019): 712–722.

Brehm, John O., and Scott Gates. *Working, Shirking, and Sabotage: Bureaucratic Response to a Democratic Public.* Ann Arbor: University of Michigan Press, 1999.

Campbell, Andrea Louise. "Policy Makes Mass Politics." *Annual Review of Political Science* 15 (2012): 333–351.

Carpenter, Daniel P. "Adaptive Signal Processing, Hierarchy, and Budgetary Control in Federal Regulation." *American Political Science Review* 90, no. 2 (1996): 283–302.

Chappell, Bill. "Coronavirus: COVID-19 Is Now Officially a Pandemic, WHO Says." National Public Radio, March 11, 2020. https://www.npr.org/sections /goatsandsoda/2020/03/11/814474930/coronavirus-covid-19-is-now-offi cially-a-pandemic-who-says.

Cho, Yoon Jik, and Gregory B. Lewis. "Turnover Intention and Turnover Behavior: Implications for Retaining Federal Employees." *Review of Public Personnel Administration* 32, no. 1 (2012): 4–23.

Cohen, David M. "Amateur Government." *Journal of Public Administration Research and Theory* 8, no. 4 (1998): 450–497.

Corrigan, Jack. "The Hollowing Out of the State Department Continues." *Atlantic*, February 11, 2018. https://www.theatlantic.com/international / archive/2018/02/tillerson-trump-state-foreign-service/553034/.

Davenport, Carol. "Federal Agencies Told to Halt External Communications." *New York Times*, January 25, 2020. https://www.nytimes.com/2017 /01/25 /us/politics/some-agencies-told-to-halt-communications-as-trump-admin istration-moves-in.html.

Davis, Wynne. "It's Not Just the Park Service: 'Rogue' Federal Twitter Accounts Multiply." National Public Radio. January 27, 2020. https://www.npr .org/sections/alltechconsidered/2017/01/27/512007632/its-not-just-the -park-service-rogue-federal-twitter-accounts-multiply.

Dennis, Brady, Juliet Eilperin, and Andrew Ba Tran. "Staff Exodus Hits EPA Under Trump: 'I Could Do Better Work to Protect the Environment Outside.'" *Washington Post*, September 8, 2018. https://www.chicagotribune .com/nation-world/ct-epa-workforce-trump-analysis-20180908-story.html.

Doherty, Kathleen M., David E. Lewis, and Scott Limbocker "Presidential Control and Turnover in Regulatory Personnel." *Administration & Society* 51, no. 10 (2018): 1606–1630.

Durant, Robert F., and Adam L. Warber. "Networking in the Shadow of Hierarchy: Public Policy, the Administrative Presidency, and the Neoadministrative State." *Presidential Studies Quarterly* 31, no. 2 (2001): 221–244.

Edwards, George C. III. "Why Not the Best? Loyalty-Competence Tradeoffs in

Presidential Appointments." In *Innocent until Nominated: The Breakdown of the Presidential Appointment Process*, edited by G. Calvin MacKenzie, 81–106. Washington, DC: Brookings Institution Press, 2001.

Edwards, George C. III, Kenneth R. Mayer, and Stephen J. Wayne. *Presidential Leadership: Politics and Policy Making.* New York: Rowman & Littlefield, 2020.

Elis, Niv. "Trump Reverses on Request to Cut CDC, NIAID Funding." Hill. com. March 19, 2020. https://thehill.com/policy/finance/488521-trump -reverses-on-request-to-cut-cdc-niaid-funding.

Etzioni-Halevy, Eva. *Bureaucracy and Democracy.* New York: Routledge, 2013.

Freking, Kevin. "Trump Derided Obama's Executive Orders as 'Power Grabs.' But in Each Year of His Presidency, Trump Has Surpassed Obama's Total over the Same Time Span." *Chicago Tribune,* October 19, 2019. https:// www.chicagotribune.com/nation-world/ct-nw-trump-obama-executive-or ders-20191019-fkj23rhqgncdfd7dkmztimofky-story.html.

Galston, William A. "Why the 2005 Social Security Initiative Failed, and What It Means for the Future." Brookings.edu. September 21, 2007. https://www .brookings.edu/research/why-the-2005-social-security-initiative-failed -and-what-it-means-for-the-future/.

GAO. "Government Wide Political Appointee Data and Some Ethics Oversight Procedures at Interior and SBA Could Be Improved." GAO. Retrieved January 18, 2019. https://www.gao.gov/assets/700/697593.pdf.

George, Susannah. "Lawmakers Hammer Trump's Proposed State Department Cuts." AP News. March 27, 2019. https://apnews.com/28ff8bd1e1ee 477b837eb938db0b6f1c.

Golden, Marissa Martino. *What Motivates Bureaucrats?: Politics and Administration during the Reagan Years.* New York: Columbia University Press, 2000.

Goldstein, Amy. "Court Ruling Could Help Keep Obamacare Subsidies." *Washington Post,* August 1, 2017. https://www.washingtonpost.com/na tional/health-science/court-ruling-could-help-keep-obamacare-subsi dies/2017/08/01/85b3ab66-7727-11e7-9eac-d56bd5568db8_story.html ?itid=lk_inline_manual_4.

Gore, Al. "Creating a Government That Works Better and Costs Less: Reinventing Environmental Management. Accompanying Report of the National Performance Review." United States, September 1, 1993.

Graham, David A. "Ratcliffe's Withdrawal Reveals Trump Still Doesn't Understand Appointments." *Atlantic.* August 2, 2019. https://www.theatlantic .com/ideas/archive/2019/08/whom-do-political-appointees-serve /595342/.

Gvosdev, Nikolas K., Jessica D. Blankshain, and David A. Cooper. *Decision-Making in American Foreign Policy: Translating Theory Into Practice.* New York, NY: Cambridge University Press, 2019.

Hechinger, Fred M. "The Reagan Effect: The Department that Would not Die." *New York Times,* November 14, 1982. https://www.nytimes.com/1982

/11/14/education/the-reagan-effect-the-department-that-would-not-die
.html.

Hirschman, Albert O. *Exit, Voice, and Loyalty: Responses to Decline in Firms, Organizations, and States.* Cambridge: Harvard University Press, 1970.

Hult, Karen, and Robert Maranto. "Does Where You Stand Depend on Where You Sit? Careerists' Attitudes toward Political Appointees under Reagan." *American Review of Politics* 31 (2010): 91–112.

Isenstadt, Alex, and Andrew Restuccia. "Civil War Rages Throughout Trump Administration." Politico.com. April 6, 2017. https://www.politico.com /story/2017/04/trump-white-house-civil-war-236917.

Joung, Madeline. "Trump Has Now Had More Cabinet Turnover than Reagan, Obama, and the Two Bushes." *Time,* July 12, 2019. https://time.com / 5625699/trump-cabinet-acosta/.

Kim, Sun Young, and Sergio Fernandez. "Employee Empowerment and Turnover Intention in the US Federal Bureaucracy." *American Review of Public Administration* 47, no. 1 (2017): 4–22.

Krause, George A., and Anne Joseph O'Connell. "Loyalty–Competence Trade-offs for Top US Federal Bureaucratic Leaders in the Administrative Presidency Era." *Presidential Studies Quarterly* 49, no. 3 (2019): 527–550.

Lewis, David E. *Presidents and the Politics of Agency Design: Political Insulation in the United States Government Bureaucracy, 1946–1997.* Stanford, CA: Stanford University Press, 2003.

———. *The Politics of Presidential Appointments: Political Control and Bureaucratic Performance.* Princeton, NJ: Princeton University Press, 2008.

———. "Deconstructing the Administrative State." *Journal of Politics* 81, no. 3 (2019): 767–789.

Lewis, David E., Patrick Bernhard, and Emily You. "President Trump as Manager: Reflections on the First Year." *Presidential Studies Quarterly* 48, no. 3 (2018): 480–501.

Lewis, David E., and Terry M. Moe. "Struggling Over Bureaucracy: The Levers of Control." In *The Presidency and the Political System,* 10th ed., edited by Michael Nelson. Washington, DC: CQ, 2013.

Lipton, Eric, and Binyamin Applebaum. "Leashes Come off Wall Street, Gun Sellers, Polluters, and More." *New York Times,* March 5, 2017. https://www .nytimes.com/2017/03/05/us/politics/trump-deregulation-guns-wall-st -climate.html.

Lowande, Kenneth S., and Sidney M. Milkis. "'We Can't Wait': Barack Obama, Partisan Polarization and the Administrative Presidency." *Forum* 12, no. 1 (2014): 3–27. De Gruyter.

Lu, Denise, and Karen Yourish. "The Turnover at the Top of the Trump Administration." *New York Times,* March 16, 2018. https://www.nytimes.com /interactive/2018/03/16/us/politics/all-the-major-firings-and-resigna tions-in-trump-administration.html.

Lutz, Eric. "Poll: Most Americans Aren't Trusting Trump on Coronavirus." *Vanity Fair*, March 17, 2020. https://www.vanityfair.com/news/2020/03/poll-most-americans-arent-trusting-trump-on-coronavirus.

Mark, Michelle. "McCain Slams Trump's Transgender Military Ban, Says It's Why 'Major Policy Announcements Should not Be Made via Twitter.'" *Business Insider*, July 26, 2017. https://www.businessinsider.com/john-mccain-trump-transgender-military-ban-tweets-2017-7.

McIntire, Mike, Karen Yourish, and Larry Buchanan. "In Trump's Twitter Feed: Conspiracy-Mongers, Racists and Spies." *New York Times*, November 2, 2019. https://www.nytimes.com/interactive/2019/11/02/us/politics/trump-twitter-disinformation.html.

Meier, Kenneth J., Laurence J. O'Toole, Jr., and Laurence J. O'Toole. *Bureaucracy in a Democratic State: A Governance Perspective*. Baltimore: Johns Hopkins University Press, 2006.

Michaels, Jeffrey, and Heather Williams. "The Nuclear Education of Donald J. Trump." *Contemporary Security Policy* 38, no. 1 (2017): 54–77.

Milkis, Sidney M., and Nicholas Jacobs. "'I Alone Can Fix It': Donald Trump, the Administrative Presidency, and Hazards of Executive-Centered Partisanship." *Forum* 15, no. 3 (2017): 583–613. De Gruyter.

Miller, Gary J. "The Political Evolution of Principal-Agent Models." *Annual Review of Political Science* 8 (2005): 203–225.

Mitchell, Ellen. "Military Pushes Back on Trump's Transgender Ban." Hill.com. August 13, 2017. https://thehill.com/policy/defense/346261-military-pushes-back-on-trumps-transgender-ban.

Moe, Terry M. "Control and Feedback in Economic Regulation: The Case of the NLRB." *American Political Science Review* 79, no. 4 (1985): 1094–1116.

———. "The Politicized Presidency." In *The New Direction in American Politics*, ed. John Chubb and Paul Peterson, 235–271. Washington, DC: Brookings Institution, 1989.

Moynihan, Donald P., and Sanjay K. Pandey. "The Ties That Bind: Social Networks, Person-Organization Value Fit, and Turnover Intention." *Journal of Public Administration Research and Theory* 18, no. 2 (2008): 205–227.

Moynihan, Donald P., and Alasdair S. Roberts. "The Triumph of Loyalty over Competence: The Bush Administration and the Exhaustion of the Politicized Presidency." *Public Administration Review* 70, no. 4 (2010): 572–581.

Nathan, Richard P. *The Administrative Presidency*. Hoboken, NJ: John Wiley & Sons, 1983.

Noah, Timothy, and Cogan Schneier. "Trump Poised to Erase Obama Policies." Politico.com. November 10, 2016. https://www.politico.com/story/2016/11/trump-erase-obama-policies-231156.

O'Connell, Anne Joseph. "After One Year in Office, Trump's Behind on Staffing but Making Steady Progress." Brookings.edu. January 23, 2018.

https://www.brookings.edu/research/after-one-year-in-office-trumps-be
hind-on-staffing-but-making-steady-progress/.

———. "Actings." *Columbia Law Review* 120, no. 613 (2020): 3–728.

O'Leary, Rosemary. *The Ethics of Dissent: Managing Guerrilla Government.* 3rd
ed. Washington, DC: CQ, 2019.

Ouyang, Yu, Evan T. Haglund, and Richard W. Waterman. "The Missing Element: Examining the Loyalty-Competence Nexus in Presidential Appointments." *Presidential Studies Quarterly* 47, no. 1 (2017): 62–91.

Partnership for Public Service. "Political Appointee Tracker." Retrieved March
22, 2020, from https://ourpublicservice.org/political-appointee-tracker/.

Peters, B. Guy. "The Politics of Bureaucracy." In *The Politics of Bureaucracy*, 5th
ed. New York: Routledge, 2014.

Phillips, Amy. "Trumps Tweets Keep Being Used against Him in a Court of
Law." *Washington Post*, August 2, 2017. https://www.washingtonpost.com
/news/the-fix/wp/2017/08/02/trumps-tweets-keep-being-used-against
-him-in-a-court-of-law/.

Picchi, Aimee. "Social Security: Here's What Trump's Proposed Budget
Could Mean for Your Benefits." usatoday.com. February 12, 2020. https://
www.usatoday.com/story/money/2020/02/12/social-security-trump
-budget-aims-cuts-disabled-workers-program/4738795002.

Popvich, Nadja, Livia Albeck-Ripka, and Kendra Pierre-Louis. "95 Environmental Rules Being Rolled Back under Trump." *New York Times*, December
21, 2019. https://www.nytimes.com/interactive/2019/climate/trump-en
vironment-rollbacks.html.

Raines, Howell. "Reagan Adopts Plan to End Energy Dept. and Shift Its Duties."
New York Times, December 17, 1981. https://www.nytimes.com/1981/12/17
/us/reagan-adopts-plan-to-end-energy-dept-and-shift-its-duties.html.

Rohr, John Anthony. *To Run a Constitution: The Legitimacy of the Administrative
State.* Lawrence: University Press of Kansas, 1986.

Romero, Dennis. "John Kelly Says He Told Trump a 'Yes Man' Would Get
Him Impeached." *NBC News*, October 26, 2019. https://www.nbcnews.com
/politics/donald-trump/john-kelly-says-he-told-trump-yes-man-would-get
-n1072491.

Rosenbloom, David H. "Public Administrative Theory and the Separation of
Powers." *Public Administration Review* 43, no. 3 (1983): 219–227.

Rourke, Francis E. "Burcaucracy in the American Constitutional Order." *Political Science Quarterly* 102, no. 2 (1987): 217–232.

Rucker, Phillip, and Robert Costa. "Bannon Vows a Daily 'Deconstruction
of the Administrative State.'" *Washington Post*, February 23, 2017. https://
www.washingtonpost.com/politics/top-wh-strategist-vows-a-daily-fight-for
-deconstruction-of-the-administrative-state/2017/02/23/03f6b8da-f9ea
-11e6-bf01-d47f8cf9b643_story.html.

Rudalevige, Andrew. "The Administrative Presidency and Bureaucratic Control: Implementing a Research Agenda." *Presidential Studies Quarterly* 39, no. 1 (2009): 10–24.

Rung, Margaret C. "Richard Nixon, State, and Party: Democracy and Bureaucracy in the Postwar Era." *Presidential Studies Quarterly* 29, no. 2 (1999): 421–437.

Schoen, John W. "Regulation Buster Trump Takes Aim at the EPA." CNBC. November 10, 2016. https://www.cnbc.com/2016/11/09/regulation-buster-trump-takes-aim-at-the-epa.html.

Shear, Michael D., Julie Hirschfeld Davis, and Adam Liptak. "How the Trump Administration Eroded Its Own Legal Case on DACA." *New York Times.* November 11, 2019. https://www.nytimes.com/2019/11/11/us/politics/supreme-court-dreamers-case.html.

Tenpas, Kathryn Dunn. "White House Staff Turnover in Year One of the Trump Administration: Context, Consequences, and Implications for Governing." *Presidential Studies Quarterly* 48, no. 502 :(2018) 3–516.

Thompson, Matt. "How to Spark Panic and Confusion in Three Tweets: Do Impulsive Twitter Messages from the President Count as Formal Policy Action?" *Atlantic,* January 13, 2019. https://www.theatlantic.com/politics/archive/2019/01/donald-trump-tweets-transgender-military-service-ban/579655/.

Thrower, Sharece. "Policy Disruption through Regulatory Delay in the Trump Administration." *Presidential Studies Quarterly* 48, no. 3 (2018): 517–536.

Thurber, James A. "Political Power and Policy Subsystems in American Politics." In *Agenda for Excellence: Administering the State,* ed. B. Guy Peters and Bert A. Rockman, 403–408. Chatham, NJ: Chatham House, 1996.

Tillmann, Peter. "Trump, Twitter, and Treasuries." *Contemporary Economic Policy* 2020. doi:10.1111/coep.12465.

Trump, Donald. [@realDonaldTrump]. June 3, 2015. Bureaucratic red tape and overregulation are discouraging the American dream. It's time for a bold new direction! [Tweet]. Retrieved from https://twitter.com/realdonaldtrump/status/606172248995692544.

———. [@realDonaldTrump.] May 10, 2017a. James Comey will be replaced by someone who will do a far better job, bringing back the spirit and prestige of the FBI. [Tweet]. Retrieved from https://twitter.com/realdonaldtrump/status/862265729718128641.

———. [@realDonaldTrump.] June 5, 2017b. That's right, we need a TRAVEL BAN for certain DANGEROUS countries, not some politically correct term that won't help us protect our people! [Tweet] Retrieved from https://twitter.com/realdonaldtrump/status/871899511525961728.

———. [@realDonaldTrump.] May 23, 2018a. Look how things have turned around on the Criminal Deep State. They go after Phony Collusion with Russia, a made up Scam, and end up getting caught in a major SPY scandal the likes of which this country may never have seen before! What goes around, comes around! [Tweet]. Retrieved from https://twitter.com/real donaldtrump/status/999242039723163648.

_____. [@realDonaldTrump.] August 9, 2018b. Space Force all the way! [Tweet]. Retrieved from https://twitter.com/realdonaldtrump/status /1027586174448 218113.

_____. [@realDonaldTrump.] December 7, 2018c. Mike Pompeo is doing a great job, I am very proud of him. His predecessor, Rex Tillerson, didn't have the mental capacity needed. He was dumb as a rock and I couldn't get rid of him fast enough. He was lazy as hell. Now it is a whole new ballgame, great spirit at State! [Tweet]. Retrieved from https://twitter.com/realdon aldtrump/status/1071132880368132096.

_____. [@realDonaldTrump.] January 20, 2019d. Don't forget, we are building and renovating big sections of Wall right now. Moving quickly, and will cost far less than previous politicians thought possible. Building, after all, is what I do best, even when money is not readily available! [Tweet]. Retrieved from https://twitter.com/realdonaldtrump/status /1086991976598245377.

_____. [@realDonaldTrump.] May 13, 2019e. Today, I officially updated my budget to include $18 million for our GREAT @SpecialOlympics, whose athletes inspire us and make our Nation so PROUD! [Tweet]. Retrieved from https://twitter.com/realdonaldtrump/status /1128052763 118718976.

_____. [@realDonaldTrump.] May 13, 2019a. Under my Administration, we are restoring @NASA to greatness and we are going back to the Moon, then Mars. I am updating my budget to include an additional $1.6 billion so that we can return to Space in a BIG WAY! [Tweet]. Retrieved from https://twitter.com/realdonaldtrump/status/1128050996545036288.

_____. [@realDonaldTrump.] May 13, 2019b. We must protect our Great Lakes, keeping them clean and beautiful for future generations. That's why I am fighting for $300 million in my updated budget for the Great Lakes Restoration Initiative. [Tweet]. Retrieved from https://twitter.com /realdonaldtrump/status/1128051913419837442.

_____. [@realDonaldTrump.] October 17, 2019c. Tonight, we forcefully condemn the blatant corruption of the Democrat Party, the Fake News Media, and the rogue bureaucrats of the Deep State. The only message these radicals will understand is a crushing defeat on November 3, 2020! #KAG2020. [Tweet]. Retrieved from https://twitter.com/realdonaldtrump/status /1185029472132698113.

_____. [@realDonaldTrump.] November 15, 2019d. So they now convict Roger Stone of lying and want to jail him for many years to come. Well, what about Crooked Hillary, Comey, Strzok, Page, McCabe, Brennan, Clapper, Shifty Schiff, Ohr & Nellie, Steele & all of the others, including even

Mueller himself? Didn't they lie?. . . . [Tweet]. Retrieved from https:// twitter.com/realdonaldtrump/status/1195389483664990208.

_____. [@realDonaldTrump.] January 2, 2020. A lot of very good people were taken down by a small group of Dirty (Filthy) Cops, politicians, government officials, and an investigation that was illegally started & that SPIED on my campaign. The Witch Hunt is sputtering badly, but still going on (Ukraine Hoax!). If this . . . [Tweet]. Retrieved from https://twitter .com/realdonaldtrump/status/1212734794762784768.

Viswanatha, Aruna, and Sadie Gurman. "New Developments Feed Debate on Justice Department Independence." *Wall Street Journal*, February 14, 2020. https://www.wsj.com/articles/trump-again-tweets-about-justice-depart ment-after-barr-urges-a-stop-11581692081.

Waldo, Dwight. *The Administrative State: A Study of the Political Theory of American Public Administration*. New York: Routledge, 1948.

Ward, Myah. "Trump: 'Life Would've Been a lot Easier' Had I Picked Barr over Sessions." *Politico*, February 13, 2020. https://www.politico.com/news /2020/02/13/trump-bill-barr-jeff-sessions-114918.

Waterman, Richard W. "The Administrative Presidency, Unilateral Power, and the Unitary Executive Theory." *Presidential Studies Quarterly* 39, no. 1 (2009): 5–9.

Wilson, James Q. *Bureaucracy: What Government Agencies Do and Why They Do It*. New York: Basic, 1989.

Wilson, Woodrow. "The Study of Administration." *Political Science Quarterly* 2, no. 2 (1887): 197–222.

Wood, B. Dan, and Richard W. Waterman. *Bureaucratic Dynamics: The Role of Bureaucracy in a Democracy*. Boulder, CO: Westview, 1994.

Workman, Samuel. *The Dynamics of Bureaucracy in the US Government: How Congress and Federal Agencies Process Information and Solve Problems*. New York, NY: Cambridge University Press, 2015.

Workman, Samuel, JoBeth S. Shafran, and Tracey Bark. "Problem Definition and Information Provision by Federal Bureaucrats." *Cognitive Systems Research* 43 (2017): 140–152.

Zuckman, Jill. "AARP: Don't Mess with Social Security." *Chicago Tribune*, January 30, 2005. https://www.chicagotribune.com/news/ct-xpm-2005-01-30 -0501300337-story.html.

CHAPTER 9

Trump and the Judiciary: Courting Conservatives and Controversy

Thomas Rogers Hunter

INTRODUCTION

Almost every American president has had an at least somewhat contentious relationship with the federal judiciary. More than any of his
predecessors, however, President Donald Trump has openly criticized
both individual judges as well as entire courts, with such even leading
to a rebuke from United States chief justice John Roberts. Ironically,
though, the president at least partially owes his election to his promise
to appoint conservatives to the federal judiciary. In this he has both
stayed true to his word and been quite successful, although some of
these appointments have raised much controversy. This chapter will
detail President Trump's relationship to the American judiciary, both
in the statements he has made and, more importantly, in the judges
he has appointed.

COMMENTS ON COURTS AND JUDGES

Conflicts between presidents and the federal judiciary go back almost
to the founding of the nation. Thomas Jefferson, for instance, de-
spised his cousin Chief Justice John Marshall, and it was Jefferson's ad-
herents in the US House who impeached Marshall's colleague Samuel

Chase—had they been successful in removal, Marshall himself would have likely been next (Beveridge 1919, 157–222). More recently, Franklin Roosevelt was so upset with decisions striking down chunks of his New Deal that he attempted to "pack" the Supreme Court with up to six additional justices (Solomon 2009; Shesol 2010).

Such frontal assaults on the judiciary have been extraordinarily rare, however, with a more common occurrence being an offhand presidential comment about a particular justice or decision. For instance, Theodore Roosevelt felt that he "could carve out of a banana a judge with more backbone" than Oliver Wendell Holmes, while Harry Truman called appointee Tom Clark "a dumb son of a bitch" (Purdum 2005). Dwight Eisenhower likewise told a leading newsman that the two biggest mistakes of his presidency were "both sitting on the Supreme Court," those being William Brennan and Chief Justice Earl Warren (Hentoff 1990). Even Barack Obama had the temerity to call out the Supreme Court and its *Citizens United* decision during his 2010 State of the Union address, which caused Justice Samuel Alito to shake his head and mouth the words "not true" (Toobin 2012, 192–199).

Still, Donald Trump's criticisms of the federal judiciary, especially the lower federal courts, have been both significantly more numerous and, given the amplifying effects of social media, more widely noticed. Throughout his private career, Trump and his businesses had numerous interactions with the judicial system, and since his election as president, he has found "himself in both personal and professional legal jeopardy. Several of his former aides and advisors have been criminally indicted. The administration's every move is subject to major lawsuits" (Jaffe 2019). Whenever the justice system has threatened to upend the president's plans or bring discomfort to his friends, he has been quick to take to social media with harsh criticism.

That the president would be so combative in this realm is not surprising, given his statements during the 2016 campaign. In the spring of that year, candidate Trump began attacking US District Court judge Gonzalo Curiel, who was hearing cases brought by former attendees of "Trump University"—a misnamed expensive real estate and wealth-creation course. Upset about some of the judge's rulings, Trump launched personal attacks against Curiel, both because he had been appointed to the bench by Barack Obama and because of the judge's Mexican heritage—while Judge Curiel had been born in Indiana, his parents had earlier emigrated from Mexico. Even when such attacks caused almost universal condemnation—including Republican

Speaker of the US House Paul Ryan labeling them a "textbook definition of a racist comment"—Trump doubled down on his allegations.
In a June 2016 interview on CNN, he told Jake Tapper, "I've had ruling
after ruling that's been bad rulings, OK? I've been treated very unfairly.
. . . Let me just tell you, I've had horrible rulings, I've been treated
very unfairly by this judge. Now, this judge is of Mexican heritage. I'm
building a wall, OK?" When Tapper mentioned that it was problematic
to "invoke [the judge's] race as a reason why he can't do his job," the
candidate responded, "I think that's why he's doing it. I think that's
why he's doing it" (Brennan Center 2020; Wolf 2018; Hulse 2019, 146).

Trump's attacks were not just reserved for a federal trial court judge
who was hearing a case that directly affected him. At a town hall in
South Carolina the previous December, he told the crowd that Chief
Justice John Roberts's decision to uphold the Affordable Care Act was
"disgraceful," adding, "I think he did it because he wanted to be popular in the beltway or something" (Phelps 2015).

Such early attacks on the judiciary, and other governmental institutions, caused Justice Ruth Bader Ginsburg, in July 2016, to tell the *New
York Times*, "I can't imagine what this place would be—I can't imagine
what the country would be—with Donald Trump as our president."
The justice followed this up with an interview where she called Trump
a "faker," adding, "He has no consistency about him. He says what-
ever comes into his head at the moment." Ever the counterpuncher,
Trump tweeted in response, "Is Supreme Court Justice Ruth Bader
Ginsburg going to apologize for her misconduct? Big mistake by an
incompetent judge!" This was followed by, "Justice Ginsburg of the
U.S. Supreme Court has embarrassed all by making very dumb political statements about me. Her mind is shot—resign!" (Brennan Center
2020; Biskupic 2016).

Trump's comments about judges would only get more notorious
once he was elected and cases were brought claiming that various actions of his were illegal. Just a week into his presidency, Trump issued
his "travel ban," an executive order that, among other provisions,
curtailed immigration from seven countries with significant Muslim
populations. A US District Judge in the state of Washington, James
Robart, issued a temporary restraining order (TRO) against the ban,
which the government unsuccessfully sought to have stayed by the US
Court of Appeals for the Ninth Circuit. The Trump administration
then rewrote the travel ban, but enforcement of this second executive
order was again stayed by another District Judge, this one in Hawaii.

While the travel ban was being litigated in the federal courts, the president made a number of tweets and other statements criticizing these decisions and the judges and courts that had made them—with one constant irritant being the Ninth Circuit. This reaction started immediately after Judge Robart issued the TRO against the executive order, with the president tweeting, "The opinion of this so-called judge, which essentially takes law-enforcement away from our country, is ridiculous and will be overturned!" Over the following days, there were additional tweets, including that it was a "terrible decision" and a "horrible, dangerous and wrong decision." As for Robart, the president fulminated, "Just cannot believe a judge would put our country in such peril. If something happens blame him and court system. People pouring in. Bad!" Needless to say, when the Ninth Circuit refused to stay the TRO, Trump tweeted, "Our legal system is broken!" (Brennan Center 2020).

Likewise, in March after Judge Derrick K. Watson stayed the second travel ban, Trump told a rally in Nashville that it was a "terrible ruling" and "unprecedented judicial overreach." He then added, "You don't think this was done by a judge for political reasons do you? This ruling makes us look weak, which we no longer are, believe me." Several days later at a Washington fundraiser, he again lashed out at the decision, saying, "The courts are not helping us I have to be honest. It's ridiculous. Somebody said I should not criticize judges. Okay, I'll criticize judges" (Brennan Center 2020).[1]

The following month, a US district court judge in California, William Orrick III, temporarily blocked Trump's executive order withholding funds from those jurisdictions declaring themselves "sanctuary cities." Confusing the US Court of Appeals for the Ninth Circuit with a district court that is within the circuit, Trump tweeted, "First the Ninth Circuit rules against the ban & now it hits again on sanctuary cities—both ridiculous rulings. See you in the Supreme Court!" A statement from the White House then opined, "the rule of law suffered another blow, as an unelected judge unilaterally rewrote immigration policy for our Nation." Judge Orrick's "erroneous ruling is a gift to the criminal gang and cartel element in our country, empowering the worst kind of human trafficking and sex trafficking, and putting thousands of innocent lives at risk." This was "yet one more example of egregious overreach by a single, unelected district judge" (Brennan Center 2020).

Trump's disgust with the Ninth Circuit again arose when, on November 20, 2018, one of its judges, Jon Tigar, ruled against the administration's recent pronouncement that one crossing the border from Mexico somewhere other than at an official port of entry would be barred from receiving asylum. The president responded by stating that the opinion was "a disgrace" and that Tigar was "an Obama judge." He also again attacked rulings coming from the Ninth Circuit, stating, "That's not law. Every case that gets filed in the Ninth Circuit we get beaten" (Brennan Center 2020).

President Trump's attack on an "Obama judge" led to an almost unheard-of response from Chief Justice John Roberts, who stated that the federal judiciary did not contain "Obama judges or Trump judges, Bush judges or Clinton judges. What we have is an extraordinary group of dedicated judges doing their level best to do equal right to those appearing before them. . . . The independent judiciary is something we should all be thankful for" (Brennan Center 2020).

To this rebuke, the president bristled and, of course, sent out a series of tweets: "Sorry Chief Justice John Roberts, but you do indeed have 'Obama judges,' and they have a much different point of view than the people who are charged with the safety of our country. It would be great if the 9th Circuit was indeed an 'independent judiciary,' but . . . these rulings are making our country unsafe! Very dangerous and unwise! . . . Judicial Activism, by people who know nothing about security and the safety of our citizens, is putting our country in great danger. Not good!" The chief justice's response was still eating at the president the following day when he tweeted, "Justice Roberts can say what he wants, but the 9th Circuit is a complete & total disaster. It is out of control, has a horrible reputation . . ." (Brennan Center 2020; Sherman 2018).

By November 2019, one federal judge had had enough of Trump's criticisms. Senior US District Judge Paul Friedman chose the annual Judge Thomas A. Flannery Lecture to detail and denounce the president's attacks on the judiciary. Before more than two hundred attorneys in the federal courthouse in Washington, Friedman stated that while other presidents had been "frustrated with judicial outcomes . . . what we are witnessing today and over the last few years is markedly different." The president's rhetoric "violates all recognized democratic norms" and was helping "undermine faith in the rule of law." According to the judge, "We are witnessing a chief executive who criticizes virtually every judicial decision that doesn't go his way and denigrates judges who rule against him, sometimes in very personal terms. He seems to view the courts and the justice system as obstacles to be attacked and undermined, not as a co-equal branch to be respected even when he disagreed with its decisions." At the conclusion of the lecture, the judge received a "standing ovation which went on for some minutes" (Shepherd 2019; LeBlanc and Polantz 2019).

The president was not at all chastened by such remarks. Several months later, in February 2020, Trump tweeted about US district judge Amy Berman Jackson, who was scheduled to sentence presidential friend Roger Stone: "Is this the Judge that put Paul Manafort in SOLITARY CONFINEMENT, something that not even mobster Al Capone had to endure? How did she treat Crooked Hillary Clinton? Just asking!" A week later, leading attorney George Conway III, husband of one of Trump's primary advisors, opined that while "Trump's ostensible purpose was to intimidate [Judge] Jackson into going easy on Stone . . . Trump's beef has always been not merely with individual federal judges who don't bend to his will, but with the idea of an independent federal judiciary generally." As evidence, Conway cited a recent book anonymously penned by an administration official that quoted the president asking, "Can we just *get rid* of the judges?" (Conway 2020).

While such a view, if truly believed and widely held, would be disastrous for the rule of law, it is to be hoped that the larger impact of Donald Trump's presidency on the federal judiciary will only be in the substantial number of conservative judges he has managed to appoint.

FILLING THE FEDERAL BENCH

In late December 2019, a *Washington Post* article stated, "After three years in office, President Trump has remade the federal judiciary, ensuring a conservative tilt for decades and cementing his legacy no matter the outcome of November's election" (Itkowitz 2019). Five days later, conservative *Post* columnist Marc Thiessen listed "The 10 Best Things Trump Did in 2019," with first place reading: "He has continued to appoint conservative judges at a record pace" (Thiessen 2019). Even those on the left have had to recognize the president's success in this area, with one writing, "Trump hasn't simply given lots of lifetime appointments to lots of lawyers. He's filled the bench with some of the smartest, and some of the most ideologically reliable, men and women to be found in the conservative movement. Long after Trump leaves office, these judges will shape American law—pushing it further and further to the right even if the voters soundly reject Trumpism in 2020" (Millhiser 2019).

The president has been justly proud of his administration's attempt to turn the judiciary to the right, even if some of his statements have not been entirely accurate. At a rally at a Hispanic Miami megachurch on January 3, 2020, Trump spent several minutes touting his views about, and successes in, appointing "187 unbelievably talented brilliant young judges. They'll be there for 40 years some of them." Trump felt that, as president, "the most important thing you have to do is judges and Supreme Court Justices," and the primary reason for his success was that he had inherited "142 slots. It never happened before. The most anyone's ever had is like one. Maybe none. You never, that's like gold. That's why it's so important. You have 142. I said 'how many slots do I have?' They said, 'sir, you have 142.' It's never happened before. That's why we're setting all these records. Nobody's ever done this. Because of President Obama. I don't know what happened. But I had 142" (C-SPAN 2020).

While the president has consistently claimed that he inherited 142 judicial vacancies, in reality, he had inherited only 104: one on the US Supreme Court, seventeen on the US courts of appeals, and eighty-six on the US district courts. In addition, while this was a substantial number, the president's assertion that such was a record, and that his predecessors had never had any more than "like one," is far from true. As seen in table 9.1, every president since Jimmy Carter has left at least thirty-five vacancies on the federal courts. The record for vacancies at the end of a presidency is not Barack Obama's 104, but, rather, the slightly higher 107 left in 1993 by George H. W. Bush.[2] In addition, Bill Clinton left nine more vacancies on the important US courts of appeals than did Barack Obama.

There are three primary reasons why Donald Trump inherited these 104 vacancies, all of which in some way involve US Senate majority leader Mitch McConnell. First, at some point near the end of a president's tenure, the Senate will stop considering a president's judicial nominees, leaving them instead for the following administration. This is sometimes referred to as the "Thurmond Rule," although it is not a strict rule at all but at best an extremely malleable tradition. Because a president's party almost always loses congressional seats in midterm elections, the past five presidents have all faced a US Senate controlled by the opposition party during their final two years in office—despite that, all but the first Bush began their tenures with

Table 9.1: Judicial Vacancies at the End of Presidential
Administrations

President	Supreme Court	Courts of Appeals	District Courts	Total
Obama	1	17	86	104
GW Bush	0	13	40	53
Clinton	0	26	54	80
GHW Bush	0	17	90	107
Reagan	0	10	29	39
Carter	0	5	30	35

their own party controlling the chamber. It is only natural that late in a president's term, an opposition party would rather save vacancies for what they hope will be a president of their own party.

While some have posited a cut-off date of July 1 of an election year, the dates of last confirmations in a presidential term have somewhat varied. For every president from Ford through George W. Bush, the last date for the confirmation of a nominee to a US district court was in September or October of the election year. With the Senate being led by Mitch McConnell, Barack Obama's last confirmation for a district court seat was ten weeks earlier, on July 6. As for the US courts of appeals, this date has apparently been moving earlier. While both Reagan and George H. W. Bush were able to have Circuit judges confirmed in October, Bill Clinton's last confirmation was in July, and George W. Bush's in June. Under the McConnell-led Senate, however, Barack Obama's final confirmation of a judge to the US courts of appeals occurred on January 11.

Even prior to this norm setting in, however, once the Republicans gained control of the Senate in January 2015, Majority Leader McConnell was able to successfully block the vast majority of President Obama's judicial nominations. Over the 114th Congress, Barack Obama nominated sixty-one individuals to the US district courts, only eighteen of whom were confirmed. Even more futile were his choices for the courts of appeals, for there, only two of his nine nominees were approved. Overall, only 28.6 percent of Obama's nominees to the district and circuit courts were confirmed during his final two years in office. This percentage is less than half of that for any other recent president, for even with the Senate in opposition control, 66.7 percent of George W. Bush's final nominees were confirmed, and the numbers were similar or better for Bill Clinton (61.5 percent), George H. W. Bush (68.6 percent), Ronald Reagan (79.8 percent), and, with same party control, Jimmy Carter (91.7 percent).[3]

Although Democrats and their allies have been quick to bash McConnell and the Republicans for refusing to confirm Obama's nominees, there is actually an important backstory to this seeming obstructionism. During the George W. Bush administration, Democrats began filibustering several nominees to the US courts of appeals, especially those who were either quite conservative or conceivable future Supreme Court nominees. In response, Republicans began discussing the "nuclear option," that is, changing the rules such that only a simple majority, rather than the traditional sixty votes, would be needed to end filibusters on judicial nominees. While tempers somewhat cooled after moderate senators worked out a 2005 compromise, they again heated up following the 2010 midterm elections, when an emboldened Republican minority began to filibuster Obama nominees (Hulse 2019, 65–113). This led to Democrats now advocating for the nuclear option, with Republicans warning against such. Chuck Grassley, ranking Republican on the Judiciary Committee, threatened, "Be careful what you wish for. . . . Remember, it was the Democrats who first used the filibuster to defeat circuit judges. . . . So, if the Democrats are bent on changing the rules, go ahead. There are a lot more Scalias and Thomases out there we'd love to put on the bench" (Hulse 2019, 107).

Grassley's words emboldened Senate majority leader Harry Reid, who used all of his skills to cobble together a 52–48 majority for ending the sixty-vote cloture requirement for judicial filibusters. Thus, as of November 21, 2013, all it would take to bring cloture on a nominee for either the district courts or the courts of appeals was a simple majority. At the time, Minority Leader Mitch McConnell stated, "I say to my friends on the other side of the aisle, you will regret this, and you may regret it a lot sooner than you think" (Hulse 2019, 111).

Harry Reid's employment of the "nuclear option" allowed the nomination floodgates to open, and Barack Obama was able to have 88.6 percent of his judicial nominees confirmed during the 113th Congress, the highest percentage since Bill Clinton's first Congress. Especially notable is the twenty-three of twenty-six nominees Obama successfully nominated to the courts of appeals (88.5 percent), which is the highest percentage since the first two years of George H. W. Bush's administration. Thus, if one looks at the final four years of a president's tenure, rather than just the final two, Barack Obama's record does not look all that out of line with his predecessors, especially in nominations to the courts of appeals.[4]

In addition, given that so many of Obama's nominees had been successfully confirmed during 2013–2015, there were not as many vacancies to fill during his final two years. The sixty-one persons Obama nominated to the US district courts during his final two years is the lowest number for any Congress since the fifty nominated by the first President Bush in 1989–1991. Even more surprising is that the nine nominations Obama made to the courts of appeals during this period is the fewest number of circuit judges nominated in a Congress since Harry Truman and the Eightieth Congress (1947–1949), when that court was significantly smaller.

Of course, the small numbers nominated should not mask the fact that, in retaliation for Harry Reid invoking the nuclear option, once he became majority leader in January 2015, Mitch McConnell did all he could to block the judicial nominations made by Barack Obama. In a December 2019 interview of McConnell on Fox News, Sean Hannity mentioned his great surprise at the large number of judicial vacancies Donald Trump had inherited. With much laughter, the senator replied, "I'll tell you why. I was in charge of . . . what we did the last two years of the Obama administration" (Campbell 2019; McCarthy 2019).

A third reason for the large number of vacancies Obama left is the "blue slip," which is a way for home-state senators to block lower federal court nominees. Ever since 1917, the Senate has had a tradition that when a president nominates someone to the district courts or courts of appeals, both senators from the home state of the nominee will be given a piece of blue paper, which the senators will then return to the chair of the Judiciary Committee with comments on the nomination. What happens if a senator withholds a blue slip, or returns one with a negative recommendation, has varied over time, but some chairs, such as James Eastland, have mandated that their committee will not consider such a nominee. Over the past two decades, Orrin Hatch, during the Bush administration (2001, 2003–2005), held that "return of a negative blue slip by one or both home-state senators does not prevent the committee from moving forward with the nomination—provided that the administration has engaged in pre-nomination consultation with both of the home-state senators." Following this, Arlen Specter, chair from 2005 to 2007, allowed one of the senators from a nominee's state to veto a district court nominee but not one for the courts of appeals. Specter was then followed by Democrat

Table 9.2: Federal Judges Confirmed during the First Three Years of a Presidency

President	Supreme Court	Courts of Appeals	District Courts	Total
Trump	2	50	133	185
Obama	2	25	97	124
GW Bush	0	30	138	168
Clinton	2	30	152	184
GHW Bush	2	31	95	128
Reagan	1	23	96	120
Carter	0	46	149	195
Ford	1	12	52	65
Nixon	4	34	123	161
LB Johnson	1	29	81	111
Kennedy	2	20	102	124
Eisenhower	2	17	55	74
Truman	2	10	33	45
FD Roosevelt	0	11	29	40

Patrick Leahy, who, over the following eight years (2007–2015), went back to the traditional rule where one home-state senator could veto a nomination. Leahy stated in 2012, "I have steadfastly protected the rights of the minority. . . . I have done so despite criticism from Democrats. I have only proceeded with judicial nominations supported by both home state senators." After the Republicans took control of the Senate in 2015, the same rule was apparently followed by Chair Chuck Grassley—at least while Barack Obama was president. This strict interpretation of the blue-slip process during his presidency meant that Obama had great trouble filling several vacancies, most notable being two Texas seats on the Fifth Circuit. Despite vacancies that opened in August 2012 and December 2013, the president was unable to find nominees acceptable to Senators Cornyn and Cruz, so Obama chose not to nominate anyone for these seats (Millhiser 2018; Tobias 2018).

Given the vacancies he inherited, it is not surprising that Donald Trump has been successful in confirming a large number of judges. As seen in table 9.2, during his first three years in office, Trump successfully nominated 2 justices to the Supreme Court, a record 50 to the courts of appeals, and 133 to the district courts.[5] In American history, this total of 185 is second only to Jimmy Carter's 195, although Trump bested Bill Clinton by just a single judge.

A president placing multiple justices on the Supreme Court during his first three years in office is not surprising, and neither were Trump's choices of Neil Gorsuch and Brett Kavanaugh—one could easily see any of the 2016 Republican presidential candidates picking both for the high court. Still, how Trump received his first vacancy and the extreme contentiousness surrounding the Kavanaugh nomination were quite unusual. While much has been written about the two confirmation battles, especially Kavanaugh's (Hulse 2019; Marcus 2019; Hemingway and Severino 2019; Kaplan 2018), a few words may be in order concerning both the vacancy that Trump inherited and how his actions in response helped secure his election.

On February 13, 2016, with Barack Obama still having eleven months to serve in office, Justice Antonin Scalia unexpectedly died. Hours later, Senate majority leader McConnell released a statement that ended, "The American people should have a voice in the selection of their next Supreme Court justice. Therefore, this vacancy should not be filled until we have a new President" (Hulse 2019, 17). Despite this pronouncement, Obama nominated Merrick Garland, a highly respected judge on the Court of Appeals for the District of Columbia Circuit. Under McConnell's leadership, however, the Senate refused to consider the nomination, not even giving Judge Garland a hearing in the Judiciary Committee.

Democrats were quick to label this action "unprecedented." In fact, no nominee had suffered such a fate over the past twelve decades. What almost all observers have ignored, however, is that with American politics becoming especially contentious, the Supreme Court confirmation process has started to revert to how it was over most of the nineteenth century. From 1828 to 1895, almost 40 percent of all nominations for the high court were unsuccessful, and this included ones that were not acted upon or were "postponed" until a new president came into office. Thus, Barack Obama joins John Quincy Adams, John Tyler, Millard Fillmore, James Buchanan, Rutherford B. Hayes, and the more recent Lyndon Johnson in being unable to fill an end-of-term vacancy (Abraham 2008).

While Mitch McConnell's actions should not be that surprising, the 2016 election did witness one action that was unprecedented. Given that he was a thrice-married New York businessman and TV personality who had once been pro-choice on abortion, Donald Trump was greatly in need of shoring up support from wary social conservatives. To help do this, on May 18, 2016, he became the first presidential candidate, or even president, to release publicly a list of individuals he would consider for the Supreme Court. This list contained the names of eleven very conservative sitting judges, and four months later, to secure the endorsement of Senator Ted Cruz, Trump released an updated, twenty-one-person list, pledging that his Supreme Court appointments would come only from those named (Marcus 2019, 18–28; Hulse 2019, 50–56, 138–143).

After releasing the lists, Trump began to emphasize to voters, especially evangelicals, how vital the issue of Supreme Court justices was in the election. At a rally in Cedar Rapids, he intoned, "If you really like Donald Trump, that's great. But if you don't, you have to vote for me anyway. You know why? Supreme Court judges, Supreme Court judges. Have no choice. Sorry, sorry, sorry. You have no choice" (Hulse 2019, 149; Marcus 2019, 28). The candidate obviously knew that, "for voters in the Republican base—far more than for Democrats—courts, and the Supreme Court in particular, are always a motivating force" (Marcus 2019, 16).

The Scalia vacancy, and Trump's list of possible nominees, may have been the most important reason why the controversial candidate was able to turn out enough evangelical voters to eke out victories in such pivotal states as Wisconsin, Michigan, and Pennsylvania. Months after the election, Mitch McConnell told a reporter, "At the end, this issue more than any other, elected Donald Trump" (Drucker 2017). Likewise, presidential advisor Steve Bannon recalled, "That list, that was a massive seller, which is, hey, you may hate Trump, you may not trust him, but it's got to be this ten, and I don't think he'd be president without that list" (Supreme Revenge 2019).

The 2016 exit polls bear out these assertions. Respondents were asked about the importance of "supreme court appointments" to their vote, and the 21 percent who said it was "the most important factor" voted for Trump over Clinton 56 percent to 41 percent. By contrast, the 14 percent who chose the answer "not a factor at all," voted for Clinton, 55 percent to 37 percent (CNN 2016). Mitch McConnell was quite proud of the role he had taken in this controversy, later telling Sean Hannity, "The most important decision I've made in my entire political career was not to fill the Supreme Court vacancy when Justice Scalia passed away" (Campbell 2019).

McConnell, of course, has also been instrumental in seeing Trump fill the lower federal courts with staunch judicial conservatives. In addition to the number of vacancies left at the end of the Obama administration, there are several reasons for Trump's success in this area. One is that his administration has consolidated the power to choose nominees in the White House Counsel's office, and under the leadership of Trump's first White House counsel Don McGahn, the office was quite efficient in forwarding names for the president to rubber-stamp. When McGahn accepted Trump's offer to be his Counsel, he, apparently under the tutelage of Mitch McConnell, asked for "almost unfettered authority to pick candidates for the federal courts" and the president "granted his request with no resistance." Once in office, McGahn "made judicial selection his top priority," and he "jealously guarded that prerogative, much to the displeasure of others not only in the Justice Department but also elsewhere in the White House" (Hulse 2019, 182; Marcus 2019, 30, 78). Unlike some other administrations, judicial nominees began quickly rolling out of the Trump White House, and even after McGahn left the Counsel's position in late 2018, nominees have continued to be quickly put forth.

Once before the Senate, these nominations have also been hastily confirmed. This, in large measure, is because of the importance Mitch McConnell gives to filling the bench with conservative judges. Shortly after the 2016 election, McConnell told his chief of staff, "We are going to move judges like they are on a conveyor belt." He then visited the president-elect and emphasized the importance of filling judicial vacancies over any other administration objective, telling Trump, "The thing that will last longest is the courts." Trump clearly heard and internalized this priority, for he has since stated, "I've always heard, actually, that when you become president, the most—single most important thing you can do is federal judges" (McCarthy 2019).

Thanks to the earlier blunder by Harry Reid in invoking the nuclear option, McConnell would not have to worry about the pesky filibuster stopping any of Trump's nominees. Democrats, thus, have found themselves powerless to stop the wave of conservative judges appointed by Trump, including those seen as rising legal stars and those whose ideology might be considered outside of the judicial mainstream (McCarthy 2019).

In addition to no longer having to worry about the filibuster, Trump's nominees have also greatly benefited by the decision of Chuck Grassley, kept by his successor in the Judiciary Chair, Lindsey Graham, to ignore the withholding of blue slips, especially for nominees to the courts of appeals. Accordingly, sixteen of Donald Trump's nominees to the courts of appeals have been confirmed even though

Table 9.3: Nominations and Confirmations to US Courts of Appeals

President	Nominations	Confirmed	% Confirmed	Average Negative Votes
Trump	54	51	94.4	36
Obama	68	55	80.9	9.6
GW Bush	86	61	70.9	8.6
Clinton	90	65	72.2	4.7
GHW Bush	53	42	79.2	0.9
Reagan	94	83	88.3	—
Carter	60	56	93.3	—
Ford	13	11	84.6	—
Nixon	47	46	97.9	—

at least one of their home-state senators did not return the slip—and for seven of these nominees, both senators objected. Such is in sharp contrast to past practice, for between 1979 and the start of the Trump administration, "only three judicial nominees out of hundreds were approved after receiving a negative blue slip from one senator; none were approved with negative blue slips from both." As noted by one journalist, "The blue slip had been such a potent weapon mainly because it had been backed up by the threat of a filibuster on the floor," but now, with such being unavailable, a majority party could ignore the objections of home-state senators (Hulse 2019, 186, 187, 190).

More minor, but still notable, reasons why Trump's nominees have sped through the Senate include that McConnell, in April 2019, limited the time for debate on district court nominees from thirty hours to just two (Senate Resolution 2019). In addition, Republicans have packed a number of nominees into a single Judiciary Committee hearing, eight times having panels of five or more district court nominees testifying at the same time, and on thirteen occasions having multiple courts of appeals nominees (Lambda Legal 2019). In addition, in 2018, without the consent of the minority, the Judiciary Committee held confirmation hearings during a Senate recess, which, under protest, every Democrat boycotted.

As Mitch McConnell desired, his judges project has run something like a conveyer belt. In 2019, while more than three hundred House-passed bills lay dormant in the Senate, the one thing the upper chamber showed great alacrity in processing was Trump's judicial nominations. Longtime Senate staffer Richard A. Arenberg has calcu-

Table 9.4: Confirmed Nominations to US District Courts, Percentage of Those with No Opposition and Those Receiving Forty or More Negative Votes

President	Number Confirmed	Number Opposed	Forty+ Negative Votes
Trump	137	33.6	20.4
Obama	268	70.9	4.9
GW Bush	261	98.1	0.4
Clinton	305	94.1	0
GHW Bush	148	100	0

lated that "an amazing and unprecedented 45 percent of all Senate votes in 2019 related to judicial nominations" (Arenberg 2020).

For every president since Nixon, table 9.3 lists the number of individuals the president has nominated to the courts of appeals, the number and percentage of those confirmed, and the average number of negative votes those confirmed nominees have received. As can be seen, as of February 21, 2020, Trump has filled fifty-one seats on this court, 28.5 percent of its 179 judges. Given that he is the only president on the list besides Carter not to have faced a Senate controlled by the opposition party, the 94.4 percent of his nominees confirmed should not be surprising. With neither the filibuster nor the blue slip, the only way Democrats have been able to show their displeasure is to cast negative votes against these nominees. Thus, Trump's nominees to the circuit courts have averaged thirty-six negative votes apiece, nearly four times as many as that for any other president. Exactly two-thirds of these fifty-one confirmed nominees have received more than forty negative votes.

Donald Trump has also been quite successful in his nominations to the district courts. As of this same date, Trump has successfully placed 137 (out of a total 677) judges on this federal trial court, with only ten of his nominees being withdrawn for various reasons. Traditionally, most district court nominees have been confirmed by either unanimous consent or on a voice vote. Since the nuclear option, however, the percentage of nominees forced to undergo a roll call vote, as well as the number of negative votes received, has increased—and such numbers have skyrocketed under Donald Trump.

Only thirty-three of Trump's district court nominees (24.1 percent) have been confirmed by voice vote, and of the remaining three-

Table 9.5: Demographics of Those Nominated to US Courts of Appeals

President	Average Age	% Minority	% Female	% White Male
Trump	47	14.8	18.5	74.1
Obama	50.6	32.4	45.6	30.9
GW Bush	50.5	12.8	23.3	67.4
Clinton	51	26.7	30	51.1
GHW Bush	48.4	9.4	15.1	75.5
Reagan	50.2	3.2	9.6	87.2
Carter	51.9	20	18.3	63.3
Ford	50.4	0	0	100
Nixon	53.9	2.1	0	97.9

quarters who underwent roll call votes, only thirteen were confirmed unanimously. Thus, as seen in table 9.4, only 33.6 percent of those Donald Trump has placed on the US district courts were confirmed with no opposition, compared to the more than 94 percent of those nominated by the two Bushes and Bill Clinton. In addition, more than half of Trump's nominees have received at least ten negative votes, with more than one-fifth receiving forty or more negative votes. The average negative vote for all of Trump's district court nominees, including those confirmed on voice vote, is 17.2, while for those facing a roll call vote, it is 22.6.

So, what type of judge has Donald Trump been appointing to these courts? Compared to Barack Obama's nominees, Trump's choices on average have been younger, more often white, more often male, better credentialed—although a small handful were considered unqualified—and, most importantly for the Republicans, extremely conservative.

During a November 2019 press conference touting his judicial selections, the president stated, "The average age of my newly appointed circuit judges is less than 50. They're young, smart. That's 10 years younger than President Obama's nominees" (Aronoff 2019).[6] As seen in table 9.5, which gives demographic information for all those nominated to the courts of appeals since 1969, Trump's statement was exaggerated, but it contained some truth; his Circuit nominees have been slightly younger than those of any president since at least Richard Nixon. This is important because younger nominees have a

Table 9.6: Age of Persons Nominated to US Courts of Appeals
(Percentage by Category)

President	Forty-Four and Younger	Fifty-Five and Older
Trump	38.9	9.3
Obama	14.7	36.8
GW Bush	20.9	25.6
Clinton	15.6	28.9
GHW Bush	24.5	17
Reagan	19.1	31.9
Carter	16.7	45
Ford	7.7	30.8
Nixon	6.4	38.3

chance at serving longer in office, and they also "have a better opportunity to plan their retirement, giving them the ability to give up a spot
for the president to fill if they are of the same party, or perhaps wait for
a more favorable shift in executive power" (Aronoff 2019).[7]

As seen in table 9.6, which shows the percentage of courts of appeals nominees under the age of forty-five, compared to those fifty-five
and above, more than any other president, Donald Trump has been
desirous of appointing young judges to the bench. At the January
2020 rally quoted above, he stated, "We have a judge in Texas, I don't
know what we do, but we have a Judge in Texas. I believe he's 38 years
old and went to Harvard and was the top student. I believe he went to
Oxford, something like that. He is 38 years old. Going to be there for
50 years. That's what we want, right? Right? That's what we want, and
that is what we are doing. Young, brilliant, and these are, uh, tremendously talented people" (C-SPAN 2020). The nominee mentioned was
the actually thirty-nine-year-old Andy Oldham, who had attended law
school at Harvard but had received a graduate degree (M.Phil.) from
Cambridge, not Oxford.

Oldham is one of five persons Trump has nominated to the courts
of appeals while still in their thirties. In American history, nominating
judges of this age has been rare but certainly not unheard of—and
those who are so nominated are usually considered to be exceptionally talented. For instance, there was only one such Circuit nominee
during the Nixon and Ford administrations, Californian Anthony
Kennedy. Jimmy Carter chose three individuals in their thirties, and
Ronald Reagan picked seven. While none of these would make it to

the Supreme Court, Reagan's group included such noted judges such as J. Harvie Wilkinson III, Frank Easterbrook, Ken Starr, Alex Kozinski, and Edith Jones. Beginning with the George H. W. Bush administration, presidents began having trouble getting these young nominees confirmed, for of the fourteen thirty-somethings nominated from then through Barack Obama's tenure, only eight were confirmed. Still, these fourteen individuals included five (three confirmed and two not) who would eventually serve on the Supreme Court—Roberts, Alito, Kagan, Gorsuch, and Kavanaugh. Thus, it will be interesting to follow the careers of Donald Trump's youngest nominees: the aforementioned Oldham, Eric Murphy, Daniel Aaron Bress, Allison Jones Rushing, and Andrew L. Brasher.

Trump has also appointed sixteen courts of appeals judges who were between forty and forty-four, a percentage (29.6) more than double that of any other president except George W. Bush (15.1). Those over the past forty years appointed to the courts of appeals at this age include four Supreme Court nominees, Stephen Breyer, Clarence Thomas, Merrick Garland, and Douglas Ginsburg, as well as such other noted judges as Richard Posner and Richard Arnold.

As for race and gender, every Democratic president since Lyndon Johnson has had a goal of diversifying the federal bench, and they have appointed a much greater percentage of women and minorities than have Republican presidents—although the Republican percentages were increasing until the current administration. It would likely surprise many that the last white male Christian successfully nominated to the Supreme Court by a Democratic president was Byron White, appointed by John F. Kennedy in 1962, and straight white men made up only 27.9 percent of those appointed to the courts of appeals by Barack Obama.

As for Donald Trump, it has been calculated that of the 185 judges confirmed during his first three years, 85 percent were white, 76 percent were male, and white men made up 64 percent (Nazaryan 2020; Alliance for Justice 2020). Of Trump's fifty-four nominees to the courts of appeals, ten were female, seven were of Asian heritage, and one was Hispanic—Trump has yet to appoint an African American to this court. The president has appointed a slightly more diverse group of individuals to the district courts, for of his first 157 nominees, forty were female, nine were African American, seven Hispanic, and five Asian. Given that Trump has not followed the Obama administration's focus on appointing women and minorities, there has been outcry

Table 9.7: Credentials of Those Nominated to the US Courts of Appeals

President	Top-Fourteen Law School	Federal Court Clerk	Supreme Court Clerk	US District Court Judge
Trump	72.2	88.9	37	18.5
Obama	54.4	64.7	22.1	32.4
GW Bush	54.7	38.4	14	25.6
Clinton	54.4	37.8	14.4	26.7
GHW Bush	37.7	22.6	11.3	52.8
Reagan	45.7	19.1	7.4	37.2
Carter	60	25	11.7	30
Ford	30.8	15.4	0	69.2
Nixon	53.2	10.6	4.3	48.9

from the left that the president was "making the judicial branch white and male again." At least one of these critics, however, has conceded that "Trump's picks are in keeping with the demographics of the [overall] legal profession" (Nazaryan 2020).

Turning to the credentials of those appointed, progressive Ian Millhiser has written, "It's tempting to assume that Trump's judicial appointees share the goonish incompetence of the man who placed them on the bench, but this assumption could not be more wrong. His picks include leading academics, Supreme Court litigators, and already prominent judges who now enjoy even more power within the judiciary" (Millhiser 2019). Table 9.7 shows the percentage of courts of appeals nominees for each administration since 1969 who graduated from one of the "top 14" law schools for their first law degree, who clerked for a federal judge, who clerked for a judge on the US Supreme Court, and who was already a sitting federal district court judge at the time of their appointment.

As can be seen, Trump's appointees have the highest percentage of graduates from top law schools, and by far the highest for those who had clerked for both federal judges overall and the Supreme Court. For the two clerkship categories, it is notable that Obama's numbers were significantly higher than those for previous presidents, and it has been said that a noticeable change occurred at the time of the nuclear option. Before then, "a sterling resume was often a liability for a judicial nominee because it flagged the nominee as a potential candidate for a future Supreme Court appointment." After the change, however,

"Democrats controlled the Senate for less than 14 months . . . yet nearly half of the former Supreme Court clerks Obama appointed to federal appellate judgeships were confirmed during this brief period. . . . Similarly, nearly three-quarters of Obama's post-reform appointees to the federal appellate bench clerked for a courts of appeals judge. One immediate impact of filibuster reform, in other words, is that it made it far easier for nominees with elite credentials to become federal judges." This trend of appointing courts of appeals judges with such credentials has only accelerated under Donald Trump (Millhiser 2019).[8]

Although the numbers have not been calculated for other presidents, it may also be a record that 61.1 percent of Trump's circuit court nominees had earlier worked for the federal government—in a position other than a clerkship, judgeship, or in the military. Interestingly, however, the Trump administration has not followed the tradition of choosing a large number of their courts of appeals nominees from those already serving on the district court. In the eight years of the Nixon and Ford administrations, as well as the four of George H. W. Bush's, more than half of all those nominated to the courts of appeals were then serving on the district courts. The numbers for Democratic presidents have been somewhat lower, but Carter, Clinton, and Obama all also chose a number of individuals serving on the highest state courts, such that at least 46.7 percent of their circuit court nominees were sitting judges. By contrast, a record low 18.5 percent of Trump's nominees were serving on the district courts, and less than 40 percent were in any type of judicial position.

While almost all of Trump's judicial appointees are well-credentialed, a notable, and record, handful have been deemed "Not Qualified" by the American Bar Association (ABA). For more than sixty years, the ABA has been rating judicial nominees, with such ratings now consisting of three possibilities: Well Qualified, Qualified, and Not Qualified. Prior to the George W. Bush administration, presidents would have the association vet candidates before their nomination, and administrations would pull back from nominating those deemed not qualified. Since the Reagan administration, which saw several courts of appeals possibilities scuttled because of these ratings, conservatives have complained about the unfairness of this process. Thus, both the George W. Bush administration and the Donald Trump administration have not submitted names to the ABA prior to nomination—although the organization has continued to investigate and rate candidates that have been named.

In the past, presidents on very rare occasions have gone ahead and nominated candidates deemed "Not Qualified," and, prior to Trump, four presidents had seen such nominees confirmed—four Lyndon Johnson and George W. Bush nominees were so confirmed, as were three chosen by Jimmy Carter and Bill Clinton. Donald Trump, however, has set a record by having nine of his nominees rated "Not Qualified," seven of whom have been confirmed—three to the courts of appeals, and four to the district courts (Aronoff 2019; Lambda Legal 2019).

While most of these nominees were so deemed because they did not yet have enough legal experience, a few were given this rating because of presumed personality defects. L. Steven Grasz, for instance, was found to have "temperament issues, particularly bias and lack of open-mindedness" (Weiss 2017), while Lawrence J. C. VanDyke was said to be "arrogant, lazy, an ideologue, and lacking in knowledge of the day-to-day practice including procedural rules." In the sixty interviews the ABA conducted, "There was a theme that the nominee lacks humility, has an 'entitlement' temperament, does not have an open mind, and does not always have a commitment to being candid and truthful" (Hubbard to Graham and Feinstein 2019). Grasz and VanDyke were both confirmed to the courts of appeals, as was the "Not Qualified" Jonathan A. Kobes, who became the first federal judge ever to win approval, 51–50, upon the tie-breaking vote of the vice president.

While the record of some of Trump's nominees may be troubling, it should also be noted that the vast majority of his two-hundred-plus judicial nominees have not raised such concerns. As of the end of 2018, Trump was tied with Obama for having the largest percentage (80 percent) of nominees to the courts of appeals rated "Well Qualified," and the 62.3 percent of his district court nominees so rated was the second highest of all time, trailing only George W. Bush.[9]

As for judicial ideology, during the 2016 campaign, Trump told Breitbart radio, "We're going to have great judges, conservative, all picked by the Federalist Society" (Millhiser 2019). The Federalist Society for Law and Public Policy Studies began in 1982 as a debating society where conservatives could discuss and promote ideas—such as originalism and textualism—that were not then prevalent within the academic legal community. Over time, however, the organization, which grew to contain tens of thousands of members, developed a purpose of "attracting, developing, and credentialing the foot soldiers of the burgeoning conservative legal movement. . . . Like a stocked pond from which to fish, the Federalist Society supplied the kind of originalist judges that Reagan attorney general Edwin Meese and his successors had committed to putting on the bench" (Marcus 2019, 21).[10] In fact, the Society "has evolved into the de facto gatekeeper for right-of-center lawyers aspiring to government jobs and federal judgeships under Republican presidents" (Farrell 2017).

Needless to say, the vast majority of Trump's judicial nominees have been members of the Federalist Society, including 85.2 percent of his choices for the courts of appeals. Interestingly, those who were not members have had a much easier time being confirmed in the Senate. The only two Trump courts of appeals nominees who were confirmed unanimously (Michael Scutter and Amy St. Eve) were both nonmembers, as were the two who received just one (Ralph Erickson) and two (William Nardini) negative votes apiece. Altogether, of Trump's fifty-one confirmed nominees to this court, the eight who were not members of the Federalist Society averaged just 14.1 negative votes, compared to an average of 40 for those who were members.

Donald Trump's picks for the lower federal courts are some of the most conservative judges in recent memory, and it has been said that "filibuster reform did not just improve the quality of nominees' resumes. It also cleared the path for known ideologues to join the bench" (Millhiser 2019). Not surprisingly, many on the left have been greatly upset about these choices, with the Alliance for Justice issuing a report detailing how multiple Trump nominees have taken concerning positions on twenty-one different legal topics (Alliance for Justice 2020).

Several nominees have raised much controversy because of their past writings and statements. To mention just a few, Trump's confirmed choices for the courts of appeals include John K. Bush, who authored anonymous blog posts on abortion and gay rights that troubled many; Neomi Rao, who felt obligated to apologize for collegiate writings on such topics as date rape, multiculturalism, and feminism; and Kenneth Lee, who admitted embarrassment over college writings on AIDS and sexual assault. All three nominees were confirmed on strict party-line votes. Likewise, with only Susan Collins switching sides, Sarah Pitlyk was confirmed to the district courts, despite being both unanimously rated "Not Qualified" by the ABA and being "lambasted by reproductive rights advocates for her vigorous opposition to abortion, surrogacy and in vitro fertilization" (Thebault 2019).

On several occasions, however, nominees have raised such opposition that their names have had to be withdrawn or their nominations have been allowed to lapse. Two of these, Ryan Bounds for the Ninth Circuit and Thomas Farr for the Eastern District of North Carolina, appeared to be headed for rejection after Senator Tim Scott of South Carolina voiced his objections over their past actions or writings regarding racial issues. In another highly publicized case, Republican Senator John Neely Kennedy of Louisiana conducted "one of the most painful inquisitions in Senate memory," by highlighting district court nominee Matthew Petersen's "total absence of trial experience. . . . The exchange disclosed that Petersen, a regulatory lawyer, had never tried a case to a verdict in any court, had never taken a deposition on his own, was not at all familiar with the rules of trial procedure or evidence, and could not define a motion in limine" (Hulse 2019, 196–197).

Possibly the most interesting unsuccessful nomination involves District Judge Halil Suleyman "Sul" Ozerden, who was nominated for a seat on the Fifth Circuit. Ozerden was "a close friend of acting White House chief of staff Mick Mulvaney," who pushed his nomination "over the objections of the White House Counsel's office." Various persons influential in the conservative legal movement, especially Carrie Severino of the Judicial Crisis Network, railed against the selection, especially because the nominee during his decade on the bench had not proved his commitment to originalist and textualist interpretations of the law. In short, he was not as pure a conservative as could be had. Based on this, Senators Ted Cruz and Josh Hawley announced their opposition, and the administration allowed the nomination to lapse (Everett 2019).

Such shows the powerlessness of Donald Trump should he wish to stray from the desires of the conservative legal movement. In all other cases, however, the president has been happy to nominate those judges funneled to him, and it has produced what is surely "the single most successful aspect of Trump's presidency" (Marcus 2019, 79).

Since early in the Trump administration, an oft-repeated liberal refrain has been that Republicans are supporting the president only because of "tax cuts and judges." In December 2019, for instance, a contributor to the *Washington Monthly* opined, "The Republican Party made a choice over the last three years to sell their own souls and the fate of the country to a morally depraved grifter under the spell of a foreign tyrant. They did this in exchange for some tax cuts and especially for a bevy of judges" (Atkins 2019). Interestingly, however, at that time even Republicans would admit that the two most successful aspects of the Trump administration were the booming economy and the large number of very conservative judges appointed to the federal bench. For instance, Donald Trump himself tweeted on January 26, 2020, "95% Approval Rating in the Republican Party. Thank you! 191 Federal Judges (a record), and two Supreme Court justices, approved. Best Economy & Employment Numbers EVER. Thank you to our great New, Smart and Nimble REPUBLICAN PARTY. It's where people want to be!" (Trump 2020).

Over the following several months, however, as the novel coronavirus (COVID-19) began to spread in the United States and lockdown orders were put in place, the stock market plunged while unemployment claims skyrocketed. Thus, it may very well be that the only bragging point Donald Trump will be left with for his entire administration is his stable of extremely conservative judges. Ironically, this is the one area of his administration where Trump has taken a complete hands-off approach and has quite willingly followed the suggestions of those with more knowledge.

Even in the midst of a national pandemic, Mitch McConnell's so-called judges project has continued apace, with the majority leader personally contacting Republican-appointed federal judges eligible for taking senior status, to feel them out about possibly retiring while Trump could still nominate their replacements (Hulse 2020). In an interview with the *Washington Post* in late March 2020, McConnell intimated that he would not adhere to the norm of the Senate refusing to consider judicial nominations after a certain point in the year of a presidential election, stating, "This Congress goes on until Dec. 31, and we intend to confirm all of the judges that are sent up to us this year" (Kim 2020). It is unknown how many additional appointments Donald Trump will have to the federal courts, yet even with just those already appointed, the president's selection of very conservative federal judges will continue to impact American law for decades to come.

NOTES

1. In his tweets, Trump would also state that the Ninth Circuit was overturned the most of any of the courts of appeals, but this was incorrect, for cases coming from the Third, Sixth, and Eleventh Circuits have a higher percent of reversals in the Supreme Court. See Woodward and Sherman 2020.

2. For table 9.1, numbers for January 2017 (end of the Obama adminis-tration) can be found at US Courts Judicial Vacancies 2017, while, following the links from this page, those from January 2009 (G. W. Bush), January 2001 (Clinton), January 1993 (G. H. W. Bush), January 1989 (Reagan), and January 1981 (Carter) can be accessed. In addition to these 104 vacancies in the primary Article III courts, as of the beginning of 2017, there were also two vacancies in the US Court of International Trade, and six in the US Court of Federal Claims. Thus, some in the media report Trump as having inherited 112 judicial vacancies, rather than 104.

3. These numbers are taken from table 3 in Congressional Research Service 2019.

4. There has been a noticeable trend of the Senate increasingly refusing to confirm a president's nominees during his final term in office, for while Ronald Reagan saw 89 percent of his nominees confirmed to the District and Circuit courts during his final four years in office, this number was 76.6 percent for George H. W. Bush, 71 percent for Bill Clinton, 61 percent for George W. Bush, and 50.8 percent for Barack Obama. Just for the Court of Appeals, however, Obama's success rate of 71.4 percent during his final term was actually higher than that for two predecessors who had to contend with the filibuster, George W. Bush (51.1 percent) and Bill Clinton (54.7 percent).

5. For this chapter, all information on federal judges has been taken from the Federal Judicial Center 2020. Unless otherwise noted, aggregate information has been compiled from all those nominated—not just those confirmed—and the above citation gives listings of all those unsuccessfully nominated. Note that Judge Murray Gurfein, who was nominated to the Second Circuit by Richard Nixon (on July 11, 1974) but confirmed under Gerald Ford (August 22, 1974), will be counted for this study under Nixon (he apparently did not require renomination), but Thomas Meskill, who was nominated by Nixon on his last day in office but, after the sitting Congress did not act on the nomination, was renominated by Ford, is counted as a Ford nominee.

6. This claim was also repeated in a fact sheet handed out by the White House.

7. As noted above, unlike other studies, the numbers used for this chapter are for all nominees, not just those confirmed, and ages have been calculated at the time of nomination.

8. The widely used term "Top 14 Law Schools" refers to those schools consistently so ranked by *US News & World Report*: Yale, Stanford, Harvard, Chicago, Columbia, NYU, Penn, Virginia, Michigan, Duke, Northwestern, Cal-Berkeley, Cornell, and Georgetown. Of the twenty nominated by Trump to the Court of Appeals who had clerked for a Supreme Court justice, all the justices were Republican appointees. Thomas led with seven, followed by four for Scalia, three for Alito and Kennedy, and one apiece for O'Connor, Rehnquist, and Souter.

9. See table 11 in the Congressional Research Service 2019.

10. See also Matthews and Pinkerton 2019. On the Society generally, see Hollis-Brusky 2015 and Teles 2008, 135–180.

REFERENCES

Abraham, Henry J. *Justices, Presidents, and Senators: A History of U.S. Supreme Court Appointments from Washington to Bush II.* Lanham, MD: Rowman & Littlefield, 2008.

Alliance for Justice. "Trump's Attacks on our Justice System, 2017–2019." 2020. https://www.afj.org/wp-content/uploads/2020/01/3-Year-Retrospective-1.14.20.pdf.

Arenberg, Richard A. "The Trumpification of the Federal Courts."Hill. January 6, 2020. https://thehill.com/opinion/judiciary/476796-the-trumpification-of-the-federal-courts.

Aronoff, Mitchell. "Trump's Exaggerated Judicial Boasts." factcheck.org. November 15, 2019. https://www.factcheck.org/2019/11/trumps-exaggerated-judicial-boasts/.

Atkins, David. "The GOP Traded Their Souls for Tax Cuts and Judges. Dems Should Take Them Away in 2021." *Washington Monthly*, December 21, 2019. https://washingtonmonthly.com/2019/12/21/the-gop-traded-their-souls-for-tax-cuts-and-judges-dems-should-take-them-away-in-2021/.

Beveridge, Albert J. *The Life of John Marshall*, vol. 3. New York: Houghton Mifflin, 1919.

Biskupic, Joan. 2016. "Justice Ruth Bader Ginsburg Calls Trump a 'Faker,' He Says She Should Resign," CNN. July 13, 2016. https://www.cnn.com/2016/07/12/politics/justice-ruth-bader-ginsburg-donald-trump-faker/index.html.

Brennan Center for Justice. "In His Own Words: The President's Attacks on the Courts." 2020. https://www.brennancenter.org/our-work/analysis-opinion/his-own-words-presidents-attacks-courts.

Campbell, Jason S. [@JasonSCampbell]. December 12, 2019, 9:27 PM [Tweet containing snippet of McConnell interview with Hannity].

CNN. "Election 2016: Exit Polls." https://www.cnn.com/election/2016/results/exit-polls.

Congressional Research Service. "Judicial Nomination Statistics and Analysis: U.S. District and Circuit Courts, 1977–2018," *Congressional Research Service*, March 21, 2019. https://fas.org/sgp/crs/misc/R45622.pdf.

Conway, III, George T. "Opinion: Trump's 'King Kong' Nickname Has Come into Full Fruition," *Washington Post*, February 19, 2020. https://www.washingtonpost.com/opinions/george-conway-trumps-pardons-are-impulsive-expressions-of-his-spite/2020/02/19/399485a0-5363-11ea-929a-64efa7482a77_story.html.

C-SPAN. Remarks Transcribed by Author from C-Span's video of Trump's January 3 Speech at El Rey Jesus. https://www.c-span.org/video/?467813-1 /president-tump-speaks-evangelical-rally-miami%start=505. 2020. (Trump's remarks on the judiciary are from 31:50 to 36:25 on the video).

Drucker, David M. "McConnell: Vacant Supreme Court Seat Won the Election for Trump." *Washington Examiner*, April 7, 2017. https://www.washington examiner.com/mcconnell-vacant-supreme-court-seat-won-the-election -for-trump.

Everett, Burgess, et al. "Ted Cruz Will Oppose Trump's Judicial Nominee." Politico. September 12, 2019. https://www.politico.com/story/2019/09/12 /ted-cruz-halil-sul-ozerden-nomination-1492305.

Farrell, Henry. "Trump's Values Are Abhorrent to the Federalist Society of Conservative Lawyers: That Doesn't Stop Them from Helping Him." *Washington Post*, May 17, 2017. (quoting Amanda Hollis-Brusky). https:// www.washingtonpost.com/news/monkey-cage/wp/2017/05/17/trumps -values-are-abhorrent-to-the-federalist-society-of-conservative-lawyers-that -doesnt-stop-them-from-helping-him/.

Federal Judicial Center. "Biographical Directory of Article III Federal Judges, 1789–Present." 2020. https://www.fjc.gov/history/judges.

Hemingway, Mollie, and Carrie Severino. *Justice on Trial: The Kavanaugh Confirmation and the Future of the Supreme Court*. Washington: Regnery, 2019.

Hentoff, Nat. "The Constitutionalist," *New Yorker*, March 12, 1990. http:// www.newyorker.com/magazine/1990/03/12/the-constitutionalist.

Hollis-Brusky, Amanda. *Ideas with Consequences: The Federalist Society and the Conservative Counterrevolution*. New York: Oxford University Press, 2015.

Hubbard, William C., to Lindsey Graham and Dianne Feinstein, October 29, 2019, copied in https://twitter.com/RalstonReports?ref_src=twsrc%5E google%7Ctwcamp%5Eserp%7Ctwgr%5Eauthor.

Hulse, Carl. *Confirmation Bias: Inside Washington's War over the Supreme Court, from Scalia's death to Justice Kavanaugh*. New York: Harper, 2019.

———. "McConnell Has a Request for Veteran Federal Judges: Please Quit." *New York Times*, March 16, 2020. https://www.nytimes.com/2020/03/16 /us/politics/mcconnell-judges-republicans.html#click=https://t.co/uX yNktqawW.

Itkowitz, Colby. "1 in Every 4 Circuit Court Judges Is Now a Trump Appointee," *Washington Post*, December 21, 2019. https://www.washingtonpost .com/politics/one-in-every-four-circuit-judges-is-now-a-trump-appointee /2019/12/2.

Jaffe, Harry. "Meet the Man Curbing Trump's Power without Anyone Noticing." *Politico Magazine*, February 23, 2019. https://www.politico.com/magazine /story/2019/02/23/karl-racine-profile-attorney-general-emoluments-law suit-trump-2020-225200.

Kaplan, David A. *The Most Dangerous Branch: Inside the Supreme Court's Assault on the Constitution.* New York: Crown, 2018.

Kim, Seung Min. "Trump Taps Former Kavanaugh Clerk to Fill Vacancy on Powerful D.C. Appeals Court," *Washington Post,* April 3, 2020. https://www.washingtonpost.com/politics//trump-taps-former-kavanaugh-clerk-to-fill-vacancy-on-powerful-dc-appeals-court/2020/04/03/3ddb5e50-7446-11ea-ae50-7148009252e3_story.html#click=https//t.co/PwLKqG6HJG.

Lambda Legal. "Special Report 2019: Trump's Judicial Assault on LGBT Protections." 2019. https://www.lambdalegal.org/sites/default/files/publications/downloads/trump-judicial-nominees-report-2019.pdf.

LeBlanc, Paul, and Katelyn Polantz. "Federal Judge Assails Trump's Attacks on Judiciary: He's Feeding a 'Destructive Narrative.'" CNN. November 7, 2019. https://www.cnn.com/2019/11/07/political/federal-judge-slams-trumps-attacks-judiciary/index.html.

Marcus, Ruth. *Supreme Ambition: Brett Kavanaugh and the Conservative Takeover.* New York: Simon & Schuster, 2019.

Matthews, Dylan, and Burd Pinkerton. "The Incredible Influence of the Federalist Society, Explained." Vox. June 3, 2019. https://www.vox.com/future-perfect/2019/6/3/18632438/federalist-society-leonard-leo-brett-kavanaugh.

McCarthy, Tom. "Trump's Dark Legacy: A US Judiciary Remade in His Own Image." *Guardian.* December 25, 2019. https://www.theguardian.com/us-news/2019/dec/25/trump-judiciary-judges-legal-america.

Millhiser, Ian. "Senate Democrats Get a Harsh Lesson on Why They Should Never, Ever Play Nice with Republicans," *Think Progress,* May 11, 2018. https://thinkprogress.org/democrats-play-nice-blue-slip-02b474ece78f/.

——. "What Trump Has Done to the Courts, Explained," Vox.com. December 9, 2019. https://www.vox.com/policy-and-politics/2019/12/9/20962980/trump-supreme-court-federal-judges.

Nazaryan, Alexander. "Trump Is Making the Judicial Branch White and Male Again." Yahoo! News. January 14, 2020. https://news.yahoo.com/trump-is-making-the-judicial-branch-white-and-male-again-100059913.html.

Phelps, Jordyn. "Donald Trump: Chief Justice Upheld Obamacare 'To Be Popular in the Beltway.'" ABC News, December 12, 2015. https://abcnews.go.com/Politics/donald-trump-chief-justice-roberts-upheld-obamacare-popular/story?id–35734063.

Purdum, Todd S. "Presidents, Picking Justices, Can Have Backfires." *New York Times,* July 5, 2005. https://www.nytimes.com/2005/07/05/politics/politicsspecial1/presidents-picking-justices-can-have-backfires.html.

Senate Resolution. "A Resolution Improving Procedures for the Consideration of Nominations in the Senate." 2019, 116th Cong., 1 Sess. S. Res. 50.

Shepherd, Katie. "Trump 'Violates all Recognized Democratic Norms,' Federal Judge Says in Biting Speech on Judicial Independence." *Washington Post*, November 8, 2019. https://www.washingtonpost.com/nation /2019/11/08/judge-says-trump-violates-democratic-norms-judiciary -speech/.

Sherman, Mark. "Roberts, Trump Spar in Extraordinary Scrap over Judges." *Associated Press*, November 21, 2018. https://apnews.com/c4b34f9639 e141069c08cf1e3deb6b84.

Shesol, Jeff. *Supreme Power*. New York: W. W. Norton, 2010.

Solomon, Burt. *FDR v. The Constitution*. New York: Walker, 2009.

Supreme Revenge. Interview with Steve Bannon in the PBS Frontline documentary *Supreme Revenge* (quote starts at 37:57). 2019.

Teles, Steven M. *The Rise of the Conservative Legal Movement*. Princeton, NJ: Princeton University Press, 2008.

Thebault, Reis. "Trump Nominee Who Is Anti-IVF and Surrogacy Was Deemed Unqualified. She Was Just Confirmed." *Washington Post*, December 4, 2019. https://www.washingtonpost.com/politics/2019/12/04/trump-nominee -who-is-anti-ivf-surrogacy-was-deemed-unqualified-she-just-got-confirmed/.

Thiessen, Marc A. "The 10 Best Things Trump Did in 2019." *Washington Post*, December 26, 2019. https://www.washingtonpost.com/opinions/2019/12 /26/best-things-trump-has-done/.

Tobias, Carl. "Senate Blue Slips and Senate Regular Order." *Yale Law & Policy Review: Inter Alia* (November 20, 2018): https://ylpr.yale.edu/inter_alia /senate-blue-slips-and-senate-regular-order.

Toobin, Jeffrey. *The Oath*. New York: Doubleday, 2012.

Trump, Donald J. [@realDonaldTrump]. January 26, 2020, 11:24 AM [Tweet].

US Courts Judicial Vacancies. 2017. https://www.uscourts.gov/judges-judge ships/judicial-vacancies/archive-judicial-vacancies/2017/01/summary.

Weiss, Debra Cassens. "ABA Committee Explains Its 'Not Qualified' Rating for 8th Circuit Nominee." *ABA Journal*, October 31, 2017. https://www .abajournal.com/news/article/aba_committee_explains_its_not-qualified _rating_for_ 8th_circuit_nominee.

Wolf, Z. Byron. "Trump's Attacks on Judge Curiel Are Still Jarring to Read." CNN.com. February 27, 2018. https://www.cnn.com/2018/02/27/poli tics/judge-curiel-trump-border-wall/index.html.

Woodward, Calvin, and Mark Sherman. "AP FACT CHECK: Trump's Judicial Comments Appear Misinformed." 2020. https://apnews.com/a2a6 c429068b4401 a40fd83d35fb912d.

PART III

Trump and Public Policy

CHAPTER 10

Swamping the Drain: Lobbying, Advocacy, and Influence in the Trump Administration

Burdett Loomis

THE LOBBYIST

In 2016, almost no one in Washington had heard of Brian Ballard, a veteran Florida lobbyist and fundraiser. He had no presence in the capital. Less than two years later, Ballard had established a DC lobbying firm and had already moved from his modest initial offices into more spacious and luxurious quarters. Starting with no national clients and no physical presence in 2016, in less than a year Ballard partners had signed up dozens of clients, ranging from the government of Turkey and an opposition leader in the Democratic Republic of the Congo to a host of major American firms (Meyer 2018). As a major fundraiser for the incoming president, Ballard parlayed his relationship, albeit not a long-term one, into the creation of a powerful, lucrative lobbying firm.

As Politico noted:

Ballard's relationship with Trump has helped him solve a lucrative puzzle that has frustrated more established players. For all of the president's "drain the swamp" rhetoric, the new administration has given corporate America and its lobbyists the opportunity to revive dreams of tax cuts, regulatory rollbacks and rule changes

that were mothballed during the Obama administration. But
Trump also presents a challenge for the influence business—a
White House in which key positions at least initially were as
likely to be staffed by Trump loyalists as by old Washington
hands with ties to K Street. Ballard has helped to bridge the gap.
He's a Trump-friendly out-of-towner who can connect with the
establishment—he is a close ally of Senator Marco Rubio as well as
Charlie Crist, the former centrist Republican governor of Florida
who is now a Democratic congressman—and make corporate
clients comfortable (Meyer 2018).

Ballard brought together—in himself and his firm—close ties to
the incoming president, coupled with a capacity to navigate policy seas
that were simultaneously familiar and turbulent. The regular channels
of access appeared open and negotiable, but this was often an illusion,
given Trump's lack of experience, his mercurial, narcissistic personality, and his general absence of traditional DC ties. Ballard's personal
linkages to the president provided him with immediate access and the
subsequent capacity to rapidly build a conventional Washington lobbying firm, which produced revenues of $437.2 million in 2018–2019
(Johnson 2019).

THE INSIDER

In Donald Trump's cabinet, noted for its frequent shake-ups and many
"acting" secretaries, Secretary of Commerce Wilbur Ross stands as an
example of how political insiders with personal agendas have survived,
and even flourished, in the wake of the 2016 elections. At the age
of eighty-three (in 2020), Ross took this position as the culmination
of a career of wealth-building and venture capitalism, often through
adept, if controversial, acquisition of distressed assets (Tindera 2017).

Given his advanced age and lack of governmental experience, Ross
was an unlikely candidate for a cabinet slot. Although he won confirmation relatively easily, compared to a truly problematic nominee
like Education Secretary Betsy DeVos, his promise to disclose and di-
vest his extensive, complicated financial holdings proved a continuing
source of controversy. Indeed, he may well have grossly and purpose-
fully misstated his net worth during his confirmation hearings (Alexander 2017).

Ross's status as a highly placed insider has allowed him—like many others in the administration—to mix his private and public roles on a regular basis. Like DeVos, Ross is wealthy enough not to need any post-cabinet economic windfalls, based on his status. At the same time, he has continued to control enough of his assets, despite his pledges to the contrary, which allow him to profit from his cabinet position, most notably regarding American trade interests with China. Ross's conflicts of interest typify those of several Trump cabinet members, but his policy impact has been modest, save to generally favor business interests at every turn. This does fit with the general Trump agenda, and Ross's further value as an insider has been to champion, with remarkable loyalty, those interests that the president has emphasized. For example, Ross pursued the inclusion of a citizenship question in the 2020 census, which is administered by the Commerce Department. Knowing Trump's preference for this question, Ross sought its inclusion in 2017 and then in 2018 lied to a congressional committee about where the request had originated (Rizzo 2018). On this issue and others, Ross demonstrated unswerving loyalty to the president. Combining his cabinet position with consistent, unreflective support of Donald Trump, Ross continues to exercise influence, not with his policy ideas or advocacy but by the fact that he can influence policies through his perch within the administration. Like Betsy DeVos and many others, he is a fox in Trump's policy-making henhouse.

As we shall see, Brian Ballard and Wilbur Ross are not exceptions as advocates in the Trump era; rather, they reflect central aspects of the Trump presidency, which encourages access to politics from both the inside and the outside of the policy-making process on issues large and small.

WASHINGTON, DC, LOBBYING: A BASELINE

As the federal government has grown through the New Deal, World War II, the Cold War, the Great Society, and beyond, so has the Washington advocacy community. Although lobbyists are often disparaged, they stand as essential and constitutionally protected participants in the policy-making process (Shabad 2013).

The Size and Scope of the Advocacy Community

Virtually all interests in American society do obtain some organized representation. The wealthy and large corporate interests do better in getting what they want, but groups do represent even the most disadvantaged sectors of American society, such as the severely disabled (American Association of Physical Disabilities), the homeless (National Association for Homelessness), or even undocumented immigrants (RAICES and ACLU). We know a lot about the number and range of lobbyists, because in 1995 (and modified in 2007) the Congress required lobbyists to register with the secretary of the Senate or the clerk of the House. The Congress compiles these reports, as does the nonprofit Center for Responsive Politics, which provides data on lobbyists and interest groups. Most advocates who lobby in Washington do register with the Congress, but many individuals who advocate on behalf of interests do not do so, given the definition of lobbying in the law (LaPira and Thomas 2013). Indeed, lobbying the executive or regulatory bodies falls outside the purview of registration, and grassroots lobbying is similarly exempt. All in all, the DC-influence community is far larger than the twelve-to-fourteen thousand lobbyists who do register.

The number of registered lobbyists grew to almost fifteen thousand before the 2007 revisions to the reporting legislation; since then, fewer individuals have registered, but there is no evidence that the volume of lobbying has decreased, even as the number of registrations has leveled off at between eleven thousand and twelve thousand.[1] Indeed, reported lobbying on spending has remained roughly constant during the Trump administration. More importantly, as with the reported number of lobbyists, the spending figures address only congressional advocacy, and even they are substantially understated, in that a great deal of advocacy is carried out informally and by those who need not register. As to the Trump administration, if there was a "swamp" when he entered office, there is no indication that it has been drained at all.

Not only are there well over twenty thousand individuals in the DC lobbying community, but advocacy attracts huge amounts of spending, which has stabilized at more than a reported $3 billion per year, according to reported numbers.[2] As with the number of advocates, the formal figures on spending represent only a portion of the actual expenditures. Indeed, one estimate places actual business lobbying costs at approximately twice their reported expenditures (Perez et al. 2019). Although various tactics are used to avoid reporting of advocacy efforts, the most widely used action comes from inventive applications of tax regulations, often described as loopholes. Corporations and trade associations can form tax-exempt 503 (C) (6) organizations, which allows them to pool money and engage in advocacy campaigns that go beyond direct lobbying. These funds receive relatively little scrutiny, and trade associations can develop social media campaigns, advertise, do polling, and conduct myriad other activities that can affect policy arguments and outcomes.

Members of Congress have decried this practice, as seen in Senator Shelton Whitehouse's statement: "From fossil fuel companies blocking climate action to the [National Rifle Association] shilling for firearms corporations, these influence schemes help hundreds of millions of dollars flow through sophisticated campaigns.... Big trade groups like the U.S. Chamber of Commerce shouldn't be allowed to swamp our government to enrich a few of their hidden backers. A lot of sunlight is needed to disinfect this area" (Perez et al. 2019). A few specific examples demonstrate the reach of such spending beyond the formal lobbying numbers. In 2017, the Blue Cross Blue Shield Association spent $174 million on consulting, while PhRMA, the drug group, spent $82 million. Much went to advocacy efforts, broadly defined. And the American Chemistry Council spent $30 million on consulting and $3.5 million more on "public policy" (Perez et al. 2019).

In sum, these off-the-books advocacy efforts likely double the amount of reported lobbying money. Beyond this, especially in light of recent Supreme Court rulings on campaign contributions and expenditures, there is effectively no limit on campaign spending for corporations, labor unions, and, most notably, the wealthy. Putting any Trump effect aside, the size and scope of the American advocacy industry is huge. Its growth and nourishment, often related to the growth of public policy, is a fact of political life in a country whose Constitution protects advocacy at a fundamental level (e.g., freedom of speech and assembly, along with the right to petition the government).

LOBBYISTS, GOVERNMENT, AND THE "REVOLVING DOOR"

Given its size and scope, members of the DC lobbying community come from diverse backgrounds, but the largest single source of advocates is the federal government, including Congress (members and staff), the executive branch, independent agencies, and regulatory bodies. In the seminal revolving-door study by LaPira and Thomas (2017), more than half their sample of lobbyists had previous federal government experience. Although "revolvers," to use Hall and

Lorenz's (2018) term, often possess considerable policy expertise, their greater value derives from the access to governmental officials.

The revolving door has swung between government employment and the private sector for decades, with perhaps the most notable early exemplar being Tommy "The Cork" Corcoran, who left the Franklin Roosevelt administration to form a highly profitable and long-lived lobbying firm (McKean 2004). Although many members of Congress relocate to K Street, the literal and metaphorical home of many lobbying firms, their numbers are dwarfed by congressional staffers, who stay long enough on the Hill to establish expertise and personal ties, only to double or triple their salaries as they move into the world of advocacy.

All this movement occurs regularly and accelerates after elections, especially when there is a change in partisan control at either end of Pennsylvania Avenue. The literature on revolvers has grown substantially over the past decade, with most of the research focused on government employees entering the private sector as lobbyists or consultants. To a certain extent, the outflow of governmental officials into the lobbying community drains the executive and legislative branches of talents and recirculates these individuals into the lobbying community. New recruits populate the ranks of executive and congressional staffs, providing fresh perspectives and energy for these branches. At the same time, many lobbyists *return* to governmental service with changes in partisan control of the presidency or the Congress. The motives for these moves are mixed, involving political, policy, and personal reasons; former lobbyists can move their issues in a favorable political environment and add to their resumes for a move back through the revolving door and a more lucrative position. As we shall see, both Republicans (in 2016) and Democrats (in 2018) attracted many lobbyists back to the government, often with major cuts in pay but with the chance to have major impacts on policy. Although most of the focus here is on Republican lobbyists entering the Trump administration (see below), when Democrats won control of the House in 2018, they attracted many lobbyists back to Capitol Hill. The revolving door in DC turns for everyone.

Writ large, lobbying and lobbyists constituted much of the "swamp" that Donald Trump sought to drain. Given lobbying's deep constitutional roots and its wide practice, any attempt to limit it and the implied power of advocates was likely doomed. But the populist rallying cry of "Drain the Swamp" made for good politics in 2016, even if it lacked substantive meaning. As one article observed, "Trump argued that he was the only candidate to clean up government because his opponents were 'controlled by lobbyists, controlled by their donors, controlled by special interests.' Lobbyists, he often said or implied, were part of Washington's 'culture of corruption.'" (Whitney 2018). As Trump transitioned from candidate to chief executive, the advocacy community paid close attention to whether his deeds would match his words.

ADVOCACY AND UNCERTAINTY IN THE TRUMP ERA

Given the solidly entrenched Washington advocacy establishment, even a self-proclaimed disrupter like Donald Trump would have a difficult time producing great structural change, whether or not he sincerely desired to do so (Baumgartner et al. 2009). Nevertheless, no contemporary administration has produced as much uncertainty as has Trump's. Lobbyists and organized interests dislike great uncertainty, even though on occasion it can provide them with real opportunities. Regardless, they had to deal with many kinds of uncertainty as the Trump presidency unfolded.

Most important has been the president himself. First, despite his claims to the contrary, Trump is an amateur in both policy making and governance. Those traits alone would generate great uncertainty within the community of Washington policy professionals, regardless of their views. Equally important, nothing indicates that Donald Trump has any identifiable ideology or coherent set of policy preferences, which analysts observed well before the 2016 election (Lowery 2015). Even on signature issues for this campaign, like immigration or abortion, Trump had no well-developed worldview; rather, he would say one thing to one interviewer and something different to another, despite the fact that both would be universally open to scrutiny. Moreover, Trump has continually disparaged experts and expertise, whether on health care, the military, immigration, or agriculture, among many subjects. Thus, the ordinary expectations that organized interests and lobbyists might have for an incoming administration often proved open to question. Again, policy advocates desire predictability, and Trump has reveled in chaos. Indeed, one sub-theme of his "Drain the Swamp" mantra was that much of the swamp was located within the civil service, with its own entrenched interests. Hence the frequent attacks on "the deep state" that provided much of the predictability with American government, especially on the implementation of public policy. The "deep state" theme emerged almost immediately in the Trump presidency and has remained a staple critique from both the president and his allies outside of government. As his chief strategist, Steve Bannon, concluded in Trump's early days in office, "Every day would be a battle for 'deconstruction of the administrative state'" (Clark n.d.).

One way to counteract the power of the permanent bureaucracy, which almost all presidents have tangled with, is to appoint strong cabinet secretaries who possess the political clout to guide policy changes through a sometimes recalcitrant set of civil servants. In some instances, as with Trump's Education Secretary DeVos and Labor Secretary Elaine Chao, this has succeeded, but far more common have been continuing rounds of cabinet shake-ups, the long-term presence of acting secretaries, and temporary assignments of personnel in important sub-cabinet positions (Blake 2020). The membership of the Trump cabinet turned over more in its first two years than did any of the previous three administrations in their full first four-year term (Tenpas 2019). This is likewise true for the top-level members of the Executive Office of the President (Tenpas 2020). Thus, rather than damping down the uncertainty generated by an unconventional incoming president, the tenuous status of many political appointees has amplified it. For lobbyists, this means establishing new ties and new lines of communication with substantial numbers of political appointees as well as with career civil servants, who also exist in a world of heightened uncertainty.

If continuing uncertainties over politics and policies make up a core element of the Trump regime, it is a context that lobbyists, whether registered or not, must address, even as the ground shifts under their feet. In general, the constants of DC advocacy remain in place—in the number of lobbyists, their tactics, and the amount of spending. Like Congress and the presidency, organized interests and their lobbyists constitute political institutions that do not change quickly or easily. Still, President Donald Trump presents a confounding force for all political actors, including lobbyists and their sponsoring organizations, from Ford Motors to the AFL-CIO to the American Civil Liberties Union. Thus, we can assess contemporary advocacy as the actions of a political institution (the lobbying community) that operates in well-developed patterns, even as it reacts to the often unusual and unpredictable initiatives of a singular president.

LOBBYING IN THE TRUMP ERA

Despite many continuities, lobbyists have encountered both great challenges and substantial opportunities in the wake of the 2016 election. While many, if not most, of the regular patterns of advocacy remain in place, the Trump presidency has affected these patterns in many ways. Affecting all actions is the fact that almost everything is "up for grabs." The Trump-era uncertainty means that many well-established policies may be modified or reversed. This is especially true for immigration, energy, and the environment, but almost all policy areas offer lobbyists the possibility of change, and sometimes profound change (e.g., military spending in context of NATO). This also means that those interests that play defense or protect the status quo must also engage actively on a wide range of issues. Beyond this baseline of uncertainty, the major elements of the Trump era include:

Lobbying beyond Capitol Hill. Although congressional lobbying continues at predictable levels, for many interests the potential to affect policy is greater inside the bureaucracy or regulatory bodies like the Securities and Exchange Commission. Operating in these multiple venues may require groups to employ more lobbyists and ones with different skills and backgrounds than for conventional work on Capitol Hill.

Lobbying Donald Trump, in various ways, can produce results. Presidents are often difficult to lobby, given the layers of policy scrutiny that exist in most administrations. With President Trump, direct appeals (from Kim Kardashian on pardons to Veterans Affairs advocates at Mar-a-Lago) have succeeded (Baker 2018). This kind of lobbying includes cronies, which is not all that unusual, but it also can encompass reaching Trump's media favorites on Fox, who may influence his decisions (Mullins 2019).

Foxes in the henhouse. Some of the most effective exertion of policy influence comes not from outside lobbyists but from within the top levels of the administration itself. Lobbyists have long known how helpful it is to have a "champion" *within* the policy-making process. Time after time, Trump has appointed cabinet secretaries and other top administrators with long records of opposing the policies of their agencies. What could school privatization advocates hope for more than for Betsy DeVos to run the Department of Education?

Beyond these three major aspects of lobbying, from its very inception, the Trump White House has been, at the least, indifferent to foreign lobbying and has often seemed to encourage it. Inside the administration (National Security advisor Ray Flynn), within Trump's political sphere (Michael Cohen and Paul Manafort), and for the outside (numerous lobbying firms), foreign interests have concluded that lobbying the administration can pay off, across a wide range of subjects in an era when the president often seeks to rewrite the rules of international engagement (Meyer 2019).

Overall, while there remains substantial stability within the lobbying community, Trump not only failed to "drain the swamp" but often opened up one channel (e.g., rolling back environmental regulations) while muddying the waters on many other issues, ranging from immigration to health care to defense spending. Nevertheless, more than any modern American president, Trump has, perhaps temporarily, bypassed many of the regular rules of lobbying and caused interest groups, corporations, and lobbyists to rethink their strategies of influence.

LOBBYING THE BUREAUCRACY AND THE REGULATORY AGENCIES

Despite holding slender Republican majorities in both the House and the Senate, President Trump found it difficult to pass much major legislation. Aside from 2017's large tax cut, that most fundamental of Republican priorities, Trump's policy successes with Congress were modest in 2017–2018. After the Democrats won control of the House in 2018, they slowed even further. Indeed, save for his partnership with the Senate majority leader in confirming record numbers of conservative judges, Trump demonstrated little capacity to act as a legislative leader. But that does not matter much to a president who was determined to roll back dozens of Obama-era (and prior) regulations and administrative rules that he and his supporters, many of them organized interests, deemed detrimental to business.[3]

Regulatory lobbying constitutes a substantial amount of activity across all administrations, but in the Trump presidency, as attempts to reverse regulatory actions have grown, such lobbying necessarily increases. For example, environmental regulations have come under special attack, as many Trump appointees have proved receptive to claims within the business community that these rules have been unduly restrictive. Since 2017, sixty-eight separate environmental regulations have been challenged by the administration, prompting enhanced actions by hundreds of environmental lobbyists.[4]

The *increase* in regulatory lobbying has occurred despite a *decrease* in rule-making in the Trump administration. One early study of relevant regulatory meetings found that despite a clear decline in rule-making, lobbying on regulatory issues increased, in large part because of the attempts to roll back or eliminate existing regulations. Compared to the first year of the Obama administration, regulatory lobbying in the Trump administration rose sharply in five cabinet domains: Health and Human Services, Labor, Commerce, Interior, and the Environmental Protection Agency (EPA). While the EPA has consistently generated lots of lobbying, the other areas reflected Trump administration priorities as to labor and business restrictions, the Affordable Care Act, and federal land policies (Potter 2018). While businesses and trade associations continued to provide the bulk of the lobbying in 2017, nonprofit/public interest lobbying rose sharply, as these groups generally defended the existing rules, promulgated under past administrations.

As a Brookings study concludes, "Focusing on those meetings about rules that were deregulatory (i.e., those that explicitly dealt with rescissions or implementation delays), nonprofit groups dominated, holding 1.2 meetings for every one held by a business or industry group. Put simply, much of the surge in nonprofit lobbying was a direct response to the administration's deregulatory agenda" (Potter 2018).

In part, such nonprofit advocacy flowed directly from the Trump administration's hiring policies, in that the number of former lobbyists in government jobs in 2017–2018 was four times that total for the first six years of Obama's presidency (see below for more on the revolving door into government) (Mora 2019).

Although regulatory lobbying grew from 2017 on, its practice looked a lot like such advocacy in previous administrations, albeit with different emphases. But that cannot be said of two other means for exerting influence in the Trump administration: (a) lobbying the president personally and through directed media and (b) placing advocates inside the administration.

LOBBYING THE PRESIDENT: A TIME LIKE NO OTHER

It's two different worlds. Under President Obama, the government was a finely tuned instrument, all the parts working together to produce a single note. You needed to work with everybody to calibrate the sound. Today, for the most part, it's a one-man band, the

President in a never-ending guitar solo on the White House lawn, overpowering all the
other instruments.
—Eric Bovim, public-affairs agency managing director

In past administrations, directly lobbying the president was difficult
and rare, although not unheard of; all presidents have their friends
and confidants, some of whom may use their ties to push particular
policies. Still, most presidents resist special pleading, per Eric Bovim's comments on policy making under Obama, where all the parts
needed to fit together. Given his personality and lack of governmental
experience, Trump has placed far fewer barriers between himself and
those who seek to influence him. Like most presidents, he meets more
with principals—major corporation executives to top trade association leaders—than with lobbyists, and it is unclear what arguments
sway his decisions. And even with his informal administrative style,
immediate White House access is difficult to obtain.[5]

So how do organized interests approach Trump, who is simultaneously unpredictable and yet generally favorable to traditional Republican interests of low taxation and less regulation? Perhaps the
most powerful tactic for organized interests is to have one of their
advocates appointed to crucial offices, such as cabinet positions and
agency heads. This will be discussed in detail below, but while Trump
often gives trusted lieutenants, like Betsy DeVos, free rein, he often
keeps other top administrators on much shorter leashes. Even at the
very top levels, where continuity is ordinarily valued highly, Trump's
executive office and cabinet personnel have turned over far more frequently in his first three years than did those of his three predecessors
over their full first term (Tenpas 2020).[6]

For Trump, relying on acting officials may make short-term sense,
in that they have less latitude than do permanent and often Senate-
confirmed appointees. He observed, "I like acting because I can move
so quickly. It gives me more flexibility" (Samuels 2019). These individuals are highly dependent on the president's approval and are less
likely to form strong bonds with organized interests that populate the
policy community that surrounds a cabinet department or agency. If
interests cannot anticipate that an acting secretary will be able to address their issues, they may well seek to influence the president himself, despite the difficulty and uncertainty involved.

Buying Time

Donald Trump is unique within the American experience in that he has remained involved in his family's extensive investments, largely through their hospitality and real estate properties. Such potential conflicts of interest have raised serious (and unresolved) constitutional questions; what remains clear, however, is that many organized interests, corporations, and foreign nations believe that, by visiting Trump properties, most notably the Trump International in Washington and Mar-a-Lago in Palm Beach, they can (a) curry favor with the president and (b) have the chance for a direct conversation, one unlikely to occur through official White House channels.

Simply holding a major event at the Trump International means that the president's firm will profit; combining such an event with participation by the president or top-level administration officials could well provide enhanced access. For example, when the conservative women's group, Concerned Women for America, celebrated its fortieth anniversary in October 2019, it held the event at the Trump International. Among the guests were Secretary of State Mike Pompeo and Vice President Mike Pence. Even more important was a congratulatory letter and video from President Trump. "That is the gold standard," said Kenda Bartlett, Concerned Women for America's executive director. "If we can get that, the rest of this is just dressing" (Lipton and Karni 2019).

Of course, merely staying at the Trump International or dining at Mar-a-Lago offers no guarantee of influence. Still, at least twenty-two foreign governments spent money at Trump properties worldwide during the first two years of his presidency, including the government of Cyprus underwriting a "Justice for Cyprus" conference that sought to counter prospective Turkish influence within the island nation. And one Saudi sheik who hoped to influence American policy spent tens of thousands of dollars for a twenty-six-day stay at the Trump International (Lipton and Karni 2019).

If Trump's Washington hotel allows for occasional personal access, his Mar-a-Lago resort provides a more relaxed and informal setting, one in which the president frequently interacts with members and their guests. Indeed, as Axios reported: "At Mar-a-Lago, we're seeing a whole new form of lobbying. People pay dues to the private club of the president of the United States, then try to influence him in person on government policy—all outside the normal watchdogs and strictures and surveillance of Washington."[7]

Again, access scarcely leads to influence, but at least in one policy arena—the Veterans Administration (VA)—personal contacts almost certainly affected policy. Three club members consistently intervened in VA policies in 2017–2018, often addressing core personnel issues and developing new initiatives. If and when they ran into trouble, one of this group, Marvel Comics chairman Ike Perlmutter,[8] could call his close friend President Trump to run interference (Arnsdorf 2018). Although this group argues, at least implicitly, that they were simply attempting to help a troubled agency, their actions sometimes became self-serving. What is remarkable is that this informal arrangement, which frequently had the group bullying the VA secretary, Daniel Sulkin, continued over a lengthy period and with the knowledge of hundreds of VA officials.

Such a relationship between outsiders and top-tier administrators is unusual, perhaps even unique. It was made possible because President Trump endorsed the arrangement, either tacitly or directly, and his friendship with Perlmutter undergirded these informal ties. At least for a while, VA policy was largely run by Trump's Mar-a-Lago cronies. But personal access to the president stood as only one of many tools for seeking influence.

An Audience of One

Even the most casual observer of Donald Trump understands that he consumes media, and especially television, voraciously. He spends his mornings and evenings watching both his favored network (Fox) and those with whom he most disagrees (MSNBC, CNN). He talks regularly with Fox's Sean Hannity and the crew at Fox and Friends. Moreover, we know of his habits through his almost-daily rantings about unfavorable coverage ("Fake news!").

Although Trump's media habits are worthy of extended analysis, for policy advocates, the very fact of his media appetite opened a new, remarkable avenue for influence. Relatively early in his administration's tenure, lobbyists and consultants came to understand that they could reach the president's eyes and ears by making their case on Fox. They could accomplish this in at least two ways: by convincing program hosts (Hannity, O'Reilly, and Carlson, among others) to address their specific issues or by getting the hosts to book guests who would make their case.

The president's media habits related directly to the serious problems faced by Washington lobbyists after Trump took office in 2017. As one story put it: "From the beginning, pressing a case with Trump was difficult for a run-of-the-mill lobbyist: Veteran GOP influencers—the establishment—didn't have many friends in Trump's inner circle. With the administration struggling to fill agency positions, even many well-connected consultants and lobbyists didn't have a lot of other corners of the government to go to for help. Instead, the focus was on Trump" (Mullins 2019). Advocates sought ways to get their ideas before the president by getting favorable stories into his morning brief or by indirectly seeking to influence his daughter and son-in-law. Still, those strategies paled before the emerging tack of appealing to Trump through his obsessive television viewing. As one Republican consultant noted, "The President's favorite topic is himself. What better way to get him interested in a message than by providing him with the thing that he's most obsessed with?" (Mullins 2019).

Buying advertising time on shows that Trump is likely to watch, including golf tournaments and a host of Fox shows, while potentially effective, is also expensive and unreliable. Policy advocates continue the advertising strategy but have added another element—booking spokespersons on key shows, mostly on Fox, who will deliver an apparently objective message to their audience of one. To be sure, these Trump-centric media initiatives are difficult to assess for their effectiveness, but in a situation in which conventional lobbying is problematic, due to policy uncertainties and personnel shuffling, seeking Trump's attention has become a continuing, viable strategy.

FOXES IN THE HENHOUSE: INFLUENCE WITHIN THE TRUMP ADMINISTRATION

Even with President Trump becoming the focal point of many lobbying efforts, the most profound and systematic change in the politics of influence within his administration has come with the appointment of many advocates to major positions of power. Given that much of the Trump deregulation agenda depends on rolling back Obama-era rules, cabinet secretaries and agency heads wield disproportionate power through administrative decision-making, even when an issue is highly controversial. Take the case of changing the rules on so-called payday lending (Confessore and Cowley 2020).

Payday lending has long attracted substantial lobbying, including more than an average of $4 million in expenditures between 2009 and

2019.[9] Regulations promulgated by the Obama administration were finalized in 2017 and were due to go into effect in 2020. This effort by the Consumer Financial Protection Bureau (CFPB) constituted the first national regulation of this highly profitable industry that prospered by charging exorbitant interest rates on short-term loans, largely to the poor. The brainchild of Elizabeth Warren, before she became a US senator, the CFPB was energetically opposed by many Republicans and the business community, even as it won passage in 2010. Although President Obama appointed Warren to help set up the agency, he did not nominate her to head it because he anticipated Republican opposition in the Senate.

Since its inception in 2011, the CFPB has returned more than $12 billion to consumers in judgments, but Republicans and the Trump administration have continued to see it as a prime example of regulatory overreach. Former House member and then budget director Mick Mulvaney was appointed acting CFPB director in 2017; one of his major missions was to undo the pending payday loan regulations, which the industry had continued to lobby against. One major problem was that attempts to overturn many Obama-era regulations had ended up in court, slowing down and sometimes stopping the initiatives. Mulvaney's CFPB sought to overcome such court actions by providing research that would demonstrate that loosening the payday loan restrictions would not do much, if any, harm to consumers. Career civil-servant economists, including one who wrote a scathing letter upon his retirement, disagreed sharply with the preferred proposals of Mulvaney and other political appointees who opposed the regulations.

In late 2018, Kathleen Kraninger pushed ahead to produce revised, industry-friendly rules, which were based on flawed economic assumptions and received virtually no economic-based scrutiny. Like Mulvaney, Kraninger came to the CFPB from the Office of Management and Budget, where she had worked under Mulvaney. With opponents of strict payday loan regulations directing the CFPB, the industry had an overwhelming advantage in reducing the rules' impact. Although payday loan firms spent more than $3 million in 2019, their most important advocates by far were Mulvaney and Kraninger, who directed the agency and served as champions of modifying the regulations.

The CFPB case is just one of dozens, across many issue areas, in which top administrators came into office with clear policy agendas of their own, most often in concert with industry interests and, more broadly, President Trump. On environmental policy, for example, the *New York Times* reported that "of 20 key officials across several agencies, 15 came from careers in the oil, gas, coal, chemical or agriculture industries, while another three hail from state governments that have spent years resisting environmental regulations. At least four have direct ties to organizations led by Charles G. and the late David H. Koch, who have spent millions of dollars to defeat climate change and clean energy measures" (Friedman and O'Neill 2020).

More broadly, as of late 2019, 281 former lobbyists were working in the Trump administration; this represents four times the number of lobbyists as worked in the Obama administration over its first six years. This is a "staggering figure," said Virginia Canter of the DC-based legal nonprofit Citizens for Responsibility and Ethics in Washington. "It suggests that lobbyists see themselves as more effective in furthering their clients' special interests from inside the government rather than from outside" (Mora 2019). In other words, the foxes are not only in the henhouses, they are running them in the Trump era.

Most of these lobbyists-turned-administrators will return to the private sector, often to profit from their stay in government. That's part and parcel of the revolving door in Washington, DC. But some top officials enter government service not for future financial rewards but rather to further their own policy agendas in ways that go far beyond anything they could do on the outside. The poster child for this kind of fox in the henhouse is Secretary of Education Betsy DeVos. Amid much cabinet shuffling, she has held firm at the Department of Education, continuing an unrelenting series of attacks on public education that grow out of her long career as an advocate for less federal involvement in education and increased funding for private schools (Kaplan and Owings 2018).

With a long background in Michigan and national Republican politics, a net worth of a billion dollars or so, and a fervent desire to "reform" American education, DeVos brought clout and zealotry to her position as education secretary. To be sure, many cabinet secretaries bring personal agendas with them into office, but few have pursued their goals in such a single-minded fashion as DeVos. Broadly speaking, she has pushed school privatization in a host of ways, from defending questionable for-profit colleges to urging that funding follow students, wherever they choose to go, including religious schools. President Trump has expressed relatively little interest in this subject but has allowed Secretary DeVos, with her financial clout and partisan

ties in Michigan and beyond, to push as hard as possible for her anti–
public school agenda.

Even as DeVos has run into bipartisan congressional criticism, she
has plowed ahead with her administrative agenda (Binkley 2020), and
she has carried out the president's hostility to immigrants in denying
DACA students grants from the coronavirus rescue package. In carrying out both her agenda and the president's, her actions mirror those
of many other top administrators in the Trump administration, who
have aggressively favored fossil fuel interests and worked to reduce
the scope of public lands that grew under the Obama administration.

One authoritative study found that Trump's policies, carried out
by appointees at the Interior Department and the Bureau of Land
Management, has led to the largest rollback in public lands in American history (Golden-Kroner et al. 2019). One former Obama administration Interior appointee observed, "There's a quiet, almost covert,
effort to dismantle the public lands management infrastructure. It's
very effective. I call it evil genius." In short, who needs lobbyists if the
most important advocates for change occupy the top positions at the
relevant agencies?

SUMMARIZING LOBBYING IN THE TRUMP ERA

After more than three years in office, Donald Trump's impact on advocacy continues to be broad and possibly deep. Without question,
another four-year term would allow him to institutionalize many of
the changes that he has fomented, including drastically changing the
politics of deregulation, maintaining a focus on the presidency as a
locus for top-level lobbying, and encouraging more and more foxes
into the henhouse of public policy making. As one critic concluded,
"Trump has organized the executive branch as a mechanism to re-
ward allies and their political power. Lobbyists are hired not because
they're great at the specific matter that they lobby for but because
their specialty is delivering political results" (Mora 2019).

That is not to say that conventional lobbying has dried up. Far
from it. As the coronavirus pandemic exploded, many firms increased
their lobbying budgets. Perhaps most notably, Gilead Pharmaceuti-
cals upped its reported spending by almost one-third (32 percent)
in the first quarter of 2020 as it sought approval to use one of its established drugs (for malaria) to combat the effects of COVID-19.[10]
Despite mixed results from various studies, Gilead did win approval

to use Remdesivir for this purpose. More generally, drug companies increased their lobbying as billions of dollars became available for a host of pandemic initiatives.

Beyond the pharmaceutical industry, well-connected Trump administration lobbyists have signed up scores of new clients to soak up the waves of new spending that have replenished the swamp that the president never drained, despite some initial regulations of post–executive branch lobbying (Ye Hee Lee et al. 2020). As one former Trump administration official-turned-lobbyist stated, "The government is picking winners and losers in industries, so being able to have an understanding of … the pulse of this administration and thought patterns, and their processes as to how they got to these decisions years ago, provides help."

From the revolving door to lobbying the president personally or through the media to packing the administration with friendly advocates, the advocacy community has prospered in the Trump years. And rather than draining the swamp, the inside influence of many interests has swamped the drain within the executive branch.

NOTES

1. See www.opensecrets.org; US Senate, via Statista.

2. See www.opensecrets.org; US Senate, via Statista.

3. For the extent of this rollback, see "Tracking Deregulation in the Trump Era," Brookings Institute, January 12, 2020, https://www.brookings.edu/interactives/tracking-deregulation-in-the-trump-era/.

4. For these actions, see "Tracking," https://www.brookings.edu/interactives/tracking-deregulation-in-the-trump-era/.

5. With apologies to Doris Kearns Goodwin.

6. For this turnover, see "Tracking," https://www.brookings.edu/research/tracking-turnover-in-the-trump-administration/.

7. See "Why Trump Is a Florida Man," Axios, June 9, 2019, https://www.axios.com/why-trump-is-a-florida-man-c3bc5117-db13-427b-8a5e-b27e7205c278.html.

8. Yes, Marvel Comics.

9. See "Industry Profile: Payday Lenders," OpenSecrets, accessed February 3, 2020, https://www.opensecrets.org/federal-lobbying/industries/summary?id=F1420&year=2019.

10. See "Gilead Lobbying Rose as Interest in COVID-19 Treatment Climbed," NPR, May 2, 2020, https://www.npr.org/sections/health-shots/2020/05/02/849149873/gilead-lobbying-rose-as-interest-in-covid-19-treatment-climbed.

REFERENCES

Alexander, Dan. "The Case of Wilbur Ross' Phantom $2 Billion." *Forbes Magazine,* December 12, 2017.

Arnsdorf, Isaac. "The Shadow Rulers of the VA." *ProPublica,* August 7, 2018.

Baker, Peter. "Alice Marie Johnson Is Granted Clemency by Trump after Push by Kim Kardashian West," *The New York Times,* June 6, 2018.

Baumgartner, Frank R., Jeffrey M. Berry, Marie Hojnacki, Beth L. Leech, and David C. Kimball. *Lobbying and Policy Change: Who Wins, Who Loses, and Why.* Chicago: University of Chicago Press, 2009.

Binkley, Collin. "Senate Passes Rebuke of DeVos Over Student Loan Forgiveness." *Associated Press,* March 11, 2020.

Blake, Aaron. "Trump's Government Full of Temps." *Washington Post,* February 21, 2020.

Clark, Charles, S. "Deconstructing the Deep State." *Government Executive.* N.d.

Confessore, Nicholas, and Stacy Cowley. "Trump Employees Manipulated Agency's Payday Lending Research, Ex-Staffer Claims." *New York Times,* April 29, 2020.

Friedman, Lisa, and Claire O'Neill. "Who Controls Trump's Environmental Policy?" *New York Times,* January 14, 2020.

Golden-Kroner, Rachel E., Siyu Quin, Carly N. Cook, Roopa Krithivasan, Shalynn M. Pack, Oscar D. Bonilla, Kerry Anne Cort-Kansinally, Bruno Coutinho, Mingmin Feng, Maria Isabel Martínez Garcia, Yifan He, Chris J. Kennedy, Clotilde Lebreton, Juan Carlos Ledezma, Thomas E. Lovejoy, David A. Luther, Yohan Parmanand, César Augusto Ruíz-Agudelo, Edgard Yerena, Vilisa Morón Zambrano, and Michael B. Mascia. "The Uncertain Future of Protected Lands and Waters." *Science,* May 31, 2019.

Hall, Richard, and Geoffrey Lorenz. "Revolving Door Access: Insider Ties, Legislative Allies, and Lobbying on the Affordable Care Act." Working paper. University of Michigan, 2018.

Johnson, Brian. "Trump-Connected Lobbying Firms Brought in Record Revenues in 2019." *Open Secrets News,* January 29, 2019.

Kaplan, Leslie S., and William A. Owings. "Betsy DeVos's Education Reform Agenda: What Principals—and Their Publics—Need to Know." *NASSP Bulletin* 102, no. 1 (2018): 58–84.

LaPira, Timothy M., and Herschel Thomas. "Just How Many Newt Gingrich's Are There on K Street? Estimating the True Size and Shape of Washington's Revolving Door." April 2, 2013. Available at SSRN: https://ssrn.com/abstract=2241671 or http://dx.doi.org/10.2139/ssrn.2241671.

LaPira, Timothy M., and Herschel F. Thomas. *Revolving Door Lobbying: Public Service, Private Influence, and the Unequal Representation of Interests.* University Press of Kansas, 2017.

Lipton, Eric, and Annie Karni. "Checking in at Trump Hotels for Kinship (and maybe Some Sway)." *New York Times,* October 25, 2019.

Lowery, Rich. "The Phenomenal Incoherence of Donald Trump." Politico, August 12, 2015.

McKean, David. *Tommy the Cork: Washington's Ultimate Insider, From FDR to Reagan.* Lebanon, NH: Steerforth, 2004.

Meyer, Theodoric. "The Most Powerful Lobbyist in Trump's Washington." Politico, April 2, 2018.

———. "Trump-Connected Lobbying Firms Cash In with Foreign Governments." Politico, March 15, 2019.

Mora, David. "Update: We Found a 'Staggering' 281 Lobbyists Who've Worked in the Trump Administration." *ProPublica,* October 15, 2019.

Mullins, Luke. "How Lobbying Has Changed in Donald Trump's Washington." *Washingtonian,* March 10, 2019.

Perez, Andrew, Abigail Luke, and Tim Zelina. "Business Group Spending on Lobbying in Washington Is at Least Double What's Being Reported." *Intercept,* August 6, 2019.

Potter, Rachel Augustine. "Regulatory Lobbying Has Increased under Trump Administration, but the Groups Doing the Lobbying may Surprise You." *Brookings Institution,* July 11, 2018.

Rizzo, Salvadore. "Wilbur Ross's False Claims to Congress That the Census Citizenship Question Was DOJ's Idea." *Washington Post,* June 30, 2018.

Robbins, Jim. "Open for Business: The Trump Revolution on America's Public Lands." *Yale Environment 360,* October 8, 2019.

Samuels, Brett. "Trump Learns to Love Acting Officials." Hill, April 14, 2019.

Shabad, Rebecca. "Lobbyists, Lawmakers Rated Dishonest, Unethical in Poll." *Hill,* December 16, 2013.

Tenpas, Kathryn Dunn. "Archive Version of Brookings White House Turnover Tracker." *Brookings Institution,* 2019. https://www.brookings.edu/research/appendix-archive-version-of-brookingss-white-house-turnover-tracker/.

———. "Tracking Turnover in the Trump Administration." *Brookings Institution,* 2020. https://www.brookings.edu/research/tracking-turnover-in-the-trump-administration/.

Tindera, Michela. "How Wilbur Ross Made a Fortune in Blue-Collar Industries." *Forbes Magazine,* January 18, 2017.

Whitney, Jake. "Trump Bashed Lobbyists. Now He's Their BFF." *Daily Beast,* August 18, 2018.

Ye Hee Lee, Michelle, Tom Hamburger, and Anu Narayanswamy. "Well-Connected Trump Alumni Benefit from Coronavirus Lobbying Rush." *Washington Post,* April 30, 2020.

CHAPTER 11

The Rhetoric of Disruption:
Trump and the Media

Matthew Eshbaugh-Soha and Joshua P. Montgomery

INTRODUCTION

Donald Trump's strategy of media leadership has elicited much commentary and speculation. Some see Trump as a master manipulator of
the media, driving news coverage in bursts of excitement, not unlike
on an episode of *The Apprentice*. A tale of incompetence is woven by
those who seek to undermine the Trump presidency, spreading "fake
news" stories and other inaccuracies (Dawes 2017). Others contend
that the daily chaos visible from the White House is a clear illustration
of this president's ineptitude (Waldman 2017). Nowhere would this
be more evident than in the president's handling of the news media,
his strategy of antagonism, and his seeming inability to build upon
communication successes, like his first Address to a Joint Session of
Congress, which was widely praised (Blake 2018). Rather, President
Trump appears too frequently to fall into the Twitter trap, blasting
enemies to create a buzz yet failing to generate a steady stream of
policy news coverage essential to presidential leadership and goal
accomplishment.

A clear example of Trump's strategy for media leadership occurred
even before the president took the oath of office. On January 11, 2017,
President-elect Donald Trump held a press conference. Preceded by

Sean Spicer and Vice President–Elect Mike Pence, the initial focus of the press conference—although it also included details about the presidential transition and Trump's economic, domestic, and foreign policies—was to sternly refute a report from Buzzfeed that speculated about the existence of a presidential dossier that had compromising information about the president-elect. Whether or not it was prudent of Buzzfeed to run the story, Trump was combative and critical of "fake news" coverage, and his demeanor previewed the many testy exchanges he would have as president with mainstream media (Trump 2017).

Presidents attacking the media is a phenomenon as old as the nation. George Washington is purported to have complained that coverage of his administration displayed "all the invective that disappointment, ignorance of facts, and malicious falsehoods could invent to misrepresent my policies" (Shogan 2001, 10). And it may be a good strategy for presidents to attack the news media, given the overall lack of trust Americans have in media institutions. Trust in media bottomed out at 32 percent during the 2016 presidential election, providing the Trump communications team with some data to justify their approach to media relations. Nevertheless, the increase in trust to 41 percent as of September 2019 (Gallup 2019) and the seemingly constant distractions that @realDonaldTrump appears to generate daily raise the question of whether Trump's antagonistic media strategy is effective or not, and, if so, in what ways.

If the president's goal in antagonizing the media is to create negative news coverage as a way to leverage support from his hardened supporters, then he has achieved his goal. President Trump has simply generated more negative coverage than any recent presidential administration. According to Patterson (2017, 8), 80 percent of President Trump's early news coverage was negative. This easily surpasses the negative coverage that burdened Presidents Obama (41 percent negative), Bush (57 percent negative), and Clinton (60 percent negative). Moreover, Trump's coverage was more negative on all broadcast and cable news outlets, including Fox News Channel. Negative coverage persisted across issue areas, with only coverage of the economy approaching 50 percent positive (Patterson 2017, 11). The president has also led the amount of news, initiating the most news coverage about his presidency and being cited most frequently (Mitchell et al. 2017). His own words, especially, dominate television news, as 65 percent of TV talking time is devoted to the president (Patterson 2017, 5).

In spite of predominately negative news coverage, the tangible costs to the president appear minimal. Trump's job approval ratings have remained relatively constant throughout his presidency and have been especially high among Republicans (Gallup 2020), and his success in Congress has been more or less as predicted (Bond 2019a). Yet, it remains unclear what impact his strategy of antagonism has had on news coverage of specific policy priorities. The purpose of this chapter is to take a closer look at the relationship between President Trump and the news media by detailing news coverage of two significant events during the first part of the Trump presidency: the nomination of Neil Gorsuch and the failed attempt by Congress to repeal Obamacare. How often did the president make news coverage of these issues across different media? Was the news more likely to cover the president's tweets or his speeches?

This topic is important for several reasons. First, it applies data to an enduring debate of the Trump presidency: whether the president's strategy of antagonizing the news media has produced significant benefits for the president or whether it has hindered his ability to generate news about his administration's priorities. Second, it extends our understanding of presidential leadership of the news media by examining the president's use of Twitter alongside traditional public remarks. No president has used Twitter as Trump has, and this study allows us to see whether Twitter is an effective vehicle of news leadership, and if it adds to or detracts from traditional forms of presidential communication, like speeches. Third, the implications of the findings speak to the independence of news media, including whether they continue to cover the president professionally even amid heightened criticism from the White House and whether news coverage of Trump's priorities has varied by traditional or online news sources.

WHAT WE KNOW ABOUT THE PRESIDENCY AND THE MEDIA

The give-and-take between presidents and the news media is central to what we know about presidential news coverage. Our understanding of media–president relations is founded upon one enduring feature: mutual benefit and antagonism (Grossman and Kumar 1981). After all, nothing requires the president and media to interact, but each needs the other to do their jobs optimally. At the same time, neither is ever satisfied with what the other brings to a relationship that generates significant conflict, especially since Watergate (Clayman et al. 2005).

Even as new media technologies afford presidents more opportunities to reach the public directly, presidents still require news media to reach national, local, and increasingly fragmented public audiences. This claim is supported by four areas of research, each of which connects the president to the public through news coverage. First, news coverage affects the public's agenda or those issues the public finds important (Iyengar 1991; Iyengar and Kinder 1987). Second, media coverage—perhaps of the president's agenda—affects the public's familiarity with and knowledge of issues (Page and Shapiro 1992). Third, media coverage of issues primes the public to evaluate the president favorably or unfavorably, depending on the issues covered (Edwards, Mitchell, and Welch 1995; Krosnick and Kinder 1990). In other words, when the media report extensively on an issue, the public uses that issue to evaluate the president's job performance, controlling for other dominant factors like party identification. Finally, media framing matters to the public's perception of issues (Gilliam and Iyengar 2001). If presidents are to influence the way the media covers an issue, they will need to engage the media to ensure that their views are part of the public's views on policies. In all, presidents typically enjoy twice the broadcast news coverage of Congress and nearly ten times more coverage than the US Supreme Court over a calendar year (Graber and Dunaway 2015, 175).

The media benefit from covering the president in a variety of ways. First, the president's words and actions are clearly newsworthy. Thus, simply by reporting on the president of the United States, journalists can meet their professional goal to cover timely and important issues (Graber and Dunaway 2015). Second, news coverage of the president is likely to drive profit (see Hamilton 2004). Since the public is most interested in the president (among politicians), newscasts about the president guarantee sufficient viewers to generate profit, especially among news organizations whose primary task is to cover presidential politics.

Even so, news media have other priorities besides covering the president. Media desire profit and tend to prefer soft, entertainment and celebrity-related news, rather than hard policy-related news. Much negative coverage of the presidency may not even center on policies but on superficial or other scandalous stories that attract more viewers. Patterson (2017) shows, for example, that news is less likely to have a policy component and more likely to be sensational and presented as soft, rather than hard, news. Even local news coverage, which provides an opportunity for the president to generate more positive coverage, also tends to be less substantive. About half of the front-page, local newspaper coverage of President George W. Bush's Social Security reform tour was descriptive, for example (Eshbaugh-Soha and Peake 2006). Furthermore, presidential news coverage has declined over time, as measured by stories printed in the *New York Times* or broadcast on network television (Cohen 2008). It is no surprise that presidents adjust their media outreach strategies in the face of changing traditional news coverage, which perhaps contributed to the rise of Twitter under Trump.

Perhaps the most reliable result of the president–media relationship is negative coverage. Using content analysis of news coverage from the early months of the Reagan, Bush, Clinton, and George W. Bush administrations, Farnsworth and Lichter (2006, 51) show that only 1989—the first year of George H. W. Bush's presidency—produced news coverage that was more than 40 percent positive. Even President Obama, who enjoyed more positive coverage than his predecessors, quickly found that negative news coverage was likely when his honeymoon period was over. In fact, news coverage of Obama's policies was not overly positive, as he received only 37 percent positive coverage on his economic policy (Schwab 2009). Networks also report more frequently on the president's approval rating when it declines (Groeling and Kernell 1998), and this pattern of coverage varies by the partisan slant of a television news station (Groeling 2008). Even local news coverage that centers on policy, such as the Iraq War in 2003, produces more negative than positive coverage (Eshbaugh-Soha and Peake 2008).

PRESIDENTIAL LEADERSHIP OF THE NEWS MEDIA

Presidents have many opportunities to lead the news media and generate news coverage of their administrations, and White House staff go to great lengths to facilitate public outreach. On the one hand, the Office of Communications helps the president reach media outside of Washington, DC (Maltese 1994). In particular, it helps cultivate relationships with local and regional media by granting interviews and providing valuable information (Kumar 2007). On the other hand, the Press Office interacts predominately with the Washington Press Corps (Walcott and Hult 1995), with the press secretary being the primary conduit between the press and the president's preferences and points of view (Kumar 2007). It is not simply the president, therefore, that affects leadership of the news but also White House institutions and the individuals who lead them.

There are three primary ways that presidents target news coverage through traditional speeches. First, the national address provides presidents with the best opportunity to lead news coverage. Regardless of the policy area, presidents have some success leading news coverage through national speeches, although it is far from guaranteed that the president will increase news coverage of his policy priorities (Peake and Eshbaugh-Soha 2008; see Wanta et al. 1989). Second, "going local," when presidents travel domestically, allows them to target local media and audiences to generate news coverage. Presidents stage scripted "media events," designed to attract support for presidents and their policies. The White House knows that local reporters, who are less experienced than members of the Washington Press Corps (Kaniss 1991), may be more likely to cover the president in a positive way (Cohen 2010). Results support this expectation, especially in geographic areas that already support the president (Barrett and Peake 2007). Third, presidential press conferences also tend to set the news agenda (Eshbaugh-Soha 2013), especially when they are solo (and thus more newsworthy) press conferences. In all of these instances, presidents generate news coverage because they are accessible to the media, which reduces the cost of creating presidential news.

Two other factors are relevant to presidential leadership of the news. First, issue salience may be the single most important factor that predicts presidential leadership of the news. Simply put, presidents succeed in leading the news on issues that are not salient (Eshbaugh-Soha and Peake 2011; Peake 2001) yet respond to news coverage on salient foreign policy (Edwards and Wood 1999) and economic (Eshbaugh-Soha and Peake 2005) issues. In short, when presidents act entrepreneurially and prioritize a policy not previously on the news, they are more likely to dictate news coverage of those issues. Second, the president's ability to focus on a topic and direct news coverage to it alone can enhance news coverage. Although the *New York Times* and *Washington Post* cover the president's legislative appeals only about 40 percent of the time (Barrett 2007), presidents can shape news coverage strategically by focusing extensively on a single policy in their speech or speaking in multiple speeches about the same topic (Cohen 2010, 116). Newer media holds promise for presidential leadership, too. According to Eshbaugh-Soha (2016), cable news programs, *Special Report* (Fox) and *Hardball* (MSNBC), covered the president's speeches most frequently, on forty of the fifty-four days in which the president delivered a speech. Traditional news sources covered the president an average of twenty-two out of fifty-four days the president gave a speech compared with even less coverage, about twenty days, on online news sources (Drudge Report, Fox News, and Huffington Post). Taken together, these findings show both the potential for presidential leadership of the media and the limitations to doing so consistently, even with more news outlets available.

PRESIDENT TRUMP AND THE NEWS MEDIA

The conventional wisdom is that Donald Trump has changed the president's relationship with the news media. Certainly, the opening vignette of this chapter illustrates a clear and concerted effort by President Trump and his administration to antagonize the news media, much to the delight of the president's core supporters. That press briefings under Sarah Sanders were infrequent (and under Stephanie Grisham nonexistent) undoubtedly inflamed tensions between the press and the president, simultaneously diminishing the president's ability to lead the news agenda. President Trump is also the first president to actively use Twitter to lead the news media. Twitter may also allow President Trump to bypass the media all together, communicating directly with core supporters and other followers. Even though we associate Trump with Twitter, the president still uses traditional means of public outreach, suggesting his presidency illustrates both differences and similarities with other recent presidencies.

How Trump Is Different from Other Presidents

There are many ways that Trump is different from other presidents. To begin, President Trump has a unique style of media engagement. Although the president has been more available to reporters than President Obama was (Bedard 2018)—in the cabinet meeting room, while walking to and from Marine One, or in joint press conferences with foreign leaders—he has shunned solo press conferences and national addresses. Indeed, a casual observer might infer that Trump's January 2019 national address was pushed on him by his staff, that they urged him to try something he had yet to do: speak from the Oval Office to gain control of the debate surrounding the government shutdown and reassert his version of the story. Stylistically, President Trump looked uncomfortable in the Oval Office setting and ultimately failed to achieve what he wanted: an increase in funding for his border wall.

The president looks much more comfortable and appears to enjoy speaking in prime-time in a campaign rally format.[1] These speeches tend to be broadcast live on the array of conservative cable television stations, for example, Fox News Channel, Fox Business Channel, and One America News Network, and they allow him to engage directly with ardent supporters and criticize his opponents, much to the crowd's delight. Just as the president will claim credit for a strong economy, successful trade deals with China, and military action against Iran, he transitions easily to superficial (but perhaps popular) topics, fixating on dishwashers and lightbulbs, for example (Weinberg 2020). Even though these comments contain an underlying policy element, they are not part of a consistent message, which seems necessary for effective public leadership (Edwards 2003).

Among the ways in which President Trump may be most different from other presidents in media outreach is his use of Twitter. Simply put, Trump is the first president to actively and consistently use Twitter on a daily basis. Yes, the Obama administration used Twitter occasionally and was even the first White House to emphasize "specialty media" in its Media Affairs Office (White House Transition Project 2019). It has been the Trump administration, however, that championed Twitter during the presidential election campaign—its negative news coverage and all (Patterson 2017)—and has used the medium frequently in office. He has tweeted a range of sentiments, from the more ceremonial—Happy Mother's Day!—to setting policy, for example, banning transgender individuals from serving in the US Armed Forces.

Has the president's use of Twitter driven news coverage and in what way? There are several reasons to think that Twitter would be effective for presidential leadership of the news. First, it is relatively easy for media to report a president's tweets. When the costs associated with covering the president are lower than its benefits (Cohen 2010), coverage is likely to increase. Moreover, when presidents can control their message, they may not be as reliant on traditional media. These consequences have traditionally been associated with national addresses, press conferences, and going local (Cohen 2010; Eshbaugh-Soha and Peake 2006). For Trump, Twitter provides another available and completely accessible means of presidential communication, one that simply requires journalists to check the president's Twitter feed every now and again for a scoop. As Major Garrett notes, however, this can be exhausting and require caution regarding what journalists report and when and how they report it (Bedard 2018). Trump seems to use Twitter to appeal to the superficial, negative, and entertainment-oriented coverage preferred by news media and the public. This is not without blowback: Trump is the first president to have a regular count of lies, as reported in the *Washington Post,* and his inconsistent statements on his presidency and policy complicate understanding the president's true public positions (see Bond 2019b). Trump has regularly called for changes to gun control laws, for example, only to walk back his comments days after a mass shooting.[2]

Even though Twitter affords the president another opportunity to lead news coverage, the nature of that coverage may not be consistent with the president's policy goals. The superficial distracts from policy, and given that media prefer the superficial to the substantive, a Tweet may generate news coverage, though not always the coverage that helps the president achieve his policy goals. This suggests that even if tweeting increases the volume of news coverage, it is unlikely to affect the content or tone of that coverage. Of course, some contend that President Trump is more concerned about ratings and reelection than he is about policy, but we still assume—as we do with all presidents—that good policy is a top goal, even when one president emphasizes it less than others have. Thus, we assume that President Trump intends to use Twitter to help achieve his goals, adding tweets to the more traditional use of speeches to do so.

Currently, we know very little about whether or not the content of Trump's tweets influences the news. Initial studies of President Trump's social media use describe the uncivil tone of Trump's tweets (Ott 2017) or show a consistent and negative tone to candidate Trump's tweets (Gross and Johnson 2016). Even with this research, it is not entirely clear what the president's tweets about top administration priorities look like or how media cover them. On the one hand, President Trump's tweets could reflect the tenor of those used during the campaign. This may generate news coverage, but coverage that is likely to be negative and superficial and unhelpful in the president's policy goal achievement. On the other hand, President Trump's tweets could underscore the importance of his top priorities, generating news coverage that is more focused on the more substantive of the president's priorities. If used in this manner, Twitter could provide the president with another avenue for leading the news, not unlike recent presidents who used newer media effectively, for example, Ronald Reagan and television (Welch 2003) or George W. Bush, who went local successfully (Eshbaugh-Soha and Peake 2006).

How Trump Is Similar to Other Presidents

Even when presidents introduce disruptions to traditional media outreach strategies, they still rely on accepted strategies for media leadership. President Nixon, for example, institutionalized the Office of Communications upon taking office (Maltese 1994) but gave numerous addresses to Congress—a staple of prior presidents—to generate news coverage. President Reagan relied upon national addresses to communicate his top priorities (Kernell 1997) but also engaged the press in prime-time press conferences, not unlike John F. Kennedy. Moreover, Bill Clinton balanced first-of-its-kind policy bus tours with national addresses and press conferences (Kernell 1997). Even as the means of media outreach diversify, presidents still rely on other means of communication.

Indeed, presidents have long used a variety of speeches to communicate with the news media and have had some success driving news coverage doing so. This success extends to national addresses (Bradshaw, Coe, and Neumann 2014; Peake and Eshbaugh-Soha 2008), press conferences (Eshbaugh-Soha 2013), radio addresses (Horvit, Schiffer, and Wright 2008), and local speeches (Cohen 2010). The success presidents have may depend on the policy itself. Presidents tend to lead news coverage on issues not previously salient (Edwards and Wood 1999) and on those that are among their top policy priorities (Barrett 2007).

Along with Twitter, President Trump engages in traditional public outreach. Through October 2019, for example, President Trump delivered 336 remarks, with a whopping 90 (or 27 percent) listed as an "exchange with reporters" (American Presidency Project 2020). This outreach strategy is similar to that of other presidents, as President Obama, for example, had delivered 312 remarks through October 2011. These counts show that President Trump's public relations strategy is similar to other presidents, and his ability to generate news coverage of his policies should reflect findings of past research: presidents face minimal and mixed coverage except under negative conditions. After all, media have a journalistic incentive—even facing a daily barrage of criticism from the White House—to cover that which is newsworthy and to report the official line of the administration (Bennett 1990). Since this incentive has not changed, we do not expect coverage of Trump's speeches to vary significantly from previous presidencies.

CASE STUDIES: HEALTH-CARE REFORM AND THE GORSUCH NOMINATION

In this section, we examine President Trump's media outreach strategy. We report on Trump's use of Twitter, on the one hand, and his use of traditional speeches, on the other. Although we lack firm expectations for how media will respond to presidential tweets, we think that journalists consider the president's tweets to be newsworthy and that they should generate news coverage because they are relatively easy to report. We are curious about how media cover tweets on the president's priorities versus how they cover speeches on the same subjects, and whether speeches are more or less likely to be covered by news media given Trump's heavy reliance on Twitter.

We examine separately two of President Trump's top priorities during his first three months in office: his effort to repeal and replace Obamacare and the nomination of Neil Gorsuch to the US Supreme Court. Both issues were top campaign promises and, aside from a series of executive orders that also generated interest from the public and news media, were the president's primary goals upon taking office. We describe both the president's remarks—taken from his Twitter account and his public speeches, found in the *Public Papers of the Presidents*—and associated news coverage in the *New York Times* and two liberal online news sources, Slate and Politico, which we expect to cover Trump priorities negatively.[3]

Repeal and Replace Obamacare

Calls to repeal and replace Obamacare became a Republican rallying cry not long after Barack Obama signed it into law. Distaste for the Affordable Care Act helped to galvanize opponents of the former president, helping Republicans to take control of the House of Representatives in 2010 and the Senate in 2014. The call to repeal was a major feature of President Trump's 2016 presidential election campaign (Donovan and Kelsey 2017), and it became his first legislative priority.

Trump demonstrated his commitment to health-care reform early on, devoting a considerable amount of public attention to the issue, even as he delegated policy formulation to House Republicans. Along with outlining four specific features of a bill he would sign, including health insurance for those with preexisting conditions, tax credits, Medicaid flexibility at the state level, and the ability to purchase health care across state lines,[4] the president devoted thirty-eight spoken remarks or written statements to health care in the *Public Papers of the Presidents* and twenty-five tweets to repeal-and-replace efforts.[5] The president was critical in his commentary, focusing extensively on the "Obamacare disaster."[6] He regularly supported the Republican effort to repeal and replace Obamacare, tweeting the following as a bill was progressing through the House while simultaneously taking a jab at the news media: "Despite what you hear in the press, healthcare is coming along great. We are talking to many groups and it will end in a beautiful picture!" (@realDonaldTrump, March 9, 2017, 12:01pm). The president often remarked about the "great" health-care reform that would replace the Affordable Care Act and resisted tweeting anything critical about the Republican's efforts after the bill failed the House.[7] The Senate later killed a second attempt to reform health care in July.

New York Times coverage of the legislative effort to repeal and replace Obamacare was extensive. We found a total of 104 stories that covered it across 46 days from January 20 through March 30, 2017. Among these stories, twenty-nine (or 28 percent) were negative, amounting to an overall positive tone of coverage. Just as most stories referenced Donald Trump in one way or another, not all reported on the president's public outreach. Only fourteen stories cited a Trump tweet on health care. Coverage of the president's speeches was more frequent, as 32 out of the 104 stories specifically referenced the president's comments in a traditional speech. Yet, only one speech—his national address on February 28—generated more than one story. Because Trump did not offer his own proposal and, according to the *New York Times*, did not "jump in" to the health-care-bill debate until mid-March (Haberman and Pear 2017), most coverage, fifty-nine stories in total, centered on congressional efforts to achieve health-care reform. Among the remaining articles, twenty-one covered Tom Price's role in the health-care-reform process.

News coverage of health-care reform published in Slate and Po-

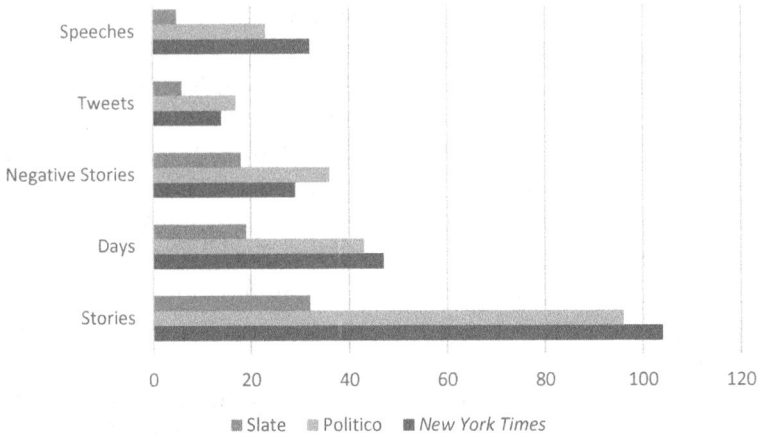

Figure 11.1: News Coverage Characteristics of Health-Care Reform. *Source:* Collected by the authors from the *Public Papers of the Presidents,* LexisNexis, Politico, and Slate.

litico is distinct. Both sources covered the president and his tweets at roughly the same percentage. Yet, Politico was more like the *New York Times* in terms of its amount of coverage, number of days with stories, number of negative stories, and tweets and speeches covered, as shown in figure 11.1. Slate offered less coverage and was more negative. We would have expected the online sources to be more similar than different in covering this topic, given their similar ideological leaning. As figure 11.1 shows overall, Trump's online and traditional news coverage was similar, and traditional speeches still drove news coverage more than the president's tweets did.

The Gorsuch Nomination

President Trump seized his first opportunity to nominate a justice to the US Supreme Court one month after taking office. Like health-care reform, the Supreme Court was a top issue during the 2016 presidential campaign. As Merrick Garland's nomination to replace the late Antonin Scalia stalled in the Senate, candidates Clinton and Trump both used the issue to motivate supporters. Whereas the fate of health-care reform was always likely to be unpredictable and complicated, given a Republican majority in the Senate, it follows that a dedicated public relations campaign was not needed to convince senators to confirm the president's nominee.

The data reflect this and show that Trump attended to the Gorsuch nomination in both his speeches and on Twitter, producing twenty-four remarks and twenty-six tweets between January 20 and March 30, 2017.[8] Most of the president's twenty-four remarks were short, at less than 150 words, suggesting from this sample, at least, that the brevity of Trump's traditional remarks could be influenced by his penchant for tweeting in brief. His five more prominent remarks included the prime-time announcement of Gorsuch's nomination. All tweets were matter-of-fact, with nothing particularly reminiscent of the more negative tweets reported during the 2016 presidential election campaign (Ott 2017) or that we revealed in the previous section about the effort to repeal and replace Obamacare. In fact, Trump tended to cheerlead this nomination, tweeting positively about Neil Gorsuch, his nomination, and the confirmation process.

New York Times coverage was modest, reporting less frequently on Gorsuch than on health-care reform. Through March 30, 2017, the *Times* produced twenty stories on the Gorsuch nomination. Although there were some moments of tension, including invoking the "nuclear option" to ensure Gorsuch's confirmation, the entire confirmation process was relatively uncontroversial. Indeed, the *New York Times* dubbed the hearings "the empty Supreme Court confirmation hearing," given Judge Gorsuch's tendency to avoid answering specific questions (Greenhouse 2017). Absent significant conflict, coverage is likely to be sparse and neutral, reflecting only the major events related to a story. This contrasts with repeal-and-replace efforts, which Donald Trump later learned was, in fact, complicated. Indeed, a Supreme Court nomination—absent a bombshell scandal like the one that Trump's second nominee, Brett Kavanaugh, faced—is relatively easy for administrations to control, much easier than shepherding a detailed policy proposal through a divided Congress.

Among the twenty stories that covered Gorsuch, most squarely covered the nomination process. The lack of conflict with the nomination itself led the *New York Times* to frame its Gorsuch coverage in relation to other elements of the Trump presidency. Two stories, for example, centered on how the Gorsuch nomination might factor into a Supreme Court battle related to the constitutionality of Trump's travel ban. The *Times* also connected Trump's campaign calls to revise libel laws to Gorsuch's record on freedom of the press issues. Of course, the substance of this coverage varies widely. Several focused on the Senate's approach to confirmation. Yet, the press did challenge

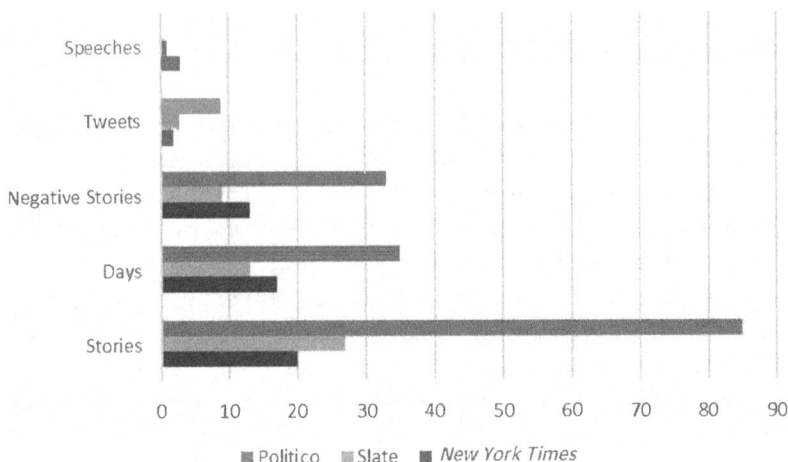

Figure 11.2: News Coverage Characteristics of the Gorsuch Nomination.
Source: Collected by the authors from the *Public Papers of the Presidents*,
LexisNexis, Politico, and Slate.

the president when it appeared that Gorsuch chided the president for
criticizing a "so-called judge." Covering elements related to Gorsuch
but not central to a relatively smooth confirmation process helped
contribute to more than half of the *Times* stories being more negative than positive. As figure 11.2 illustrates, only two stories covered
a tweet, and three stories covered a traditional speech, with two of
these stories centered on Trump's January 31, 2017, nomination announcement.

Examining online news coverage, we see precisely the opposite of
what we reported for coverage of health-care reform. *Times* coverage
was less and was more in line with Slate's coverage than with Politico's.
Politico continued to offer extensive coverage of the nomination—
and the most coverage among our three sources—with eighty-five stories over thirty-five days. Although it referenced nine tweets, Politico
did not cite a presidential speech. A lot of coverage referenced Trump
in relation to potential swing voters in the Senate. Among others, Politico ran stories on Claire McKaskill (D-MO), Bill Nelson (D-FL), and
Joe Manchin (D-WV). Of course, their votes ended up mattering very
little to the outcome of Gorsuch's nomination after Majority Leader
Mitch McConnell (R-KY) invoked the "nuclear option" to eliminate
the filibuster for Supreme Court nominations. The nuclear option was
covered extensively, including in twenty stories published by Politico.

CONCLUSION

Political scientists know a great deal about the presidency and the news media. Presidents and the media work in a symbiotic relationship, with elements of both antagonism and mutual benefit. Despite generating the most news coverage of any single political figure, presidents struggle to set the policy agenda and direct the news media to offer positive coverage of their policies and presidencies. With the advent of Twitter as a new means to influence news coverage, this chapter is an early attempt to see whether Twitter has indeed changed presidential news coverage.

In spite of Twitter's potential to enhance the president's public relations strategy, news coverage of the Trump presidency is not so different from that of other presidencies. As our data illustrate, traditional speeches still play a prominent role in news coverage, especially for health-care reform. Although coverage of speeches and tweets was more similar for the Gorsuch nomination, our findings do not support the implication of early studies, namely, that Twitter had significantly changed presidential communications (Ott 2019). Because we report considerably more coverage of tweets than speeches during the Gorsuch nomination on Politico, we concede that other news stories or online news outlets could also rely on presidential tweets more than on speeches.[9] After all, it may be that the culture of online newsrooms may be more receptive to Twitter than other media and as these sources continue to gain market share—and have more space to cover presidential news (Eshbaugh-Soha 2016)—they may increase their reliance on tweets in covering the presidency. Yet, despite the ease with which reporters may simply comment on and offer their opinions on the president's morning barrage of tweets, the substantive impact of the president's media strategy does not appear to have increased his influence over media, not unlike prior presidents' use of novel media relations strategies like going local. Moreover, Trump's antagonistic strategy does not appear to have hurt the president's relationship with the news media, as coverage is about what we expect absent a significant scandal that may have driven more stories and more negative coverage.

Without question, the Trump presidency is qualitatively different than other presidencies. The president appears to be more antagonistic and combative with the media, just as he is also more accessible and engaged in back-and-forth with reporters (Bedard 2018). His public style is unique, and he often ad-libs, falls off script, and offers inconsistent and contradictory statements (to himself and others in the administration) in his public accounts. None of this appears to have affected the motivation for news coverage for President Trump, at least on his top priorities, however. If our inferences are supported in other research, we conclude that, in spite of his antagonistic media relations strategy, news media have continued to act as an independent voice in American politics, covering President Trump's public statements on policy similarly to how they have covered other administrations. President Trump's primary difference from other presidencies may be that he has taken advantage of media's desire for superficial and scandalous coverage by using Twitter to dictate the daily news cycle with tweets related to superficial complaints and the myriad scandals afflicting the White House. This chapter does not explore this particular question at length, of course. A future research project should investigate the circumstances under which the president's tweets are likely to make the news. Perhaps the president's policy tweets will continue to fall silent, suggesting that although Twitter is now a part of the modern presidency, it may not help presidents reach the media and generate news coverage to secure their top policy priorities.

NOTES

1. This is not to say that Trump is the only president who likes this format. George W. Bush also appeared more engaged when he spoke before a crowd. Moreover, each president chooses their own ways to present a message. President Obama chose to announce the death of Bin Laden from the end of the Cross Hall in the White House, standing at a podium after walking down the red carpet. Another president may have chosen the Oval Office to make a similar announcement.

2. See "Remarks in an Exchange with Reporters Prior to Departure for Dayton, OH," August 7, 2019, and "Remarks Prior to a Meeting with President Klaus Iohannis of Romania and an Exchange with Reporters," August 14, 2019.

3. We searched for "Trump and Health Care" and "Gorsuch and Nomination" in our news sources. The *New York Times* is available on LexisNexis, and we used Google to search for these terms in both Politico and Slate.

4. "Address before a Joint Session of Congress," February 28, 2017.

5. We collected Tweets from both @POTUS (eight tweets) and @realDonaldTrump (seventeen tweets). Only one was a duplicate tweet.

6. "Our wonderful new Healthcare Bill is now out for review and nego-tiation. ObamaCare is a complete and total disaster—is imploding fast!" @realDonaldTrump, March 7, 2017, 7:13am.

7. "The President's News Conference with Chancellor Angela Merkel of Germany," March 17, 2017.

8. We collected Tweets from both @POTUS (sixteen tweets) and @real DonaldTrump (ten tweets). Although four were duplicate tweets, most were unique messages.

9. Our out-of-sample data from Breitbart produced coverage of only two presidential tweets, however.

REFERENCES

American Presidency Project. *Public Papers of the Presidents.* 2020. http://www .presidency.ucsb.edu/.

Barrett, Andrew. "Press Coverage of Legislative Appeals by the President." *Political Research Quarterly* 60 (2007): 655–668.

Barrett, Andrew W., and Jeffrey S. Peake. "When the President Comes to Town: Examining Local Newspaper Coverage of Domestic Presidential Travel." *American Politics Research* 35 (2007): 3–31.

Bedard, Paul. "CBS' Garrett: More Access to Trump than Obama, Bush, 'We See Him all the Time.'" *Washington Examiner,* October 9, 2018. https:// www.washingtonexaminer.com/washington-secrets/cbs-garrett-more -access-to-trump-than-obama-bush-we-see-him-all-the-time.

Bennett, W. Lance. "Toward a Theory of Press-State Relations in the U.S." *Journal of Communication* 40 (1990): 103–125.

Blake, Aaron. "Breaking Down Trump's Much-Praised 2017 Address to Con-gress: Where We Stand Today." *Washington Post,* January 30, 2018. https:// www.washingtonpost.com/news/the-fix/wp/2018/01/30/breaking -down-trumps-much-praised-2017-address-to-congress-where-we-stand -today/?utm_term=.696be959d682.

Bond, Jon R. "Contemporary Presidency: Which Presidents Are Uncommonly Successful in Congress? A Trump Update." *Presidential Studies Quarterly* 49 (2019a): 898–908.

———. "Validity and Reliability of Identifying Presidential Positions on Roll-Call Votes in the Age of Trump." *Presidential Studies Quarterly* 49 (2019b): 153–167.

Bradshaw, Seth C., Kevin Coe, and Rico Neumann. "Newspaper Attention to Major Presidential Addresses: A Reexamination of Conceptualizations, Predictors, and Effects." *Communication Reports* 27 (2014): 53–64.

Clayman, Steven E., Marc N. Elliot, John Heritage, and Laurie L. McDon-ald. "Historical Trends in Questioning Presidents: 1953–2000." *Presidential Studies Quarterly* 36 (2005): 561–583.

Cohen, Jeffrey E. *The Presidency in an Era of 24-Hour News.* Princeton, NJ: Princeton University Press, 2008.

———. *Going Local: Presidential Leadership in the Post-Broadcast Age.* New York: Cambridge University Press, 2010.

Dawes, Nic. "Trump Versus the Media: How to Cover a Hostile President." *Nation,* March 1, 2017. https://www.thenation.com/article/trump-versus-the-media-how-to-cover-a-hostile-president/.

Donovan, Chris, and Adam Kelsey. "Fact-checking Trump's 'Repeal and Replace' Obamacare Timeline." *ABC News,* March 24, 2017. https://abcnews.go.com/Politics/fact-checking-trumps-repeal-replace-obamacare-timeline/story?id=46360908.

Edwards, George C. III, William Mitchell, and Reed Welch. "Explaining Presidential Approval: The Importance of Issue Salience." *American Journal of Political Science* 39 (1995): 108–134.

Edwards, George C. III, and B. Dan Wood. "Who Influences Whom? The President, Congress, and the Media." *American Political Science Review* 93 (1999): 327–344.

Eshbaugh-Soha, Matthew. "Presidential Leadership of the News Media: The Case of the Press Conference." *Political Communication* 30 (2013): 548–564.

———. "Presidential Agenda-Setting of Traditional and Nontraditional News Media." *Political Communication* 30 (2016): 1–20.

Eshbaugh-Soha, Matthew, and Jeffrey S. Peake. "Presidents and the Economic Agenda." *Political Research Quarterly* 58 (2005): 127–138.

———. "The Contemporary Presidency: 'Going Local' to Reform Social Security." *Presidential Studies Quarterly* 36 (2006): 689–704.

———. "The Presidency and Local Media: Local Newspaper Coverage of President George W. Bush." *Presidential Studies Quarterly* 38 (2008): 606–627.

———. *Breaking through the Noise: Presidential Leadership, Public Opinion, and the News Media.* Stanford, CA: Stanford University Press, 2011.

Farnsworth, Stephen J., and S. Robert Lichter. *The Mediated Presidency: Television News and Presidential Governance.* Lanham, MD: Rowman & Littlefield, 2006.

Gallup. "Americans' Trust in Mass Media Edges Down to 41%," September 26, 2019. https://news.gallup.com/poll/267047/americans-trust-mass-media-edges-down.aspx.

———. "Trump Job Approval." 2020. https://news.gallup.com/poll/203207/trump-job-approval-weekly.aspx.

Gilliam, Franklin D., Jr., and Shanto Iyengar. "Prime Suspects: The Impact of Local Television News on the Viewing Public." *American Journal of Political Science* 44 (2000): 560–573.

Graber, Doris, and Johanna Dunaway. *Mass Media and American Politics,* 9th ed. Washington, DC: CQ, 2015.

Greenhouse, Linda. "The Empty Supreme Court Confirmation Hearing."

New York Times, March 30, 2017. https://www.nytimes.com/2017/03/30/opinion/the-empty-supreme-court-confirmation-hearing.html.

Groeling, Tim. "Who's the Fairest of the Them All? An Empirical Test for the Partisan Bias on ABC, CBS, NBC, and Fox News." *Presidential Studies Quarterly* 38 (2008): 631–657.

Groeling, Tim, and Samuel Kernell. "Is Network News Coverage of the President Biased?" *Journal of Politics* 60 (1998): 1063–1087.

Gross, Justin, and Kaylee Johnson. "Twitter Taunts and Tirades: Negative Campaigning in the Age of Trump." *PS: Political Science* 49, no. 4 (2016): 748–754.

Grossman, Michael, and Martha Kumar. *Portraying the President: The White House and the News Media*. Baltimore, MD: Johns Hopkins University Press, 1981.

Haberman, Maggie, and Robert Pear. "Trump Jumps In, Trying to Propel Health Care Bill." *New York Times*, March 9, 2017, A1.

Hamilton, James T. *All the News That's Fit to Sell*. Princeton, NJ: Princeton University Press, 2004.

Horvit, Beverly, Adam. J. Schiffer, and Mark Wright. "The Limits of Presidential Agenda Setting: Predicting Newspaper Coverage of the Weekly Radio Address." *International Journal of Press/Politics* 13 (2008): 8–28.

Iyengar, Shanto. *Is Anyone Responsible?* Chicago: University of Chicago Press, 1991.

Iyengar, Shanto, and Donald R. Kinder. *News That Matters: Television and American Opinion*. Chicago: University of Chicago Press, 1987.

Kaniss, Phyllis. *Making Local News*. Chicago: University of Chicago Press, 1991.

Kernell, Samuel. *Going Public: New Strategies of Presidential Leadership*, 3rd ed. Washington, DC: CQ, 1997.

Krosnick, Jon A., and Donald R. Kinder. "Altering the Foundations of Support for the President through Priming." *American Political Science Review* 84 (1990): 497–512.

Kumar, Martha Joynt. *Managing the President's Message: The White House Communications Operation*. Baltimore, MD: Johns Hopkins University Press, 2007.

Lockhart, Michele, ed. *President Donald Trump and His Political Discourse: Ramifications of Rhetoric via Twitter*. New York: Routledge, 2018.

Maltese, John Anthony. *Spin Control: The White House Office of Communications and Management of Presidential News*. Chapel Hill: University of North Carolina Press, 1994.

Mitchell, Amy, Jeffrey Gottfried, Galen Stocking, Katerina Matsa, and Elizabeth M. Grieco. "Covering President Trump in a Polarized Media Environment." *Pew Research Center*, October 2, 2017.

Ott, Brian L. "The Age of Twitter: Donald J. Trump and the Politics of Debasement. *Critical Studies in Media Communication* 34 (2017): 59–68.

————. *The Twitter Presidency: Donald J. Trump and the Politics of White Rage.* New York: Routledge, 2019.

Page, Benjamin, and Robert Shapiro. *The Rational Public: Fifty Years of Trends in Americans' Policy Preferences.* Chicago: University of Chicago Press, 1992.

Patterson, Thomas E. "News Coverage of Donald Trump's First 100 Days." Shorenstein Center on Media, Politics and Public Policy. Harvard Kennedy School. 2017.

Peake, Jeffrey S. "Presidential Agenda Setting in Foreign Policy." *Political Research Quarterly* 54 (2001): 69–86.

Peake, Jeffrey S., and Matthew Eshbaugh-Soha. "The Agenda-Setting Impact of Major Presidential TV Addresses." *Political Communication* 25 (2008): 113–137.

Schwab, Nikki. "Media Coverage of Obama Grows More Negative." usnews .com. September 9, 2009. http://www.usnews.com/articles/news/wash ington-whispers/2009/09/14/media-coverage-of-obama-grows-more-neg ative.html.

Shafer, Byron, and Regina L. Wagner. "The Trump Presidency and the Structure of American Politics." *Perspectives on Politics* 26 (2019): 340–357.

Shogan, Robert. *Bad News: Where the Press Goes Wrong in the Making of the President.* Chicago: Ivan R. Dee, 2001.

Trump, Donald. "Press Conference." *New York Times,* January 11, 2017, https://www.nytimes.com/2017/01/11/us/politics/trump-press-confer ence-transcript.html.

Walcott, Charles Eliot and Karen Marie Hult. *Governing the White House: From Hoover through LBJ.* Lawrence: University Press of Kansas, 1995.

Waldman, Paul. "Trump Says He Runs a 'Fine-Tuned Machine.' Here Are the Ways That's Not True." *Washington Post,* February 17, 2017. https:// www.washington post.com/blogs/plum-line/wp/2017/02/17/trump-says -he-runs-a-fine-tuned-machine-here-are-all-the-ways-thats-not-true/?nore direct=on&utm_term=.74d5e3f155a3.

Wanta, Wayne, Mary Ann Stephenson, Judy Van Slyke Turk, and Maxwell E. McCombs. "How Presidents State of Union Talk Influenced News Media Agendas." *Journalism Quarterly* 66 (1989): 537–541.

Weinberg, Abigail. "While the Democrats Debate, Trump is Complaining about Dishwashers," January 15, 2020. https://www.motherjones.com /politics/2020/01/while-the-democrats-debate-trump-is-complaining-about -dishwashers/.

Welch, Reed L. "Presidential Success in Communicating with the Public through Televised Addresses." *Presidential Studies Quarterly* 33 (2003): 347– 356.

White House Transitions Project. "Individual Office Organization Charts." 2019. http://www.whitehousetransitionproject.org/transition-resources-2 /office -briefs/.

CHAPTER 12

Trump's Destructively Aberrant Approach to Federal Budgeting

Roy T. Meyers

INTRODUCTION

President Trump's budgetary behavior has been a strange blend of orthodox and unorthodox behavior and decisions. Trump's advocacy for tax cuts has been orthodox for his party, similar to the actions of Presidents Ronald Reagan and George W. Bush. His rhetoric about spending policies, mostly tweets, has at times been *heterodox* to his party, opposing cuts to popular entitlements yet frequently attacking major Democratic spending priorities via his administration's budget policies and regulatory actions. But unorthodox is an accurate description of President Trump's budgeting style, which is quite unlike previous presidents' approaches to their budgetary responsibilities.

The extent of this unorthodox style has been so great that it may be even more accurate to label his approach as destructively aberrant. The timing could not be worse. There is a widespread consensus that the federal budget process is broken or, to attach blame more directly, that recent Congresses and presidents have often failed in their duty to budget responsibly and intelligently. The extensive partisan polarization that so afflicts national politics is no doubt part of the cause, though it has not been the only reason why the norms that once supported the process have lost much force. Trump's actions have added to this problem by supporting policies that increased budget deficits even though the economy was strong and by reducing the effectiveness of the executive budget preparation and execution processes. Trump's personal financial behavior has often been irreconcilable with fundamental principles of good budgeting. In addition, Trump acted to weaken the power of the purse held by Congress, in part through violations of the Antideficiency Act during the longest partial government shutdown in history. More important were the transfer of funds appropriated for defense to border-wall construction, even though his previous appropriations request for that purpose had been denied by Congress, and the withholding of appropriated security assistance to Ukraine.

TRUMP: NOT LIKE IKE

Describing what has been unorthodox about Trump's approach to budgeting requires defining orthodox budgeting behavior by presidents. In the budget world, the budget absent any changes in policy is defined as the "baseline." And like developing a budget baseline, projecting what presidents are expected to do is more complicated than many might think.

A starting point is provided by a personal anecdote related to President Eisenhower. After my grandmother passed away, my father went through her effects and found a letter, which he framed and sent to me; it now hangs on my office wall. Dated March 19, 1957, it was signed by Sherman Adams, the former chief of staff to Eisenhower; Adams later resigned for having accepted a vicuna coat and an oriental rug from an influential businessman. My grandmother did not have such elite status, but she was not shy—in his response, Adams thanked her for what he called "a forthright expression of your views." Her letter to Eisenhower had demanded that her taxes be reduced.

Tax reduction has long been central to Republican Party strategy, especially after California's Proposition 13 property tax revolt in 1978. But Adams did not give in to my grandmother's demand. Instead, he wrote:

> Few things could give the President greater pleasure than to be able to recommend tax reductions over and beyond the $7.4 billion reduction accomplished in 1954. That reduction, incidentally, was the largest in our history and gave relief to millions of taxpayers who had suffered unusual hardships and inequities under old

tax laws. Just as soon as the budgetary situation permits, he will recommend such reductions to the Congress. Of course, tax cuts must give way under present circumstances to the cost of meeting urgent national responsibilities. Substantial cuts now without a corresponding reduction in Government expenditures would renew deficit financing and gravely risk renewed inflation which, in the fifteen years before 1953, cut in half the purchasing power of the dollar. In the meantime, I can assure you this administration will continue to work diligently to keep spending under tight control and to increase the efficiency of Government operations.

Adams expressed the orthodox Republican view about the danger of budget deficits. Concern about inflation being caused by government policy was particularly strong in the year before Eisenhower was elected; due in part to Korean War spending, inflation was in double-digit territory. This was also the result of a long-standing policy that the Federal Reserve would support the sale of Treasury bonds during wartime by keeping interest rates low. The 1951 "accord" between the Treasury and the Fed freed the latter from having to monetize government debt over the long run. Thus the Eisenhower era began with the view that both monetary and fiscal policy had to be cautious in order to keep inflation in check. Throughout his administration, Eisenhower was committed to the control of spending, denying agencies budget increases and using his veto power on spending bills (Penner 2014).

As the rest of this chapter will show, Trump's budgetary policies and style have been the reverse of Eisenhower's. Consider Trump's August 23, 2019, tweet that asked: "My only question is, who is our bigger enemy, Jay Powell or Chairman Xi?," which rejected the strong norm against presidents publicly pressuring the Fed.[1] Ike conducted a "hidden-hand presidency"; its documentation was a revelation to observers of the presidency (Greenstein 1994). In contrast, it should surprise no one that Trump's continual public pronouncements, featuring itchy trigger thumbs for unrestrained tweeting, would be inconceivable to his predecessor.

DISREGARD OF BUDGETARY EXPERTISE

Another fundamental difference of style between Trump and all of his predecessors, rather than just Ike, has been Trump's willful isolation from executive branch budgetary expertise. Since the 1920s, presidents have been supported by a central budget office, which is now called the Office of Management and Budget. It is one of the legacies of a report issued by President Taft's Commission on Economy and Efficiency in 1912, twenty-five years before the Brownlow Committee's declaration that "the President needs help." The commission was chaired by Frederick Cleveland, a leading advocate of the "executive budget" approach that was being adopted by reformist cities and states.

An important argument for the executive budget was that it would promote government accountability to citizens, empowering the executive to prepare a comprehensive budget request for transmission to the legislature and to oversee agencies' execution of the legislatively approved budget so that spending limits would not be exceeded. This model assumed that either the chief executive would have sufficient character and skill to promote "economy and efficiency" or, if lacking those qualities, the public would punish that deficiency by replacing the chief executive in the next election (Meyers and Rubin 2011).

While it took nearly a decade for Congress to agree to the reform, after passage of the 1921 Budget and Accounting Act, the executive lost no time in building its technical capacity to support the president. Since then the presidential budget office has been an elite institution of career staff who have served presidents regardless of their partisan affiliations (Mosher 1984). That ethos was expressed well in a speech by the agency's former deputy director, Paul O'Neill, a copy of which is routinely given to new hires.

> It is of the greatest importance that there be a point of
> institutional memory and neutral competence, better yet, neutral
> brilliance, available to the President and the Presidency. We are
> doomed to repeat the mistakes of the past if we lack a trusted
> cadre of experts who can span the issues of partisan politics
> and survive the transition between parties in power. This is the
> role that is the raison d'etre of this office. If it slips further from
> your grasp it will, I suspect of necessity, be placed elsewhere. If
> that should happen, OMB will become another point of special
> interest, yet another office the president must protect himself
> from rather than one he can count on as his own. (O'Neill 1988)

Presidents prior to Trump, either at their inauguration or shortly thereafter, have understood what a valuable asset their budget professionals were. In the Trump administration, the role of OMB has instead been downgraded, but not because of the failure of staff to aim for "neutral brilliance." Rather, that supply of insightful advice has no demand from #45. As someone who is convinced of his own genius, Trump regularly rejects new information, especially when it conflicts with his own prior beliefs. Averse not only to briefings that last longer than a few minutes but also to reading of any kind, by all reliable reports he usually does not consider advice generated through a typical executive branch policy review process (Rucker and Leonnig 2020; Dionne et al. 2017). This situation is far worse than previous turns toward an anti-analytical presidential style (Williams 1990; Rocco 2017). One of the results is that the impact of OMB career staff has decreased; their work, which is traditionally filtered through political staff, is less likely to make it to the top, where it really matters. Anticipation and recognition of this malign neglect may have contributed to the quit rate of OMB staff in fiscal 2017: from the base number of career staff at the end of fiscal year 2016, in the next fiscal year 31 percent left OMB, with 71 percent of those quitting the federal government. That's extraordinary turnover.[2]

Another important change has been with how OMB agency leaders have been treated. Mick Mulvaney served as director during 2017–2018, before being appointed acting White House chief of staff in January 2019, where he continued to exercise influence over budget policy at the president's direction. This fit with Trump's predilection for having his leadership corps in "acting status," with Mulvaney's ostensible replacement, Russell Vought, being named only as acting OMB director. Also notable was that during much of Mulvaney's formal direction of OMB, more than a full-time job in itself, he was also acting director of the Consumer Financial Protection Bureau, where he worked to eviscerate that agency (Thrush and Rappeport 2018).

But arguably the most important leadership within OMB is its top civil servants, the deputy associate directors (DADs) and branch chiefs who are the organization's institutional memory and quality control experts. OMB works well only when the agency's program associate directors (PADS), who are political appointees, empower their subordinates, as a transition report put it: "Behind every good PAD there is a great DAD or two" (Redburn and Posner 2017). A troubling example that the legitimate functions of DADs have not been honored came to light in the withholding of Ukraine security assistance, where the PAD atypically took over the DAD's highly technical responsibility for apportioning appropriated funds to agencies (see below).

It is difficult to specify the extent to which the executive branch's overall budgeting capacity has suffered because of Trump's indifference. There are, of course, still many competent budget staff members across the diverse agencies of the executive branch, and much of the executive branch budget process has rolled on from year to year. On the other hand, it is not unreasonable to be concerned that the Trump administration, which Michael Lewis has shown is injuring the government's general administrative capacity, will leave the next president with an impaired ability to budget (Lewis 2018; Hiatt 2018).

THE BULLSHIT PULPIT AND FINANCIAL CORRUPTION

A related issue is the need for honesty in budgeting. A common saying among budget professionals is that "the numbers don't lie." Accurate data is the base of good budget analysis. This is not to say that budget forecasts and estimates should be viewed as indisputable. Most budget analysis includes some level of uncertainty, which should be estimated and described. When uncertainties are concealed, and worse, when budget projections are intentionally biased, decision-makers and the public are ill-served.

Previous presidents have not been blameless in this regard. But the problem here is that Trump is a serial liar without compare in American political history.[3] This extensive dishonesty could create the peripheral damage that public trust in government budget information will decline. This is the opposite of what the country needs, for public confusion about budget realities, created in part by the messaging from both parties, makes it more difficult to agree on sustainable policies. To counter this, some advocates of budget reform have suggested that presidents be charged with the duty of speaking annually on the fiscal state of the nation. While that proposal may be overly optimistic about the potential of using the bully pulpit, a continuation of Trump's bullshit pulpit is certain to worsen the budget process.[4]

Finally, a man who cannot be trusted to tell the truth should be expected to be untrustworthy with other people's money. There was voluminous evidence in Trump's history before he became president: multiple declarations of bankruptcy, numerous complaints by contractors whom Trump had stiffed out of bills he owed, and an exceptional record of litigation over money matters. In 2016, David Fahrenthold of the *Washington Post* reported a series, which the next year won a Pulitzer Prize, on Trump's fraudulent operation of his charity. Attentiveness to these facts signaled that candidate Trump would be unlikely to adhere to government norms of good budgeting and financial management.

Those signals were confirmed by the candidate's often bizarre claims about his financial wizardry that went far beyond the puffery that is common among those from the real estate industry. Fact-checkers did their duty here, such as Glenn Kessler's "four Pinocchio" takedown of Trump's ridiculous assertion that he was so skilled in renegotiating contracts that he could eliminate the nation's $19 trillion in debt in just eight years (2016). However, those corrections had little influence with many voters who had been conditioned by Trump's celebrity from *The Apprentice*, believing the fiction that he had the business acumen needed in spendthrift Washington (never mind Trump's ostentatious personal consumption).

More damning evidence about the president's financial past came to light as he was president, including a deeply sourced *New York Times* investigation that showed Trump and his family had cheated on their taxes; no penalty would be paid because of the statute of limitations that applied (Barstow et al. 2018). Trump had controversially refused to release his tax returns during the campaign and fought off numerous suits while president in order to keep them secret. He refused to withdraw from influence over his real estate operations, one of which, the Trump Hotel on Pennsylvania Avenue, was leased from the General Services Administration, which reports to the president. It became a popular hangout for Trump supporters and a venue that billed at top dollar to foreign and state government clients, producing charges that Trump was violating the two clauses in the Constitution that forbid presidential acceptance of emoluments. Trump's other refuges—golf course resorts in New Jersey and Virginia and the Mar-a-Lago Club in Florida, where Trump spent about one-third of his presidency—were handsomely compensated for Secret Service expenses (Fahrenthold 2020).

Historians will have the opportunity to compare the Trump administration's corruption to those of Grant, Harding, and other presidents. For now, the damage assessments could begin by asking by how much Trump's behavior has signaled to taxpayers that they should not comply voluntarily with the tax code and to contractors and government employers that they should not observe legal standards for federal financial management. Those signals do not meet the constitutional standard that a president must take care that the laws be faithfully executed. But meeting that standard is not all that we expect from a president regarding the budget. Particularly since the Budget and Accounting Act of 1921, the executive budget has allowed presidents to show foresight and leadership by how they proposed to allocate funds. Trump's cavalier approach to budgeting has prevented him from exploiting that opportunity.

FROM REAGAN TO TRUMP: THE NEW ORTHODOXY OF CONSTRAINED BUDGET OPPORTUNISM

While Trump's *style* in dealing with the budget clearly differs from that of his predecessors, comparing his budget *policy* to those of his predecessors is more difficult. Eisenhower's balanced budget orthodoxy was partially rejected soon after he left Washington, beginning with President Kennedy's advocacy of a stimulative tax cut. The redefinition of what presidents were allowed to do with their budget policies continued to evolve in succeeding administrations.

This is not to say that presidents fully rejected the ideal of a balanced budget, both as a symbol and as a real policy goal, for remnants of that ideal were endorsed and reinterpreted by Ike's successors in various ways, as has happened throughout the country's history (Savage 1988). Yet from Kennedy through Obama, acceptance of large deficits was converted from unorthodox to orthodox status, aside from the interregnum of the late 1990s when deficits were surprisingly converted to surpluses.

The clearest examples are Republican presidents' advocacy of large tax cuts, beginning with Reagan in 1981. (Developments from LBJ through Carter are not covered here because of space limits.) Supporters argued at first, using the guise of supply-side economics, that tax cuts would pay for themselves, with induced economic growth offsetting initial revenue losses. But even if that didn't work, as Representative Jack Kemp put it, "We Republicans no longer worship at the altar of the balanced budget." Deficit hawk Republican senators disagreed, leading the effort that scaled down tax cuts in 1982 and 1984 legislation. They later joined with Reagan and Democrats to adopt the 1986 Tax Reform Act, which reduced tax expenditures and lowered marginal rates, in turn keeping the law deficit neutral. On the spending side of the budget, though Reagan pushed big domestic cuts through Congress in 1981, overall his spending policies did not match his small government rhetoric, particularly because of a major buildup of the defense budget.

Reagan was followed by two presidents who reversed the country's fiscal course. In 1990, the landmark Budget Enforcement Act established caps on discretionary spending and required that new mandatory spending and/or tax cuts be offset through the "PAYGO" procedure. This happened only after President George H. W. Bush abandoned his 1988 nominating convention pledge of "Read My Lips: No New Taxes"; his deal with congressional Democrats reduced deficits by about half a trillion dollars over five years, with the savings roughly split between tax increases and spending cuts. That action also split his party, helping Newt Gingrich set the unyielding path that congressional Republicans have followed in many years since, weakening support for the incumbent president who was parodied by comedian Dana Carvey for rejecting policies because they "wouldn't be prudent." However, Bush's action was reflective of popular concern about deficits, as represented by the 19 percent of the 1992 popular vote given to deficit hawk independent candidate Ross Perot.

The winner, Bill Clinton, had campaigned on a stimulative platform, but in 1993 he convinced his party to adopt a similarly sized deficit reduction plan that relied heavily on tax increases. It garnered no support from Republicans, who in 1994 ousted some Democrats from swing districts who had voted for the plan, contributing to the GOP's capture of the House.

The remaining years of divided government were far from routine, with government shutdowns in 1995 and 1996 because of differences between the parties followed by the bipartisan Balanced Budget Act of 1997. Aided by abnormally high economic growth and the dissolution of the Soviet Union, which made it possible to downsize the military, budget balance then was reached. That result was also due to the restrictive budget policies and deficit control–oriented procedures adopted earlier in the decade. Adhering to those policies and procedures hurt Clinton's attempt to expand government health insurance but helped his opposition to the tax cuts that Republicans pushed once surpluses appeared.

Election of the next Republican president, George W. Bush, broke the impasse, enabling major tax cuts in 2001 and 2003. In internal debates about the latter, when faced with opposition from the Treasury secretary (the same Paul O'Neill who is quoted above), Vice President Cheney riffed on Kemp's abandonment of a balanced budget declaration by stating "Reagan proved that deficits don't matter," adding "We won the midterms. This is our due" (Suskind 2004, 291). After the 9/11 attack, large increases in military spending from war fighting in Afghanistan and Iraq also generated deficits. Bush also supported the Medicare Modernization Act (MMA) that created Part D of Medicare, providing coverage for prescription drugs without offsetting the added spending.

With the election of Obama, history repeated itself again, but only in part. As did George W. Bush, Obama expanded government spending on health care when his party had unified control of Congress, using the reconciliation process after the party lost its filibuster-proof majority in the Senate. The difference from the MMA was that the Affordable Care Act (ACA) did not add to the deficit (Elmendorf 2014). And as did Clinton, Obama reversed some of the tax cuts previously adopted under Republican predecessors. Obama's presidency was like Clinton's in another respect, in that both saw their party lose control of Congress in their first midterm elections, followed by strident opposition by an influential House Republican leader. Obama's antagonist was Budget Committee chair Paul Ryan, the author of a series of plans, none of which became law, that would have substantially reduced entitlement spending.

Obama's election and actions had stimulated the mobilization of Tea Party Republicans, who renewed the party's rhetorical opposition to large deficits. Deficits had already increased substantially because of the Great Recession. That downturn began at the end of the Bush second term; preventing the collapse of the financial system required extraordinary actions by the Fed and Treasury and difficult votes in Congress for a bailout plan. Bush's leadership on those remedies was followed by President Obama's 2009 advocacy of a countercyclical stimulus bill, the size of which was limited by pivotal Republican senators who voiced concern about growing deficits. Much of that deficit growth was the natural result of the budget's automatic stabilizers; the additional deficits were layered over the baseline deficits created during the Bush #43 administration.

To deal with this situation, in 2010 Obama created by executive order a National Commission on Fiscal Responsibility and Reform, a bipartisan group intended to produce a "grand bargain" between the parties that would reduce deficits. A proposal by its chairs failed to gain enough support and was followed by difficult negotiations between Obama and Speaker Boehner (R-OH) that also failed. Then, at the last minute, before brinksmanship would have led to default, the parties agreed on the Budget Control Act of 2011 (BCA), which has structured budgeting since then. The law established tight caps on discretionary spending, created a bipartisan "supercommittee" in another attempt at a grand bargain, and reincarnated a "sequestration" process that would automatically reduce discretionary spending caps, and cut Medicare, if a grand bargain wasn't made.

Sequestration was central to the 1985 "Gramm-Rudman-Hollings" budget law, but it failed to force Reagan and Congress to agree on deficit reductions, because the parties agreed instead to avoid that hard penalty. This time a partisan impasse over the spending cap reduction led to a government shutdown in October 2013. Cooler heads then prevailed with adoption of the Bipartisan Budget Act of 2013, which split the difference between Republican- and Democratic-preferred appropriations levels for two years. With that agreement, the political steam went out of this approach to deficit reduction, though fiscal austerity policy continued for another two years.[5] In 2015, Obama and the Republicans again increased the discretionary spending caps. As the economy recovered slowly but steadily, the net effect was that by fiscal year 2016, the deficit had declined from its fiscal 2009 high of 9.8 percent of GDP to 3.2 percent of GDP.

That was as low as the Obama administration wanted to go, particularly as its advisors in the economics profession had concluded real interest rates were also likely to stay low, which made the debt burden less worrisome (Summers 2016). And despite the sustained criticism of "Obama's deficits" from Republicans through most of his administration, many Republicans also went silent on the issue as Trump ran on a platform that would increase deficits, primarily by cutting taxes (Zeller 2016).

Long before then, the Nobel economist and liberal columnist Paul Krugman had repeatedly complained about the "fiscal hypocrisy" of Republicans for their persistent blaming of Democrats for deficits when Republicans didn't hold the presidency and their credit claiming for deficit-increasing tax cuts when they did hold the presidency (for a recent version, see Krugman 2020). His colleague David Leonhardt provided data in support: Republican presidents' periodic success in cutting taxes is a major reason why deficits, beginning with the Reagan administration, increased during each Republican presidency and decreased during Democratic ones (with the deficits calculated excluding the effects of automatic stabilizing policies that result when the economy is operating below its potential capacity) (Leonhardt 2018).

During the 2016 presidential campaign, the deficit hawk group

Committee for a Responsible Federal Budget predicted that if the candidates' promises were honored in office, that pattern would continue:
deficits over ten years would increase by $5.3 trillion under Trump,
mostly due to tax cuts, while they would be roughly stable under Clinton, though both revenues and spending would increase (2016).

It was a prescient prediction, for one of the few legislative accomplishments of the Trump administration has been the law popularly
known as the Tax Cuts and Jobs Act (TCJA) of 2017. Though the
Congressional Budget Office (CBO) projected that TCJA would increase deficits by $1.5 trillion over ten years (not counting additional
debt service or macroeconomic effects), it was adopted by a unified
party that claimed the tax cuts would pay for themselves and that used
the budget reconciliation process to prevent a Democratic filibuster.
CBO's analysis from 2018 put the cost at $1.9 trillion, including debt
service and macroeconomic effects. Unlike Reagan's Tax Reform Act,
the TCJA increased horizontal inequities in the tax code by creating
more special preferences than it abolished (Slemrod 2018).

On the spending side of the budget, President Trump and Congress,
following the 2013 and 2105 bipartisan budget agreements, adopted
similar agreements in 2018 and 2019 that increased discretionary
spending substantially above the BCA caps. Chairs of the House and
Senate Budget Committee maintained that these agreements elim-
inated the need to adopt budget resolutions, though changing the
permissible levels for 30 percent of spending is far from developing a
comprehensive plan for the government's finances. The CBO still prepared comprehensive budget baseline projections in January 2020,
expecting a fiscal year 2020 deficit of $1.0 trillion. The deficit came at
a time when the economy was temporarily above its calculated maxi-
mum of long-term output (2020a). The agency projected that deficits
over the next ten years would average $1.3 trillion, about three-fifths
higher than their average over the previous fifty years.

From this history, it should be clear that presidents can no longer
be expected to carry the torch of balanced budget orthodoxy and
certainly that Trump did not do this. What has taken its place? The
new orthodoxy can be described as a strategy of constrained budget
opportunism. That opportunism can be seen most clearly when presidents with majority support in Congress took advantage of procedural
opportunities afforded by the budget process to advance their parties'
major priorities. In particular, reconciliation, which prevented filibusters by the minority party, enabled passage of controversial bills that

cut spending (Reagan), cut taxes (Reagan, Bush #43, and Trump), and changed health policy (Bush #43 and Obama).

This opportunistic strategy was periodically constrained by pressure to respond to concerns about excessive deficits. That pressure was a complicated function of actual and projected increases in deficits, the stage of the business cycle, changing expert beliefs about the macroeconomic role of deficits, and the public opinion effects of cues from co-partisan elites. When pressure was high, then the budget process stood ready to be used for the cause of deficit reductions, as it was in the 1990s (Meyers and Joyce 2005).

Regardless of the presence or absence of such pressure, much of the executive budget process followed tradition prior to Trump. Its norms included comprehensive transparency of government finances, following a detailed annual schedule, and completing negotiations within the executive branch to arrive at specified allocations and acceptable totals. For example, agencies had to comply with OMB's budget circular A-11, with its more than a thousand pages of detailed directives about how agencies should prepare their budget requests and how they should execute the budgets enacted by Congress. In contrast, budgetary relations between the president and Congress worsened, to the point that years before the beginning of the Trump administration, major parts of the budget process were widely viewed as "broken" (Meyers 2009, 2014). A downward spiral of hyper-partisan conflict interacting with the weakening of traditional congressional norms helped make late appropriations even more frequent, caused the nonadoption of budget resolutions, and stimulated recurrent brinksmanship. This atrophy of process caused much frustration but also permitted additional budget opportunism.

This weakness of budgetary constraints must have been welcome to President Trump, who disdains constraints to such an extent that, as Hennessey and Wittes describe in their insightful evaluation, he has invented what they call an "expressive" presidency: "Whereas the traditional presidency developed process because administering government effectively required it to work optimally, Trump is proposing a kind of disconnect between the workaday functions of government and the show going on at the top. He doesn't care if it works optimally; optimal effectiveness is not the goal. He wants to mouth off and announce things and have the executive branch below effectuate his will" (2020, 52). Trump's application of this style to budgeting can be summarized by going beyond Cheney's statement about deficits not mattering: not only does Trump believe deficits don't matter, but he also believes the budget process doesn't matter. Yet despite this president's disinterest in budgeting, the administration still sent budget requests to Congress and negotiated over spending and tax bills. The next section describes those actions, and then reviews how Trump used his budget execution powers, part of his extremely aggressive administrative presidency.

TRUMP'S BUDGET REQUESTS, NEGOTIATING APPROACH, AND THE WALL SHUTDOWN

When Trump ran for the nomination, voters viewed him differently than they did other Republican candidates because some of his positions were heterodox to standard GOP ones. On trade, he sounded like anti-NAFTA Democrats, and like almost all Democrats he pledged to protect entitlement programs. The latter stance periodically reappeared when he wasn't preoccupied with immigration and investigations; or when the budget was news, Trump tweeted two days before his FY21 budget request that it "will not be touching your Social Security or Medicare."

In this modern era, when parsing presidential statements has sunk to the depth of considering the meaning of "is," the accuracy of this tweet depends on one's interpretation of "touching your." In fact, like every presidential budget request for many years, the FY21 budget proposed savings from Medicare to reduce its rate of growth; almost all would reduce payments to providers and likely not reduce care received by beneficiaries. But in her initial response to Trump's budget, Speaker Nancy Pelosi (D-CA) read from page one of the Democratic playbook, accusing the president of making "savage cuts." This is a Democratic variant of the fiscal hypocrisy problem that Krugman ascribed to Republicans, because the ACA was full of provisions designed to reduce health spending while protecting quality (which, of course, Republicans criticized, another example of partisan blame generation in budgeting).

Looking at his budget requests over four years, Trump's heterodox tweeting should be viewed mostly as distraction. His budgets matched GOP orthodoxy, greatly resembling Paul Ryan's plans. The first budget, as is usual for new administrations, was submitted late, in May. Also usual was that the administration, given the challenge of quickly staffing up, drew much of its first budget's contents from outside groups allied with the administration. It relied especially on the Heritage Foundation's annual "Blueprint for Balance" publication and continued to do so in later years. In 2019, Heritage celebrated its strong connection with the Trump administration: "Of the 175 Bluen print proposals, 66 are fully included in the president's budget, and another 41 are partially included. This means the Heritage Blueprint and the president's budget share about 61 percent in common, according to these criteria" (Boccia and Ditch 2019).

Skipping ahead to his fourth budget, transmitted to Congress in an election year, the FY21 budget shared basic features with Trump's previous requests. It increased funding for homeland security and defense, though the increases were smaller than in previous years. The budget attacked nondefense discretionary spending, in two ways. First, it proposed big cuts to selected agencies, such as 27 percent less for the EPA, which would complement the administration's broad reversal of Obama's regulations. Second, the "two-penny plan" would cut this category by 2 percent a year in nominal dollars, which over ten years would shrink its contribution to GDP from 3.3 percent to 1.6 percent. This was not the first time that a ten-year budget plan suggested a future government whose size resembled those that predated the New Deal, but it was just as fictional. Also unlikely to occur was the administration's prediction of rapid economic growth coincident with low interest rates, far more optimistic than expected by CBO or almost all independent forecasters. Finally, the budget made major cuts to means-tested entitlement programs, such as Medicaid and food assistance (Kogan, Romig, and Beltran 2020).

Given the Democratic minority's remaining influence in the Senate, and after 2018 the Democrats' control of the House, many proposals in Trump's four budgets were fated to suffer immediate rejection. Even so, the effective requirement to get a presidential signature on appropriations bills is a very real constraint for the president's opponents, so Trump's budget requests for discretionary spending could not be ignored. Further incentivizing both sides to compromise was that honoring the BCA caps would bite heavily into the priorities of both Democrats (nondefense) and Republicans (defense and homeland security).

Partisan polarization assured that negotiations over increasing the caps would be difficult, but they were far worse because of Trump's temperamental negotiating style. Appropriators, whether Democrat or Republican, are skilled negotiators who do not value unpredictability. The president, in contrast, is known for his lack of concentration and shifting positions, often based on whoever meets with him last.

The high consequences of this style were especially visible in the conflict over Trump's request for wall construction funding (from Congress, that is, rather than from Mexico). The president blew up in a photo opportunity on December 11, 2018, after being egged on by Senator Schumer, saying what no previous modern president would have said: "I am proud to shut down the government for border security, Chuck, because the people of this country don't want criminals, and people that have lots of problems, and drugs, pouring into this country." While Mulvaney supported this strategy, other advisors to Trump felt it was ill-advised. Once Congress said for the last time that it would not provide the $5.7 billion in funding for the wall that Trump had demanded in the fall, months after his FY19 budget had requested only $1.6 billion, the partial shutdown for lack of appropriations began. It lasted thirty-five days, the longest in US government history.

When the branches settled their differences, the appropriation for the wall was only $1.375 billion, but Trump still declared victory. That was probably accurate, for Trump also declared a national emergency, which he said allowed the transfer and reprogramming of an additional $6.5 billion for wall construction, mostly from accounts for military construction and defense counter-drug activities. In theory these shifts were legally questionable, but since appropriations law is highly complex, space is lacking here to discuss the issue in necessary detail. In practice, plaintiffs opposing the shifts filed suits but found it difficult to gain standing in the courts. In the field, execution of the funds was slow because of technical difficulties, leading to a large balance of unspent money. This balance was one reason House Democrats appropriated only another $1.375 billion for the wall, below what Trump had requested, in the FY20 bill that was enacted in December 2019.

Trump had followed his 2019 shift of funds by asking Congress to use the FY20 bill to backfill the accounts from which the transfers had come. This was tempting to Congress because the activities defunded by Trump's shifts, such as repairing dilapidated barracks, are popular with constituents, but Congress did not comply with the request. Trump did enjoy another victory in the FY20 appropriations bill, however, because Democrats could not convince Republicans to support legislative language that would have prevented additional transfers to supplement the appropriated amount for the wall. In February 2020, Trump announced he was again moving funds for the wall, $3.8

billion worth, this time from procurement accounts for all four uniformed services, targeting appropriations that exceeded administration requests.

The administration's actions during the shutdown and after it were major challenges to the power of the purse granted to Congress in Article I of the Constitution. Concerned about being blamed for the lack of government services during the shutdown that Trump said he was proud to force, the administration loosened a strict policy, promulgated by President Carter's attorney general, that prevented unfunded agencies from carrying out routine operations (Rein et al. 2019). This was arguably a violation of the Antideficiency Act (see Candreva 2019). The more worrisome issue is how the appropriations process will evolve because Trump refused to follow congressional directives on how money should be spent. The congressional power of the purse will become meaningless if future presidents repeatedly use Trump's strategy. In the past, violations of congressional spending directives have often led Congress to withdraw the flexibilities it had previously granted the president. While such assertion of control was often necessary, in some cases it also reduced agencies' abilities to operate efficiently.

BUDGET EXECUTION DECISIONS—INCLUDING THE WITHHOLDING OF UKRAINIAN SECURITY ASSISTANCE

Trump made other budget execution decisions that have illustrated how strong the effect of the administrative presidency's powers can be on the budget. On the revenue side, his Commerce Department's expansive interpretation of the Trade Expansion Act of 1962, which for example found that national security was threatened by other countries' trade in auto parts, allowed Trump to unilaterally declare tariff increases. This increased tariff revenues, which Trump celebrated as being paid by opponents in the trade war. In fact, most of the burden of the trade restrictions, which were akin to a tax, was borne by American consumers. Trump's aggressive policies also led targeted countries to respond in kind, such as by buying fewer of America's farm exports. To protect his political base, Trump then used existing authority to make "market facilitation payments" to some farmers for their losses from the trade war, at a budget cost of $28 billion.

Other significant administrative actions that could or did affect spending for means-tested entitlements include proposing waivers for

Medicaid that would establish work expectations and reduce ACA en-
rollment expansions, restrictions on SNAP (food stamps) eligibility,
and tightening "public charge" requirements for those seeking immigration and naturalization approvals. Major changes to how border
protection agents dealt with undocumented people, including requiring separation of children from adult family members, required more
spending to deal with violations of standards for adequate treatment
of these individuals. The latter contrasts with the Obama administration's Deferred Action for Childhood Arrivals policy, which rational-
ized the loosening of requirements for a subset of the undocumented
in part on grounds that the budget included insufficient resources to
strictly follow the law; deportation activities were instead focused on
criminals. While CBO incorporates the estimated budget effects of
proposed and final rules into its baseline, these effects are generally
invisible to the public.

The most politically important budget execution action by Trump
was his insistence that $392 million in security assistance funding be
withheld from Ukraine. This act was part of the basis of the House's
impeachment of Trump, although the Senate decided not to remove
Trump from office. This was not the only controversial case of the
administration withholding appropriated funds, among which was the
refusal to send emergency relief funds to Puerto Rico on suspicion
that the money would be spent corruptly.

Without getting into the details of the impeachment case, the
relevant point here is that the withholding of funds violated the Impoundment Control Act (ICA). Adopted in 1974 along with the Congressional Budget Act, the ICA allows the president to defer spending,
but only when he notifies Congress that he is doing so legally and
when the deferral would not in effect be a rescission, or cancellation,
of funds, because the deferral would last up to the date when the
funds would no longer be legally available for obligation. In this case,
the required notification of Congress did not occur. The deferral was
camouflaged by adding footnotes to documents that "apportioned"
funds, that is, that told agencies the amounts of their appropriations
they could spend during a certain period. The footnotes required that
the Ukrainian assistance funds *not* be obligated and in most cases were
added by the national security PAD, with the support of the OMB general counsel, both political appointees. This direction was the subject
of extensive disagreements with the Defense Department and is said
to have caused the resignation of two OMB staff and a lot of angst

among other involved career staff. Prior to the impeachment trial, GAO ruled that the withholding of funds was a violation of the ICA (2020). However, just as in the case of the wall, most Republicans were unwilling to take on the president, even though his action reduced congressional power.

BUDGETING AT THE START OF THE PANDEMIC

Because the novel coronavirus is extremely contagious, social and economic disruption was inevitable even under the best possible governance. That the actual disruption was greater is due in part to some decisions made before the Trump administration that weakened pandemic containment and mitigation capacities. Trump made the problem much worse by ignoring warnings of pandemic risks and failing to provide the central direction and public communications needed to mobilize an effective quick response. Many governors took the lead to fill that void, mandating physical distancing in order to avoid exceeding the health system's ability to care for patients. This produced an extraordinary negative economic shock, with CBO projecting a 39.6 percent decline in real gross domestic product for the second quarter of 2020 (CBO 2020b).

In response, by the time this chapter was completed, the federal government had enacted four bills to provide massive relief for many sectors of the economy and also finance additional public health spending. Trump delegated most responsibility for negotiating the terms to Treasury Secretary Mnuchin, who bargained with congressional leaders, representing the many legislators whose ability to fulfill their constitutional role was severely constrained by the lack of a plan to maintain congressional continuity during crises. When combined with revenue declines, the additional spending led CBO to project that the fiscal year 2020 budget deficit would be 17.9 percent of GDP, an increase of 13 percent of GDP above the previous projection.

As in World War II, this period was one in which it was right to temporarily ignore any concern about the growth of deficits, if the adopted policies effectively speeded the end of the pandemic and provided needed relief. However, delivering that much aid was bound to be challenging for agencies like the Small Business Administration. Trump again revealed his dislike of financial probity by removing the acting inspector general who had been selected by peers to conduct oversight of pandemic spending (Hudak 2020). Another major budget problem was that Trump encouraged states to acquire essential medical supplies on their own, rather than maximizing use of federal powers to increase supplies and limit price increases. Even worse, he was reluctant to provide significant financial relief to the states, despite their vanishing sales and income tax revenues. When added to the states' extraordinary public health costs and expectations that the states balance their operating budgets, this would guarantee that states would have to make procyclical deficit reductions, thereby delaying any economic recovery that would be central to Trump's reelection strategy.

CONCLUSION

The long-term impact of Trump's approach to budgeting will obviously be greatly affected by the results of the 2020 election. Regardless of that result, though, the evidence presented in this chapter may inspire some to think about the current presidential selection process. In *Federalist*, no. 68 Alexander Hamilton defended the proposed Electoral College for its ability to establish a minimum standard for selection: "The process of election affords a moral certainty, that the office of President will never fall to the lot of any man who is not in an eminent degree endowed with the requisite qualifications."

To this author, the moral certainty is that President Trump lacks those qualifications, calling into question our process for selecting presidents. While there are many reforms worth considering in order to meet Hamilton's standard, one that relates to budgeting is replacing the seemingly endless series of events during the nomination process that are improperly called "debates." In reality, they are unreality TV shows in which candidates have incentives to use the time they have available, no longer than the length of a few sound bites, to make improbable promises of policies with no mention of unavoidable tradeoffs involved. A better approach would be to have a round-robin of moderated one-on-one debates between two candidates, which would be more likely to help citizens estimate whether each candidate has the virtue to make responsible and responsive budget decisions once in office (Langer 2019).

Another lesson that might be learned is that some of President Trump's actions have been possible because of the vacuum created by congressional budgetary dysfunctions. In half of the fiscal years since 1999, Congress has not adopted budget resolutions. The failure to enact regular appropriations bills on time has worsened, and the same goes for regular reauthorizations of major programs. It has also often failed to use performance information from the executive branch to conduct effective oversight.[6]

The most recent attempt to improve the process, by the Joint Select Committee on Budget and Appropriations Process Reform, ended in failure (Joyce and Meyers 2020). However, the cap structure from the BCA will expire next year, opening a window for another attempt to consider how Congress could fulfill its responsibilities over the power of the purse, including assuring that appropriated funds are spent as intended. They should try again.

NOTES

1. Powell was chair of the board of governors of the Federal Reserve System of the United States, and Xi was the general secretary of the Communist Party of China and president of the People's Republic of China.

2. Calculated from the Office of Personnel Management's FedScope separation database. Thanks to Michael Hassett and Ryan Wilkens for accessing these data.

3. For one compilation of lies, see https://projects.thestar.com/donald-trump-fact-check/.

4. The president has repeatedly used this profanity in public, including in a public event held on the day after the Senate voted to find him not guilty of impeachment charges.

5. The Hutchins Center Fiscal Impact Measure shows that in the second quarter of 2011, the combined effects of government spending and taxing became contractionary. A stimulative trend didn't emerge until 2018–2019. https://www.brookings.edu/interactives/hutchins-center-fiscal-impact-measure/.

6. For a broader analysis of the congressional capacity to budget, see Meyers 2017.

REFERENCES

Barstow, David, Susanne Craig, and Russ Buettner. "Trump Engaged in Suspect Tax Schemes as He Reaped Riches from His Father." *New York Times*, October 2, 2018.

Boccia, Romina, and David Ditch. "Trump's Proposed Budget Adopts 61% of Heritage Proposals." *Heritage Foundation*, June 4, 2019.

Candreva, Philip J. "The Federal Antideficiency Act at 150: Where Do We Stand?" *Public Budgeting and Finance* 39 (2019): 75–93.

Committee for a Responsible Federal Budget. "Promises and Price Tags: An Update." September 22, 2016.

Congressional Budget Office. *The Budget and Economic Outlook: 2020–2030.* January 2020a.

———. "CBO's Current Projections of Output, Employment, and Interest Rates and a Preliminary Look at Federal Deficits for 2020 and 2021." April 24, 2020b.

———. *The Budget and Economic Outlook: 2018 to 2028.* Appendix B. April 2018.

Dionne, E. J. Jr., Norman J. Ornstein, and Thomas E. Mann. *One Nation After Trump.* New York: St. Martin's, 2017.

Elmendorf, Douglas. "Estimating the Budgetary Effects of the Affordable Care Act," *Congressional Budget Office,* June 17, 2014.

Fahrenthold, David A. "What President Trump's company charges the Secret Service." *Washington Post,* March 5, 2020.

Government Accountability Office. "Office of Management and Budget Withholding of Ukraine Security Assistance." January 16, 2020.

Greenstein, Fred I. *The Hidden-Hand Presidency.* Baltimore, MD: Johns Hopkins University Press, 1994.

Hennessey, Susan, and Benjamin Wittes. *Unmaking the Presidency: Donald Trump's War on the World's Most Powerful Office.* New York: Farrar, Straus and Giroux, 2020.

Hiatt, Fred. "Trump Is Destroying a National Treasure." *Washington Post,* January 12, 2018.

Hudak, John. "Inspectors General Will Drain the Swamp, If Trump Stops Attacking Them," *Brookings Institution,* April 16, 2020.

Joyce, Philip G., and Roy T. Meyers. "The Problem and the Process Are Both Problems: Why the Joint Select Committee on Budget and Appropriations Process Reform Failed." Working paper. 2020.

Kessler, Glen. "Trump's Nonsensical Claim He Can Eliminate $19 Trillion in Debt in Eight Years." *Washington Post,* April 2, 2016.

Kogan, Richard, Kathleen Romig, and Jennifer Beltran. "Trump's 2021 Budget Would Cut $1.6 Trillion from Low-Income Programs." *Center for Budget and Policy Priorities,* March 9, 2020.

Krugman, Paul. "The Triumph of Fiscal Hypocrisy: What We Can Learn from Trump's Deficitpalooza." *New York Times,* February 6, 2020.

Langer, Andrew. "How to Reform Our Flawed System of Presidential Debates." *Real Clear Politics,* January 31, 2019.

Leonhardt, David. "The Democrats Are the Party of Fiscal Responsibility." *New York Times,* April 15, 2018.

Lewis, Michael. *The Fifth Risk.* New York: W. W. Norton, 2018.

Meyers, Roy T. "The 'Ball of Confusion' in Federal Budgeting: A Shadow Agenda for Deliberative Budget Process Reform." *Public Administration Review* 69 (March 2009): 211–223.

———. "The Implosion of the Federal Budget Process: Triggers, Commissions, Cliffs, Sequesters, Debt Ceilings, and Shutdown." *Public Budgeting and Finance* 34 (Winter 2014): 1–23.

———. "Is the U.S. Congress an Insurmountable Obstacle to Any 'Far-Sighted Conception Of Budgeting?'" *Public Budgeting and Finance* 37 (Winter 2017): 5–24.

Meyers, Roy T., and Philip G. Joyce. "Congressional Budgeting at Age 30: Is It Worth Saving?" *Public Budgeting and Finance*, Special Silver Anniversary Issue (2005): 68–82.

Meyers, Roy T., and Irene S. Rubin. "The Executive Budget in the Federal Government: The First Century and Beyond, with Irene S. Rubin." *Public Administration Review* 71 (May 2011): 334–344.

Mosher, Frederick C. *A Tale of Two Agencies.* Baton Rouge: Louisiana State University Press, 1984.

O'Neill, Paul. Presentation to OMB staff, September 6, 1988.

Penner, Rudolph G. "When Budgeting Was Easier: Eisenhower and the 1960 Budget." *Public Budgeting and Finance* 34 (Winter 2014): 24–37.

Redburn, Steven, and Paul Posner, eds. *The Office of Management and Budget: An Insider's Guide.* Baker Institute for Public Policy, 2017.

Rein, Lisa, Juliet Eilperin, and Jeff Stein. "'We're Left in the Dark': As Many Industries Get Shutdown Relief, Those without Political Clout Feel Left Behind." *Washington Post*, January 19, 2019.

Rocco, Philip. "The Anti-Analytic Presidency Revisited," *Forum* 15 (July 2017).

Rucker, Philip, and Carol Leonnig. *A Very Stable Genius: Donald J. Trump's Testing of America.* New York: Penguin, 2020.

Savage, James D. *Balanced Budgets and American Politics.* Ithaca, NY: Cornell University Press, 1988.

Slemrod, Joel. "Is This Tax Reform, or Just Confusion?" *Journal of Economic Perspectives* 32 (Fall 2018): 73–96.

Summers, Lawrence. "The Age of Secular Stagnation: What It Is and What to Do About It." *Foreign Affairs*, February 15, 2016.

Suskind, Ron. *The Price of Loyalty.* New York: Simon & Schuster, 2004.

Thrush, Glenn, and Alan Rappeport. "'Like a Mosquito in a Nudist Colony': How Mick Mulvaney Found Plenty to Target at Consumer Bureau." *New York Times*, May 7, 2018.

Williams, Walter. *Mismanaging America: The Rise of the Anti-Analytic Presidency.* Lawrence: University Press of Kansas, 1990.

Zeller, Shawn. "Not Your Father's GOP: The Deficit Debate Has Disappeared." Roll Call, September 26, 2016.

CHAPTER 13

From Comey to COVID-19: Assessing President Trump's Twitter Activity and Equity Market Uncertainty

Christopher Olds

RESEARCH BACKGROUND

Going public has been recognized in the political science literature as a strategic tool that presidents can use to engage with the public to generate support for an administration's preferred policy priorities (Kernell 2007). There are a variety of avenues in which a president can adopt going public as a strategy, such as making visits to local communities within the country, making televised addresses directed to the public at large, or attempting to dominate the news cycle by consistently mentioning a top policy priority in all public communications (Eshbaugh-Soha 2016).

One of the underlying elements for applying going public as a strategy is the notion that presidential power is the power to persuade, meaning that presidents use the prominence of the office of the presidency and their own respective communications skills to get other actors in the political system to think or act in ways they would not normally unless there is intervention from the president (Neustadt 1991). A new tool in the twenty-first-century digital age available in a president's arsenal in efforts to persuade is Twitter, one of numerous social media platforms whereby individuals can exchange information with one another. President Trump, an active user of Twitter for years prior to his election under the handle @realdonaldtrump, is a useful case in which to assess the potential consequences of how others respond and react to what is disseminated through a political leader's social media account.

Most scholarly treatments of President Trump's usage of Twitter have sought to make connections to how Twitter has brought about change to the public discourse. For example, Ott's (2017) study suggests that Trump's Twitter feed is demonstrative of public discourse that is low on civility and high on simplistic statements devoid of critical thinking or analysis. Others have highlighted that President Trump chooses to use Twitter as a platform to engage in self-promotion and castigate those who speak poorly of him or criticize his decisions (e.g., Kreis 2017). Tweeting with a focus on personal enemies suggesting the presence of conflict and the need to classify these perceived enemies as "the other" worthy of scorn appear to be common tactics exercised by Trump (Pelled et al. 2018).

Specific analyses of Trump's Twitter comments on matters surrounding the economy have also occurred. Tillmann (2020) finds that statements from Trump about the Federal Reserve have led to lower long-term interest rates, a finding that is in line with a separate study by Bianchi, Kung, and Kind (2019) that demonstrates that President Trump's tweets about the Federal Reserve lower Federal funds rate expectations. Work from Salem, Younger, and St. John (2019) on behalf of the investment bank and financial services company JP Morgan Chase suggests that tweets from President Trump on matters like trade and monetary policy increase interest rate volatility. Tweets from President Trump that strongly criticize a company's actions have been found to reduce the market value of that particular company (Brans and Scholtens 2020). President Trump's tweets pertaining to the US trade war with China had a negative effect on S&P 500 returns; this relationship was found to be unidirectional, meaning Trump's tweets were influencing S&P 500 returns and not the other way around (Burggraf, Fendel, and Huynh 2019).

While all of these works have undoubtedly made a meaningful contribution to knowledge regarding the consequences of the messages being spread through President Trump's Twitter account, there are two underlying considerations that remain. The first is that the research examining the consequences of Trump's Twitter feed on the economy are focused on specific comments pertaining to matters involving the economy. Adopting this approach ignores the possibility that given the prominence of the office of the presidency, anything being communicated through Trump's Twitter account can have ramifications on the economy, regardless of whether any aspect of the economy is explicitly invoked or whether the comments are not being directly made by President Trump himself and instead are merely retweets of what others are saying.

An issue area commonly mentioned on the @realdonaldtrump Twitter account that can potentially influence perceptions others have about the economy without the economy even being invoked at all is immigration. Passel and Cohn's (2018) research finds that undocumented immigrant workers constitute 25 percent of the workforce in farming occupations, 15 percent of the workforce in construction occupations, 8 percent of the workforce in either production or service occupations, and 6 percent of the workforce in transportation occupations. Their report estimated that at least 7.8 million undocumented immigrants aged eighteen and over in 2016 were a part of the US labor force. President Trump's tweets and retweets about the need to rapidly change immigration laws, the need for local law enforcement to cooperate with federal immigration authorities, the need to build a border wall along the southern border shared with Mexico, and how illegal immigration poses a serious threat to the country can have possible implications on the economic perceptions and choices that are made by the assortment of businesses and companies in diverse sectors of the economy that employ undocumented immigrant workers.

The second consideration that remains given prior work on President Trump's Twitter account is whether economic indicators can alter the daily behavior observed from the @realdonaldtrump account; is the president's daily social media approach shaped in any way by what information is available about the economy on a day-to-day basis? This chapter makes a positive early attempt to address both elements through an emphasis on the concepts of information overload and responsive presidential leadership.

The assumption of much of the current literature on the impact of President Trump's Twitter feed on the economy is that specific mentions of the economy are what will direct economic shifts. Making this assumption ignores a long-standing concept in the academic literature that spans multiple disciplines: information overload. Information overload has been a concept discussed in areas as diverse as medical imaging (Duncan 2017), mass media reports of scientific information (Jensen et al. 2017), using restaurant review platforms to decide where to eat (Sun, Guo, and Zhu 2019), and whether wearable technology that transmits information helps or hinders athletic performance (Halson, Peake, and Sullivan 2016). While in the past there has been discussion of the role of the American president being rife with information overload (Fiske 1993), there has not been nearly as much review of whether a president's communication approach can produce information overload for the nation as a whole and what the consequences of this information overload can be.

Information overload can simply be described as someone receiving too much information. Heightened feelings of stress, anxiety, and diminished decision quality are common findings of the response to information overload. The body of scholarship seems to suggest there is a threshold point; yes, individuals can make quality decisions when the amount of information they receive increases, but this effect exists only up to a certain point. When information continues to be provided, the decision-making capabilities of people will decline. When overloaded with information, individuals assigned to a decision task will express confusion and the inability to establish and focus on priorities and will struggle to remember prior information given to them (Schick, Gordon, and Haka 1990). Consequences such as these explain why the concept of information overload has led scholars to branch out and look at similar concepts like information fatigue syndrome (Eppler and Mengis 2004). Too much information can overwhelm those trying to process and evaluate available information when faced with a decision task.

Findings in various fields of inquiry support the position that information overload can bring about negative consequences for those making a choice or decision. Allen and Shoard (2005) demonstrate that providing police officers with mobile devices where they are able to access greater collections of information more rapidly than before increased approximation behavior, which means responding to situations in a less clearly defined and ambiguous way. In an experimental study of accounting, individuals presented with an abundance of information about a decision task were found to make inconsistent decisions and express less consensus with others involved in a decision (Chewning and Harrell 1990). Presenting multiple different characteristics about products makes consumers express a lower level of confidence and a higher level of confusion surrounding a decision, whereby too much information about products breeds symptoms of information overload (Lee and Lee 2004).

With too much information to process, determining what is relevant and irrelevant becomes increasingly difficult (Jacoby 1977), which can result in delays in making decisions (Jacoby 1984). If individuals are asked to process a significant amount of information in a finite amount of time, making unrealistic demands on information processing capabilities, information overload can result. Information overload should be a particularly acute problem when people have to assess the usefulness of all the information that is out there (Keller and Staelin 1987). Although people, even in the presence of cognitive limitations, are able to process and make decisions that are satisfactory to them by relying on cues, such as the observation of fairly consistent patterns within the decision-making environment (Simon 1991), such decision-making becomes more difficult when there is a deluge of information available in the decision-making environment. There will be those instances where making decisions will necessitate information-processing requirements that are significantly greater than the information-processing capabilities of people. There can be an abundance of information necessary to complete a decision-making task but just a small amount of information that individuals can actually review and incorporate into their own personal decision-making process (Galbraith 1974).

It is not just the sheer quantity of information itself that can produce information overload. Trying to evaluate the characteristics or traits of the information can induce overload. The attributes of available information can be ambiguous, uncertain, and/or complex, which only helps to make completion of the decision-making task more complicated. The diverse attributes of information available in the environment creates difficulties whereby decision-makers cannot make the connection between the details of information and how this information relates to the overall decision-making task (Schneider 1987). Put more succinctly, wading through information and attempting to determine whether it is credible, relevant, and useful can induce information overload.

With new communication technologies that expedite and lower the costs of information being spread, digital advances have been singled out as a potential cause for the rise in information overload. With means of getting massive amounts of information out quickly and easily, the digital age can cause what is known as information paralysis, which is the inability to integrate and apply new information when making decisions (Bawden 2001). Digital communications bringing about information overload should be particularly important when discussing President Trump's Twitter account.

President Trump and his staff on any given day can use his Twitter account to submit information for the public to consider, be it written tweets from Trump himself, tweets from staff members, links to media clips that have to be viewed or listened to, or retweets of what others have posted. As each day progresses and more content is being posted from the @realdonaldtrump Twitter account, people are led to potentially review more information and to try to interpret how that information applies to choices they personally have to make. As a case study, let us explore two consecutive days in the Trump presidency, March 7 and March 8, 2019. On March 7, three tweets came from Donald Trump's @realdonaldtrump Twitter account, none of which have anything directly to do with the economy: one asserting that the accusation he violated campaign finance laws was "fake news," one touting apprehension levels along the southern border shared with Mexico, and one commenting on an MSNBC story about his former lawyer Michael Cohen. The Dow Jones Industrial Average closed that day at 25,473.23.

The next day, on March 8, thirty-five tweets came from Donald Trump's @realdonaldtrump account, an increase of thirty-two tweets from the day before. There were tweets ranging from the following: discussions of the border barrier being constructed, words of appreciation for the television show Fox & Friends, complaints that the media is dishonest, a lamentation that he is the victim of "presidential harassment," a comment that the "Russian Witch Hunt" continues, a retweet of talk radio personality Mark Levin calling Florida governor Ron DeSantis "America's governor," retweets of Ivanka Trump and First Lady Melania Trump in recognition of International Women's Day, and a video clip of the president's visit to Alabama after a tornado. Only five of the thirty-five tweets had any clear tie to the economy:

- A tweet agreeing with a quote from Fox Business host Stuart Varney that it is a good time to be an American worker.
- A tweet touting the drop in the women's unemployment rate compared to 2011 levels.
- A retweet of Ivanka Trump discussing the administration's job apprenticeship and on-the-job training programs.

- A tweet talking about aluminum prices falling and how the usage of tariffs on aluminum dumping will provide additional funds and jobs for the United States.
- A retweet of Fox Business host Charles Payne talking about growth in non-supervisory wages and wages overall.

Despite the fact that there was more cheerleading about the economy in these tweets than anything else, the Dow Jones Industrial Average closed at 25,450.24, about a 23-point drop from the day before. In addition, the index measure developed by Baker, Bloom, and Davis (2012) to measure uncertainty in the equity market increased from a level of about 38 on March 7 to about 67 on March 8. The stock market dropped, and an indicator of equity market uncertainty increased in the span of one day. What happened?

A potential explanation is that the president's shift in Twitter behavior produced an information overload that introduced a lack of clarity into the marketplace. A jolt of thirty-two additional tweets on a variety of topics increases the amount of effort members of the general public, the press, and other political actors have to exert to review and evaluate what the president's policy priorities and goals are, if any exist. If the president is tweeting about so many different areas, it leaves one to wonder whether there is a clear direction or path forward for the country. Trying to discern the credibility of not just President Trump's written comments but the credibility of the information the president or staff retweets on his account makes it difficult to integrate any new information into decision-making given the prior discussion on what information overloads can do. In just one day of what can be considered a Trump tweetstorm (numerous tweets in close proximity to each other), the stock market dropped and equity market uncertainty increased, even though the tweets involving the economy were positive in tone. A potential explanation is that President Trump's Twitter account introduced an information overload that made the task of determining where the country's economic policy stands much more complicated. With the frequent usage of social media, especially if posts are from multiple sources and about incongruous topics, anyone occupying the office of the presidency has the potential to provide too much information that reduces decision quality.

Information overload can derive from other sources as well. For example, information overload can occur during election cycles where firms need to map out potential scenarios of specific election outcomes and predict the ramifications of elections on future economic policy. An abundance of information about multiple candidates and their policy stances have to be reviewed and processed to make informed projections of the composition of government institutions that shape economic policies; attempts to complete this work can help to heighten economic uncertainty and result in risk-averse behaviors (Julio and Yook 2016).

The second major component in the existing literature that needs to be addressed here involves how responsive presidents are to cues in the political environment. Eshbaugh-Soha and Peake (2011) discuss presidential leadership that is responsive in nature to what is currently happening. Presidents will attempt to address matters that others in the political system find salient or troubling. Canes-Wrone (2001) and Edwards (2009) both believe that successful presidential administrations are those that will take advantage of opportunities in the political environment to bring about change. For example, if there is support within the public for criminal justice reform, a strategic president can observe this and use this as a reason to pressure Congress into taking meaningful policy action on criminal justice reform. The logic of a responsive presidency should apply to the economy. If there is uncertainty in economic markets, a president will feel compelled to do something to assuage concerns. As a result, a presidential administration will use the tools they commonly use to address what they observe in the political environment, such as social media. A result can be an increase in the number of tweets emanating from the @realdonaldtrump account, resulting in more tweetstorms. Tweetstorms have the potential to directly address the issue or attempt to deflect attention away from it by discussing other issues.

A responsive leader observing increased public dissatisfaction with their performance can attempt to change the subject altogether. As a case in point, a frustrated President Trump, reeling from criticism about his response to a white supremacist rally in Charlottesville, Virginia, can start increasingly talking about the need for Americans to exhibit patriotism and not be disrespectful to the US flag or the national anthem, especially if those perceived to be disrespecting the country are well-compensated athletes kneeling during the national anthem. A change in economic conditions presents another opportunity for a president to either address the subject directly or try to divert attention from it, depending upon the strategic calculations made by a specific president. Regardless of the choice made, a potential likely outcome is the same in the case of the Trump presidency: an increase in the number of tweets disseminated from the @realdonaldtrump account.

RESEARCH THEORY AND HYPOTHESIS

Presidents have to balance their need to persuade others with the need for a healthy economy. Economic conditions are the primary area in which the public crafts presidential evaluations of performance (Eshbaugh-Soha and Peake 2011). Public perceptions of economic performance could predict entirely the electoral fortunes of an incumbent president seeking reelection, as well as the performance of candidates running for office under the same party ticket as the president (Erikson 1989). Findings like these provide an incentive for presidents to behave strategically given economic conditions, such that their public remarks have the goal of increasing the chances of their own reelection and their party gaining seats in the legislature (Wood 2007).

In attempts to optimize the probability of his reelection, President Trump can choose to disseminate more content for the public to consume on Twitter in the face of changing economic conditions (regardless of whether this content explicitly invokes the economy), a sign of responsive leadership. Nonetheless, this increase in the volume of tweets from the @realdonaldtrump account, if prolonged, can potentially result in information overload. Although going public in the digital age is quick and relatively easy, there comes a point when too much information is being presented for the public to consume.

Information overload, as discussed in the prior section, can increase the level of uncertainty surrounding a decision, which can increase the likelihood of adverse or suboptimal choices being made. One consequence that can come about is a feedback loop. A president that frequently takes to social media in response to shifts in economic conditions can, through their increased dissemination of information, lead economic conditions to move in a less than preferable direction. What results is akin to a catch-22. If a president feels compelled to make public remarks in response to economic conditions in order for the public to adopt the president's preferred viewpoint or outlook, there is the chance that all of these public remarks can produce an information overload that ultimately worsens economic conditions. Whether or not there is evidence of this in the context of the Trump presidency is evaluated in this project.

A worsening of economic conditions brings about an increase in anxiety within the public. When individuals are made to feel anxious, they engage in efforts to learn more about the source of that feeling in an attempt to ascertain why it produces that feeling. When people are made to feel like they are experiencing uncertain or unfamiliar circumstances, they are compelled to figure out why they happen to feel this way (Marcus 2003). The activity of individuals searching for more information at times of uncertainty again creates a sort of catch-22 situation: a president might increase uncertainty by making people feel overwhelmed with information, which might help to elevate levels of uncertainty surrounding the economy, which then compels people (who can already feel overwhelmed with information) to search for even more information in efforts to better understand what exactly is happening as it relates to certain aspects of the economy. Examining whether there is any evidence of these causal linkages during Trump's time in office is the intent of the empirical work in this study.

With all of this in mind, the following empirically testable hypotheses can be predicted:

Hypothesis one—A prior increase in the intensity of presidential tweet volume can significantly predict an increase in equity market uncertainty.

Hypothesis two—A prior increase in equity market uncertainty can significantly predict an increase in the intensity of presidential tweet volume.

Hypothesis three—A prior increase in the intensity of equity market uncertainty can significantly predict an increase in the extent to which the public searches for information about equity markets.

Given that the predictions offered in these hypotheses involve inferences about dynamic relationships between concepts/variables, a dataset must be collected and analyzed using methods of analysis that can evaluate temporal factors.

RESEARCH DESIGN AND METHODS

Since the project evaluates dynamic information about President Trump's tweet volume, equity market uncertainty, and public information search about equity markets, any research method applied must account for the possibility of feedback between variables. The usage of vector autoregression and moving-average representation time series analyses can help to determine whether support for multidirectional relationships between variables exists. Before moving on to a description of these techniques, a description of the variables collected and measured through these analytical techniques is necessary.

Information about daily tweet volume from the @realdonaldtrump Twitter account comes from the Trump Twitter Archive, a digital repository of President Trump's Twitter account. All tweets are collected through Twitter's application programming interface using a programming library called Tweepy. Each tweet is collected and then converted to when it was released in the Eastern Standard time zone. An advantage of the site is that it captures and maintains tweets that are deleted. Tweets that are deleted should count in terms of measuring tweet volume. When each tweet is sent out, people have to determine what the intention was behind the tweet. If a tweet happens to be deleted, that does not mean that any effort exerted in interpreting the tweet vanishes. It is essential to account for deleted tweets when measuring for the possibility of information overload. Repeated instances of tweets that are written, deleted, and get posted up again with slight modifications or significant changes can contribute to the amount of information being processed that can produce symptoms tied to overload.

Trying to figure out why tweets are deleted and either do not return or pop up again in altered form requires cognitive effort. The total number of tweets disseminated from the @realdonaldtrump Twitter account each day since President Trump's inauguration on January 20, 2017, up to April 24, 2020, serves as the measure of presidential tweet volume in this project. There is no attempt to distinguish whether President Trump personally posted a tweet or retweeted someone else's tweet, as there is no clear empirical indication that the general public can determine whether President Trump himself or a staff member is disseminating the post.

For information about the extent of uncertainty in the US equity market, content analysis procedures originally developed by Baker, Bloom, and Davis (2012) are used. Having a daily measure is important because it provides details about all seven days of the week, since trading hours in the major stock market exchanges are conducted Monday through Friday of each week. The closure of major stock exchanges on weekends necessitates using credible information about the level of uncertainty present in the equity market during Saturday and Sunday of each week.

For every day during the period studied, programming work established by Baker, Bloom, and Davis (2012) chronicles the usage of specific keywords in more than one thousand US newspapers available through the Access World News NewsBank service. For a newspaper article to be included in the index, articles must contain the terms "uncertain" or "uncertainty," the terms "economy" or "economic," and one of several phrases that pertain to the stock market: "equity market," "stock market," "equity price," and "stock price." The terms all intend to capture stories suggesting uncertainty in the economy that is tied to the stock market.

The index for equity market uncertainty scales the raw daily count of articles collected by the total number of overall articles in the newspapers. The result is a daily index whereby low numbers closer to zero suggest negligible levels of equity market uncertainty and numbers far away from zero suggest higher equity market uncertainty.

A graphic plot contrasting President Trump's daily tweet volume with the daily measure of equity market uncertainty over the same period is presented in figure 13.1 below. The figure indicates that the volume of tweets disseminated from the @realdonaldtrump Twitter account has increased markedly since the beginning of the impeachment inquiry initiated in the House of Representatives. While there have been multiple brief spikes during the period studied, the level of equity market uncertainty has skyrocketed in the face of the COVID-19 pandemic.

To capture in some capacity the level to which people are searching for information about the equity market, a sum of the daily number of page views on Wikipedia of several pages pertaining to the stock market are collected. The five pages are as follows: "Dow Jones Industrial Average," "stock market," "stock market index," "stock market prediction," and "stock market index future." The daily count of page views for each page is collected by the Wikimedia page-views application programming interface and hosted on the Wikimedia Toolforge service. Higher levels of page views about the equity market suggest a higher level of interest in learning more about the stock market. A higher level of interest involves a search for pertinent information.

Although by no means all-encompassing, this daily measure works as an adequate approximation of public information search about the equity market, as the Wikimedia page-views application programming

President Trump Tweet Volume (Daily Number of Tweets Disseminated)

Equity Market Uncertainty Index (Daily Index Value)

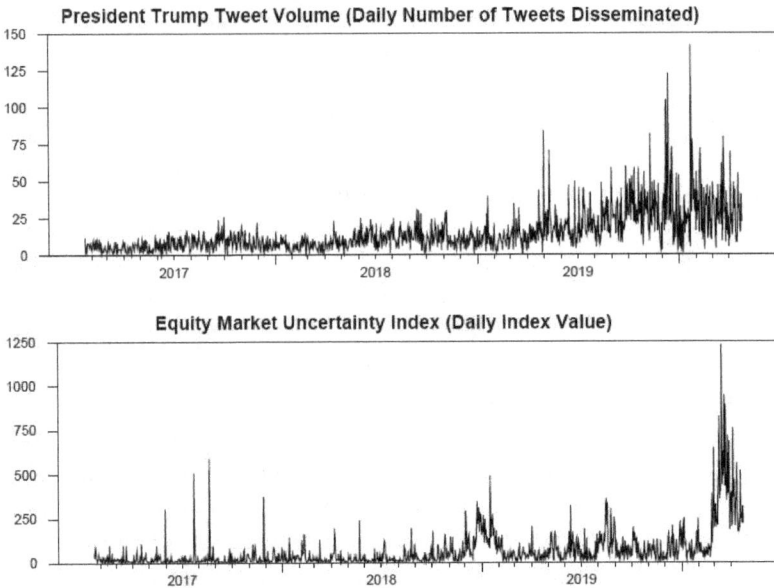

Figure 13.1: Contrasting Daily Time Series of Trump Tweet Volume and Equity Market Uncertainty. *Note:* Visual produced in WinRATS Standard 9.2.

interface is able to detect and exclude significant shifts in page views that are attributable to automatic or programmed web crawlers that scan the Internet. The analytics on page views are from people that search for a page or are redirected to a page through an organic information search.

To perform the traditional vector autoregression and moving-average representation techniques, all three of the core variables in the project must be stationary. Time series information with stationary properties do not have trend or seasonal effects, which means each time series has properties that do not depend on the time in which a particular series is observed. The probability characteristics and statistical properties do not depend on the time reference point used; the mean, variance, autocorrelation, and all other properties are constant over time. Table 13.1 below presents the diagnostic tests for each variable. After reviewing the three sets of results, it is clear all three variables are stationary. Since each variable is stationary, the combination of all three variables will not be cointegrated. Cointegration means variables share a common trend across time that makes estimation

Table 13.1: Augmented Dickey-Fuller t-tests for Presence of Unit Roots

Variable	Equity Market Uncertainty	Trump Tweet Volume	Wikipedia Page Views
Test Statistic	–3.56*	–3.96*	–4.36*
Critical value .01	–3.43	–3.43	–3.43
Critical value .05	–2.86	–2.86	–2.86
Critical value .10	–2.57	–2.57	–2.57
Number of Lags	7	7	12

Note: Number of lags determined by Bayesian Information Criteria. For the test statistics of all variables at all critical values, the null hypothesis of a unit root present in the variable can be rejected. All variables in the system are stationary, such that standard vector autoregression and moving average representation techniques can be applied.

of relationships using standard time-series techniques difficult. The results indicate that this is not a concern, which means standard vector autoregression and moving-average representation analyses can be performed.

To account for the potential effect of exogenous factors, indicator variables for major events during the Trump administration are included in the analyses. Exogenous variables do not depend on shifts in the variables studied (Trump tweet volume, equity market uncertainty, and information search about equity markets). Still, exogenous variables should be included and accounted for since they have the potential to alter values of the three aforementioned variables. One can think of exogenous variables in time-series analyses as essentially control variables that help to determine the true extent of the relationship between the core variables studied. The dichotomous dummy variables are scored as a 1 for being in the period of relevance to a major event and as a 0 for being outside of the period of relevance. The full list of exogenous control factors is presented in table 13.2 below. The list was developed by performing search queries through Google News for those events that received a high number of mass media outlet coverage over the period studied for the project.

The time-series approach used in efforts to determine causal direction is known as vector autoregression (VAR), while attempts to gauge the magnitude (size) and polarity (direction) of relationships are evaluated through moving-average representation (MAR). In vec-

Table 13.2: List of Exogenous Events Accounted for in Analysis

Event (Variable Name)	Time
James Comey Fired (comey)	May 9, 2017
Special Counsel to Investigate Russian Interference Begins/Appointed (sca)	May 17, 2017
US Withdraws from Paris Climate Agreement (pca)	June 1, 2017
Affordable Care Act Repeal Fails (acaf)	July 28, 2017
Tax Cuts and Jobs Act of 2017 Signed into Law (tcjas)	December 22, 2017
January 2018 Government Shutdown (shut1)	January 20, 2018, to January 22, 2018
2018 Midterm Elections (mid18)	November 6, 2018
2018 to 2019 Government Shutdown (shut2)	December 22, 2018, to January 25, 2019
Special Counsel Investigation Concludes (scic)	March 22, 2019
Impeachment Inquiry Initiated in House (iiih)	September 24, 2019
Al-Baghdadi Raid and Death (abrd)	October 26, 2019, to October 27, 2019
Revised Version of USMCA Signed by US, Mexico, and Canada (usmca)	December 10, 2019
House Votes to Impeach Trump (hvit)	December 18, 2019
China Reports Cases of Pneumonia in Wuhan (crpw)	December 18, 2019
Qasem Soleimani Baghdad International Airport Strike (qsbas)	January 3, 2020
First Recorded Case of COVID-19 Outside China (fccoc)	January 13, 2020
Senate Impeachment Trial (sit)	January 16, 2020, to February 5, 2020
First Known Case of COVID-19 Confirmed in U.S. (fkcusa)	January 20, 2020
White House Coronavirus Task Force Established (whctf)	January 29, 2020
Proclamation on Suspension of Entry from China (ban)	January 31, 2020
Trump Oval Office Primetime National Address about COVID-19 (trumpad)	March 11, 2020
Coronavirus Aid, Relief, and Economic Security Act Signed into Law (cares)	March 27, 2020

Note: For each exogenous variable, the dataset marks the date(s) when the event occurs with a "1" and marks all other times before and after the event with a "0." Variable name designates how the event is listed in the dataset and presented in the vector autoregression findings of table 13.3.

tor autoregression, the analysis checks to see whether prior values of a variable can predict current values of other variables measured in the vector autoregression system. Since prior values of each variable are included in the analysis, the inertial qualities of a variable are accounted for (meaning that current values of a variable can potentially be predicted by prior values of the variable itself).

Vector autoregression is a useful approach in efforts to learn about whether a potential causal relationship exists between variables. The problem with vector autoregression is that it does not provide a precise estimate of the polarity or magnitude of any relationship between variables. The reason for this is that due to the usage of prior values (lags) in the statistical procedure, any coefficient estimates have multicollinearity concerns that need to be addressed. Accounting for multicollinearity necessitates the usage of moving-average representation.

Through moving-average representation, a simulated change (known as a shock) is imposed on a single specific variable to see how other variables being studied react across time. In other words, if we are to simulate an increase in one variable, it is possible to detect whether other variables increase or decrease in response and also to observe how long the increase or decrease persists. After introducing a change (shock) to a variable, we monitor how other variables react over time. For a more intuitive interpretation of the extent of change across the variables studied, each variable is standardized. A standardized variable is rescaled to have a mean of zero and a standard deviation of one. Rescaling the variables in this way places each on a common metric.

RESEARCH FINDINGS

The empirical findings of the time-series analyses support all three research hypotheses of the project. There is a feedback relationship that exists between President Trump's tweet volume and equity market uncertainty. It also appears that a second feedback relationship exists between equity market uncertainty and information search about equity market uncertainty on Wikipedia. The full results of the vector autoregression analysis are presented in table 13.3 below.

Prior levels of Twitter activity from the @realdonaldtrump account Granger-causes equity market uncertainty (p-value = 0.01). When looking at the moving-average representation results after Trump's tweet volume is increased by one standard deviation, the level of eq-

Table 13.3: Vector Autoregression (VAR) Granger Test Results

Independent Variable	Dependent Variable	p-value [F-statistic]
Trump Tweet Volume ➔	Trump Tweets	0.00* [59.2983]
Equity Market Uncertainty ➔		0.03* [2.1653]
Information Search/ Wikipedia Page Views		0.61
Exogenous Controls comey (ns), sca (ns), pca (ns), acaf (ns), tcjas (ns), shut1 (ns), mid18 (ns), shut2 (ns), scic (ns), iiih (ns), abrd (–), usmca (ns), hvit (+), crpw (+), qsbas (ns), fccoc (ns), sit (+), fkcusa (ns), whctf (–), ban (–), trumpad (ns), cares (ns)		
Trump Tweet Volume ➔	Equity Market Uncertainty	0.01* [2.5966]
Equity Market Uncertainty ➔		0.00* [61.1461]
Information Search/ Wikipedia Page Views ➔		0.00* [10.8953]
Exogenous Controls comey (ns), sca (ns), pca (ns), acaf (ns), tcjas (ns), shut1 (ns), mid18 (ns), shut2 (+), scic (ns), iiih (ns), abrd (ns), usmca (ns), hvit (–), crpw (ns), qsbas (ns), fccoc (ns), sit (ns), fkcusa (ns), whctf (ns), ban (+), trumpad (ns), cares (–)		
Trump Tweet Volume	Wikipedia Page Views	0.15 [1.5025]
Equity Market Uncertainty ➔		0.00* [10.3052]

Information Search/
　Wikipedia Page Views ➔　　　　　　　　　　　0.00*
　　　　　　　　　　　　　　　　　　　　　　　　[129.3375]

Exogenous Controls
　comey (ns), sca (ns), pca
　(ns), acaf (ns), tcjas (ns),
　shut1 (ns), mid18 (ns),
　shut2 (ns), scic (ns), iiih
　(ns), abrd (ns), usmca (ns),
　hvit (ns), crpw (ns), qsbas
　(ns), fccoc (ns), sit (ns),
　fkcusa (ns), whctf (ns), ban
　(ns), trumpad (ns), cares
　(ns),

Note. The arrows and asterisks indicate Granger-causality from the block of coefficients for the independent variable to the designated dependent variable based on 0.05 significance levels. All *p*-values derive from F-tests for the null hypothesis of no Granger-causality. The system includes a deterministic constant. The results of the exogenous controls are based on t-test results based on 0.05 significance levels. A plus sign represents a positive significant relationship, a negative sign represents a negative significant relationship, and "ns" represents not significant. Each of the independent variables in the system includes eight daily lags to control for the inertia of the variables. Lag length is selected by Bayesian Information Criterion (BIC). VAR estimation with lags performed with information on 1,183 daily usable observations (January 2017–April 2020).

uity market uncertainty remains significantly bounded away from the standardized mean of 0 based on the 95 percent confidence interval for sixteen of the nineteen days following the simulated shock. The estimate for all of these sixteen days is around 0.05 standard deviations above the mean, indicating that a positive relationship exists. An increase in the level of Twitter activity from the @realdonaldtrump account brings about an increase in the equity market uncertainty index. The more Trump tweets, the higher the level of equity market uncertainty will be. The dynamics of the moving-average representation are presented in figure 13.2 below. Hypothesis one appears to have full support in the findings from the vector autoregression and the moving-average representation.

The multidirectional relationship between Trump's tweet volume and equity market uncertainty is made clear when looking at the vector autoregression results again in table 13.3. Prior equity market un-

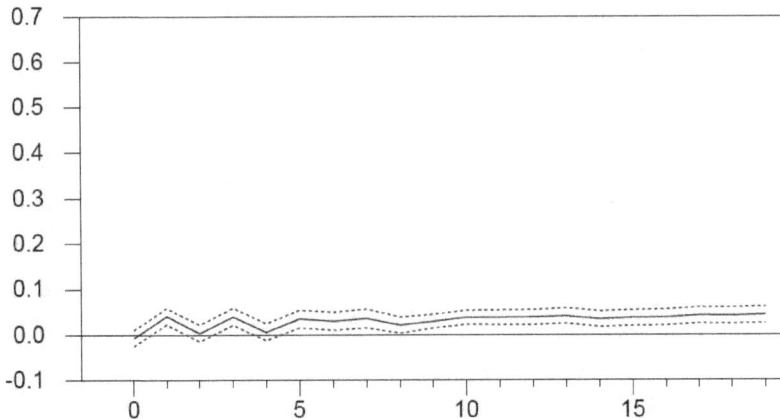

Figure 13.2: Impulse Response of Equity Market Uncertainty Following Shock to Level of Trump Tweets. *Note*: Dashed lines represent 95 percent confidence intervals. The x-axis represents the number of days following the shock to the level of Trump tweets, while the y-axis represents the level of standard deviation change in equity market uncertainty resulting from this shock. For a more intuitive interpretation of change across variables in the system, each variable in the system is standardized. Standardization means each variable is rescaled to have a mean of zero and a standard deviation of one.

certainty levels Granger-causes Trump's tweet volume (p-value = 0.03). Prior change in the equity market uncertainty index predicts current levels of Twitter activity from the @realdonaldtrump Twitter account. When looking at the moving-average representation results presented in figure 13.3 below, a one standard deviation positive shock to the equity market uncertainty index brings about a statistically significant increase in Trump's tweet volume that persists for the majority of the nineteen days following the simulated shock. The presence of a reciprocal positive relationship between this pair of variables means that views on equity markets are responsive to the extent of Trump's Twitter activity and vice-versa. Hypothesis two is supported by the combination of vector autoregression and moving-average representation results.

The vector autoregression results in table 13.3 illustrate that prior change in equity market uncertainty Granger-causes information search on Wikipedia about equity markets (p-value = 0.00). Figure 13.4 below presents the moving-average representation response of Wikipedia page views about equity markets following a one standard

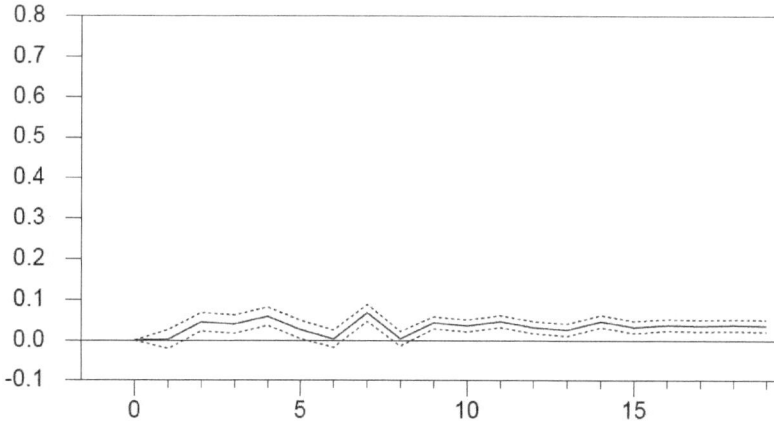

Figure 13.3: Vector Autoregression (VAR) Granger Test Results. *Note:* The arrows and asterisks indicate Granger-causality from the block of coefficients for the independent variable to the designated dependent variable based on 0.05 significance levels. All *p*-values derive from F-tests for the null hypothesis of no Granger-causality. The system includes a deterministic constant. The results of the exogenous controls are based on t-test results based on 0.05 significance levels. A plus sign represents a positive significant relationship, a negative sign represents a negative significant relationship, and "ns" represents not significant. Each of the independent variables in the system includes eight daily lags to control for the inertia of the variables. Lag length is selected by Bayesian Information Criterion (BIC). VAR estimation with lags performed with information on 1,183 daily usable observations (January 2017–April 2020).

deviation positive increase to the equity market uncertainty index. At the point of the shock to the equity market uncertainty index and throughout the nineteen days following the shock, the level of Wikipedia page views about equity markets is bounded away from 0 in a positive direction. A result like this means that an increase in the equity market uncertainty index increases the level of information search about equity markets. Three days following the shock to the equity market uncertainty index, we can expect the level of information search on Wikipedia to be around 0.15 standard deviations above the mean. Elevated equity market uncertainty means more information search about equity markets on the Internet given the results seen here. The collection of vector autoregression and moving-average representation results support hypothesis three of the project.

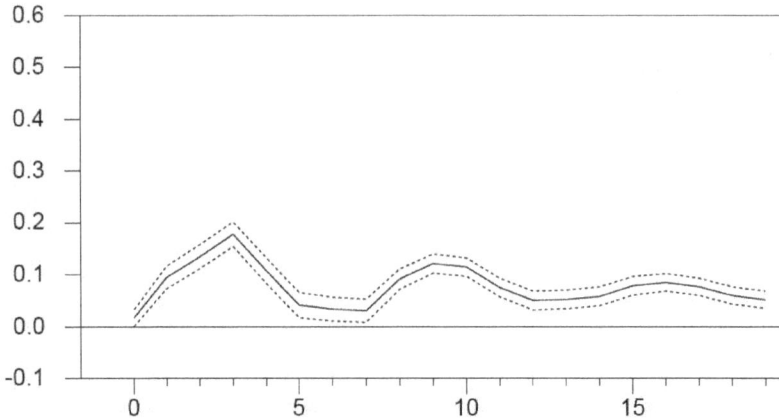

Figure 13.4: Impulse Response of Wikipedia Views Following Shock to Level of Equity Market Uncertainty

It is worth noting that prior change in information search on Wikipedia about equity markets predicts equity market uncertainty (p-value = 0.00). Taking this result into account with the moving-average representation dynamics presented in figure 13.5, it is clear there is another feedback relationship present in the dataset. An increase in information search on Wikipedia about equity markets increases equity market uncertainty, and vice-versa.

Prior change in Trump's Twitter volume fails to significantly Granger-cause information search on Wikipedia about equity markets (p-value = 0.15), and prior change in information search on Wikipedia about equity markets fails to significantly Granger-cause Trump's Twitter volume (p-value = 0.61). While these variables might not have a direct influence on each other, all of the results in this project indicate that they might have an indirect effect on each other with the equity market uncertainty index acting as an intermediary. Increases in tweets from Trump elevate equity market uncertainty. The increase in equity market uncertainty increases online information search about equity markets. On the flip side, an increase in information search online about equity markets increases equity market uncertainty. The increase in equity market uncertainty increases Trump's Twitter volume. Given the evidence available in the project, it appears that Trump's Twitter activity, equity market uncertainty, and information search on Wikipedia on equity markets all have some relationship with each other, be it direct or indirect.

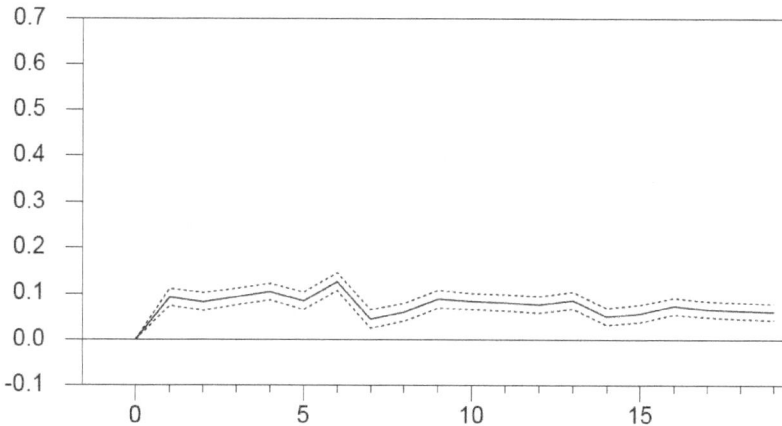

Figure 13.5: Impulse Response of Equity Market Uncertainty Following Shock to Wikipedia Page Views

RESEARCH DISCUSSION

The results of this project are certainly not definitive, but they are still sobering. President Trump's Twitter feed appears to heighten the level of uncertainty about the markets in a fashion that suggests more tweets means more uncertainty. Additional tweets disseminated from the @realdonaldtrump account can create symptoms tied to information overload. Observable symptoms of information should strategically make President Trump reluctant in disseminating too many messages on Twitter than can lead to information overload, particularly in periods when equity market uncertainty is already high, such as what has been observed in the aftermath of the COVID-19 pandemic. The findings here in this project though indicate that more equity market uncertainty compels President Trump to tweet more, a sign of a potentially pernicious cycle in the economy.

While responsive presidential leadership does indicate that presidents will react to cues in the political environment, especially if doing so helps them electorally, President Trump's response to an indicator relevant to the stock market can actually be self-defeating. Instead of responding in a way that ameliorates the level of equity market uncertainty, President Trump's behavior on social media increases equity market uncertainty.

President Trump's Twitter usage might be a defining feature of a rather unorthodox presidency. Instead of carefully and selectively using Twitter as a part of a strategic public communications strategy that attempts to persuade others, President Trump is using Twitter as a personally preferred modality to express his own thoughts, feelings, and concerns at any given point in time (Ott and Dickinson 2019). Packer (2019) believes that Trump's behavior is indicative of high levels of emotional reactivity, the expression of what can be impulsive or almost uncontrollable emotional reactions to events or stimuli. Rather than using Twitter as a part of a portfolio of available tools in a going-public campaign, President Trump could be employing Twitter as an outlet to express his emotional reactions to what he is experiencing without extensive consideration of the potential consequences or ramifications of doing so (such as creating symptoms of information overload for members of the general public). A tweetstorm of numerous tweets and retweets within a single day is not necessarily a part of making the case for a policy agenda but instead is a possible indicator of how President Trump is reacting to things in real time. A president's social media presence as a makeshift mood detector is not aligned with traditional perceptions of what a president's public communications style consists of (Hart 1987).

Whether or not the results observed in this project will hold for future presidential administrations or simply reinforce the perspective that President Trump's time in office deviates from prior empirical regularities observed in the presidency literature is a key aspect for scholars to contemplate. The analyses performed here should inspire additional work that explores whether alternative economic indicators show the same results, whether alternative indicators of public information search offer the same results, and whether an alternative indicator of Trump's public remarks (e.g., content analysis from the Public Papers of the Presidents) demonstrate the same results. While being an initial step in this area of inquiry, the early results here suggest that President Trump's Twitter activity has the potential to do more economic harm than good. It could very well be that for some presidents some things are better left unsaid (or un-tweeted).

REFERENCES

Allen, David K., and M. Shoard. "Spreading the Load: Mobile Information and Communications Technologies and Their Effect on Information Overload." *Information Research: An International Electronic Journal* 10, no. 2 (2005): n2.

Baker, Scott R., Nicholas Bloom, and Steven J. Davis. *Policy Uncertainty: A New Indicator.* No. 362. Centre for Economic Performance, London School of Economics, 2012.

Bawden, David. "Information Overload." *Library & Information Briefings* 92 (2001): 1–15.

Bianchi, Francesco, Howard Kung, and Thilo Kind. *Threats to Central Bank Independence: High-Frequency Identification with Twitter.* No. w26308. National Bureau of Economic Research, 2019.

Brans, Heleen, and Bert Scholtens. "Under His Thumb: The Effect of President Donald Trump's Twitter Messages on the US Stock Market." *PloS one* 15, no. 3 (2020): e0229931.

Brown, Brandon. "Trump Twitter Archive." Last modified April 25, 2020. http://www.trumptwitterarchive.com/.

Burggraf, Tobias, Ralf Fendel, and Toan Luu Duc Huynh. "Political News and Stock Prices: Evidence from Trump's Trade War." *Applied Economics Letters* (2019): 1–4.

Canes-Wrone, Brandice. "The President's Legislative Influence from Public Appeals." *American Journal of Political Science* (2001): 313–329.

Chewning Jr., Eugene G., and Adrian M. Harrell. "The Effect of Information Load on Decision Makers' Cue Utilization Levels and Decision Quality in a Financial Distress Decision Task." *Accounting, Organizations and Society* 15, no. 6 (1990): 527–542.

Duncan, James R. "Information Overload: When Less Is More in Medical Imaging." *Diagnosis* 4, no. 3 (2017): 179–183.

Edwards III, George C. *The Strategic President: Persuasion and Opportunity in Presidential Leadership.* Princeton, NJ: Princeton University Press, 2009.

Eppler, Martin J., and Jeanne Mengis. "The Concept of Information Overload: A Review of Literature from Organization Science, Accounting, Marketing, MIS, and Related Disciplines." *Information Society* 20, no. 5 (2004): 325–344.

Erikson, Robert S. "Economic Conditions and the Presidential Vote." *American Political Science Review* 83, no. 2 (1989): 567–573.

Eshbaugh-Soha, Matthew. "Going Public and Presidential Leadership." In *Oxford Research Encyclopedia of Politics.* 2016. DOI: 10.1093/acre fore/9780190228637.013.57.

Eshbaugh-Soha, Matthew, and Jeffrey S. Peake. *Breaking through the Noise: Presidential Leadership, Public Opinion, and the News Media.* Redwood City, CA: Stanford University Press, 2011.

Fiske, Susan T. "Cognitive Theory and the Presidency." *Researching the Presidency: Vital Questions, New Approaches* (1993): 233–265.

Galbraith, Jay R. "Organization Design: An Information Processing View." *Interfaces* 4, no. 3 (1974): 28–36.

Halson, Shona L., Jonathan M. Peake, and John P. Sullivan. "Wearable Technology for Athletes: Information Overload and Pseudoscience?" *International Journal of Sports Physiology and Performance* 11, no. 6 (2016): 705–706.

Hart, Roderick P. *The Sound of Leadership: Presidential Communication in the Modern Age.* Chicago: University of Chicago Press, 1987.

Jacoby, Jacob. "Information Load and Decision Quality: Some Contested Issues." *Journal of Marketing Research* 14, no. 4 (1977): 569–573.

———. "Perspectives on Information Overload." *Journal of Consumer Research* 10, no. 4 (1984): 432–435.

Jensen, Jakob D., Manusheela Pokharel, Courtney L. Scherr, Andy J. King, Natasha Brown, and Christina Jones. "Communicating Uncertain Science to the Public: How Amount and Source of Uncertainty Impact Fatalism, Backlash, and Overload." *Risk Analysis* 37, no. 1 (2017): 40–51.

Julio, Brandon, and Youngsuk Yook. "Policy Uncertainty, Irreversibility, and Cross-Border Flows of Capital." *Journal of International Economics* 103 (2016): 13–26.

Keller, Kevin Lane, and Richard Staelin. "Effects of Quality and Quantity of Information on Decision Effectiveness." *Journal of Consumer Research* 14, no. 2 (1987): 200–213.

Kernell, Samuel. *Going Public: New Strategies of Presidential Leadership.* 4th ed. Washington, DC: CQ, 2007.

Kreis, Ramona. "The 'Tweet Politics' of President Trump." *Journal of Language and Politics* 16, no. 4 (2017): 607–618.

Lee, Byung-Kwan, and Wei-Na Lee. "The Effect of Information Overload on Consumer Choice Quality in an On-Line Environment." *Psychology & Marketing* 21, no. 3 (2004): 159–183.

Marcus, George E. "The Psychology of Emotions and Politics." In *Oxford Handbook of Political Psychology*, 182–221. Oxford: Oxford University Press, 2003.

Neustadt, Richard E. *Presidential Power and the Modern Presidents: The Politics of Leadership from Roosevelt to Reagan.* New York: Simon & Schuster, 1991.

Ott, Brian L. "The Age of Twitter: Donald J. Trump and the Politics of Debasement." *Critical Studies in Media Communication* 34, no. 1 (2017): 59–68.

Ott, Brian L., and Greg Dickinson. *The Twitter Presidency: Donald J. Trump and the Politics of White Rage.* New York: Routledge, 2019.

Packer, Gail S. "Conflict, Culture, and Community: Dispute Resolution after Trump." *Negotiation Journal* 35, no. 1 (2019): 173–176.

"Pageviews analysis," Wikimedia Toolforge, accessed April 25, 2020, https://tools.wmflabs.org/pageviews/?project=en.wikipedia.org&platform=all-access&agent=user&redirects=1&start=2017-01-20&end=2020-04-24&pages=Dow_Jones_Industrial_Average|Stock_market|Stock_market_index|Stock_mrket_prediction|Stock_market_index_future.

Passel, Jeffrey S., and D'Vera Cohn. "U.S. Unauthorized Immigrant Total Dips to Lowest Level in a Decade." Last modified November 27, 2018. https://

www.pewresearch.org/hispanic/2018/11/27/unauthorized-immigrant -workforce-is-smaller-but-with-more-women/.

Pelled, Ayellet, Josephine Lukito, Fred Boehm, JungHwan Yang, and Dhavan Shah. "'Little Marco,' 'Lyin' Ted,' 'Crooked Hillary,' and the 'Biased' Media: How Trump Used Twitter to Attack and Organize." In *Digital Discussions*, 176–196. Routledge, 2018.

Salem, M., J. Younger, and H. St. John. "Introducing the Volfefe Index." *North American Fixed Income Strategy* (2019).

Schick, Allen G., Lawrence A. Gordon, and Susan Haka. "Information Overload: A Temporal Approach." *Accounting, Organizations and Society* 15, no. 3 (1990): 199–220.

Schneider, Susan C. "Information Overload: Causes and Consequences." *Human Systems Management* 7, no. 2 (1987): 143–153.

Simon, Herbert A. "Bounded Rationality and Organizational Learning." *Organization Science* 2, no. 1 (1991): 125–134.

Sun, Lihua, Junpeng Guo, and Yanlin Zhu. "Applying Uncertainty Theory into the Restaurant Recommender System Based on Sentiment Analysis of Online Chinese Reviews." *World Wide Web* 22, no. 1 (2019): 83–100.

Tillmann, Peter. "Trump, Twitter, and Treasuries." *Contemporary Economic Policy* (2020) doi:10.1111/coep.12465.

Wood, B. Dan. *The Politics of Economic Leadership: The Causes and Consequences of Presidential Rhetoric*. Princeton, NJ: Princeton University Press, 2007.

CHAPTER 14

Trump's Unorthodox Foreign Policy

Jeffrey S. Peake

INTRODUCTION

Donald J. Trump's presidency is not a normal presidency. This is especially clear with regard to the president's foreign policy, which differs substantially from that of his predecessors. Trump's differences in foreign policy focus on how he conducts himself in office, makes key decisions, interacts with world leaders, and constructs foreign policies. While the substance of US policy has maintained some stability from prior administrations, with some notable differences, the process by which Trump formulates foreign policy is markedly different. The differences largely stem from Trump's overt hostility toward the foreign policy establishment and norms that typically limit presidential action in foreign policy, as well as toward constitutional checks on his own authority. In this chapter, I summarize the characteristics of Trump's foreign policy process that set him apart from his predecessors, providing numerous examples where those differences matter for US foreign policy. I conclude with a brief commentary on the broader significance of Trump's departure from what typifies presidential behavior in foreign policy.

In many respects, President Donald J. Trump's foreign policy is typical. For example, wars started during the George W. Bush administration, and continued by Barack Obama, persist. American combat troops remain deployed in conflict zones ranging from Afghanistan to West Africa. The tactics used by prior administrations in these conflicts also persist, as many of the details of policy making occur within the foreign policy bureaucracy. Numerous early accounts of President Trump's foreign policy emphasized the degree to which it represented conventional Republican foreign policy (Abrams 2017; Kroenig 2017), yet there was broad disagreement on this account among foreign policy scholars (for a summary, see Benkowski and Potter 2017). While much of President Trump's foreign policy represents a continuation of American policy, that is not the case in all areas, particularly with regard to international trade. Moreover, his approach to policy making is unorthodox, particularly in terms of style and process.

A shift in style and process was evident in President Trump's embrace of nationalism with his inaugural address, which emphasized the mantra "America First." The speech was a continuation of his campaign and suggested to allies and competitors alike that there would be a notable shift in American foreign policy. Early moves, including withdrawing from the Trans-Pacific Partnership (TPP), fulfilled campaign promises and suggested a very different approach to foreign policy. Other moves, however, indicated more of the same in foreign policy. Trump's decision to punish the Syrian regime for its use of chemical weapons, using cruise missile strikes, during the first months of his presidency is similar to previous presidents' uses of force. While a fair assessment of Trump's foreign policy would note the continuity in many areas, it is difficult to set aside Trump's stark differences in style and process that distinguish him from his predecessors.

What sets President Trump apart from his predecessors, then? President Trump routinely violates norms of foreign policy, in terms of both process and style. It is precisely these sorts of norm violations that led to Trump's impeachment in December 2019. Trump is only the third president to ever be impeached by the US House of Representatives and the first to be impeached for alleged abuses of power in the realm of foreign policy, a field where presidents are typically deemed to have broad latitude in action. These violations of basic norms significantly limit the degree to which his foreign policy actions are hemmed in by the foreign policy establishment and the separation of powers system—a system that has come under significant strain due to hyper-partisanship. As a result, while President Trump has been able to act unilaterally to enact foreign policy change, the policies are seen as less legitimate and are likely to be less resilient than policies enacted through the normal process and in keeping with the basic guardrails of American foreign policy making.

As Diana Panke and Ulrich Petersohn write, "Norms are standards of appropriate behavior and are an integral part of international and domestic politics and policies" (2017, 574). There is a vast literature on norms in international relations, much of it focusing on the role played by the United States, the only global hegemon, in policing appropriate behavior by states and upholding the liberal international order it helped build after World War II. Many of the criticisms of Trump's foreign policies focus on how his policies and diplomatic style, such that it is, violate these basic international norms (Cohen 2019). President Trump's America First approach to foreign policy presents a direct challenge to the historical leadership role played by the United States, and critical assessments of his foreign policies have been fairly strident (Benkowski and Potter 2017; Cohen 2019; Drezner 2019a; Farrow 2018; McGurk 2020).

While standards of appropriate behavior (i.e., norms) are critically important to international relations, they are also relevant to the domestic sources of US foreign policy. The Constitution established a singular executive, provisioning the presidency with significant authority in the creation and conduct of foreign and national security policy. To constrain the executive, the framers also set up an elaborate system of shared powers and checks and balances so that other institutions, most notably the Congress, could check this singular executive. Presidency scholar Edward Corwin summarized this as an "invitation to struggle" (1958). Over time, however, the constitutional guardrails on presidential authority, particularly in foreign policy, have eroded, as Congress has delegated substantial additional authority to the executive, including in war powers, trade, agreement making, and even spending authority (Binder, Goldgeier, and Saunders 2020; Fisher 2000; Rudalevige 2005). The courts largely stayed on the sidelines during constitutional conflicts between the branches, particularly in foreign policy, and when they did intervene they typically sided with the executive (Fisher 2017). The constitutional checks on the executive are further weakened by extreme partisanship (Fallows 2017; Goldgeier and Saunders 2018; Schulz 2017). The president's party is less interested in oversight in foreign policy, suggesting that recent presidents have even greater latitude than their predecessors (Fowler

2015). When Congress does try to check the president directly, leaders are unable to marshal the supermajorities required to do so.

Given the general weakness of these checks and balances, and their erosion over time, international and domestic political norms have been critical in checking presidential actions in the foreign policy realm. Norms that undergird American democracy have weakened over time, however. Levitsky and Ziblatt (2018) write, "Two basic norms have preserved America's checks and balances in ways we have come to take for granted: mutual toleration, or the understanding that competing parties accept one another as legitimate rivals, and forbearance, or the idea that politicians should exercise restraint in deploying their institutional prerogatives." These norms have eroded over time, particularly since the end of the Cold War, and their erosion has accelerated under President Trump. While the separation of powers system is critical here, given its erosion, perhaps the greatest enforcement mechanism today is the significant importance of the foreign policy establishment and the widespread acceptance of both the international and the domestic political norms within that establishment. For Trump to effectively shift US foreign policy toward his "America First" mantra, he had to tackle head-on this establishment tendency to resist change and promote basic norms of behavior.

TRUMP TAKES ON THE FOREIGN POLICY ESTABLISHMENT

President Trump has relied less on establishment expertise than his predecessors, altering the basic policy-making process in foreign policy and producing tremendous turnover in national security staff during his first three years. Trump's war on the policy-making establishment has proven difficult to win, however. One front in this war relates to leaks. While leaks from inside the executive branch are a problem faced by all modern presidents, such leaks increased significantly during Trump's first term, including the transcripts of phone calls between Trump and foreign leaders.[1] An unprecedented op-ed was published by the *New York Times*, written by an anonymous "senior official in the Trump administration," which detailed how "many of the senior officials . . . are working diligently from within to frustrate parts of his [Trump's] agenda and his worst inclinations" (Anonymous 2018). The op-ed writer pointed directly to President Trump's foreign policy, suggesting there were two tracks: one where Trump routinely violated norms and another where the establishment worked hard to uphold the very norms Trump was assaulting. Another front in this war relates to the president's communication strategy, which relies heavily on unfiltered communication via Twitter. President Trump's Twitter habit routinely contradicts official US policy, often leaving his advisers scrambling to respond and supporting charges of incoherency in foreign policy (Shepp 2018).[2] Whistleblowers from within the executive branch have also proven problematic for Trump. Trump's impeachment, which dominated Washington politics for the last few months of 2019 through early 2020, was instigated by a whistleblower report that emanated from the intelligence community. While only a partial list, none of these things are normal for presidents and presidential foreign policy.

Turnover among presidential advisers is a typical problem for modern presidents. However, turnover among President Trump's top advisers has outpaced recent presidents, which significantly hampered the advisory process in foreign policy (Tenpas 2020a). Among the president's "A team," defined as those top-level advisers who are not statutory members of the cabinet, turnover was at 80 percent for the Trump administration's first three years, and more than one-third of those positions had turned over multiple times. This is a higher rate of turnover than for the entire first terms of Presidents Reagan through Obama. Turnover in the cabinet was also higher for Trump—his cabinet turned over in ten of thirteen positions in just three years. The closest comparison among Reagan through Obama is George H. W. Bush, who experienced turnover of eight cabinet secretaries during his four-year term (Tenpas 2020b).

The Trump administration experienced turnover at the highest levels in foreign policy, with departures of the director of National Intelligence (twice), the director of the Central Intelligence Agency, the secretary of Homeland Security (twice), the secretary of State, the secretary of Defense, and the secretary of Energy. Turnover was especially pronounced for national security staff positions. Before the end of his third year, Trump had fired his third national security adviser (NSA), John Bolton, and the National Security Council (NSC) staff was on its sixth deputy NSA.[3] Of the seven most senior NSC staff positions, five had turned over at least once in the first seven months of the Trump administration, and all seven had turned over at least once during the first three years. Kathryn Dunn Tenpas (2020a) writes, "This turnover rate is simply off the charts—no prior president comes close to this level of NSC instability. In stark contrast, both Presidents Bush and President Clinton had single National Security Advisers throughout the first term; President Obama had two and President Reagan had three. Similarly, while the sixth Deputy National Security Adviser is serving for President Trump, Presidents Clinton and George W. Bush had one during the first term, Presidents Obama and George H.W. Bush had two and President Reagan had three."

Such turnover, particularly with the NSA and the NSC, undermines the effectiveness of the national security decision-making process and leads presidents to act in foreign policy without a clear strategy or understanding of the broader consequences of their actions (Daalder and Destler 2019). The unprecedented turnover led to significant worry among journalists covering foreign policy, with concern that the "axis of adults" that had surrounded Trump during his first two years had all left, leaving him with sycophants and yes-men (Wright 2019). One of the most important elements of any foreign policy advisory system is that the president gets the information and advice on complex foreign policy issues they need, rather than the advice they want. In this regard, early assessments of Trump's advisory system are concerning (Daalder and Destler 2019; Da Vinha 2019).

The foreign policy bureaucracy did not fare much better under Trump's leadership. His initial budget sought to slash State Department funding by nearly one-third, and career foreign service officers resigned or took early retirement in droves as morale plummeted during 2017 (Gramer, De Luce, and Lynch 2019). The situation only worsened under Mike Pompeo, Trump's second secretary of state, who replaced Rex Tillerson in early 2018. In its 2019 report, the State Department's Inspector General Office stated, "staff shortages, frequent turnover, poor leadership, and inexperienced and under-trained staff" were undermining the department's mission. Much of the problem was linked to a sixteen-month hiring freeze that started in 2017, the brain drain that resulted from the rash of retirements and resignations, and the numerous ambassadorial vacancies (Lynch and Gramer 2018). The Trump administration was particularly slow in filling top staff positions in the State Department: "When Trump fired Rex Tillerson . . . in February 2018, eight of the top ten positions at the State Department were vacant" (Drezner 2019b, 726).

When asked about the high-level vacancies, Trump responded, "I'm the only one that matters, because when it comes to it, that's what the policy is going to be" (Chappell 2017). Tillerson's efforts at redesign and reform at State were spectacular failures and further diminished morale (Farrow 2018). There were also serious concerns that political appointees at the State Department routinely disregarded or undermined the work of career professionals and regularly bullied civil servants, contributing to low morale and significantly diminishing the effectiveness of information flow from the bureaucracy to decision-makers in the White House (Bublé 2020).

Daalder and Destler (2019) describe the difficulty of successfully managing the national security process for President Trump, arguing that the typical models of the NSA as "honest broker or straightforward adviser" do not work "for a president who disdains process and tends to follow his 'gut.'" Presidency scholars find that presidents typically organize their policy advice based on three standard management approaches: the formalistic or hierarchical model; the collegial or spokes of the wheel model; and the competitive model. The models vary in terms of the amount of delegation presidents provide to gatekeepers (e.g., the chief of staff), the amount of cooperation that exists between advisers, and the degree to which the president is directly involved in policy formulation (Snow and Haney 2018).

Early accounts of the Trump presidency suggest his management style most closely approximates the competitive model that President Franklin Roosevelt favored: he encourages competition among advisers who have overlapping responsibilities, those advisers communicate directly with the president, and the president selectively engages in policy discussions. The approach seemed to best fit his management style of decision-making based on instincts; however, Trump lacks the vast political experience and skills needed to successfully pull off such a model (Da Vinha 2019). Trump entered office with the impression that he had strong management skills as a successful businessman. This was a view made popular through his successful stint as a reality television star in *The Apprentice*, which emphasized direct competition between contestants looking to be hired by Trump. Unfortunately, running a real estate business and reality television show do not approximate the difficulties of working through complex issues with advisers to make sound foreign policy decisions.

Despite his lack of government experience, Trump was extremely confident in his management prowess, such that he ignored advice on how to best set up his advisory system. During Trump's first year, it became abundantly clear that he lacked patience with the national security process put into place by his second NSA, H. R. McMaster (Daalder and Destler 2019). Da Vinha's (2019, 290) account of Trump's decision-making in foreign policy suggests that his process is a "byproduct of [his] policy detachment and proclivity for making improvised decisions based on his gut feeling." Trump encouraged competition between advisers in "order to foster different ideas," which is an important component of the competitive model. However, "despite having access to divergent information and advice, he has consistently followed his initial instincts and disregarded the counsel of his national security team" (Da Vinha 2019, 301). Such an approach led to significant problems during his first term.

The disregard for the foreign policy establishment and an effective national security process, both features of President Trump's approach to national security, led numerous foreign policy commenters, particularly in the pages of *Foreign Affairs*, to label Trump's foreign policy as "incoherent," as "retrograde," and as fundamentally undermining American leadership of the liberal international order (Drezner 2019a; McGurk 2020). During President Trump's first term, weekly news cycles were replete with examples of the president shirking basic expectations of modern presidents in the foreign policy process. Examples include the president's unwillingness to read the daily intelligence brief (Leonnig, Harris, and Jaffe 2018; Schlesinger 2019; Walcott 2019), his assigning significant foreign policy responsibilities to his son-in-law, Jared Kushner, despite his lack of experience and the denial of a security clearance (Lafraniere et al. 2017; Gramer and Gandhi 2019), his defense policy pronouncements on Twitter (Nelson et al. 2017; Associated Press 2017), and his routine attacks on the intelligence community (Geltzer and Goodman 2020; Viswanatha 2019), just to name a few.

Bright Line Watch is a research project focused on monitoring, through surveys of political scientists and the American public, "democratic practices, their resilience, and potential threats."[4] In addition to surveying experts and the public on the importance and performance on twenty-eight principles for American democracy, the surveys query experts as to the importance and relative abnormality of ongoing events during the Trump administration. The surveys between August 2018 and October 2019 asked expert respondents to rate ninety-three Trump events. Thirty-two events were rated, on average, as at least "mostly abnormal" and "mostly important." Nine of these thirty-two events relate directly to foreign and national security policy, including (in order of significance):

1. President Trump pressuring Ukraine to investigate former vice president Biden while withholding $391 million in military aid during the summer of 2019;
2. President Trump's summit in Helsinki with Russian president Vladimir Putin in July 2018, where he appeared to side with Putin against the US intelligence community regarding Russian interference in the 2016 presidential election;
3. President Trump's February 2019 declaration of a national emergency at the Mexico-US border, in order to transfer military construction funds to construct the border wall, in the face of congressional opposition to funding the wall;
4. President Trump announcing US troops would be withdrawn from Syria by tweet without consulting his aides in December 2018, precipitating the resignation of the secretary of defense, James Mattis;
5. President Trump's labeling the European Union a "foe" ahead of his July 2018 summit with Putin;
6. President Trump's direct criticism of German leader Angela Merkel and the United Kingdom's prime minister Theresa May in July 2018;
7. President Trump's deployment of troops to the Mexican border just prior to the 2018 midterm elections;
8. President Trump's tweet of a spy photo of an Iranian rocket launch site, August 2019;
9. President Trump's approving arms sales to Saudi Arabia despite congressional opposition in May 2019.[5]

The foreign policy events identified above as both important and abnormal provide a partial picture of how scholars generally view President Trump's foreign policy actions. The two events listed as most important and most abnormal, the Ukrainian affair and the Putin summit, merit additional discussion here. Each of these events illustrate broader trends in Trump's foreign policy process identified by scholars. Trump often disregards foreign policy advice and a regularized policy process, and as a result abnormal events are a likely result. In both instances, Trump stepped outside of the formal policy-making process.

Against the advice of his advisers, Trump met alone with Putin during their first summit in Helsinki on July 16, 2018.[6] During the post-meeting press conference, Trump appeared to accept Putin's statement that Russia had nothing to do with the 2016 election, putting him directly at odds with the American intelligence community's universal conclusion that Russia had hacked the Democratic National Committee and had sought to manipulate, through a variety of methods, the 2016 election in favor of candidate Trump. The press conference was universally panned, as pundits and politicians from across the political spectrum excoriated Trump for kowtowing to Putin before the cameras (Tharoor 2018). The summit came at the end of the president's European tour, where he directly criticized allied leaders, including Prime Minister May of the United Kingdom and Chancellor Merkel of Germany, and referred to the European Union as a "foe," actions that also appear on the Bright Line Watch list above. It was quite a week!

In the wake of the press conference, Director of National Intelligence Dan Coats stated that the US intelligence community had clear and convincing evidence that Russia had, in fact, meddled in the 2016 election and that Russian meddling efforts were ongoing. Following the meetings, much was made of Trump's refusal to discuss the specifics of his conversation with Putin and his unwillingness to turn over notes or other documents related to his past communications with the Russian president. Trump's unwillingness to share the details of these one-on-one meetings with other US officials or to keep notes on the meetings was unusual, by historical standards, as the president's advisers and other officials need to understand what was said at those meetings in order to formulate policy recommendations.[7] Trump's alone time with Putin fits a more general pattern, where the president appears to want to develop personal relationships with American adversaries. For example, he was the first president to meet a leader of North Korea, and during each of those meetings, he had lengthy private meetings with Kim Jong Un.[8]

Trump's one-on-one meetings with Putin are especially problematic, given the cloud of suspicion concerning his relationship with Russia that was part of the Mueller investigation into 2016 election meddling. Moreover, Trump's apparent embrace of Putin was in stark contrast to the policies of his administration, which ramped up its support for Ukraine in its war against Russian separatists, pointedly reaffirmed the US position that rejects Russia's annexation of Crimea, and reiterated the threat of retaliation against Russian interference into US elections (Taussig 2018; Weiland 2019). Elliott Abrams (2019) refers to this disconnect between Trump's rhetoric and inconsonant official US policy as "Trump versus the government."[9] It suggests considerable unpredictability when it comes to US policy, particularly if Trump is faced with a foreign policy crisis. Both allies and adversaries are unsure who speaks for the US government.

President Trump's eschewal of a national security process was especially apparent during the events that led to his impeachment by the House of Representatives in December 2019 and his eventual acquittal in the Senate in February 2020. It is hard to imagine national security professionals agreeing to Trump's plan to encourage President Zelensky of Ukraine to investigate one of the leading 2020 Democratic presidential candidates, Joe Biden, and his son Hunter Biden, at a time when the president had ordered the delay of hundreds of millions of dollars in military aid to the beleaguered ally and conditioned a White House meeting with Zelenksy on the Ukrainian president announcing the investigation.

As became clear in testimony before the House investigating committees, Ukraine policy experts were adamant that such a policy was a universally bad idea and counseled against it. For example, the president's NSA, John Bolton, abruptly ended a meeting when the plan came up and referred to the initiative as a "drug deal," cooked up by acting Chief of Staff Mick Mulvaney and the ambassador to the European Union Gordon Sondland. Bolton suggested to his aide that she go directly to NSC counsel to inform them of the situation (Wilkie 2019). As became clear during the impeachment testimony, Ukraine policy was being directed outside of the standard policy process, and the president's personal attorney Rudy Giuliani played an important role. As a result, the president's own political interests (i.e., winning reelection) subordinated official US national security goals in supporting Ukraine in its war with Russia (Mascaro 2019).

While the president was acquitted, Trump's impeachment marks only the third time in American history that a president was impeached and the first time a president was impeached over his foreign policy behavior. In summarizing the articles of impeachment, Harold Koh (2019) writes, "President Trump used the powers of the Presidency in a manner that [1] compromised the national security of the United States and [2] undermined the integrity of the United States democratic process," due to his goal of smearing Joe Biden. The surreptitious and unlawful delay placed by the Office of Management and Budget (OMB) on the duly enacted military aid for Ukraine[10] also strikes at another important trend during the Trump presidency: the unbridled expansion of unilateral executive power.

TRUMP'S EMBRACE OF UNILATERALISM IN FOREIGN POLICY

"America First" evokes the United States acting in its own self-interest, first and foremost, irrespective of how that might be received on the international stage. Under the realist school, states acting in a self-interested fashion is the basis for international politics, so when viewed from that perspective, Trump's mantra is not so unorthodox. However, when you engage with Trump's "America First" rhetoric more directly, significant unilateral strands emerge, setting him apart from prior administrations. While this is most clear on the international stage, where Trump clearly prefers bilateral to multilateral agreements because he sees multilateralism as a violation of American sovereignty (Patrick 2019), Trump's embrace of unilateralism encompasses his policy-making approach, as well.

Trump has steered American foreign policy in a decidedly unilateral direction, both in terms of the actual foreign policies (i.e., the United States acting alone) and the process by which the president secures policy change (i.e., the president acting alone, without Congress). Acting alone is not new to the presidency, as recent presidents have made significant use of the various unilateral tools available to them in order to conduct foreign policy (Howell 2003; Howell and Pevehouse 2007). The 9/11 terrorist attacks accelerated presidential unilateralism, reinvigorating what scholars term the "imperial presidency" (Rudalevige 2005). President Trump, unconstrained by a weak and divided Congress, has pushed the throttle on presidential unilateralism, particularly in foreign policy (Binder, Goldgeier, and Saunders 2020).

How does this make Trump different from his predecessors? The differences go well beyond mere rhetoric and style. In some areas of foreign policy, Trump's substantive policies are fairly orthodox for a conservative Republican president. The same can be said for his unilateral approach to policy making, particularly in his decisions to use force abroad. However, the nature of many of his actions, particularly in diplomacy, has been decidedly unilateral, in both senses of the word, as he has pushed for bilateral agreements rather than multilateral agreements, sought to withdraw the United States from significant multilateral agreements forged by his predecessors against concerted efforts by allies and advisers, and questioned the value of longtime alliances, such as NATO. His shift here, toward unilateral action, makes him quite different from his predecessors.

In terms of the policy-making process, presidential unilateralism (i.e., acting without Congress) is an important component of the modern presidency, particularly in foreign policy. Trump's predecessors routinely acted alone to forge important foreign policies, though they would often justify their actions within the separation of powers framework. Trump, on the other hand, rejects in principle limits to his foreign policy authority, and Republicans in Congress have effectively ceded their institutional authority to check him. Such checks and balances were at the heart of the impeachment effort that dominated Washington in 2019 and early 2020.

Trump's Unilateral Diplomacy

President Trump entered office clearly hostile toward treaties, the primary means by which states enter into binding international agreements. Early in his administration, a draft executive order on multilateral agreements was leaked. If implemented, the order would have created a high-level committee to review all multilateral agreements, unrelated to national security, trade, or extradition, signaling a significant change in American treaty behavior (Conrad and Rigger 2017; DeYoung and Rucker 2017).[11] While the executive order was never officially issued, it clearly signaled to State Department officials and others the new administration's hostility to current and new multilateral agreements.

Past Republican presidents have largely been supportive of multilateralism and international law.[12] President Trump appears to be changing this basic norm. During his first three years in office, Trump submitted just two treaties for Senate approval, suggesting an acceleration of Obama's avoidance of Article II treaties documented by Peake (2017), instead favoring the use of other unilateral devices, including executive agreements and political agreements, which do not require legislative approval.[13] In one of his first official foreign policy acts, Trump withdrew from the TPP, a massive free trade agreement between the United States and eleven other Pacific states, which importantly excluded China. Trump's hostility to multilateralism extends to major agreements completed by President Obama, including the Paris Agreement on Climate Change and the Iran Nuclear Agreement.[14] President Trump's aversion to traditional forms of diplomacy, including treaties and binding multilateral agreements, has had profound implications for US foreign policy. Two Trump decisions stand out as particularly important: his decisions to abrogate the Iran Nuclear Agreement and the Paris Agreement on Climate Change. Both agreements were key foreign policy successes of Obama, which Trump vowed during the 2016 election to undo. Just as Obama had entered the agreements unilaterally, without Congress, Trump left the agreements without consulting Congress. Both Obama's decision to enter the agreements and Trump's decision to vacate them reflect upon trends in presidential unilateralism. Both decisions also represent examples where the president went against counsel from his formal national security policy advisers and against the lobbying of important American allies (Da Vinha 2019).

That Trump prefers presidential unilateralism when implementing diplomacy is not surprising, given the recent erosion of norms that were developed during the twentieth century regarding treaties that satisfy both domestic and international political concerns. For example, presidents typically submit arms control agreements to the Senate as treaties in order to involve Congress and satisfy the concerns of treaty partners.[15] Similar norms exist for human rights accords, multilateral environmental agreements, and bilateral tax, extradition, and investment treaties (Spiro 2001). However, these norms broke down during the Obama presidency, given the paucity of treaties submitted by Obama to the Senate for approval and his routine skirting of congressional approval on a host of agreements that, under the norm, would seemingly require congressional input (Bradley and Goldsmith 2018; Peake 2017). Trump's behavior has solidified this breakdown in norms regarding international agreements, firmly establishing presidential unilateralism in this area. If Obama was able to make these commitments unilaterally (i.e., without Congress), then certainly Trump was within his authority to undo them.

The Iran Nuclear Agreement, or the Joint Comprehensive Plan of Action (JCPOA), is an agreement signed by the United States, Russia, Germany, the United Kingdom, China, France, and Iran that limited the capacity of Iran in terms of its nuclear program, in exchange for significant sanctions relief and other benefits. The agreement represented a major foreign policy success for President Obama; however, it faced substantial opposition from Republicans in the Congress. Because a majority of Congress opposed the JCPOA, Obama completed the agreement as a nonbinding political agreement rather than as a binding executive agreement or treaty. A political agreement did not require approval by Congress.[16]

The political agreement solution was problematic, however, as it gave credence to the Republican argument that Obama's successor was free to renege on the agreement should he or she wish to—and many of the 2016 Republican candidates for the presidency were stating they would do just that, should they be elected. During the campaign, Trump indicated his opposition to the Iran nuclear accord and signaled that he would "tear up" the agreement once he was president. After all, if President Obama had the legal authority to waive the sanctions, his successor certainly has the authority to not issue the periodic waiver, absent a congressionally authorized legally binding agreement and changes to the statutes governing Iranian sanctions.

The weakness of the agreement is clearly demonstrated by President Trump's abrogation, announced on May 8, 2018. Calling the agreement "one of the worst and most one-sided transactions the United States has ever entered into," Trump announced the termination of US participation in the JCPOA and the reimposition of the suspended sanctions on Iran (Chappell 2019; White House 2019).[17] The decision came after Trump had certified twice already that Iran was complying with the deal. His highest-level advisers on the national security team counseled against abrogating the deal. Secretary of State Tillerson and Defense Secretary Mattis, among others, believed the agreement provided stability in the region; however, Trump did not buy their arguments and fumed, wanting to keep his campaign promise to leave the agreement. According to Da Vinha (2019, 295), "McMaster and his NSC team sought to find a compromise solution that would accommodate Trump's visceral opposition to the JCPOA without abrogating it completely."

Understanding Trump's distaste for the agreement, opponents to the deal took full advantage, and a policy track outside of the NSC came together to push Trump to abrogate the agreement. Those advising against the agreement included Senator Tom Cotton, a longtime opponent to the deal; John Bolton, who had no official capacity in the administration at the time; Steve Bannon, a White House political adviser; and Nikki Haley, the US Ambassador to the United Nations. Essentially, they told Trump what he wanted to hear, pushing him to leave the agreement. Attempts by McMaster and Mattis to forge a compromise failed (Da Vinha 2019, 296). The president's decision had predictable effects. It isolated the United States from rivals and allies alike and led to a new crisis in the Persian Gulf, with direct conflict between the United States and Iran in early 2020.

The Paris Agreement on Climate Change was another major Obama foreign policy achievement that Trump unilaterally abrogated. The agreement was a watershed moment in the global fight against climate change, as it represented "the first international accord that contains policy obligations for addressing climate change for all countries" (Da Vinha 2019). During the 2016 presidential campaign, Trump made his hostility to the Paris agreement clear, and more broadly, he questioned the wisdom of action to curb climate change, as he believed the economic costs were too great and that the science was dubious. That hostility carried over to his presidency, as Trump appointed climate change skeptics to key environmental positions in the executive branch. Trump clearly had the authority to withdraw from the agreement, especially since Obama, much like with the Iran agreement discussed above, never sought congressional approval and completed the agreement unilaterally without Congress. Again, a majority of the Congress, controlled by Republicans, opposed Obama's agreement. Because of this opposition, Obama had only limited authority to complete a binding agreement, and as a result the policy commitments in the agreement were largely nonbinding (Goldsmith 2016). On June 1, 2017, Trump announced in a Rose Garden address his decision to withdraw from the Paris agreement. Trump stated that his decision to leave the agreement "represents a reassertion of America's sovereignty" (Patrick 2019, 252).

Because the agreement is a hybrid one—partially binding and partially nonbinding—the United States was not free to leave the agreement under the agreement's binding terms until November 4, 2020, the day after the 2020 presidential election. In fact, signatories were not authorized to give notice of departure until November 4, 2019, so the Trump administration's official announcement, which came in August 2017, was two years premature. Moreover, the parts of the agreement that Trump opposed included the nationally stated greenhouse emissions standards, which were voluntary. He could have voided these or unilaterally reduced US commitments, without withdrawing from the agreement (Meyer 2017). The practical effect of the withdrawal is that it cedes American leadership on international efforts to halt climate change and is a serious setback to those efforts. Much like in the decision over the Iran agreement, Trump sought out advice that coincided with his campaign promise to leave the deal and eschewed advice from within the policy process that advised him to stay in the deal (Da Vinha 2019). The decision was also a huge disappointment to American allies, who had lobbied the president to remain in the deal.

President Trump has also been hostile toward trade agreements negotiated by his predecessors, having termed just about every existing trade deal to which the United States is party as "one of the worst deals ever." He threatened to terminate the US-South Korea bilateral trade agreement, the TPP, and US participation in the North American Free Trade Agreement (NAFTA), among others. During the fall of 2017, Trump ramped up his threats to terminate NAFTA, trying to force Mexico and Canada to make significant concessions. Rather than scuttling NAFTA, Trump instead sought to "update" the agreement with a successor called the United States-Mexico-Canada Agreement (USMCA). To force America's two largest trading partners to the negotiating table, Trump issued a number of tariffs on Mexican and Canadian goods. Trump's unilaterally imposed steel and aluminum tariffs on Canada were particularly problematic. In the face of a possible ruinous trade war, Mexico and Canada relented and made some minor concessions to alter NAFTA in the form of the USMCA. The US Congress approved the agreement in early 2020. Trump is also seeking new trade deals or revisions on existing trade deals with Japan, China, the United Kingdom, and other major trading partners. It is unclear if he plans to submit these deals to Congress, like with the USMCA, though it is instructive that Trump's revisions to the trade deal with South Korea went into effect without approval from Congress.

Trump's trade war, which includes the unilateral imposition of a series of tariffs on Chinese imports, as well as imports from other countries, represents a marked change from Republican free trade orthodoxy. One of the signature foreign policy powers given directly to Congress by the Constitution is the power to regulate international commerce, yet the Congress has been unable to stop President Trump's trade war. If Congress opposes Trump's multifront trade war, why have they not been able to stop him? The story is a familiar one, actually. Throughout the twentieth century, Congress delegated its trade authority to the executive. Some of those delegations allowed the president to implement tariffs, should they certify that certain conditions apply. The best example of such a delegation, which has been abused by Trump to level tariffs on metals and autos, is Section

232 of the Trade Expansion Act of 1962, which allows the president to implement tariffs should they deem imports of certain goods to be a "threat to national security." Trump has used this authority far more than his predecessors and far afield of the law's original intent (Palmer 2018; Wassell 2018).

Using this obscure delegation of authority, Trump leveled or threatened to level tariffs on steel and aluminum from all over the world, as well as on autos from Europe.[18] He wielded this tariff authority in order to force trading partners to the table to renegotiate a range of trade deals. Republicans in Congress, once champions of free trade, have been unable to slow down Trump's trade war. Their complaints were loud, but in terms of action, nothing concrete emerged during 2018 and 2019. Republicans concluded, generally, that "past Congresses granted the White House too much authority and now there's nothing lawmakers can do about it" (Everett and Levine 2019). Short of passing veto-proof legislation to end the trade war, Congress's hands are tied. It really is a strange situation, given the clarity of the Constitution on this question, which clearly gives the trade power to Congress. Such delegations of authority, however, were not uncommon during the twentieth century. President Trump has taken advantage of these congressional abdications of power, unilaterally making foreign policy on a range of issues.

Trump's Unilateral Policy Actions

In the national security realm, President Trump has continually pushed the envelope of unilateral presidential authority. While presidential unilateralism is not new, the character and degree to which Trump has behaved unilaterally, that is, without Congress, represent an important shift in how foreign policy is made. The unilateral toolbox for presidents includes a number of policy actions: executive orders, national security proclamations, presidential uses of force, executive agreements and other international deals, and the declaration of emergencies (Howell 2003). As discussed above, Trump has expanded this list to include unilateral imposition of tariffs for "national security purposes." President Trump has utilized each of these tools to effect change in American foreign policy, often on controversial issues in contravention of the preferences of the majority of Congress. This last point is important, as a president's unilateral actions are less concerning in terms of separation of powers when they involve policies that have significant domestic and congressional support. However, when presidents unilaterally enact controversial, contested policies, concerns for checks and balances are more relevant.

The beauty of unilateral action, from the perspective of the president, is that presidents can act alone, and it is left to the other institutions to respond in order to check the president's action (Howell 2003). Presidents are further emboldened to behave unilaterally in foreign policy by the widespread belief that the executive has greater power in foreign policy than in domestic policy, something political scientists often refer to as the "two presidencies" (Wildavsky 1998). Moreover, in our current era of partisan polarization, presidential unilateralism is even more attractive. With the ability to act unconstrained due to congressional dysfunction, presidents can further push the envelope of their unilateral powers and Congress becomes less likely to be able to constrain the president (Binder, Goldgeier, and Saunders 2020). These realities were clearly evident during the Trump presidency, making unilateral policy tools especially attractive, particularly as the president looked to reshape American foreign policy.

Throughout the twentieth century, Congress delegated tremendous authority to the president. Much of this delegation came in foreign policy and includes significant abdications of congressional authority involving war powers, international agreements, spending, arms transfers, trade, and national emergencies (Fisher 2000). Most of these original delegations included a direct congressional check, typically a single-chamber legislative veto. However, such legislative vetoes were invalidated by the Supreme Court in 1983 (*INS v. Chadha*), which required the Congress to alter these laws such that single-chamber disapproval resolutions became joint resolutions of disapproval, subject to a presidential veto (Manne and Weinberger 2019). Thus, for Congress to block a presidential action in an area of congressional authority it had given to the executive decades prior, it has to muster significant supermajorities necessary to override a presidential veto (two-thirds majority in both chambers). The weakness of this approach to checking the president is plainly obvious when we review President Trump's vetoes during his first term.

When Trump entered office, much like other presidents, he got right to work implementing many of his policies unilaterally.[19] Several of these actions relate directly to foreign policy and invoked a negative response to the president's actions by Congress. In fact, each of President Trump's six vetoes,[20] as of this writing, struck down efforts by bipartisan majorities in Congress to check his unilateral action in foreign policy. All six vetoes occurred during 2019. Two relate directly to Trump's unilateral declaration of emergency at the border with Mexico, used to divert billions of dollars in military construction funds toward construction of his unpopular border wall.[21] The remaining four vetoes relate directly to Trump's support for Saudi Arabia's intervention in the civil war in Yemen. It is fairly remarkable that in every instance of President Trump's vetoes, he was striking down resolutions of disapproval for unilateral actions taken by him on behalf of his foreign policy priorities. The vetoes demonstrate the fundamental weakness of Congress in checking the president's unilateral action in foreign policy, even when those actions are unpopular and are opposed by a majority of Congress.

At the end of 2018, the US government experienced its longest shutdown in history, thirty-five days, primarily due to an impasse over funding for Trump's border wall. The spending deal that ended the shutdown did not include sufficient funding for the wall, in Trump's view, so he used delegated authority to declare a national emergency on the US-Mexican border in order to shift military construction spending toward building the wall. The National Emergencies Act of 1976 authorizes presidents to declare emergencies. The law is vague as to what constitutes an emergency, and it allows the president to redirect appropriations, subject to a joint resolution of disapproval by Congress. Congress had never passed a disapproval resolution on a national emergency. The Democratic-controlled House passed a resolution of disapproval on Trump's emergency declaration in late February 2019. The Republican-controlled Senate passed the resolution on March 14, which the president vetoed the next day (Johnson and Galioto 2019). The House failed to override the veto on March 26 (Gearan and Barrett 2019). The National Emergencies Act allows Congress to vote on the emergency declaration every six months, and in September both the House and Senate again passed a joint resolution of disapproval; however, President Trump vetoed the resolution and the Senate failed to override it (Zhou 2019).

The United States provided direct support for Saudi Arabia's intervention in the civil war in Yemen during the last two years of the Obama administration. Not only did the United States sell arms to the Saudis, but they directly participated in combat operations through in-air refueling of Saudi aircraft and the provision of intelligence. Congressional opposition to this support was slow to gel, as many in Congress saw the war as a broader regional conflict between the long-time American ally, Saudi Arabia, and enemy, Iran. As conditions in Yemen worsened and the Saudis were implicated in gross human rights abuses in 2016, opposition grew and the Obama administration announced that it would suspend the sale of certain munitions to the kingdom. Upon assuming office, Trump ordered a review of Obama's support for Saudi Arabia. Shortly before departing for the kingdom on his first international state trip, Trump announced he was proceeding with direct sales of arms, subject to congressional review. In 2017, the Senate Foreign Relations Committee considered but failed to report on a resolution of disapproval on these arms sales (Sharp, Blanchard, and Collins 2019).

Unable to block arms sales to Saudi Arabia, in 2018 opponents of the president's policy turned to the War Powers Resolution of 1973 in order to restrict American participation in the war. The initial effort stalled due to disagreement on whether US forces were engaged or potentially engaged in hostilities in Yemen. The 2018 efforts culminated in a provision in the National Defense Authorization Act that required the president to certify that US forces were not participating in refueling of Saudi aircraft that participated in prohibited activities. The provision was quite weak, however, as a waiver existed whereby the Secretary of State could waive the certification requirement for "national security purposes" (Sharp, Blanchard, and Collins 2019, 11). Secretary Pompeo issued the certification in September. After the brutal murder of *Washington Post* reporter Jamal Khashoggi in October by Saudis with close ties to Crown Prince Mohammed bin Salman, congressional opposition to support for the Saudi campaign grew. In response, Secretary of Defense Mattis announced the end of refueling operations. In December, the Republican-controlled Senate passed a joint resolution (S.J. Res. 54) directing the president to remove US forces from hostilities in Yemen; however, the Republican-controlled House did not consider the resolution. The passage of this resolution in the Senate was "the first time either chamber has used the War Powers Resolution to order an end to the use of military force" (Binder 2018).

On February 13, 2019, the new Democratic majority in the House passed a joint resolution (H.J. Res. 37) "directing the removal" of US forces from "Yemen that have not been authorized by Congress." The Senate version of the joint resolution (S.J. Res. 7) was passed by the Republican-controlled Senate on March 13, and then in the House on April 4, another historic move in that this was the first time in the history of the War Powers Resolution that both chambers had enacted a joint resolution of disapproval on a presidential use of force, sending it to the president's desk (Gramer and MacKinnon 2019). Trump vetoed the joint resolution, and his veto was sustained in the Senate on May 2. Supporters of the president's policy in Congress argued that the United States was not party to the war in Yemen, as refueling operations had ended the previous October (Sharp, Blanchard, and Collins 2019, 15). The administration continued to claim that US forces were not involved in hostilities in Yemen, making the War Powers Resolution moot on this question (Anderson 2019).

On May 24, 2019, the Trump administration announced an emergency declaration under the Arms Export Control Act (AECA) on pending arms transfers to Saudi Arabia and its ally the United Arab Emirates. The declaration sidestepped congressional review of the sales, under ordinary procedures through the AECA, and further solidified US support for the unpopular war in Yemen. The $8 billion in weapons included highly sophisticated guided munitions, used in the war in Yemen. The fact that US bombs were being employed in what many opponents saw as the indiscriminate slaughter of civilians made the sale controversial (Kessler 2019). On June 20, the Republican-controlled Senate passed three resolutions of disapproval, which were passed by the Democratic-controlled House on July 17. A week later, President Trump vetoed each of the three resolutions. The Senate failed to override each of the vetoes in votes on July 29 and the arms transfers went forward despite this bipartisan opposition (Kerr 2019).

Arms sales to the Middle East, in particular Saudi Arabia, have been controversial for some time. President Reagan had to adjust plans in order to overcome a vote to disapprove arms sales to the kingdom in both 1981 and 1986. In both cases, President Reagan adjusted the arms sales in order to make them more palatable to Congress, and they went through only after considerable lobbying and a willingness to bargain on the part of the administration (Kane 2018). In 2008, the George W. Bush administration announced a $20 billion arms deal with the Saudis. To avoid a tough battle in Congress as had occurred in the 1980s, the Bush administration kept Congress informed of the deal, and a move to block the deal sputtered (Krutz and Peake 2009, 196–197). Rather than bargain and consult with Congress like his predecessors, Trump employed the veto in order to overcome clear opposition. Congress has never successfully stopped a proposed arms sale through a joint resolution of disapproval, although it came close to doing so in 1986 (Kerr 2019), and Trump's efforts to sidestep legitimate congressional authority on arms sales represents an important assault on checking executive authority (Yousif 2019).

It is instructive that each of the vetoes discussed above stems from President Trump's unilateral use of power in the face of congressional opposition. Each case represents an instance where the separation of powers system broke down, and the president was able to implement unpopular foreign policies in the face of domestic opposition. Trump's vetoes are not examples where the president vetoed a foreign policy act passed by Congress that he considered unwise, like with Obama's veto of the 9/11 victims bill in 2016 (Eilperin and Demirjian 2016). Trump's vetoes take on a different character, as they demonstrate the inability of Congress to check presidential actions in areas of authority that are clearly within Article I of the Constitution (e.g., spending and the war power). While not drawing a joint resolution of disapproval and, thus, a veto, President Trump's order to the OMB to surreptitiously withhold $391 million in military aid to Ukraine, which sparked his impeachment in 2019, also represents presidential unilateralism in order to exert presidential control over spending, well outside of the president's legal authority. In this instance, much like with Congress's primary check, the veto, impeachment did not serve as an effective check on the president's behavior.

Much of the research on presidential unilateralism emphasizes the role of politics and congressional opposition in checking presidents when they might push too far. On the war power, Howell and Pevehouse (2007) argue that presidents are less likely to engage in presidential uses of force when Congress opposes their action, and this more commonly occurs when the opposing party controls one or both chambers of the legislature. Howell (2003), Mayer (2001), and Warber (2006) show a similar dynamic with executive orders—presidents are cognizant of their political situation and likely congressional opposition when using unilateral tools. Prior work on executive agreements finds a similar dynamic (Krutz and Peake 2009). It is questionable whether President Trump is similarly constrained by politics, however.

The examples detailed above of President Trump's unilateral actions suggest that his use of unilateral powers in foreign policy has further pushed the envelope of executive power. Even in instances where there is clear congressional opposition, Trump utilizes his unilateral tools to enact policy, acting in a much less constrained manner than his predecessors (Binder, Goldgeier, and Saunders 2020). Where Trump is clearly more orthodox, however, has been in his use of military force abroad, perhaps the most important use of unilateral authority possessed by modern presidents (Burns 2019). Much like President Obama before him, Trump entered office focused on ending the "forever wars," including bringing troops home from Afghanistan, Iraq, and Syria. Despite these initial inclinations, Trump's foreign policy has led to even greater involvement in conflicts in the Middle East, with a surge in forces in Afghanistan and an increased presence in Syria, Iraq, Saudi Arabia, and North Africa. Trump's decision to leave the JCPOA precipitated a military conflict with Iran, leading directly to conflict between the United States and Iran in January 2020. In each of these instances, like with Obama, when the Trump administration believed it necessary to legally justify their actions, they relied heavily on the 2001 Authorization to Use Military Force (AUMF) in Afghanistan in response to the 9/11 attacks and the 2002 AUMFs in Iraq, despite the fact that the new targets of military force had nothing to do with 9/11 or the Hussein regime in Iraq (Burns 2019).

Trump's penchant for unilateral action was especially evident in the use of military force to assassinate Iranian general Qasem Soleimani in January 2020. The attack represented a significant escalation in the conflict with Iran, as it was the first time the United States had taken direct action against Iranian forces. Iran responded with rocket fire on American bases in Iraq; however, no Americans were killed. To justify this unilateral action, the president's legal team pointed to the 2001 and 2002 AUMFs that gave the president authority to respond to the 9/11 attacks and gave the president broad authority in Iraq. In February 2020, both the House and Senate passed resolutions stating that the president was required to seek additional congressional authority in order to take additional military action against Iran (Zhou 2020). Because the chambers passed separate resolutions, rather than a joint resolution, the resolutions do not go to the president for signature and are not binding under law. This does not mean they are unimportant, however, as they clearly state the opinion of both chambers regarding the application of the AUMFs with regard to an expanded conflict with Iran. In the opinion of Congress, they do not provide the president that authority (Martin 2020).

President Trump's unilateral policy making is troubling to political science experts, as it suggests a significant breakdown of institutional checks and balances that are central to American democracy. The

Bright Line Watch data indicate that as the Trump presidency progressed, scholars became less upbeat about the ability of institutional checks and balances to constrain Trump's behavior. On the two democratic principles most closely associated with the institutional checks, surveyed experts indicated significantly lower ratings from one survey to the next, and the decreases were especially pronounced after the Ukraine scandal came to light. On "legislature can limit the executive" and "Constitution limits the executive," the change in experts stating that the United States fully meets or mostly meets the principle decreased by more than twenty percentage points, down from 49 percent in the prior survey.[22] Another survey of international relations experts taken during the impeachment supports the notion that Trump had "overstepped the foreign policy powers" of the office, with 74 percent of those surveyed agreeing, representing a significant increase from a survey taken in the previous year, where just 42 percent agreed (Jackson et al. 2020). The shifts in expert opinion come in the wake of a highly charged impeachment debate that centered on the question of whether President Trump abused his foreign policy powers, so follow-on surveys will need to be conducted to determine if this shift in expert opinion is lasting.

CONCLUSION

The substance of President Trump's foreign policy is fairly typical. For example, the United States remains in NATO and other alliances and continues to engage in conflicts worldwide related to terrorism and instability in the Middle East. The broad contours of American foreign policy rarely change from one administration to the next. How, then, is Trump unorthodox in terms of foreign policy? As laid out above, Trump's hostility toward the norms inherent in the foreign policy process has had a significant impact on the quality of policy and how allies view American commitments. After all, "America First," when taken at face value, denotes an American pullback from the world and, in particular, of American leadership in that world. The process norms include, primarily, having a clear national security process where the president receives and considers the most effective advice on any given issue to make the best possible decision. Trump eschews such a process. Staffing in national security positions, both appointed and in the civil service, has taken huge hits during the Trump presidency. A wealth of experience has left the government, either voluntarily or because they have been forced out due to the overt politicization of the foreign policy bureaucracy.

Another norm of American democracy is that presidents will give some consideration to the checks and balances inherent in the Constitution, even in foreign policy. Trump has abandoned any pretense of working with Congress on most foreign policy issues, including in areas where the Constitution clearly gives most of the authority to the legislature. His unilateralism abroad carries over to aggressive presidential unilateralism at home. While expedient in achieving policy change, the foreign policies enacted unilaterally are likely to be seen as illegitimate by domestic political actors and international actors alike. This is especially the case in the context of hyperpartisanship, where the focus of partisan warfare is to delegitimize the opposition.

Thus, the next administration will likely focus on reversing President Trump's foreign policies, particularly those enacted unilaterally. The unilateral actions highlight to allies and foes alike the degree to which Trump lacks domestic support for his actions, thus weakening the president on the international stage. Policies without broad political support are more easily reversed by future presidents, leading to a cycle of foreign policy shifts from one presidency to the next and a lack of stability. In terms of international agreements, who will make a deal with the United States when it is very likely the next president will undermine it? Even worse, perhaps, is that Trump's unilateralism may undermine existing American commitments that have undergirded the liberal international order. Is it potentially a problem if American participation in NATO is now seen as a legitimate political football, dependent on the winner of the next presidential election? Such considerations are bound to have lasting implications for American foreign policy and leadership.

The erosion of norms in foreign policy making—both internationally and domestically—may harm the ability of the United States to lead in the international system. It has clearly damaged our constitutional processes at home. It remains to be seen whether the damage is permanent or temporary.

NOTES

1. Reports indicate that during Trump's first two years, criminal referrals to the Justice Department related to leaks averaged 104 per year, as compared

to thirty-nine per year for the eight years of the Obama administration (Dilanian 2019).

2. For a comprehensive analysis of Trump's tweets, see Shear et al. 2019.

3. Trump's first NSA, Michael Flynn, served just twenty-four days in his post, setting a record for brevity in the post. President Trump fired Flynn for lying to the vice president about his communications with the Russian ambassador. Flynn was later indicted by the Mueller investigation for lying to the FBI regarding his communications with the Russian ambassador. Trump selected H. R. McMaster has his next NSA in February 2017 but fired him on Twitter in March 2018. Neoconservative firebrand John Bolton replaced McMaster, serving in the post until his firing in September 2019. He was replaced by Robert O'Brien.

4. https://brightlinewatch.org/. See Carey et al. (2019) for a description of the methods used by Bright Line Watch in conducting their survey of experts.

5. See Bright Line Watch (2019). Respondents were asked to rate events on the following scale of importance: unimportant, mostly unimportant, semi-important, mostly important, and important. They were also asked to judge events on the following scale of normality: normal, mostly normal, borderline normal, mostly abnormal, and abnormal. There are several additional foreign policy events that were deemed at least "mostly important" but not quite "mostly abnormal," based on average responses of the surveyed experts. They include unilaterally issuing tariffs on China; unilaterally issuing tariffs on allies based on "national security concerns"; and the summit with North Korea's Kim Jong Un. Foreign policy events found to be at least "mostly abnormal" but not quite "mostly important" include Trump's order to revoke former CIA director Brennon's security clearance; Trump calling Canadian prime minister Justin Trudeau "weak" following the G-7 summit; laughter during Trump's UN speech; and discussion of sensitive national security information in the Mar-a-Lago dining room. For comparison purposes, other events that did not meet either of these thresholds include the US withdrawal from the UNHRC; Trump's demand for increased NATO defense spending; Trump's congratulatory call to Putin on his "reelection" despite being told "do not congratulate"; Trump's threats of further tariffs against Canada; proposing a replacement for the North America Free Trade Agreement (NAFTA); meetings with the Chilean president; barring transgender troops from service; Mattis's resignation; cancelation of Putin meeting in Buenos Aries on Twitter; signing of the USMCA; and calling Saudi Arabia an ally.

6. Each president had their translator present; however, President Trump ordered his translator not to divulge what the discussion was about, and there was no official readout of the discussion. This allowed the Russians to characterize the meeting in a way that benefited them politically.

7. Helsinki was not the first one-on-one meeting between Trump and Putin where Trump did not have aides present. In fact, during his first two years, Trump met five times with Putin, and in each case, the specifics of their conversations are unknown to the president's advisers (Baker 2019; Miller 2019). This was not the first time a US president had met with the leader of Russia alone; however, the secrecy and frequency are unusual. President Reagan met with Soviet premier Gorbachev during the Geneva summit in November 1985 (Weinraub 1985).

8. Trump met alone three times with North Korean leader, Kim Jong Un, in 2018 and 2019. The first historic meeting came in Singapore, in June 2018, and included an hour-long meeting between the two leaders and just their translators (Lederman and Lee 2018). The second meeting was during a follow-on summit in Hanoi in February 2019, which also included a private meeting, but collapsed due to incompatible demands emanating from each side (Panda and Narang 2019). Trump continued his personal diplomacy with Kim in a surprise meeting at the Korean Demilitarized Zone in June 2019, which also included a private meeting (Stokols and Kim 2019).

9. This disconnect is also apparent in US policy toward North Korea. In one instance, NSA Bolton had ordered additional sanctions on a Chinese shipping company for violating international sanctions in their trade with North Korea, only to have his order reversed later by President Trump (Walcott 2019).

10. The 1974 Impoundment and Control Act (ICA) "allows the president to temporarily defer or withhold appropriated funds, but only for certain reasons and only if the president sends a special message to Congress explaining the reasons for the deferral" (Krawzak 2019). The reasons put forth by the Office of Management and Budget do not fall within the acceptable reasons listed in the ICA, and the president failed to report the deferral to Congress.

11. While the order was never implemented, it caused quite a stir in the international law community, as it signaled a shift in thinking regarding multilateral commitments and American leadership. Alternatively, it suggested that high-level officials in the White House had a serious misunderstanding of the purpose of international law, particularly with regard to human rights agreements (Sullivan 2018).

12. For a comprehensive review of the history of treaties, with a focus on the domestic politics, see Krutz and Peake (2009).

13. The two treaties submitted by Trump include an amendment to a Pacific fisheries treaty and the protocol to NATO for the accession of North Macedonia. For comparison purposes, the lowest number of treaties transmitted by a modern president during a single term is fifteen, during Obama's first term. Obama transmitted twenty-two treaties during his second term, the second lowest number of any modern president. From 1949 to 2008, the average number of transmittals per presidential term is sixty-three (Peake 2017).

14. In 2019, President Trump also ended the Intermediate Nuclear Forces (INF) Treaty with Russia, unsigned the UN Arms Trade Treaty, and threatened to leave the 144-year-old international organization governing postal services (the Universal Postal Union), which was successfully renegotiated in 2019. During his first year in office, he ended US participation in the nascent Trans-Pacific Partnership and in 2018 forced Mexico and Canada to renegotiate the NAFTA agreement. Its successor, the United States-Mexico-Canada Agreement (USMCA), was approved by Congress and signed into law by the president in January 2020. It is instructive that the president, during his three years in office, has left or announced US abrogation of more key international agreements than he has completed.

15. There is precedent for presidents to submit arms control agreements to the Congress for bicameral approval, as Nixon did with the original Strategic Arms Limitation Talks accord in 1972. The Senate jealously guards its turf on these kinds of agreements, especially.

16. The Obama administration's reasoning for going the unilateral route is, perhaps, best summed up by Secretary of State John Kerry's statement in congressional testimony, "We can't pass a treaty anymore." Congress did pass the Iran Nuclear Agreement Review Act, which required the president to subject any sanctions relief provided to Iran under the agreement to a joint resolution of disapproval by both chambers of Congress, which itself was subject to presidential veto. This required congressional opponents to muster a two-thirds majority in both chambers in order to block the agreement, rather than the typical two-thirds requirement in the Senate to approve a treaty or the simple majorities in both chambers to approve the agreement by statute. Congress took up the joint resolution of disapproval, which was passed by the Republican-controlled House but died to a Democratic filibuster in the Senate, and President Obama was able to fulfill his obligations to reduce sanctions under the JCPOA (Peake 2017).

17. The White House claimed that Iran was in breach of the agreement; however, the United Nations and the administration's own State Department had indicated numerous times that Iran had not violated the JCPOA.

18. For a timeline of Trump's trade war, see https://www.piie.com/blogs/trade-investment-policy-watch/trump-trade-war-china-date-guide.

19. A significant share (25 percent) of Trump's first-year executive orders were related to foreign policy. For example, he implemented his infamous "Muslim travel ban" through a series of executive orders (Potter et al. 2019).

20. For a list of Trump's vetoes, see here: https://www.senate.gov/legislative/vetoes/TrumpDJ.htm.

21. At the time, about 60 percent of the American public opposed further expansion of the border wall (Norman 2019; Pew Research Center 2019).

22. The surveys indicate that just 23 percent of the experts believed that US democracy meets the principle of "the legislature can limit the executive."

The figure is 26 percent for "the Constitution limits the executive" (Bright Line Watch 2019).

REFERENCES

Abrams, Elliott. "Trump the Traditionalist: A Surprisingly Standard Foreign Policy." *Foreign Affairs*, July/August 2017. https://www.foreignaffairs.com/articles/united-states/2017-06-13/trump-traditionalist.

Anderson, Scott. "Where Trump's Veto Leaves the Yemen Resolution." *Lawfare*, April 18, 2019. https://www.lawfareblog.com/where-trumps-veto-leaves-yemen-resolution.

Anonymous. "I Am Part of the Resistance Inside the Trump Administration." *New York Times*, September 5, 2018. https://www.nytimes.com/2018/09/05/opinion/trump-white-house-anonymous-resistance.html.

Associated Press. "Defense Chiefs Resist Donald Trump's Ban on Transgender Troops." *Guardian*, July 27, 2017. https://www.theguardian.com/us-news/2017/jul/27/donald-trump-transgender-ban-troops-pentagon-us-military.

Baker, Peter. "Trump and Putin Have Met Five Times. What Was Said Is a Mystery." *New York Times*, January 16, 2019. https://www.nytimes.com/2019/01/15/us/politics/trump-putin-meetings.html.

Benkowski, James, and A. Bradley Potter. "The Center Cannot Hold: Continuity and Change in Donald Trump's Foreign Policy." *War on the Rocks*, November 1, 2017. https://warontherocks.com/2017/11/the-center-cannot-hold-continuity-and-change-in-donald-trumps-foreign-policy/.

Binder, Sarah. "Analysis | Three Reasons You Should Be Startled by How the Senate Rebuked Trump." *Washington Post*, December 14, 2018. https://www.washingtonpost.com/news/monkey-cage/wp/2018/12/14/three-reasons-you-should-be-startled-by-how-the-senate-rebuked-trump/.

Binder, Sarah, James Goldgeier, and Elizabeth N. Saunders. "The Imperial Presidency Is Alive and Well." *Foreign Affairs*, January 21, 2020. https://www.foreignaffairs.com/articles/2020-01-21/imperial-presidency-alive-and-well.

Bradley, Curtis A., and Jack L. Goldsmith. "Presidential Control over International Law." *Harvard Law Review* 131, no. 5 (2018): 1203–1297.

Bright Line Watch. "Democratic Transgressions and Constitutional Hardball: Bright Line Watch October 2019 Surveys." *Bright Line Watch*, October 2019. https://brightlinewatch.org/democratic-transgressions-and-constitutional-hardball-bright-line-watch-october-2019-surveys/.

Bublé, Courtney. "Watchdog Finds Serious Staffing and Leadership Problems at State Department." *Government Executive*, January 23, 2020. https://www.govexec.com/oversight/2020/01/watchdog-finds-serious-staffing-and-leadership-problems-state-department/162621/.

Burns, Sarah. *The Politics of War Powers: The Theory and History of Presidential Unilateralism.* Lawrence: University Press of Kansas, 2019.

Carey, John M., Gretchen Helmke, Brendan Nyhan, Mitchell Sanders, and Susan Stokes. "Searching for Bright Lines in the Trump Presidency." *Perspectives on Politics* 17, no. 3 (2019): 699–718.

Chappell, Bill. "'I'm the Only One That Matters,' Trump Says of State Department Job Vacancies." *NPR*, November 3, 2017. https://www.npr.org/sections/thetwo-way/2017/11/03/561797675/im-the-only-one-that-matters-trump-says-of-state-dept-job-vacancies.

———. "Trump Says He Called Off Strike on Iran Because He Didn't See It As 'Proportionate.'" NPR, June 21, 2019. https://www.npr.org/2019/06/21/734683701/trump-reportedly-orders-strike-on-iran-then-calls-off-attack-plan.

Cohen, Eliot A. "America's Long Goodbye: The Real Crisis of the Trump Era." *Foreign Affairs*, January/February 2019. https://www.foreignaffairs.com/articles/united-states/long-term-disaster-trump-foreign-policy.

Conrad, Courtenay R., and Emily Rigger. "A Trump Moratorium on International Treaties Could Roll Back Human Rights—Here at Home." Monkey Cage Blog, *Washington Post*, March 1, 2017. https://www.washingtonpost.com/news/monkey-cage/wp/2017/03/01/a-trump-moratorium-on-international-treaties-could-roll-back-human-rights-here-at-home/.

Corwin, Edward S. *The President: Office and Powers.* 4th ed. New York: NYU Press, 1958.

Daalder, Ivo H., and I. M. Destler. "Why National Security Advisor Is the Hardest Post for Trump to Fill." *Foreign Affairs*, September 24, 2019. https://www.foreignaffairs.com/articles/2019-09-11/why-national-security-advisor-hardest-post-trump-fill.

Da Vinha, Luis. "Competition, Conflict, and Conformity: Foreign Policy Making in the First Year of the Trump Presidency." *Presidential Studies Quarterly* 49, no. 2 (2019): 280–309.

Demerjian, Karoun, and Juliet Eilperin. "Congress Overrides Obama's Veto of 9/11 Bill." *Washington Post*, September 28, 2016. https://www.washingtonpost.com/news/powerpost/wp/2016/09/27/senate-poised-to-vote-to-override-obamas-veto-of-911-bill/.

DeYoung, Karen, and Philip Rucker. "Trump Lays Groundwork to Change U.S. Role in the World." *Washington Post*, January 26, 2017. https://www.washingtonpost.com/world/national-security/trump-lays-groundwork-to-change-us-role-in-the-world/2017/01/26/812998e6-e404-11e6-a547-5fb9411d332c_story.html.

Dilanian, Ken. "Under Trump, More Leaks—and More Leak Investigations." NBC News, April 8, 2019. https://www.nbcnews.com/politics/justice-department/under-trump-more-leaks-more-leak-investigations-n992121.

Drezner, Daniel W. "This Time is Different: Why U.S. Foreign Policy Will

Never Recover." *Foreign Affairs*, April 16, 2019a. https://www.foreignaffairs.com/articles/2019-04-16/time-different.

———. "Present at the Destruction: The Trump Administration and the Foreign Policy Bureaucracy." *Journal of Politics* 81, 2 (2019b): 723–730.

Eilperin, Juliet, and Karoun Demirjian. 2016. "Congress Overrides Obama's Veto of 9/11 Bill." *Washington Post*, September 28, 2016. https://www.washingtonpost.com/news/powerpost/wp/2016/09/27/senate-poised-to-vote-to-override-obamas-veto-of-911-bill/.

Everett, Burgess, and Marianne Levine. "Republicans Surrender to Trump's China Tariffs." Politico, May 13, 2019. https://www.politico.com/story/2019/05/13/trade-china-republicans-1319024.

Fallows, James. "The Broken Check and Balance." *Atlantic*, October 31, 2017. https://www.theatlantic.com/politics/archive/2017/10/republicans-in-congress-youve-got-another-chance/544466/.

Farrow, Ronan. *War on Peace: The End of Diplomacy and the Decline of American Influence*. New York: W. W. Norton, 2018.

Fisher, Louis. *Congressional Abdication on War and Spending*. College Station: Texas A&M University Press, 2000.

———. *Supreme Court Expansion of Presidential Power: Unconstitutional Leanings*. Lawrence: University Press of Kansas, 2017.

Fowler, Linda L. *Watchdogs on the Hill*. Princeton, NJ: Princeton University Press, 2015.

Gearan, Anne, and Devlin Barrett. "Trump Issues First Veto of His Presidency over Emergency Declaration for Border Wall." *AllSides*, March 16, 2019. https://www.allsides.com/news/2019-03-16-0714/trump-issues-first-veto-his-presidency-over-emergency-declaration-border-wall.

Geltzer, Joshua, and Ryan Goodman. "The Pattern and Practice of Trump's Assaults on the Intelligence Community." justsecurity.org. February 12, 2020. https://www.justsecurity.org/66035/the-pattern-and-practice-of-trumps-assaults-on-the-intelligence-community/.

Goldgeier, James, and Elizabeth N. Saunders. "The Unconstrained Presidency: Checks and Balances Eroded Long Before Trump." *Foreign Affairs*, September/October 2018. https://www.foreignaffairs.com/articles/2018-08-13/unconstrained-presidency.

Goldsmith, Jack. "The Contributions of the Obama Administration to the Practice and Theory of International Law." *Harvard International Law Journal* 57, no. 2 (2016): 1–19.

Gramer, Robbie, Dan De Luce, and Colum Lynch. "How the Trump Administration Broke the State Department." *Foreign Policy*, July 23, 2019. https://foreignpolicy.com/2017/07/31/how-the-trump-administration-broke-the-state-department/.

Gramer, Robbie, and Maya Gandhi. "Tillerson to Kushner: We've Got to Stop Meeting Like This." *Foreign Policy*, June 27, 2019. https://foreignpolicy.com

/2019/06/27/tillerson-secretary-of-state-testimony-transcript-house-for eign-affairs-committee-jared-kushner-role-trump-administration/.

Gramer, Robbie, and Amy Mackinnon. "Congress Is Finally Done with the War in Yemen." *Foreign Policy*, April 4, 2019. https://foreignpolicy.com/2019 /04/04/congress-makes-history-war-yemen-powers-bill/.

Howell, William G. *Power without Persuasion: The Politics of Direct Presidential Action*. Princeton, NJ: Princeton University Press, 2003.

Howell, William G., and Jon Pevehouse. *While Dangers Gather: Congressional Checks on Presidential War Powers*. Princeton, NJ: Princeton University Press, 2007.

Jackson, Emily B., Eric Parajon, Susan Peterson, Ryan Powers, and Michael J. Tierney. "Analysis | Has Trump Abused His Presidential Powers, as the House Charges? Foreign Policy Scholars Think So." *Washington Post*, January 25, 2020. https://www.washingtonpost.com/politics/2020/01/25/has -trump-abused-his-presidential-powers-house-charges-foreign-policy-schol ars-think-so/.

Johnson, Eliana, and Katie Galioto. "Trump Issues First Veto of His Presidency." *Politico*, March 15, 2019. https://www.politico.com/story/2019/03/15 /trump-veto-national-emergency-1223285.

Kane, N. Stephen. *Selling Reagan's Foreign Policy: Going Public vs. Executive Bargaining*. Lanham, MD: Lexington, 2018.

Kerr, Paul K. "Arms Sales: Congressional Review Process." *Congressional Research Service*, CRS Report RL31675, January 30, 2019.

Kessler, Ethan. "Trump Vetoes Challenge to Arab Arms Sales." *Arms Control Association*, September 2019. https://www.armscontrol.org/act/2019-09 /news/trump-vetoes-challenge-arab-arms-sales.

Koh, Harold Hongju. "A National Security Impeachment." *Yale Global Online*, December 19, 2019. https://yaleglobal.yale.edu/content/national-security -impeachment.

Krawzak, Paul M. "GAO: Trump's Hold on Ukraine Aid Violated Budget Law." *Roll Call*, January 16, 2020. https://www.rollcall.com/2020/01/16/gao -trumps-ukraine-aid-pause-violated-budget-law/.

Kroenig, Matthew. "The Case of Trump's Foreign Policy." *Foreign Affairs*, May/ June 2017. https://www.foreignaffairs.com/articles/world/2017-04-17 /case-trump-s-foreign-policy.

Krutz, Glen S., and Jeffrey S. Peake. *Treaty Politics and the Rise of Executive Agreements*. Ann Arbor, MI: University of Michigan Press, 2009.

Lafraniere, Sharon, Maggie Haberman, and Peter Baker. "Jared Kushner's Vast Duties, and Visibility in White House, Shrink." *New York Times*, November 25, 2017. https://www.nytimes.com/2017/11/25/us/politics/jared -kushner-white-house-trump.html.

Lederman, Josh, and Matthew Lee. "Alone Time: Trump, Kim Jong Un Ditch Aides to Meet 1 on 1." *Associated Press*, June 12, 2018. https://apnews.com

/35c3a4dcd07b4ae9b0276f8348bc4304/Ditching-entourages,-Trump -and-Kim-Jong-Un-to-meet-1-on-1.

Leonnig, Carol D., Shane Harris, and Greg Jaffe. "Breaking with Tradition, Trump Skips President's Written Intelligence Report and Relies on Oral Briefings." *Washington Post*, February 9, 2018. https://www.washingtonpost .com/politics/breaking-with-tradition-trump-skips-presidents-written-in telligence-report-for-oral-briefings/2018/02/09/b7ba569e-0c52-11e8 -95a5-c396801049ef_story.html.

Levitsky, Steven, and Daniel Ziblatt. "This is How Democracies Die." *Guardian*, January 21, 2018. https://www.theguardian.com/us-news/comment isfree/2018/jan/21/this-is-how-democracies-die.

Lynch, Colum, and Robbie Gramer. "Federal Watchdogs Target Bullying, Retaliation at State Department." *Foreign Policy*, September 7, 2018. https:// foreignpolicy.com/2018/09/07/state-department-watchdog-probe-in to-trump-retaliation-against-career-employees-international-organization -affairs-bureau-mari-stull.

Manne, Geoffrey, and Seth Weinberger. "Time to Rehabilitate the Legislative Veto: How Congress Should Rein in Presidents' 'National Emergency' Powers." justsecurity.org. March 19, 2019. https://www.justsecurity .org/63201/congress-rein-presidents-national-emergency-power-rehabili tating-legislative-veto/.

Martin, Kate. "Congress Speaks: Trump Currently Has No Authority to Launch War with Iran." justsecurity.org. February 25, 2020. https://www .justsecurity.org/68832/congress-speaks-trump-currently-has-no-authority -to-launch-war-with-iran/.

Mascaro, Lisa. "The New 'Three Amigos' Riding into Trump Impeachment Inquiry." *Associated Press*, December 1, 2019. https://apnews.com/3d4e c2a77c244 d2b9727b50dfcaf0c95.

Mayer, Kenneth R. *With the Stroke of a Pen: Executive Orders and Presidential Power.* Princeton, NJ: Princeton University Press, 2001.

McGurk, Brett. "The Cost of an Incoherent Foreign Policy." *Foreign Affairs*, January 22, 2020. https://www.foreignaffairs.com/articles/iran/2020-01 -22/cost-incoherent-foreign-policy.

Meyer, Robinson. "Trump and the Paris Agreement: What Just Happened?" *Atlantic*, August 4, 2017. https://www.theatlantic.com/science/archive/2017 /08/trump-and-the-paris-agreement-what-just-happened/536040/.

Miller, Greg. "Trump Has Concealed Details of His Face-to-Face Encounters with Putin from Senior Officials in Administration." *Washington Post*, January 13, 2019. https://www.washingtonpost.com/world/national-security /trump-has-concealed-details-of-his-face-to-face-encounters-with-putin-from -senior-officials-in-administration/2019/01/12/65f6686c-1434-11e9-b6ad -9cfd62dbb0a8_story.html.

Nelson, Louis, Burgess Everett, Jacqueline Klimas, Matthew Nussbaum, Connor O'Brien, and Rachael Bade. "Trump Bans Transgender Individuals from U.S. Military Service." Politico, July 26, 2017. https://www.politico.com/story/2017/07/26/trump-transgender-240980.

Norman, Jim. "Solid Majority Still Opposes New Construction on Border Wall." Gallup, September 4, 2019. https://news.gallup.com/poll/246455/solid-majority-opposes-new-construction-border-wall.aspx.

Palmer, Doug. "The Cold War Origins of Trump's Favorite Trade Weapon." *Politico*, July 5, 2018. https://www.politico.eu/article/cold-war-origins-of-donald-trump-favorite-trade-weapon/.

Panda, Ankit, and Vipin Narang. "The Hanoi Summit Was Doomed from the Start." *Foreign Affairs*, March 11, 2019. https://www.foreignaffairs.com/articles/north-korea/2019-03-05/hanoi-summit-was-doomed-start.

Panke, Diana, and Ulrich Petersohn. "President Donald J. Trump—An Agent of Norm Death? *International Journal* 74, no. 4 (2017): 571–578.

Patrick, Stewart. *The Sovereignty Wars*. Washington, DC: Brookings Institution, 2019.

Peake, Jeffrey S. "Obama, Unilateral Diplomacy, and Iran: Treaties, Executive Agreements, and Political Commitments." In *Presidential Leadership and National Security: The Obama Legacy*, ed. Richard S. Conley, 142–171. New York: Routledge, 2017.

Pew Research Center for the People and the Press. "Most Border Wall Opponents, Supporters Say Shutdown Concessions Are Unacceptable." January 16, 2019. https://www.people-press.org/2019/01/16/most-border-wall-opponents-supporters-say-shutdown-concessions-are-unacceptable/.

Posner, Ted, and Simon Lester. "More from the Comments: Ted Posner on Implementing Trade Facilitation in the US." *International Economic Law and Policy Blog*, December 16, 2013. http://worldtradelaw.typepad.com/ielpblog/2013/12/more-from-the-comments-ted-posner-on-implementing-trade-facilitation-in-the-us.html.

Potter, Rachel Augustine, Andrew Rudalevige, Sharece Thrower, and Adam L. Warber. "Continuity Trumps Change: The First Year of Trump's Administrative Presidency." *PS: Political Science & Politics* 52, no. 4 (2019): 613–619.

Rudalevige, Andrew. *The New Imperial Presidency: Renewing Presidential Power after Watergate*. Ann Arbor: University of Michigan Press, 2005.

Schlesinger, Robert. "Why It Matters That Trump Doesn't Read His Daily Intelligence Briefings." *U.S. News & World Report*, February 9, 2019. https://www.usnews.com/opinion/thomas-jefferson-street/articles/2018-02-09/why-it-matters-that-trump-doesnt-read-his-daily-intelligence-briefings.

Schultz, Kenneth A. "Perils of Polarization for U.S. Foreign Policy." *Washington Quarterly* 40, no. 4 (2017): 7–28.

Sharp, Jeremy M., Christopher M. Blanchard, and Sarah R. Collins. "Congress and the War in Yemen: Oversight and Legislation 2015–2019." *Con-*

gressional Research Service, September 6, 2019. https://fas.org/sgp/crs /mideast/R45046.pdf.

Shear, Michael D., Maggie Haberman, Nicholas Confessore, Karen Yourish, Larry Buchanan, and Keith Collins. "How Trump Reshaped the Presidency in Over 11,000 Tweets." *New York Times*, November 2, 2019. https://www .nytimes.com/interactive/2019/11/02/us/politics/trump-twitter-presi dency.html.

Shepp, Jonah. "How U.S. Foreign Policy Is Being Shaped by Trump's Tweets." *Intelligencer*, January 19, 2018. https://nymag.com/intelligencer/2018/01 /how-u-s-foreign-policy-is-being-shaped-by-trumps-tweets.html.

Snow, Donald M., and Patrick J. Haney. *U.S. Foreign Policy: Back to the Water's Edge*, 5th ed. New York: Rowman & Littlefield, 2018.

Spiro, Peter J. "Explaining the End of Plenary Power." *Georgetown Immigration Law Journal* 16 (2001): 339.

Stokols, Eli, and Victoria Kim. "Trump Meets Kim Jong Un at DMZ and Becomes First Sitting U.S. President to Enter North Korea." *Los Angeles Times*, June 30, 2019. https://www.latimes.com/politics/la-na-pol-trump-korea -dmz-kim-moon-20190630-story.html.

Sullivan, Scott. "The Draft Order on Multilateral Treaties and the Trump Administration's Failure to Understand the Human Rights of National Security." justsecurity.org. July 9, 2018. https://www.justsecurity.org/37825 /dangerous-thinking-draft-order-multilateral-treaties-trump-administra tions-failure-understand-human-rights-national-security/.

Taussig, Torrey. "The Helsinki Summit and Great Power Competition." Brookings.edu. August 9, 2018. https://www.brookings.edu/blog/order-from -chaos/2018/08/09/the-helsinki-summit-and-great-power-competition/.

Tenpas, Kathryn Dunn. "Crippling the Capacity of the National Security Council." Brookings.edu. January 21, 2020a. https://www.brookings.edu /blog/fixgov/2020/01/21/crippling-the-capacity-of-the-national-security -council/.

———. "Tracking Turnover in the Trump Administration." Brookings.edu. February 21, 2020b. https://www.brookings.edu/research/tracking-turn over-in-the-trump-administration/.

Tharoor, Ishaan. "Analysis | Trump's Helsinki 'Disgrace' Caps a Destructive European Trip." *Washington Post*, July 17, 2018. https://www.washing tonpost.com/news/worldviews/wp/2018/07/17/trumps-helsinki-dis grace-caps-a-destructive-european-trip/.

Vieira, Paul. "Canada Begins USMCA Ratification Process That Won't Necessarily Be Smooth Sailing." *Wall Street Journal*, January 27, 2020. https://www .wsj.com/articles/canada-begins-nafta-ratification-process-that-wont-nec essarily-be-smooth-sailing-11580152748.

Viswanatha, Aruna. "Trump's Rocky Relationship with Intelligence Community Worsened with Whistleblower Complaint." *Wall Street Journal*, September 27,

2019. https://www.wsj.com/articles/trumps-rocky-relationship-with-intelli gence-community-worsened-with-whistleblower-complaint-11569582000.

Walcott, John. "Donald Trump Rejects Intelligence Briefing Facts." *Time*, February 5, 2019. https://time.com/5518947/donald-trump-intelligence -briefings-national-security/.

Warber, Adam L. *Executive Orders and the Modern Presidency: Legislating from the Oval Office.* Boulder, CO: Lynne Rienner, 2006.

Wassell, David. "Section 232: A Splendid Little Trade War." Hill, March 17, 2018. https://thehill.com/opinion/finance/378290-section-232-a-splen did-little-trade-war.

Weiland, Noah. "5 Times the Trump Administration Has Been Tougher Than Trump on Russia." *New York Times*, January 2, 2019. https://www.nytimes .com/2019/01/21/us/politics/trump-administration-russia-president .html.

Weinraub, Bernard. "Reagan Continues Private Meetings with Gorbachev." *New York Times*, November 2, 1985. https://www.nytimes.com/1985/11/21 /world/reagan-continues-private-meetinfs-with-gorbachev.html.

White House. "President Donald J. Trump Is Working to Bring Iran's Oil Ex- ports to Zero." April 22, 2019. https://www.whitehouse.gov/briefings-state ments/president-donald-j-trump-working-bring-irans-oil-exports-zero/.

Wildavsky, A. "The Two Presidencies." *Society* 35, no. 2 (1998): 23–31.

Wilkie, Christina. "Giuliani and Sondland Hijacked Ukraine Policy to Push for Investigations, Trump Impeachment Witness Fiona Hill Says." CNBC, November 21, 2019. https://www.cnbc.com/2019/11/21/trump-impeach ment-fiona-hill-says-giuliani-sondland-hijacked-ukraine-policy.html.

Wright, Thomas. "The Yes-Men Have Taken Over the Trump Administration." *Atlantic*, November 4, 2019. https://www.theatlantic.com/ideas/archive /2019/11/trumps-foreign-policy-getting-worse/601327/.

Yousif, Elias. "Congress Needs More Authority in International Arms Sales." Hill, July 9, 2019. https://thehill.com/opinion/international/452290-con gress-needs-more-authority-in-international-arms-sales.

Zhou, Li. "The Senate Fails to Override Trump's Veto on Its National Emer- gency Resolution." Vox.com. October 17, 2019. https://www.vox.com/2019 /10/17/20917835/senate-national-emergency-border-wall-trump-veto.

———. "The Senate Just Voted to Take Military Action Against Iran." Vox. February 13, 2020. https://www.vox.com/2020/2/13/21136242/senate -war-powers-vote-trump-iran.

Conclusion: The Unorthodox Presidency

Paul E. Rutledge and Chapman Rackaway

This project, like so many projects that have come before it, started with a good conversation among friends over a hot cup of coffee in a comfortable chair. The presidency of Donald Trump is living history. It is equal parts unprecedented and unpredictable. These factors also made this volume a significant challenge. The idea came to fruition in early 2019, when we had all of the authors on board and a contract seemed likely. On a short time line, most of the work for this volume was in first draft form by the end of 2019. As revisions were being worked on in early 2020, the House of Representatives voted to impeach President Trump, marking the third president in the history of the United States to be impeached. A short time after the Senate voted to acquit President Trump on the impeachment charges, COVID-19 reached the shores of the United States. At the time of this writing, the virus has infected more than one million Americans, and more Americans have died from the virus in just over two months than in the nineteen and a half years of American involvement in the Vietnam War. Thus, it is tremendously difficult to write about presidents in real time. Trump's unorthodox nature has, without question, exacerbated this difficulty. With this in mind, it is incumbent upon us as editors to organize this chapter as follows. First, we will explore the lessons of the volume regarding the extent to which the presidency of Donald Trump has been unorthodox, the extent to which the constraints and safeguards designed constitutionally have prevented this unorthodox approach from achieving its full fruition, and what these lessons carry forward into the future of the American presidency. Next, we will look ahead to the 2020 presidential election, with the ramifications of impeachment and especially COVID-19 as a central part of the discussion. Finally, we will wrap up the volume with a discussion of the Trump presidency within presidential history.

THE UNORTHODOX PRESIDENCY

Donald Trump's candidacy for the presidency was unorthodox in many ways. One needs to look no further than his speech to launch his campaign, in which he systematically alienated a sizable portion of the electorate. Trump's comments suggesting that illegal immigrants were among the worst in society and that those crossing the border were rapists among other incendiary accusations signaled at the earliest moments that this would be a campaign like no other. The effort from Trump to win the Republican nomination and eventually the presidency would be an effort at disruption, as Chapman Rackaway details in this volume.

The politics of disruption are not new or even original to Trump. Andrew Jackson's campaign for the presidency in 1828, following his perceived illegitimate defeat by John Quincy Adams in the House of Representatives despite winning the popular vote and failing to secure an Electoral College majority, was a major disruption to the ruling elites. Jackson sought to involve the "forgotten man," a populist message intended to rally against the ruling elites. Many other candidates, including most notably George Wallace, embraced populist disruptive politics, pitting us against them. Not even on the racial undertones of Trump's disruptive populism is he truly original, as similar if less successful approaches were taken by Wallace in his 1972 campaign. Trump's focus on white America, to the exclusion of many minority groups, is detailed in chapters 2 and 3 by Wayne Steger and Russell Brooker, respectively. Perhaps the biggest difference between Trump and other right-wing populists before him is that his campaign was a success, winning the presidency.

Not all of Trump's disruption is populist in nature. Regime-building presidents in political time are typically disruptive (Skowronek 2020). Franklin Roosevelt campaigned on, and then enacted, fundamental changes in the structure of American government. In response to the Great Depression, his New Deal program thrust the national government centrally into the economy, establishing a new social safety net and vastly expanding the reach of the national government. Roosevelt's New Deal also cast a tremendous shadow over future presidents, who would be held to a similar expectation for achievement within the first 100 days of their presidency. Ronald Reagan's campaign for president in 1980 promised to scale back the vast expansion of national government found in the New Deal regime and expanded by Lyndon Johnson's Great Society. Benefited by the most advantageous public policy mood toward a conservative in the history of the presidency (Erickson, Mackuen, and Stimson 2002) and an associated mandate election (Grossback, Peterson, and Stimson 2006), Reagan advanced a disruption by contracting much of the national government's reach in domestic policy while vastly increasing the portion of the budget allocated to defense spending. Returning many of these functions to the state was a significant effort at policy disruption, where many of his proposals to scale back the national government, such as eliminating the Departments of Energy and Education (Edwards and Barrett 2000), were met with resistance.

Trump's efforts at disruption mirrored Reagan's, a somewhat unoriginal promise to "Make America Great Again" that he borrowed from Reagan, with grand if vague proposals to secure the border, reduce taxes, and undo many of the policies of the Obama administration, most notably the Patient Protection and Affordable Care Act. Trump's campaign and agenda were far different from the Roosevelt and Reagan attempts at disruption, however, in that the policy specifics were not there. As Rebecca M. Eissler argues in chapter 6, Trump did not take much interest in the details or minutiae of the legislative process. Nor did he make much of an effort to build winning coalitions, which would require substantial work to win the margins of American politics (Edwards 1989). Instead, Trump's focus was on campaigning even while governing, preferring instead to hold large campaign rallies and preach to the converted. Trump also used Twitter as a consistent way to get unfiltered (and unpolished) messages out to his supporters, embracing the Twitter world that Chapman Rackaway calls "the political land of misfit toys," of which Trump has crowned himself king.

Perhaps most importantly, when it comes to the differences in Trump's efforts at disruption, there was no mandate for him to do so. In the cases of both Roosevelt and Reagan, the presidents were benefited by a mandate election and a willing Congress as they ushered in a new presidential regime that would restructure American government based on the associated public will to build or scale back the government. Trump's disruption efforts were backed by no such mandate. As Paul E. Rutledge details in chapter 5, Trump's opportunity to govern was quite limited by a popular vote loss to Democratic candidate Hillary Clinton. The Electoral College victory for Trump came as a result of about seventy thousand votes, concentrated mostly in the Rust Belt and built on the backs of lesser-educated white voters who were frustrated by an economic evolvement over time that has largely left both them and their regions behind. Trump's efforts to revive Reagan conservatism were also problematic in that these efforts were not very close to Reagan's vision of America, nor were they backed by any evidence of public desire for them. The public policy mood has been trending in a liberal direction, a trend that has been exacerbated under Trump's leadership as the public has reacted to his policies and actions in office. We will discuss Trump's opportunity to govern and his place in the Reagan presidential regime later in this chapter as we look forward to 2020.

President Trump is also not the first president to learn the hard lesson that unified government is not a guarantee of success. Trump started his term under a unified Republican government, with a forty-seven-seat Republican majority in the House and holding fifty-two seats in the Senate. In spite of having this advantage, however, Trump found himself unsuccessful in navigating the legislative process in many ways. Trump eschewed an opportunity to deliver on a campaign promise that is antithetical to Republican orthodoxy in working on infrastructure. While Democrats expressed a willingness to work across the aisle to achieve a major infrastructure package, Trump instead chose to first focus on repealing and replacing the Affordable Care Act. In doing so, he not only failed because he did not even have the consistent support of Republicans to repeal the program, major parts of which are backed by popular support, but he also alienated Democrats who expressed a willingness to cross party lines (Edwards 2017). Following the first two years of Trump's presidency in which little of his agenda was accomplished, Trump experienced a midterm loss of Republican control of the House of Representatives. Presidents losing seats at the midterm is the norm, and the Republican losses in the 2018 midterm elections were not unprecedented. As Tyler J. Hughes and Lawrence A. Becker point out in chapter 4, however, the loss of the House of Representatives and a Republican gain of two Senate seats were unorthodox because of the calendar being so stacked against the Democrats. For example, twenty-six of the thirty-five Senate seats up for election in 2018 were held by Democrats, leaving only nine seats for the Democrats to swing. Additionally, the improving economic conditions were clearly favorable to the president's party. However, the 2018 midterms saw a major swing in the House of Representatives to Democratic control and in a few key congressional elections that previously had been deemed safe Republican holds for decades. The evidence presented by Hughes and Becker in chapter 4 clearly indicates a strong public rebuke for President Trump in the 2018 midterms, which although not abnormal was unorthodox considering the favorable conditions for Republicans.

As Roy T. Meyers describes in chapter 12, Trump also failed to achieve funding support for his proposed border wall. In the process of battling over funding for the border wall, Trump presided over the longest government shutdown in history in an attempt to force Democrats to provide funding. When the Democrats provided partial funding for the border wall as a means to end the painful shutdown that was beginning to significantly affect many nonessential segments of the federal workforce, Trump proceeded to withhold funds allocated to defense and divert them to funding construction of the border wall to combat what he called an emergency. The budget showdown has become more of a normal practice in American politics as polarization has increased over the last two decades. However, the Trump shutdown reached a record length and was followed by a constitutionally questionable impoundment and diversion of funds.

The budget showdown is but one of many examples of a preference for unilateral action on the part of the president. Presidents historically rely on unilateral action when they are unable to get major agenda items passed through Congress. Achieving success on policy priorities in Congress, rather than through executive fiat, is far preferred and much more strategic given the permanence that comes with legislative statutes. Executive actions are much more fleeting in that the next president can undo them just as easily as they were done in the first place. Trump has been unique in his penchant for unilateral action as a first resort rather than as a final result of frustrations. As Rebecca M. Eissler details in chapter 6, President Trump opted directly for executive action for his banning from entry into the United States those who emigrated from seven majority Muslim countries, a move that was challenged in court but that the Supreme Court upheld. Trump's use of executive action stands in stark contrast to the typical uses of executive action by presidents, which usually come after a president has become frustrated by negotiating breakdowns with the opposite party–dominated Congress. However, as Eissler points out, Trump's preference for executive action is unorthodox given his experience with unified government during the first two years. This is likely, in Eissler's view, borne out of the business background Donald Trump came from prior to becoming officially involved in politics. This view is similar to Harry S. Truman's famous concerns about Dwight D. Eisenhower, quoted in Neustadt (1990): "He'll sit here, and he'll say, 'Do this! Do that!' And nothing will happen. Poor Ike—it won't be a bit like the Army. He'll find it very frustrating." The difference is that despite Eisenhower's background of military command, which is certainly much more resolute than that found in the business world, Eisenhower rose to the occasion of occupying the presidency and engaging in negotiation and compromise much more effectively than Donald Trump has.

Jonathan Lewallen argues in chapter 7 that Trump's use of the president's negative power has been unorthodox for similar reasons to those Eissler points out. At first glance, Trump has used veto bargaining in a standard way, given that his veto threats have occurred only after the Democrats had taken control of the House of Representatives following the 2018 midterm elections. However, Lewallen demonstrates that an unprecedented proportion of them have been aimed at his own party. Trump's veto threats have arisen over challenges to his foreign policy presented by the Republican-controlled Senate. Further, his veto threats have abnormally deviated from his policy agenda expressed in the State of the Union, which according to Lewallen's (2017) research is unorthodox behavior in terms of the veto bargaining among presidents.

The politics surrounding Donald Trump's appointments have been unorthodox, owing in part to his own actions but also in part to the nuclear option used by Senate majority leader Harry Reid in 2013 that has carried forward regarding judicial nominees. As Lewallen indicates in chapter 7, in spite of Republican control of the Senate, President Trump has seen more of his nominees fail to make it out of committee and has left many positions within the executive branch vacant. As Lewallen shows, the number of vacant positions within the executive branch is not unheard of, but the unorthodox component of his management of the executive branch vacancies arises in the high-profile nature of the positions he has opted to leave open or fill with temporary, acting appointments. Further, Trump has had many nominations stuck in committees that have historically been much friendlier to presidential nominees to the executive branch. Trump's difficulty here has arrived despite having Republican control of the Senate and with the filibuster removed as a weapon for the Democratic minority and is further evidenced by his rather high number of nominees withdrawn compared to predecessors.

Trump's executive branch nominees have also reflected his tendency to put "foxes in the hen house," so to speak, according to Burdett Loomis in chapter 10. Loomis writes that Trump has appointed or hired 281 former lobbyists to work in the executive branch. Trump has also established a very informal approach to allowing access to lobbyists, who will meet with the president in one of his clubs and discuss policy issues with him in a social setting. Such a strategy has proven especially successful, as Loomis details, in the area of Veterans Affairs. This approach to open access for lobbyists to lobby the top levels of American government, or even more pointedly become a part of the top levels of American government, has become the ultimate embodiment of the revolving-door politics of Washington. Loomis writes that rather than draining the swamp as Trump has promised, he has swamped the drain of the executive branch with former Washington lobbyists. This is a change in the staffing and structure of the executive branch that could provide Washington lobbyists with new and unprecedented access and is a potential unorthodox contribution of the Trump presidency that will have permanent ramifications for the executive branch moving forward.

Additionally, Trump's nominees to the federal courts have faced much more opposition than those of any previous president. As Thomas Rogers Hunter illustrates in chapter 9, Trump's nominees to the federal bench have faced a record number of no votes compared to those of previous presidents. Further, a much higher percentage of nominees to the federal courts did not make it out of committee, similar to what Lewallen observes in regard to Trump's executive branch appointments. In fact, as Hunter points out, Trump is the first president to have a nominee to the federal courts confirmed by the Senate in a 51–50 vote, with Vice President Mike Pence providing the tie-breaking vote.

Despite the unprecedented amount of negative votes many of his justices received in the Senate, President Trump's biggest success as president will likely prove to be his nominations to the federal bench. As Hunter details, in cooperation with Mitch McConnell, Trump has appointed many young, talented, and conservative justices to the federal bench whose impact on legal precedent likely will last for decades. Remaking the judicial branch was a major priority for then candidate Trump, who for the first time in history provided a public list of twenty-one justices that he would consider for Supreme Court vacancies. Candidate Trump recognized, as Hunter notes, that judicial appointments would be one of the most important activities of his presidency. Trump successfully nominated 2 Supreme Court justices, a record 50 to the appellate courts, and 133 to the district courts, a volume of success that demonstrates that his campaign rhetoric was at least somewhat prophetic. Trump benefited tremendously from the work of Senate majority leader Mitch McConnell's judicial project, which prevented Barack Obama from filling many vacancies in the last two years of his term in order to hold those vacancies for a new and potentially Republican president. Thanks in part to Harry Reid's earlier use of the nuclear option as the Democratic Senate majority leader, McConnell has been able to move through Trump nominees to the federal courts as though they are on a conveyer belt. Many of the nominees faced tremendous opposition, in fact unprecedented numbers of opposition votes, from Democrats in the Senate. However, lacking the power of the filibuster, the minority was forced to sit by rather helplessly as Trump and McConnell successfully remade much of the judicial branch of government with very young and very conservative nominees.

To this point, this chapter has uncovered many ways in which the presidency of Donald Trump has been unorthodox and some ways in which it has been rather orthodox in the history of the presidency. The unorthodox presidency of Donald Trump comes into its clearest context, however, in two ways. First, President Trump's use of Twitter has set him apart as the first president not only to really rely on social media but also to use Twitter to advance his bullying approach, which was evidenced in the earliest portions of his campaign. As Thomas Rogers Hunter details in chapter 9, Trump has used Twitter to denigrate federal judges over decisions on which he disagrees, to take aim at the Ninth Circuit Court of Appeals on numerous occasions, and to explicitly label judges in partisan ways, such as referring to justices appointed by his predecessor as "Obama judges." Trump's aberrant rhetoric resulted in several unorthodox public rebukes from Chief Justice John Roberts, a conservative appointee of President George W. Bush, who decries the idea that any justice on the federal bench is an Obama Judge, a Bush Judge, or a Trump Judge. As JoBeth Surface Shafran and Heather T. Rimes detail in chapter 8, Trump has used Twitter to take similar aim at executive branch appointees such as former secretary of state Rex Tillerson and former attorney general Jeff Sessions. Twitter has also been his forum from which to launch assaults on executive branch agencies, in some cases to make personnel changes, and to announce major policy shifts without warning. Despite his staff repeatedly pleading with him to stop using such an informal-yet-public mechanism for such important governing business, Trump has continued to use Twitter as a medium for reaching out to his supporters over their objections.

Trump's use of Twitter has also bypassed the gatekeeping function of the media to some extent. Trump used this to his advantage in the campaign for presidency, where he could reach his supporters absent filters or perspective usually provided by the media. During Trump's presidency, he has used Twitter as a venue to reach out to his supporters directly in a way to not only get around but also in many cases to attack the media as "fake news." This is reflective of the broader truculent and combative approach Trump has taken with the media, which is described in chapter 11 by Matthew Eshbaugh-Soha and Joshua P. Montgomery. Trump's unorthodox approach with the media includes a rather direct personal approach, both literally and figuratively, as Trump has preferred to go directly to the media rather than allowing his press secretaries to be much of a mouthpiece. In spite of his unorthodox approaches, the media coverage of Trump has, as Eshbaugh-Soha and Montgomery show, been largely focused on his official press conferences rather than on his Twitter activity. Further, in spite of the onslaught of insults and combative engagement, the media's coverage of Trump has been much higher but not significantly more negative than other presidents have experienced.

The most important unorthodox action of Trump's presidency has emerged in foreign policy. His approach to foreign policy, unlike the other unorthodox approaches discussed above, may be the one most likely to have lasting consequences for the office of the presidency. Jeffrey S. Peake, in chapter 14, details a number of ways in which Trump's foreign policy actions are unconventional. There have been some areas in which President Trump has continued along the path of his predecessors in foreign policy, most notably in the continuation of foreign military interventions in Afghanistan and other areas. This was true as well for Trump's military intervention in Syria in response to Bashir Al-Assad's use of chemical weapons against his own people. However, as Peake details, these areas of continuation are superseded by significant disruption in the usual practice of foreign policy.

President Trump has shown tremendous hostility toward standing multilateral agreements, ranging from trade to security. Trump sought to change the long-standing trade partnership set out in NAFTA among Canada, Mexico, and the United States. Trump's business background made him confident that in such situations he could negotiate a better deal. Likewise, Trump withdrew the United States from the Trans-Pacific Partnership trade agreement, arguing that it was a bad deal negotiated by his predecessor. Trump has been hostile to multilateral agreements with a demonstrated preference for bilateral negotiations that he expects will give him the opportunity to get a better deal for the United States. Trump was able to negotiate a new deal with Canada and Mexico, the USMCA, which despite disagreeing with replacing NAFTA, Canada and Mexico gave into in order to avoid an economic calamity as a result of a disastrous trade war.

Trump has also experienced tremendous turnover in the foreign policy establishment. As Jeffrey S. Peake details in chapter 14, Trump has experienced a personnel turnover that substantially exceeds any of his predecessors' in terms of his top foreign policy advisory positions. In addition to turnover in secretaries of state and defense, Trump has also had turnover in other key positions such as the director of National Intelligence, the director of the Central Intelligence Agency, and the secretary of Homeland Security each twice. Further, Trump has fired three national security advisors and has been through six deputy national security advisors. Similarly to many of the executive branch positions above, Trump has taken to Twitter for their criticism, dismissals, and long-lasting denigration even after their service to the administration has ended. Another similarity with his broader management of the executive branch is the length of time during which key positions in the foreign policy establishment are left vacant. Finally, there are numerous accounts and a general perception that foreign policy expertise, and executive branch expertise generally, is largely ignored or even worse, undermined, in the Trump administration. Such a practice certainly sets a bad precedent and makes it unlikely that qualified individuals will be eager to work in the Trump administration. It would be an especially difficult proposition for the United States to prosecute effective foreign policy if there is a lingering effect of this discouragement of foreign policy expertise from entering future presidential administrations, which is certainly possible.

Interestingly, Trump's general management of his cabinet has been similar to some of the best presidents in at least one way. There has been tremendous expertise within the Trump administration, and his boardroom approach given his business background has encouraged vigorous debate. Such a competitive approach has been successful for past presidents in getting the necessary policy perspectives. However, the difference for the Trump administration is that the competition is not a means to an end. There is no end, because in the end Trump does not act according to the winning arguments of the debate. Instead, the evidence of numerous accounts inside the administration suggests that in spite of such expertise, Trump acts according to his own whims.

Trump has also demonstrated many tendencies in foreign policy that have been flagged by Bright Line Watch, a cooperative academic and citizen watchdog entity that flags actions that could be deemed as a threat to democracy. As Peake details in his chapter, Bright Line has flagged numerous foreign policy actions as threats to the national security of the United States. Among the most egregious examples, Trump's dealings with Russian president Vladimir Putin especially stand out, given the evidence US intelligence agencies have presented that Russia interfered on Trump's behalf in the 2016 presidential election. Trump had a private meeting with Putin and he did not share his notes from the meeting with the foreign policy establishment, flouting the precedence that presidents do so for reasons of national security. Further, Trump also appeared to side with Putin in public against US intelligence agencies' findings following Putin's denial of Russian interference. Further, Trump has taken a more standoffish approach to known allies, including the labeling of the European Union as a foe. Finally, in an action that would ultimately lead to President Trump becoming the third president in the history of the United States to be impeached by the House of Representatives, Trump threatened to withhold aid to the Ukraine as an ultimatum to force the government of Ukraine to investigate the business dealings of Hunter Biden, the son of 2020 Democratic presidential nominee and former vice president Joseph Biden.

In the areas of foreign policy and international trade, Peake presents that the extreme partisanship evident in so many areas documented in this volume has had especially problematic consequences.

Hyper-partisanship in Congress makes checks on unilateral actions in foreign policy very difficult, given the supermajorities needed in Congress to exercise such checks on the executive. This has allowed Trump a great deal of leeway for executive unilateral action that is quite unorthodox in nature, with little opportunity for Congress to respond and protect the foreign policy establishment.

These unorthodox actions by the Trump administration in the prosecution of foreign policy, relationships with allies and enemies, and eschewing of long-standing multilateral agreements have the potential to tremendously affect US foreign policy moving forward. While it is easy to discount the actions of President Trump as but a blip on the radar, so to speak, it is quite possible that the international community will see things differently. It is quite likely that it will take time for other nations to have any strong desire to enter into agreements with the United States should they perceive that the US participation in them is so directly tied to partisanship and election results. Likewise, allies cannot be expected to so easily trust the United States after being labeled as "foes" publicly. On the other hand, enemies of the United States have likely been emboldened by Trump's friendlier approach with them, especially his willingness to directly question his own foreign policy establishment, which could be perceived as a strong indication that the United States lacks the resolve to hold foreign adversaries accountable for their actions.

2020 AND THE TRUMP PRESIDENCY IN CONTEXT

As of this writing, the Democratic presidential primary is basically over. All of the candidates other than Joe Biden have dropped out of the race, making the former vice president the presumptive Democratic nominee. When this project started in early 2019, the prospects of a Trump reelection appeared to be a mixed bag. Trump was benefited by a strong economy, with a Dow Jones Industrial Average reaching an all-time high of over 29,000. In spite of the other areas in which the Trump administration has struggled, which are detailed throughout this volume, the economy is well known to be of paramount importance to the president's standing with the public. President Trump also has benefited from unusually stable public approval ratings, which have stood in stark contrast to Paul Light's (1999) assertion of inevitable presidential cycles. Trump's approval rating has hovered, according to Gallup Polls, between 43 and 47 percent for the vast majority of his term. Similar to the last president to be impeached, Bill Clinton, impeachment did not really do tremendous damage to the president in terms of his public approval either. Again, Trump's support among his base, the minority of the population that was enough to elect him in the Electoral College, was resilient. Further, the Democratic primary elections began in early 2020, with an early lead established by Vermont senator Bernie Sanders, who has openly professed himself to be a Social Democrat. It appeared as though the Democratic primary electorate was leaning far left, which is not totally unusual for primary elections. Taken together, a strong economy, a stable base of support, a Teflon-like deflection of impeachment, and another Democratic candidate that would likely be undesirable to the more moderate voting public were all positive signs for President Trump heading into his reelection campaign in 2020. Additionally, Trump has been building a substantial war chest that he can sit on, while potential Democratic challengers had been expending a great deal of donor money on first winning the Democratic nomination.

There were two key factors in early 2020 that changed the trajectory of President Trump's reelection hopes. First, former vice president Joe Biden's campaign for the Democratic nomination, which many pundits had understandably left for dead, scored a big victory in the South Carolina Democratic primary election. Biden benefited tremendously from the African American vote in South Carolina, where Senator Bernie Sanders has lacked in his electoral coalitions across the last two presidential cycles. The momentum from the victory in South Carolina carried him through Super Tuesday and in a period of just two months cleared the path for Biden to be the Democratic nominee. Each of the former Democratic rivals that remained after Iowa, upon dropping out, have since endorsed Biden in an effort to consolidate Democratic Party voters around Biden to defeat Donald Trump. Certainly, it seems clear that an establishment candidate like Biden is more likely to pull key Trump voters, especially in the Rust Belt states, that won him the Electoral College vote over Hillary Clinton in 2016. The early consolidation of the Democratic support for a more mainstream candidate like Joe Biden, and his ability to focus both his energy and his funds on the general election, allows Biden the opportunity to exploit Trump's serial norm violations in November. This is certainly a more difficult path for Trump to be reelected than he would have faced had Bernie Sanders won the nomination or even continued to contest it over a longer period of time.

The second key factor that changed the likelihood of President Trump's success in 2020 was the global COVID-19 pandemic. The outbreak of COVID-19, a coronavirus emanating from China that as of this writing has infected more than one million Americans and claimed more lives in two months than the entire nineteen years of the Vietnam War, put a hard stop on both the Democratic primary election and the US economy. The virus has been demonstrated to spread quickly and easily with human interaction, which led to nationwide social-distancing initiatives beginning in early March and continuing through the entire month of April. Many businesses were forced to close at least temporarily, and many workers were laid off or even fired nationwide. Unemployment rates as of April 2020, resulting from the practices of social distancing, had reached double digits, with millions filing for unemployment. The economy began a free fall in March, with the Dow Jones Industrial Average sitting currently at just over 23,000. The loss of millions of jobs and 6,000 points in the Dow Jones Industrial Average has notably decreased the amount of credit Trump could claim for a booming economy.

Further hampering President Trump's reelection goal has been his response to the COVID-19 crisis. For well over a month during the national social-distancing period, Trump held daily news conferences against the advice of his advisers (Seipel 2020). In these daily news updates from the coronavirus task force, Trump was truculent with reporters, used the briefings as quasi-campaign-like credit-claiming opportunities, and touted the great job the administration was doing in response to the virus even as the United States' numbers of infections and deaths soared to become the highest in the world by mid-April. The response to COVID-19 was a continuous effort from Trump to blame China for hiding information about the virus, despite intelligence briefings indicating that the president was informed as early as January that the virus was coming. However, sources inside the White House indicate that Trump not only does not read the daily intelligence briefing that included important information early in the year, before the first COVID-19 infection hit the United States, but also becomes quickly agitated when he partially listens to them twice per week as they are read to him (Miller and Nakashima 2020). Additionally, President Trump has repeatedly pushed the responsibility for testing, securing personal protective equipment, and securing ventilators onto the states, refusing to enact the Defense Production Act for the production of necessary materials to combat the virus or release much of the equipment contained by the federal government in the US stockpile.

Becoming impatient with the damage inflicted by the virus, which continues to infect more than a million Americans and kill thousands more daily as of April 30, 2020, Trump has established guidelines for reopening the US economy and easing social-distancing guidelines beginning in early May. Again, on this, Trump has pushed the responsibility for reopening, despite establishing federal guidelines, down to the states. This has led to wildly different actions on the part of state governors, with many Republican governors acting more aggressively to reopen their economies than even the Trump-established federal guidelines recommend. For example, Georgia Governor Brian Kemp announced on April 21 that Georgia would begin reopening businesses on April 24, with tattoo parlors and bowling alleys being among the initial essential businesses to reopen. This followed an announcement by Trump establishing federal guidelines for reopening the states, which he issued the day prior, and yet Trump criticized Kemp's reopening in Georgia for being too fast the very next day, on April 22. Trump's attorney general, William Barr, has also ordered the Justice Department to investigate states for potential civil liberties violations in their mandatory quarantines as a result of the COVID-19 outbreak (Williams 2020). These actions have continued a virtual declaration of war on the part of the Trump administration toward the states, perhaps best exemplified with his encouraging social distance, on the one hand, but tweeting with literally the other hand to encourage his followers to protest in Virginia, Michigan, and Minnesota for the respective governors to open their states (Fritze and Jackson 2020).

Trump's haphazard, inconsistent, and frequently petulant response to the COVID-19 crisis has, like much of his presidency, produced significant divisions in the public evaluation of his job performance. Gallup polling indicates that Trump's initial handling of the COVID-19 crisis was supported by the majority of the public, with 60 percent approving of the job he was doing handling the crisis from March 13 to March 22. However, a second round of polling performed by the Gallup organization from April 14 to April 28 shows that his approval has slipped to 50 percent, with notable losses among Democrats and Independents as well as a small 3 percent loss among Republicans (Jones 2020). The majority of Americans also felt as of late April that the Trump administration was reopening the economy too soon (Lucey 2020). Further, only 36 percent of Americans, a much lower percentage than his usual polling base, said they trust what President Trump says about COVID-19. Nine percent of those samples in this same poll felt that Democratic rival Joe Biden would be better suited to handling the pandemic (Lucey 2020). Finally, a Pew Poll indicated that 65 percent of Americans felt that President Trump acted too slowly in responding to the COVID-19 pandemic.[1] This is in stark contrast to leaders in Europe and state governors, who are getting record high marks from their voters for their handling of the pandemic (Lerer 2020).

The polling data referenced above indicates that even the Trump base, which has been abnormally stable in polling data throughout his presidency, has begun to question his response, honesty, and suitability to handle the major crisis of his presidency. This is further evidenced by the defection from the Republican Party of long-time Republican establishment figures George T. Conway III, Steve Schmidt, John Weaver, and Rick Wilson. Wilson and his colleagues led the "Never Trump" effort during 2016 and followed through after his election with the Lincoln Project, which is aimed at defeating Trump and restoring the pre-Trump Republican Party (Conway, Schmidt, Weaver, and Wilson 2019). Former Republican House member and Freedom Caucus leader Justin Amash announced an independent bid for the presidency with the specific intent of removing Trump from office. While the defectors cite numerous areas of opposition to the Trump administration, the former Republican stalwarts are clearly citing the COVID-19 response as the last straw.

As President Trump continues to see his poll numbers decline in grading his response to the pandemic, the poll numbers are looking similarly bleak as of the last day in April for his 2020 matchup with Joe Biden. The Real Clear Politics poll average at this point has Biden with a six-point lead nationally, including leads that are larger than the margin of error in every swing state except North Carolina, where Trump has a 0.3 percent lead, well within the margin of error.[2] Coupling the COVID-19 response, the associated economic decline, and the current polling numbers with the blue wave of the 2018 midterm elections that were very clearly a referendum on President Trump makes the prospects of a Trump reelection in 2020 look bleak. This leaves open the question of where the Trump presidency, unorthodox as it has been, falls within the broad contours of presidential history.

Steven Skowronek (2020) speculates about Trump's place in presidential history in the third edition of his book *Presidential Leadership in Political Time.* Skowronek divides the history of presidential leadership in the United States into "eras" or regimes, and the current era in Skowronek's construction is defined by the Reagan presidency. In this book, released in early 2020, Skowronek projects an uncertain future regarding Trump's placement in political time. In his concluding chapter, he wonders aloud whether the Trump presidency is the disjunctive presidency of the Reagan era, which would usher in a new Democratic regime following Trump. The other possibility he considers is that presidential regimes have been left in a perpetual cycle, with a pendulum swinging power back and forth among the parties without a substantial shift in regime ideology, similar to what we have seen with the elections of Ronald Reagan in 1980 and Franklin Roosevelt before him in 1932.

With the benefit of more information at the time of this writing, we find there is substantially more evidence that the Trump presidency is indeed the disjunctive presidency of the Reagan regime. As Paul E. Rutledge details in chapter 5, Trump has faced a much more unified Democratic opposition but diffuse support among Republicans in Congress. The Republican Party was fractured during the 2016 primary and does not seem to have recovered its unity. The combination of changed allocation rules for convention delegates and Trump's disruptive strategy functionally allowed him to engage in a hostile takeover of the Republican Party. Further, as Rutledge points out, the public mood has been moving in an increasingly liberal direction since the election of Donald Trump, reaching an all-time high in 2018, which led to the Democrats recapturing the House of Representatives and winning several surprising individual races that were formally Republican strongholds, as Tyler J. Hughes and Lawrence A. Becker indicate in chapter 4. Additionally, each disjunctive president seems to be faced with scandal that helps to usher in a new regime. President Jimmy Carter, who faced a Democratic New Deal coalition that was falling apart at the seams and the Iran Hostage Crisis late in his presidency, presages Trump's Republican experience and the COVID-19 outbreak. Going back further, Herbert Hoover had lost tremendous amounts of support among Republicans in 1932 and faced the Great Depression, an economic calamity that may be the only modern economic free fall worse than what we have seen as a result of COVID-19.

In the end, predictions are a dangerous business, and this is not a forecasting model. Forecasters both inside and outside of political science circles learned the hard way in 2016 the hazards of forecasting in a highly polarized, partisan era. Forecasters, with the exception of two, correctly had Hillary Clinton winning the popular vote but also predicted a Clinton presidency. That hazard is only magnified when it comes to dealing with an unorthodox candidate like Donald J. Trump. The evidence indicates that Trump was able to defeat Clinton largely on the backs of late deciders, benefiting from the fact that although those voters did not like him, they did not like Clinton either. However, such a windfall of late deciding voters who like neither candidate seems far less likely in 2020. President Trump's likability has not improved, while Joe Biden appears to be a much more likable candidate (Enten 2020a). The most convincing evidence is presented in a poll indicating that among those who like neither candidate, Biden stands to win by more than 50 percent (Enten 2020b).

As we detail in this volume, the unorthodox presidency of Donald Trump gives plenty of ammunition to Democrats and moderates for imposing a strong electoral rebuke. Similarly, even many Republicans are becoming significantly disillusioned with the Trump approach to governing, a movement that frequently is a strong signal of the end of an established coalition. The recent circumstance of the COVID-19 response is perhaps the most convincing in a long line of evidence that suggests a resounding Trump defeat in 2020 will serve as the final nail in the coffin of the Reagan regime.

NOTES

1. "Most Americans Say Trump Was Too Slow in Initial Response to Coronavirus Threat," Pew Research Center, https://www.people-press.org/2020/04/16/most-americans-say-trump-was-too-slow-in-initial-response-to-coronavirus-threat/.

2. For Biden's projected lead, see: https://www.realclearpolitics.com/epolls/latest_polls/. Retrieved April 30, 2020.

REFERENCES

Conway, George T., Steve Schmidt, John Weaver, and Rick Wilson. "We Are Republicans, and We Want Trump Defeated." *New York Times*, December 17, 2019.

Edwards, George C. III. *At the Margins: Presidential Leadership of Congress*. New Haven, CT: Yale University Press, 1989.

———. "No Deal: Donald Trump's Leadership of Congress." Paper presented at the Annual Meeting of the American Political Science Association. September 2, 2017.

Edwards, George C. III, and Andrew Barrett. "Presidential Agenda Setting in Congress." In *Polarized Politics: Congress and the President in a Polarized Era*, ed. Jon R. Bond and Richard Fleischer. Washington, DC: CQ, 2000.

Enten, Harry. "Trump's Likeability Deficit Could Cost Him in 2020." CNN. April 26, 2020a. https://www.cnn.com/2020/04/25/politics/2020-election-trump-favorability/index.html.

———. "2020 Is Shaping Up to Be All About Trump." CNN. April 7, 2020b. https://www.cnn.com/2020/04/07/politics/trump-2020-analysis/index.html.

Erickson, Robert S., Michael B. Mackuen, and James A. Stimson. *The Macro Polity*. New York: Cambridge University Press, 2002.

Fritze, John, and David Jackson. "Trump Calls to 'Liberate' States Where Protestors Have Demanded Easing Coronavirus Lockdowns." *USA Today*, April 17, 2020.

Grossback, Lawrence J., David A. M. Peterson, and James A. Stimson. *Mandate Politics*. New York: Cambridge University Press, 2006.

Jones, Jeffrey M. "Americans Divided on Trump's Handling of COVID-19 Situation." *Gallup News*, April 30, 2020.

Lerer, Lisa. 2020. "Trump Exceptionalism: What Happened to President Trump's Approval Ratings?" *New York Times*, April 20, 2020.

Lewallen, Jonathan. "The Issue Politics of Presidential Veto Threats." *Presidential Studies Quarterly* 47, no. 2 (2017): 277–292.

Light, Paul C. *The President's Agenda: Domestic Policy Choice from Kennedy to Clinton*. Baltimore, MD: Johns Hopkins University Press, 1999.

Lucey, Katherine. "More Americans Fear Lifting Coronavirus Restrictions Too Soon, WSJ/NBC Poll Says." *Wall Street Journal*, April 19, 2020.

Miller, Greg, and Ellen Nakashima. "President's Intelligence Briefing Book Repeatedly Cited Virus Threat." *Washington Post*, April 27, 2020.

Neustadt, Richard. *Presidential Power and the Modern Presidents*. New York: Free, 1990.

Seipel, Brooke. "Trump to Scale Back Coronavirus Press Conferences after Disinfectant Comment: Report." *Hill*, April 24, 2020.

Skowronek, Stephen. *Presidential Leadership in Political Time: Reprise and Reappraisal*. 3rd ed. Lawrence: University of Kansas Press, 2020.

Williams, Pete. "Barr Directs Prosecutors to Look for State and Local Stay at Home Orders That Go Too Far." *NBC News*, April 17, 2020.

About the Contributors

Lawrence A. Becker is a professor of political science at California State University, Northridge. He is currently working on a coauthored book project (with Dr. Cahn) examining the interplay between scientific expertise and stakeholder politics in the policy process.

Russell Brooker is the director of the Politics Program at Alverno College, Milwaukee, Wisconsin, and teaches courses in American politics, social theory, statistics, Vietnam, and African American history. His doctorate focused on public opinion and political participation. He taught as a Fulbright scholar in Vietnam during the spring 2006 term and returned to Vietnam in 2007 and 2008 to teach summer school.

Rebecca M. Eissler earned her PhD from the University of Texas at Austin. She is an assistant professor in political science at San Francisco State University. She studies public policy and American politics with an emphasis on agenda-setting, the presidency, and information processing.

Matthew Eshbaugh-Soha is a professor and chair of political science at the University of North Texas and holds a PhD in political science from Texas A&M University. His research focuses on American political institutions, specifically the presidency, mass media, and public policy. He is the author of *The President's Speeches: Beyond "Going Public"* (2006) and coauthor of *Breaking Through the Noise: Presidential Leadership, Public Opinion, and the News Media* (2011).

Tyler J. Hughes is an assistant professor at California State University, Northridge. His research focuses on American political institutions and the public policy process, with a particular interest in energy and environmental policy.

Thomas Rogers Hunter holds bachelor's, master's, and law degrees from the University of Virginia and a PhD from Johns Hopkins University. A member of the North Carolina Bar, he clerked for a judge on the US Court of Appeals and has taught at the University of Arkansas Law School, Hendrix College, and Auburn University. He is currently completing books on historical patterns of congressional districting and the institutionalization of legal education and a biography of George E. Badger of North Carolina, a major nineteenth-century attorney-politician.

Jonathan Lewallen earned his PhD at the University of Texas at Austin in 2017. He is an assistant professor of political science at the University of Tampa. His research has appeared in the *Journal of Legislative Studies*, *Political Science Quarterly*, and *Presidential Studies Quarterly*, among other outlets.

Burdett Loomis is a professor emeritus of political science at the University of Kansas. The tenth edition of his coedited *Interest Group Politics* was published in 2019, and the seventh edition of his coauthored book *The Contemporary Congress* came out in 2018. He continues to work on a book on changes in Kansas politics in the 1960s and 1970s, as well as overseeing an oral history project for veteran Kansas state legislators.

Roy T. Meyers is a professor of political science at the University of Maryland, Baltimore County. He was the recipient of the 2018 Aaron Wildavsky Award from the Association for Budgeting and Financial Management. His book *Strategic Budgeting* (1994) cowon the Louis Brownlow Book Award from the National Academy of Public Administration in 1996.

Christopher Olds, PhD, Texas A&M University, is an interdisciplinary social scientist with interests in rhetoric, economic policy, information processing, and human–computer interaction. His primary research agenda looks at the causes and consequences of changes to the stylistic characteristics of public remarks from US presidents across time. He is currently coeditor of two interdisciplinary journals, the *American Journal of Medical Research* and *Economics, Management, and Financial Markets.*

Jeffrey S. Peake is a professor and chair of the Department of Political Science at Clemson University. His research interests focus on the presidency, the media, and Congress. Peake is the coauthor of two books: *Breaking Through the Noise: Presidential Leadership, Public Opinion, and the News Media* (with Matthew Eshbaugh-Soha; 2011) and *Treaty Politics and the Rise of Executive Agreements: International Commitments in a System of Shared Powers* (with Glen S. Krutz; 2009). His research has appeared in a range of scholarly journals, including *American Political Science Review, Political Research Quarterly*, and *Political Communication*, among others.

Chapman Rackaway has published more than twenty articles and book chapters as well as six books. Rackaway is the author of *Civic Failure and Its Threat to Democracy: Operator Error* (2016) and coeditor of *Amrican Political Parties under Pressure* (2017), as well as other books on American politics, political communication, and voting behavior.

Heather T. Rimes earned her PhD from the University of Georgia. She is an assistant professor and MPA director at Western Carolina University.

Paul E. Rutledge is an associate professor and chair of the Department of Civic Engagement and Public Service at the University of West Georgia. He earned his PhD in political science from West Virginia University in 2009. He teaches and conducts research on the American presidency, agenda setting, and public policy. His research has appeared in *Political Research Quarterly, Policy Studies Journal*, and *American Review of Public Administration.*

JoBeth Surface Shafran earned her PhD from the University of Texas at Austin. She is an assistant professor at Western Carolina University.

Wayne Steger earned his PhD from the University of Iowa in 1995. He is a professor of political science at DePaul University. He is the author of two books, and his research has appeared in *Presidential Studies Quarterly* and *American Politics Research*, among many other venues.

Index